The media are American

By Jeremy Tunstall

The fishermen
The advertising man
Old and alone
The Westminster Lobby correspondents
Journalists at work
Media sociology (editor)
Sociological perspectives (editor with Kenneth Thompson)
The Open University opens (editor)

In the same series

Journalists at work
Jeremy Tunstall

The making of a TV series
Philip Elliott

The political impact of mass media
Colin Seymour-Ure

The manufacture of news
Stan Cohen and Jock Young (editors)

Children in front of the small screen
Grant Noble

The Fleet Street disaster
Graham Cleverley

The silent watchdog
David Murphy

There's No Business like Show Business: South Korea, 1955

The media are American

JEREMY TUNSTALL

New York Columbia University Press 1977

Published in 1977 in Great Britain by Constable and Company Ltd and in
the United States of America by Columbia University Press

Printed in Great Britain

Library of Congress Cataloging in Publication Data
Tunstall, Jeremy.
  The media are American.

  Bibliography: p.
  Includes index.
  1. Mass media—History. 2. Mass media—United
States—History. 3. Mass media—Economic aspects.
  I. Title.
  P90.T84   1977   301.16′1′0973   77–2581
  ISBN 0–231–04292–2

For Sylvia, Rebecca and Helena

Acknowledgements

Many colleagues have helped with this book. At an early stage four people provided research assistance: David Walker for France and Germany, Margaret Gallagher for Italy, Frank Turfus for Germany and Robert Gibbs for Mexico and Argentina. All four were diligent and creative both in testing my early ideas in particular countries and in suggesting new approaches.

My thanks to the Open University for financing this research assistance, for a period of sabbatical leave, and also for funding short visits to Nairobi, Bombay, New Delhi, Mexico City and Bogota. In each of these cities very senior people – such as chief editors of leading publications and their equivalents in broadcasting – were outstandingly helpful. In the same cities I was also greatly assisted by bureau chiefs and local senior managers of Agence France-Presse; Associated Press; United Press International; Reuters; J. Walter Thompson; McCann-Erickson; Ogilvy, Benson & Mather; and the United States Information Service. Perhaps it is best to resist the temptation to thank by name individuals who were exceptionally hospitable; this is especially true in the case of Bombay.

Several pioneers in this field have provided invaluable written comments and also have kindly discussed mutual problems – usually during their visits to London. Elihu Katz has been encouraging since early days; he and his colleague George Wedell have let me see in draft their forthcoming major study of broadcasting in eleven developing countries, as well as most of the case studies of single countries. Herbert Schiller, author of the pioneering *Mass Communications and American Empire* has been a constructive critic and helpful colleague. Tom Guback, author of the relatively unknown but outstanding work, *The International Film Industry,* has been the source of sage advice and many insights. Tapio Varis, author of the pioneering television export inventory study, has supplied a steady flow of valuable comment and interesting papers – including a draft of his joint study with Tom Guback on transnational communication corporations. Wilson Dizard, author of *Television: A World View,* has also made useful suggestions.

Much of the material on the four western international news agencies comes from Oliver Boyd-Barrett's Leverhulme Trust financed study on that topic. In particular I have relied on his detailed notes from interviews with senior agency executives and bureau chiefs especially in Japan and the Far East, Egypt and the Middle East, New York and Washington; his material is exceptionally strong on Paris (where many of the interviews were conducted by Michael Palmer) and on London.

Drafts of this book were commented on in especially profuse detail by three British colleagues – James Curran, Philip Elliott, and Philip Schlesinger. While on a visit to Britain from the Soviet Union, Yuri Vlasov provided exceptionally lengthy, well informed and valuable comments.

Others who provided written comments – some long, some short, almost all very helpful and fairly critical – were: Jay Blumler, Michael Burrage, Chen Chimutengwende, Margaret Dickinson, Winston Fletcher, Herbert Gans, Peter Golding, Michael Gurevitch, Hanno Hardt, Mikko Jokela, Barry King, John Landell-Mills, Kurt Lang, Brian Lapping, Denis McQuail, J. Edward Murray, Graham Mytton, Rita Cruise O'Brien, Michael Palmer, Michael Pilsworth, Eddi Ploman, Graeme Salaman, Colin Seymour-Ure, Michael Sissons, Jean Texier, Kenneth Thompson, Jack Winkler, Frank Wolf, Janet Woollacott.

Further useful comment came from members of seminars at which papers based on this study were given: British Sociological Association; Saint Antony's College, Oxford; University of Leicester; the European Political Science Consortium meeting at Strasbourg; University of Iowa; and University of Illinois (Champaign-Urbana).

The Library staffs at the Open University, and later at the City University, have been most helpful and resourceful.

Successive drafts were efficiently typed by Pam Gardner, Marita Caffrey and Irene Cox.

My thanks to Elfreda Powell of Constable for being such a tough, supportive, and efficient editor.

Last and most, thanks to my wife, Sylvia, who made detailed suggestions which were largely followed in the rewriting of the early chapters.

Jeremy Tunstall
City University London 1976

Contents

PART THREE:

1945: AMERICAN MEDIA CONQUEST

List of illustrations

List of tables

Introduction

'The media are American. And Vodka's Russian. So what?' commented one American.

An African country of ten million people cannot make all its own feature films – so it imports them from Hollywood. It cannot collect its own international or Pan-African news – so it imports it from Reuters of London. It lacks resources to produce more than very modest quantities of recorded music, television entertainment, paperback books or comic strips; so it imports these things at low prices from American companies like UPI, RCA–NBC, Paramount, King Features and Disney or from British organizations like Reuters, the BBC or EMI.

Even an economically and artistically strong nation like Sweden, complete with its own national language, defended by state subsidies to the arts and media, and surrounded by its own circle of smaller Scandinavian states, even Sweden could not continue with its current level of media consumption without large imports of films, television series, international news, music, comics and so on. And these Swedish media imports come mainly from the United States and Britain.

In most of the world's countries the media are only there at all, on the present scale, as the result of imports in which the American media (with some British support) predominate. One major influence of American imported media lies in the styles and patterns which most other countries in the world have adopted and copied. This influence includes the very definition of what a *newspaper*, or a *feature film*, or a *television set* is.

Does the predominant form of newspaper need to be something which is printed every day and contains numerous pages of which many are advertising? For the United States, where this format was largely developed, it is convenient and suitable; but for an African nation where transport is slow, literacy low, newsprint scarce and advertising weak, this 'daily newspaper' format is less obviously suitable.

Does the predominant form of film have to be the feature film with a fictional story running for two hours or so? No, it does not, but this was the format which Hollywood evolved in the US domestic market and which all other nations including the

Soviet Union and China copied, scarcely recognizing that there was a choice.

And television? Does television have to be based on *domestic* sets – a square box which eats electricity and sits in the living room? Would not for many countries some format closer to the village hall movies have been better? Or was television necessary at all, when in many places in the world even village hall movies still have not arrived? But no, virtually every country of even a few million people has adopted the box-in-the-sitting-room concept of television even though the box may cost more than a farm family's annual cash income.

The high tide of American media exports, in their most obvious form, has passed. *I Love Lucy, Peyton Place* and *Mission Impossible* no longer rule the global village quite so masterfully as in the 1960s. But Hollywood is always dying only to be reborn with renewed vigour. And the world, by adopting American media formats, has in practice become hooked on American-style media whether these are home-made or imported.

The phenomenon discussed in this book covers all the major media–news agencies, newspapers, magazines, films, radio, television – and touches upon records and paperback books. Advertising, clearly, is also an important part of the picture. Without the century-long dominance of Anglo-American media products and styles, many aspects of life in most of the world's countries would be different – consumption patterns, leisure, entertainment, music, the arts and literature. But these media also touch politics in all lands and in many ways. People who are heavily exposed to the media usually use the media as their main raw material for perceiving what the external world is all about. In many countries not merely politics, but the very notion of a rather tenuous nation state, is perceived through and is seen to exist through the media.

'The pictures in our heads' of international reality also come largely through the media – as Walter Lippmann noted over fifty years ago. Many of these pictures are shaped and packaged on Sunset Boulevard, Madison Avenue and Fleet Street. Britain's, and later the United States', position as Number One nation in the world were both self-ascribed; each nation at the height of its political power also had the means and the will to beam its own image around the world as Number One nation.

This book covers a lot of media, a big time span and most of the world's larger countries. Not everyone is interested in both India and Germany, or in both Latin America and China. *The reader is therefore invited to skip.* The general thesis is mainly at the beginning and the end, while particular countries come in the middle. I have concentrated primarily on the argument that the media are American (with some rather strategic British help). If you as a reader find this point a trifle obvious, I hope to convince you by the end that it is neither entirely obvious nor inevitable. But if the assertion that the media are American strikes you as far-fetched, I hope to convince you that it is nevertheless true.

Inevitably with a book covering the entire world almost all readers will know more than I do about particular countries, media or time-periods. My hope, however, is to illustrate that these details do fit into a much larger jig-saw, some aspects of which can only be understood if all the media and all the countries are considered together over time.

PART ONE

News, entertainment, advertising . . . and imperialism?

CHAPTER ONE

World news : Made in USA and UK

'In 1971, the AP estimated that more than one billion persons outside the United States saw or heard AP news each day.'

Albert L. Hester

'Visnews is the world's leading supplier of international news actuality material for television. Its services are used by more than 170 broadcasters in virtually every country where television exists covering, indeed, some 99 % of all the television receivers in the world.'

Visnews 1975

The key invention in the history of world media was the modern newspaper. It gave news, entertainment and advertising their media shape. Television was the only subsequent media form to present this entire range of materials within a single media package.

The United States was the first nation to detach its press from the official machinery of government – the first amendment to the Constitution formally specified the press along with freedom of speech and worship as an area in which Congress could make 'no law'. Since government and politics cannot be carried on without the press, this decision ceded part of the apparatus of government and politics into private ownership.

Increasingly as the republic moved west 'one man, one vote' became a reality; and political power was diffused through a federal arrangement of states. The absence of political constraints and the nearly universal suffrage fuelled the growth of the press; the federal structure ensured its localism. Localism became an abiding characteristic of the US media; the detachment of the press from government and then from close party involvement led also to dependence on advertising. News and advertising grew together – as two parts of a sandwich whose filling was entertainment. News, like American politics, borrowed heavily from entertainment – in order to get the people's attention politicians employed all the available entertainment razzle-dazzle and so did editors, and so also did advertisers.

The news-entertainment-advertising medium of the newspaper had a distinct technology and raw materials; it had a peculiar double system of finance – public sales and advertising; it evolved an elaborate division of labour – printers, journalists, commercial management. All of these were developed in ways which fitted with American (and British) circumstances, and were then copied, often in countries where quite different sets of circumstances obtained.

The news-entertainment-advertising newspaper was defined as primarily a commercial product; subsequently increasing stress was given to 'independence', 'objectivity' and 'neutrality'. In subsequent chapters we will consider this value-neutral ideology and how it looks at the receiving end.

POPULAR COMMERCIAL NEWSPAPERS: KEY INVENTION

The scale and vigour of the American popular press had been known in Europe since the 1830s and at least until 1900 it remained, for Europeans, one of the great wonders of the world. Writing in 1835 a young Frenchman, Alexis de Tocqueville had this to say:

Among the twelve million people living in the territory of the United States, there is not *one single man* who has dared to suggest restricting the freedom of the press. . . .

In France little space is given over to trade advertisements, and even news items are few; the vital part of the newspaper is that devoted to political discussion. In America three-quarters of the bulky newspaper put before you will be full of advertisements and the rest will usually contain political news or just anecdotes. . . .

In the United States printers need no licences, and newspapers no stamps or registration . . . so the number of periodical and semi-periodical productions in the United States surpasses all belief. The most enlightened Americans attribute the slightness of the power of the press to this incredible dispersion. . . .

There is hardly a hamlet in America without its newspaper. . . . In France the hallmark of the spirit of journalism is a violent but lofty and often eloquent way of arguing about great interests of state . . . the hallmark of the American journalist is a direct and coarse attack, without any subtleties, on the passions of his readers; he disregards principles to seize on people, following them into their private lives and laying bare their weaknesses and their vices. . . . Above all, the result is that the personal views expressed by journalists carry, so to speak, no weight with their readers. What they look for in a newspaper is knowledge of facts, and it is only by altering or distorting those facts that the journalist can gain some influence for his views.

However, with their sources thus restricted, the power of the American press is still immense. It makes political life circulate in every corner of that vast land. Its eyes are never shut, and it lays bare the secret shifts of politics, forcing public figures in turn to appear before the tribunal of opinion. . . . Through the press the parties, without actually meeting, listen and argue with one another. . . .

Each individual American newspaper has little power, but after the people, the press is nonetheless the first of the powers.[1]

The American approach to the press began to diverge from its English origins even before Independence. The Stamp Act of 1765 struck at the printers of the colonial papers; the printers not only found various ways of evading the tax but also used their papers' columns to launch a sustained attack on the Stamp Act. The early American press concentrated on seaport commercial information and its first regular readers belonged mainly to the merchant class. Prominent in the merchant class were the printers – the first media entrepreneurs of the new nation; they were in many cases also the postmasters, responsible for mailing newspapers.

Whereas the remote London government had taxed the press, after Independence the press was widely regarded as a basic part of the new political order. The press was seen as having played a vital, indeed heroic, role in the establishment of this new order and consequently it came to seem natural that the American press should be not merely free of taxation but positively subsidized. Perhaps the most important subsidy was the practice of running the Federal Post Office as a public service. Many newspapers, both daily and weekly, were distributed by mail. Between 1790 and 1810 the number of items carried by the postal service increased fourteenfold.[2] 'Exchanges' of newspapers between printers were carried free after 1792 and small rural sheets simply lifted much of their material out of larger newspapers.

Around 1800 there were two polar types of newspaper – first, the *commercial* newspaper devoted to commercial and shipping news with a heavy advertising element; secondly, especially common after 1800 was the paper tied to a political faction – these papers were often *partisan* in an extreme and scurrilous form. But many were a mixture of the two. The press had got in on the ground floor of a new social, political and commercial order and this was to ensure that the American press through the nineteenth century grew ahead of the press of Europe.

By 1850 the United States had become the world centre of a completely new phenomenon – the *cheap daily* press. The penny, or one cent, daily paper was especially a New York phenomenon. *The Sun* had become the first penny daily in New York in 1833. In New York, and in other major eastern cities, such as Philadelphia and Boston, the daily press in 1850 was already reaching deep down among the urban manual workers, whereas in England and the rest of Europe in 1850 the daily press had not yet reached much of the *middle class*.

The New York penny press borrowed many ideas from London. *The Sun* of 1833 was intended partly as a copy of the English *Penny Magazine*. *The Sun* also copied the London technique of humorously reporting court cases; its sales system was even called the 'London Plan' and an Englishman was editor of *The Sun* from 1835 onwards. Yet these influences were combined into something not yet familiar in London, a daily paper aimed at the common man, sold for a cent, subsidized by advertising, which as early as 1836 was making a handsome profit.[3]

By 1850 a predominant pattern of city-region newspapers had emerged in all the American states. Compared with London and Paris – each a dominant capital in a small, mainly flat country – transportation even out of New York City in 1850 still presented severe hazards: to the west were high mountains, and to both north and south were large rivers, which in winter still presented difficulties for daily paper circulation. The early start of the city-region dailies firmly established many papers before the arrival of the railroad – a means by which both London and Paris newspapers achieved national dominance. Telegraph news further strengthened the American regional dailies, by enabling them to carry the major national news.

In American election campaigns from about 1830 onwards a campaign committee's 'newspaper' was usually started a few months before the voting. At least some such papers continued after the election. The Election Specials were important because in America there were more voters than in Europe, more frequent elections, longer campaigns, more offices at stake.

By 1900 special extra-fat Sunday editions were already common; so were colour sections printed on Hoe colour presses. News photographs adorned front pages, and comics were already the first and true love of circulation managers. The basic technology of 1900 was to last for over half a century – fast rotary presses, linotype machines for quick setting and edition changes, the typewriter and the telephone, the continental distribution of news by 'wire' services. The owner of a small weekly paper got much of his editorial material mailed cheaply by syndicates. Providing advertisers with women readers was a major motivation in the increase of afternoon, rather than morning, papers. The newspaper as a vehicle for collecting advertising revenue was a profitably established concept by 1900.

The American immigrant press illustrates the very sharp contrasts between the press in America and in Europe, especially Eastern Europe. Because the Jewish population was so concentrated in New York, the Yiddish press had an unusual number of *daily* papers. The Swedish press was entirely composed of small weekly papers in rural areas – in 1910 there were 348 Swedish-language weekly newspapers and periodicals published in the United States.[4] In 1892 there were 97 German-language *dailies* – New York, Philadelphia,Chicago, St Louis and Milwaukee each had at least five German-language daily newspapers in that year. As early as 1850 New York had four German daily papers, more than either Berlin or Leipzig supported at that time.[5] In the 1870s the *New Yorker Staats-Zeitung* was making a large annual profit and its circulation was probably higher than that of any paper in Germany.[6]

In Eastern Europe German-speaking and Russian colonizers had tried to impose their languages on subject peoples; what local publications did survive tended to be in a 'high' literary form of the language. When the immigrants reached New York all this changed: they were confronted with a range of papers of many political complexions, and in their own language varying from its literary form to local dialects now written down for the first time.

The ideological and religious papers in general foundered; many hundreds of Marxist publications lurched on with small and declining circulations to ultimate extinction. A common commercial type was the paper owned by the shipping company which had brought the immigrants to America and now wanted to promote visits to the 'old country' to fill empty berths on returning ships. Other 'commercial' papers were connected with immigrant banks. It was the 'americanizing' papers which were successful – although this strategy too was ultimately self-destructive.

The American popular press was powerfully shaped by the cities, the immigrants and the western frontier. All three forces were combined in the great base-camp cities of the expanding frontier such as St Louis, Chicago and San Francisco. Pulitzer learnt his journalism in St Louis, Hearst his in San Francisco. Irish immigrants played a leading part in Chicago journalism from 1848 onwards: they initiated the pattern by which the American immigrant press became a firebrand for revolutions and independence movements in Europe.

The frontier element in the American press can be illustrated by Californian journalism a generation before William Randolph Hearst took charge of the *San Francisco Examiner*. In 1850 the United States had 200 *daily* newspapers, probably more than the rest of the world combined. This was also the height of the California gold rush which left the city of San Francisco alone in 1858 with twelve *daily* newspapers. A veteran of these early San Francisco newspapers, writing in 1858, provided these recollections:

> We have gone through the long list of the periodicals started in San Francisco within the last eleven years. They number 132 in all. . . . The papers have been printed in six different languages, have represented nine different nationalities . . . have preached eight different forms of religion, and have been the organs of seven distinct political parties. Most of these papers expired within a twelve-month after they were started, and only twenty-six survive. The *Alta* and the *Herald* are the only papers in the city which date from 1850, and both have been on the verge of the newspaper grave. Not an editor or proprietor connected with the press in 1850 is to be found now in the same position. Let us remember the fate of a few of the editors and reporters . . . King and Dunn [died] at the hands of assassins. Nugent, Washburn, Loehr and Rapp have been wounded in duels, and Russell dangerously wounded with a knife – all for articles they had written. Lafuente and Walton have been sent to Penitentiaries, the former for homicide, the latter for larceny.[7]

Frontier journalists were hard-hitting in more ways than one. Many, before the gold rush, had worked as printers on big papers in New York. Many went on to found new papers elsewhere in California and the west; others carried Californian frontier styles of journalism into Latin America.

ANGLO-AMERICAN PRESTIGE PAPERS AND NEWS AGENCIES

There have been two outstandingly influential examples of the prestige newspaper: first *The Times* of London before 1918 and especially from 1830 to 1870; secondly, the *New York Times* since 1918 and especially since 1940. The leading newspapers of most other countries in the world have been closely modelled upon one or both of these *Times* newspapers. In most countries the serious newspapers also rely for much of their world news on the Anglo-American news agencies – Reuters, AP and UPI.

Prestige newspapers typically have plenty of affluent readers and classified advertising (houses, jobs, servants – and in some countries marriage partners – are acquired through the prestige paper). The paper covers finance, the arts and politics. It becomes a political force, through its news coverage and its close contacts with senior politicians. The prestige paper aims to be also a diplomatic force. For a substantial staff of its own foreign correspondents is an expensive enterprise, which a newspaper cannot justify in revenue terms. The foreign correspondents typically return home to take charge also of the domestic side of the prestige newspaper, so that it acquires a cosmopolitan, sometimes even an alien, reputation – which encourages some politicians to make accusations of lack of patriotism.

The Times was a diplomatic force throughout the mid-nineteenth-century world, and as the legal restrictions were lifted in Europe many newspapers were modelled on it; the same was true of Latin America and the British Empire. Fewer of the newspapers were able, however, to employ their own sizeable staffs of foreign correspondents – they bought their foreign news cheaply from news agencies.

In more recent years many prestige newspapers have bought a news service direct from the *New York Times*. A similar service is also provided by pooling the news services of the *Washington Post* and the *Los Angeles Times*. These latter two have since 1950 followed the *New York Times*: each has strengthened its grip on a major American urban market, has achieved some semi-monopoly security, and has moved away from a conservative past to the more liberal and internationalist stance typical of the prestige paper. In addition to the huge resources of these wealthy papers, each news service draws on other major American, and predictably British, newspaper resources. Both news services are used especially by medium-sized newspapers within the United States; in the rest of the world they are used mainly by serious papers for their feature and column coverage of the United States and for their staff foreign correspondents.

The three leading international news agencies are Associated Press and United Press International (both American) and the British Reuters. There is little doubt that 'the major part of the international news flow is carried by the four Western agencies'.[8]* Even those two dozen or so newspapers and other news organizations in the non-communist world which have substantial numbers of foreign correspondents still use the international news agencies for their basic world coverage. All of the thousands of other newspapers and radio/television stations (outside the communist countries) have little choice but to rely directly or via a national agency on the international agencies as their main source of world news.

The British agency, Reuters, for half a century after 1870 played the leading part in a world news cartel. The European news agencies in 1870 divided the world into exclusive news territories. Reuters obtained the lion's share: Britain, Holland and their combined dependencies in the world – that is, much of Asia and Africa. Havas, the French agency, was given France, Italy, Spain, Portugal and the Levant. Reuters and Havas agreed to operate jointly in the Ottoman

* The fourth major western agency is Agence France-Presse.

Empire, the Balkans, Egypt and Belgium, while the German agency merely got Germany, Scandinavia and Russia. Since 1866 (when the first Atlantic cable was successfully laid), Reuters and Havas exchanged news with the Associated Press, the leading American agency. United States news thus reached the world mainly via Reuters. In 1876 Reuters agreed to Havas having Latin America – while Reuters got Australia, China, Japan and the entire Far East, except Indo-China.

From 1870 to 1914 Reuters, based in London at the hub of the world cable system, dominated – with some French assistance – the world flow of news. Reuters specialized in financial and political news. Havas and Reuters both supplied financial news to businessmen before they began supplying news to newspapers. Both the British and French agencies operated in the world from an imperial base.

The dominance of Reuters in world news was resented by Associated Press, which itself was a rather different kind of news agency. Whereas Havas and Reuters originated as privately owned commercial companies, the Associated Press had always been co-operatively owned by 'member' newspapers; whereas the European agencies concentrated on financial, diplomatic, and national political news, the American agency supplied news across the broad range now required by US newspapers – including sport, women's features, human interest, crime and regional American news. Whereas Havas was closely tied to the French government and Reuters was loosely tied to the British Empire, the US agencies proclaimed (even if they could not entirely demonstrate) their total independence of government. Above all Associated Press was, in 1900, still entirely a *domestic* US agency – built on the immensely secure 'membership' base of 725 of the largest daily newspapers in the US.[9]*

After the 1914–18 war the American agencies began to compete with, and slowly to overhaul the European agencies on the world scene. The American agencies accused Reuters and Havas of being monopoly government agencies. The 1939–45 war and its aftermath established the dominance of the Anglo-American agencies. Since 1945 the French agency (reborn as Agence France-Presse) has been clearly in fourth place.

The American agency style also became predominant over the old British and French emphasis on diplomatic and commercial news.

---

* By 1962 AP claimed 8,000 clients, 4,109 of them in the USA. Since so many of the world's newspapers and radio/television stations are now within chains and networks, the definition of 'client' has become vague and such statistics increasingly meaningless. According to Michael Singletary (1975), 1,171 US daily newspapers took the AP service and 799 took UPI in 1973.

Reuters in the mid-1970s was successfully clinging to its tradition of financial news – and drawing at least half its revenue from non-media clients such as banks. But the American agencies have diversified into other kinds of media news – and AP and UPI both draw some 80 per cent of their income from US domestic press, radio and TV. The world-wide operation of the American agencies is heavily geared to supplying news to domestic US media; the American agencies have a strong American flavour compared with the less strong British flavour in the Reuters service.

In most of the world, notions of what a prestige newspaper should be, and how a national news agency should operate, are strongly influenced by the news which so many of them acquire from the Anglo-American prestige papers (through syndication) and from the Anglo-American news agencies. But the United States prestige papers and news agencies reflect the special circumstances of the American media.

The great United States prestige newspapers are semi-monopolies – dominating advertising (especially classified and retail) in a great urban market, such as New York, Washington or Los Angeles. In each of these cities the previously intense competition is now radically reduced. Their finances relatively assured through semi-monopoly, these great newspapers focus on maximizing their revenue in the local news, advertising and feature sections; but in the more prominent sections of the paper the concern is primarily with prestige. Prestige takes the form of objective 'neutral' news, political analysis and maintaining the paper's own formidable staff of national and international correspondents.

Power is another name for this prestige – the goal is to be an independent force in local, national and international politics. The more prestigious and independent, the more powerful; the more powerful, the more independent and prestigious. No President or Governor can easily inflict upon them more than minor wounds. They are unlikely to be outflanked – their power being such that they can buy into or otherwise defend themselves against new or rival media.* These great American semi-monopoly papers have become bastions of, and independent baronies within, the American political system. They are the prime exhibit – indeed the militant carriers – of a great and potent tradition, the free and independent press. In foreign eyes – in the eyes of journalists around the world, and of some politicians

---

* All three of these newspapers (*NYT*, *WP* and *LAT*) own newsprint mills and are diversified into other media interests – mainly television, radio, magazines and books. In all three cases, however, the newspapers remain the lynch-pins of their respective groups and none of them are overshadowed by non-media business interests.

too – these great newspapers embody American democracy more even than does Congress, more than the Presidency, more certainly than the Supreme Court. They exercise a great fascination, and lead to many attempts at imitation. Yet the prestige papers of most other lands cannot be another *New York Times*. They lack its dominance in an immensely affluent if troubled urban area, where its main competition is provided by suburban dailies.

The United States prestige newspapers' local semi-monopolies reflect a wider pattern – most American daily newspapers are complete local monopolies. There are some 1,700 daily newspapers in the USA – few of which are seriously threatened by competition. The *national* vacuum is primarily filled by the two dominant American news agencies, Associated Press and United Press International. Here there is genuine competition between two powerful forces – somewhat similar to the competition between the three broadcast networks. But this AP and UPI duopoly is itself built upon the local monopoly of nearly all of their newspaper clients.

The American pattern of local media leads to a *national* pattern of a few strong organizations which are geared to supplying far-flung local outlets – and then go on to do the same thing in the world. As with the electronic media, these exporters, while selling their own media output, also tend to influence and define news values, styles and formats around the world.

'BACKGROUND' AND OTHER ANGLO-AMERICAN NEWS FORMS

The predominant press form is the daily newspaper and the predominant syndicated service is the news agency geared mainly to the requirements of daily newspapers – specializing in a rapid supply of 'hard' news, the day's events in politics, sport and disaster. Magazines also require 'news', but of a less instant kind; the same is true of Sunday newspapers and to some extent of the daily press as well.

Thus various kinds of non-hard, less rapid, news have grown up. Weekly news magazines, feature coverage, specialized and technical news and various documentary or investigative approaches are some of the internationally best known varieties. Like hard news these various kinds of soft news have largely been defined by the Anglo-Americans – and broadly for the same reasons. Soft news, background, features, and so on, are defined as filling in the gaps, or filling the areas behind, the hard news. Thus the major forms of news in these areas grew up alongside the commercial daily newspapers and the news agencies in the Anglo-American press. They were developed earlier and taken further in the American, and to a lesser extent the British, press.

The *news magazine*'s history is usually traced from the founding of *Time* magazine in 1923. It was a response to the dominance of daily and agency news. At first *Time* was largely made up of rewritten press cuttings. Soon it developed its own reporting staff who in effect went back over last week's stories in an attempt to tell readers what 'really' happened. Much of the news magazine's appeal lay in its being available across the US in localities where the only easily available daily newspapers were dull and provincial. *Time* and its imitators offered the zip and glamour of New York, a sense of Washington's backstairs – this was appealing both in the American mid-west and later in other countries. In many countries the local adoption of American news magazine formats also conceals influences from Britain (for instance in West Germany and in India).

'Feature' coverage is one of those many words in journalism which has no satisfactory definition except in terms of yet other sorts of journalism. Features are non-hard news; features are not tied rigidly to a point in time. The larger American newspapers developed feature writing to fill out the hard news and to fill up the paper on days which were short of disasters and other instant events. These services were sold by the New York and Chicago press across the American continent by mail and in the form of 'stereotypes' ready for printing. They are the origin of the present-day newspaper international news services.

Specialized magazines also complemented the general interest news service of the agencies and the daily press. The prototype was the American farm magazine. One of the first was the *American Farmer* (launched 1818).[10] By the 1870s there were numerous American farm publications increasingly packed with advertising for farm goods and equipment.[11] American farming in productivity and output/manpower terms was throughout the nineteenth century well ahead of Europe.[12] Subsequently other kinds of technical publications emerged, and here again shrewd European 'innovators' did the usual borrowing from American examples.

The column is yet another type of news coverage which has a particular relationship to the American pattern of national news agencies and local daily newspapers. Unlike the characteristic European newspaper column emphasizing literary grace and personal opinion, the American one was usually a mixture of opinion and background news or gossip. This was true of the show business column – as represented by Walter Winchell in his brazen keyhole coverage of Broadway stars; it was equally true of the political column especially from 1933. The columns were bought at low prices by newspapers across America; they offered a mild antidote to the conventions of instancy and neutrality upheld by the agencies. The show business, and later the political, columns were also syndicated abroad.

Documentary is even less easily definable than the others. One recent writer[13] sees documentary as a peculiarly American world view – which found expression in radio journalism, photojournalism, the federal writers' projects of the 1930s, in participant observation sociology and in the writing of James Agee; he also acknowledges some European and especially British origins – notably in John Grierson's 'documentary film' movement.

SOUND AND VIDEO NEWS

Sound and video news combine the Anglo-American traditions of news agency, newspaper and Hollywood. Radio, in its early days, was seen as a threatening prospect by newspapers, and in some cases by news agencies and governments. An urge to combat Nazi foreign radio in the late 1930s led the American networks to broadcast news to Latin America and the BBC to add foreign language broadcasts to its Empire Service. This was the forerunner of a huge expansion of radio news aimed at both overseas and domestic audiences in the Second World War.

By 1945 the British and the Americans had evolved two somewhat different styles of radio news, one or both of which, after 1945, served as models for nearly every country in the world. The American news agencies developed specialized news services for the many small radio stations in the US – a pattern which they also adapted for other countries, especially in Latin America. All three Anglo-American agencies now sell 'voice' news stories from their own staff correspondents on a world-wide basis.

The regular use of photographs in newspapers began only around 1900; New York news photography quickly became available across America via the established agencies and syndication services. In the 1920s the pace was set by the New York tabloids – although the 'tabloid' also had London ancestry. In the late 1930s came the influential newsphoto techniques of *Life* magazine – developments which had first a German and then British ancestry.[14] Perhaps even more widespread in its significance was the development in the 1930s of the wirephoto machine. This technique enables a news agency to supply photographs to clients thousands of miles away within a matter of minutes. The world wirephoto market is monopolized by the two American agencies, AP and UPI; many newspaper clients take them primarily for their wirephoto service.* Newspapers which cannot afford wirephoto may subscribe to a cheap airmail photo service. The first still pictures of spectacular air crashes, floods and other disasters reach most of the world's television screens via the wirephoto services of AP and UPI.

French companies were the early leaders in cinema newsreels. This lead later passed to Hollywood[15] - and in those many countries where Hollywood films became dominant the typical pattern was of local newsreel companies which were part-owned by, or contracted with, Hollywood newsreels. The Hollywood newsreels reached their peak of world influence in 1945-50. Two news-film agencies subsequently emerged to provide the most extreme of all examples of Anglo-American dominance in a specialized media field.

Visnews is three-quarters owned in Britain - in equal parts by Reuters and the BBC; the other quarter share is owned equally by the public service broadcasting organizations in Australia, Canada and New Zealand. The second major news film agency, UPITN, is owned by the American UPI news agency and by British ITN television news. These film agencies depend upon the familiar circumstance of the Anglo-Americans selling to other countries a high cost service at a relatively low price.

UPI and Reuters respectively provide UPITN and Visnews with a ready-made international telecommunications network and a huge basic news supply. Visnews also provides BBC news-film to the American NBC network news; Visnews has based its service on selling to the world the entire news-film resources of the American NBC news,† the British BBC and the Japanese NHK news. UPITN has similarly been selling the British ITN news-film and UPI news-film from USA and overseas.

The American CBS network was in the mid-1970s also selling its domestic US television news, on videotape, to customers around the world, as were two other organizations (though on a smaller scale) - the West German DPA-Etes and the American ABC network.

The three significant sellers of daily video news in the world are all Anglo-American. The leading agency by any criterion is the British Visnews, second the Anglo-American UPITN, third the American CBS. Once again London and New York are the twin capitals of a world news operation - with Hong-Kong the main staging post on the other

* On a single day in May 1973 the author counted 32 foreign news photographs in 4 prominent Mexico City newspapers - *Excelsior, El Heraldo, El Universal* and *La Prensa*. 28 of them were from AP and UPI.
† NBC television news is also extremely dependent upon the AP and UPI agencies. In December 1968 the AP and UPI wire services provided the starting point of 70% of all stories assigned by NBC news for film coverage. Epstein (1974), p. 142.

side of the world. London has the usual advantages of a special relationship with the USA and the Commonwealth, and in video news it has the additional advantage of membership in the Eurovision news exchange. Until the early 1970s these services were based on news-film freighted by air from London. By the mid 1970s the agencies were moving away from film-by-air to videotape and satellite. Visnews has a well established 10-minute daily satellite feed to Australia.

Visnews in 1975 claimed that its news was seen on 'some 99 per cent of all the television receivers in the world'. It had network customers in all of the world's most populous nations – including China and the Soviet Union. The Visnews service was taken by every European country possessing a TV network with the single exception of Bulgaria. The largest Latin-American country *not* taking Visnews was Ecuador.

In addition to its core of BBC, NBC, and NHK news-film, Visnews has its own staff of television reporters and stringers around the world. On any day it has about 30 video stories of which some 8 or 10 are sent to any individual television client. At the Visnews headquarters, in an industrial area of west London not far from Heathrow airport, it is possible to see set out on just two sheets of paper a table indicating which of today's video stories are going to which of 193 customers in 98 countries and territories of the world. Of the 12 or 15 minutes sent each day to each client, the typical television network uses 4 or 5 minutes each day on its news bulletins, whilst some poorer television networks use the full 12 to 15 minutes day after day.

NEWS, STORIES AND THE MEDIA

Human interest is the universal element in the news. It is what gives the news story its symbolic character. . . .

It is the practice of writing up and dramatizing the news which came into existence with the so-called Yellow Press that has transformed the newspaper in the United States and, to a lesser extent, in other countries, including Japan, from a more or less sober record of events into a form of popular literature . . . stories like those recorded in the popular ballads; stories of love and of death.

. . . Mr Hearst . . . has gone out for human documents and, in doing so, has apparently been responsible for the new vogue of the so-called 'true story' magazines.[16]

'Every news story should, without any sacrifice of probity or responsibility, display *the attributes of fiction*, of drama,' Reuven Frank instructed his staff at NBC.[17]

The 'story' element is common to all the media and is referred to as such in most of the media occupations. That there should be *stories* in entertainment and advertising is more obvious than that there should be *news* stories. Nevertheless English-language journalism in general and American popular journalism in particular has emphasized this story element.

Newspapers became a mosaic of stories, the journalist a story teller. A common element for all media was thus forged within the news format and was carried into all other media by journalists who played a substantial part in populating all the other media occupations.

Press journalists went forth into films and became script writers; they worked in radio drama and pursued soap-opera story-lines; journalists were among the early pop song writers of Tin Pan Alley; they invaded television, the greatest story-telling medium of all. Journalists and their ideas of news stories also emigrated to advertising agencies where products are given 'strong stories' and sympathetic storytellers; public relations men, like their advertising cousins, are in the story-telling business. Still pictures also must 'tell a story' – no less, ideally, than political cartoons or Disney comics. Stories must 'grab' first fellow media professionals, then audiences. Even market research reports should tell a story if they are to get read.

Throughout all of the media the unadulterated fictional story has long been, and remains, strong. The media occupations are pervaded by the art of the anecdote; journalists are professional anecdotalists. Hearst's achievement was to take the American western tradition of the tall tale and to dress it in clothes of fact.

Two occupational types dominate the American media and have been imitated around the world. One is the journalist, the teller of stories and dispenser of facts. The second type is the promotional entrepreneur, the seller of stories.

CHAPTER TWO

Media imperialism?*

THE TELEVISION IMPERIALISM THESIS

Many people over the last hundred years have pointed out the importance of American (and British) media in the world.[1] The most carefully researched work on this topic is still Thomas Guback's *The
International Film Industry* (1969) which analyses Hollywood dominance in the western European film industries since 1945. However,
Herbert Schiller's *Mass Communications and American Empire*, also
by an American and also published in 1969, is a rare exception to the
general lack of Marxist empirical accounts.[2] Schiller's thesis – that
American television exports are part of an attempt by the American
military industrial complex to subjugate the world – has been followed
by other related work. Alan Wells's *Picture Tube Imperialism?* (1972)
pursues the television imperialism thesis in Latin America.

Schiller's first contention is that despite the apparently commercial
character of United States telecommunications, the American radio
spectrum has increasingly come under the control of the federal
government in general and the US Secretary of Defense in particular.
Domestic American radio and television is concerned with selling
receiving sets and advertising goods. The educational stations of early
American radio were lost as a consequence of commercialism and
greed, and Schiller would like to see a return to a more educational
and less commercial emphasis. Since 1950 and increasingly since
the Cuban Bay of Pigs fiasco of 1961, Schiller sees American television
as having come under the control of Washington; for example RCA
(which controls the NBC television and radio networks) is also a
major defence contractor – and consequently beholden to, and un-
critical of, the federal government.

The great expansion of American television into the world around
1960 – equipment, programming and advertising – is seen by Schiller
as part of a general effort of the American military industrial complex
to subject the world to military control, electronic surveillance and
homogenized American commercial culture. American television

---

* You may prefer to read about 'Media Imperialism' at a later stage, for
instance, before reading Part Four. If so, please skip.

programme exports, through their close connection with the manufacture of television receiving sets and American advertising agencies,
are also seen as the spearhead for an American consumer goods invasion of the world. This export boom has, and is intended to have,
the effect of muting political protest in much of the world; local and
authentic culture in many countries is driven on to the defensive by
homogenized American culture. Traditional national drama and
folk music retreat before *Peyton Place* and *Bonanza*. So powerful is
the thrust of American commercial television that few nations can
resist. Even nations which deliberately choose not to have commercial
broadcasting find their policies being reversed by American advertising agencies within their borders and by pirate radio stations from
without. Commercial radio and television received from neighbouring countries tend to a 'domino effect', by which commercial radio
spreads remorselessly into India, while commercial television spreads
from one west European country to the next. With the exception of
the communist countries, and perhaps Japan, few nations can
resist.

During the 1960s, Schiller argued, American policy came to focus
even more strongly on subjugating and pacifying the poor nations;
and in this strategy space satellites were to play a key part. The
United States government handed its telecommunications satellite
policy into the hands of the giant electronics companies (ATT, ITT,
RCA) and then negotiated with the western nations INTELSAT arrangements which gave the United States dominance of world communications; ultimately the policy was to beam American network television
complete with commercials straight into domestic television sets
around the world. The homogenization of world culture would then
be complete. False consciousness would be plugged via satellite into
every human home.

Alan Wells elaborates how American television imperialism works
in Latin America. Latin American television, since its birth, has been
dominated by United States finance, companies, technology, programming – and, above all, dominated by New York advertising
agencies and practices. There is a very substantial US direct ownership interest in Latin American television stations. 'Worldvision', an
ominously titled subsidiary of the US national ABC network, plays a
dominant role in Latin America; American advertising agencies not
only produce most of the very numerous commercial breaks but also
sponsor, shape and determine the whole pattern of programming and
importing from the USA. Indeed, 'approximately 80 per cent of the
hemisphere's current programs – including *The Flintstones*, *I Love
Lucy*, *Bonanza* and *Route 66* – were produced in the United States'.[3]
This near monopoly of North American television programming

within South America distorts entire economies away from 'producer-ism' and towards 'consumerism'. Madison Avenue picture tube imperialism has triumphed in every Latin American country except Cuba.

THE TELEVISION IMPERIALISM THESIS: TOO STRONG AND TOO WEAK

The Schiller-Wells account *exaggerates* the strength of American television, partly because some of their quoted figures are unreliable; they concentrate on the high point of American television exports in the mid-1960s. They also tend to accept too easily the promotional optimism of a company like ABC, whose Worldvision remained a paper 'network' only. Sometimes, too, their logic is faulty. They complain that in the poor countries only the very rich can buy tele-vision anyhow, and then they see television as subverting the whole nation. But the American influence on world television – even if not so great as these authors argue – has been very considerable.

These authors' argument is also too *weak*. They scarcely notice the tendency of television merely to repeat a previous pattern of radio and feature films. This television imperialism thesis ignores the much earlier pattern of the press and news agencies which quite un-ambiguously did have an imperial character – although the empires were European ones, mainly British, but also French, Dutch, Belgian, Portuguese.

Tapio Varis has produced (Table 1) the first reasonably compre-hensive mapping of worldwide television import patterns. Varis found for 1971 (the year before Wells's book was published) that the tele-vision channels in the larger Latin American countries (such as Argentina, Colombia and Mexico) imported between 10 per cent and 39 per cent of programming. The only one of seven Latin American countries in the Varis study to import 80 per cent of programming was Guatemala.[4] Varis also found that a substantial proportion of television imports came from countries other than USA, including imports from such Latin American countries as Mexico.

Nevertheless, the Varis 1971 study did document American tele-vision exports around the world on an enormous scale:

> Many of the developing countries use much imported material, but
> – with the exception of a number of Latin American countries
> and a few Middle East countries – television is still of minor
> importance in most parts of the developing world; when it is
> available, it is for the most part merely a privilege of the urban
> rich.

The United States and the People's Republic of China are examples of countries which currently use little foreign material – at least compared with the total amount of their own programming. Japan and the Soviet Union also produce most of their own programs. Most other nations, however, are heavy purchasers of foreign material. Even in an area as rich as western Europe, imported programs account for about one-third of total transmission time.

Most nonsocialist countries purchase programs mainly from the United States and the United Kingdom. In western Europe for example, American produced programs account for about half of all imported programs, and from 15 to 20 per cent of total transmission time. The socialist countries also use American and British material, but only TV Belgrade uses as large a share of American programs as the Western European countries.

The real social and political impact of imported programs may be greater than might be inferred from the volume of imported material, because of audience viewing patterns and the placing of foreign programming. Available studies about prime-time programming in various countries tend to show that the proportion of foreign material during these hours is considerably greater than at other times.

For each country surveyed, we looked at the categories into which imported programs fell. Program imports are heavily concentrated on serials and series, long feature films, and entertainment programs.[5]

A more recent study by Elihu Katz, George Wedell and their colleagues[6] traces the history of both radio and television in ten Latin American, Asian and African countries plus Cyprus. This study attributes a considerably larger place to British influence. The Katz-Wedell study suggests that the television imperialism thesis takes too little account of radio and of differences both within and between nations. It also strongly confirms that there was a high point of American influence on world television at some point in the 1960s. Central to the Katz-Wedell study is the notion of 'phases of institutionalization'. First there was a direct transfer or adoption of a metropolitan – usually American, British or French – model of broadcasting, with radio setting the pattern for television. Secondly, there was a phase of adapting this system to the local society. Thirdly, and ultimately, a new 'sense of direction' was introduced by the government – this typically involved removing any remaining vestiges of direct foreign ownership and increasing the direct control of government. This third phase typically occurred around 1970 and thus invalidated some of the Schiller and Wells arguments around the time they were being published.

Katz and Wedell focus heavily on the receiving countries and are excellent at detailing the endless muddles, confusion, indecisions, self-deception, conflicting goals, conflicting ministries – the general chaos which seems to characterize the appearance of television. Katz and Wedell reject any strong television imperialism thesis, and they tend to see the American and British exporters of television models and styles as no less muddled and self-deceiving than the importers.

Nevertheless despite their implicit rejection of much of the television imperialism thesis, Katz and Wedell do provide much descriptive material which fits the thesis quite well. The importance of production (transmission and studio) technology is confirmed. Like the other students of television exports, they look with horror on the weight of commercial advertising, the predominance of American entertainment series and the relative absence in most countries of high quality educational or cultural television programming.

EXPENSIVE MEDIA PRODUCT AT LOW PRICES

The economies of scale operate in many manufacturing fields, and especially in fields where the research and development costs are high – such as new drugs, aircraft production or computers. In these three fields the United States has achieved supremacy. But the economies of scale work in an even more extreme way in some media fields. In order to achieve extra overseas sales you have physically to manufacture and sell additional aircraft, or computers or pills – and a similar situation obtains with books or records. But in other media fields the additional cost of extra 'copies' is negligible. Only one copy is needed to show on a national television network. Only a smallish number of copies of feature films are required for one country. And – what few television imperialism writers have noticed – news agencies and syndication services are also subject to extreme economies of scale; once you have a news service available in a foreign capital, hooking up additional clients costs a fairly negligible amount.

Such economies of scale operate equally for all large producers, one might think. But this is not quite the case. The standard American practice in all media fields is initially to undercut the opposition through price competition; this follows from the enormous numbers of publications and broadcasts outlets in the USA. The policy is wide sales at low prices. American news agencies adopted this policy when they broke into the world market and they still operate it now. Hollywood did this so successfully with feature films that it could later raise its prices. The same tactics were pursued in television –

but the possibility of greatly raising prices has been defeated by the national television organizations which are typically strong buyers looking for bargains among competing sellers. Thus it may be true that American companies like RCA saw enormous sales of television sets and programming as a lucrative possibility; but there is also some evidence that RCA were rather hesitant, and only ABC of the US networks was really optimistic. Moreover, what happened was as bad in commercial terms as the most pessimistic predictions; starting with 'initially' very low prices, American television exporters saw their prices rise only a little and later stay steady against inflation. Exports of American television sets also did not succeed as well as many expected.

The often ferocious and often self-contradictory arguments put forward on this topic stem partly from an absence of reliable information about the actual prices paid for various services. Since an extra 'copy' of a news agency service, or the use of a feature film or a television series, has no obvious or 'rational' price there is more than the usual scope for price cutting and variation. Nevertheless, my guess is that the absence of price information results partly from embarrassment on both sides; often, I suspect, the salesmen of American companies are embarrassed by the low prices they are getting. Equally, I suspect, purchasers are embarrassed by the quantity and sometimes the *quality* of material they are receiving for such a low price.

Reasonably reliable estimates of the total overseas revenue of United States media are available in some cases, even though the nature of revenue varies greatly between media – as does the ratio of 'revenue' to profit. Probably first would come feature films; Hollywood 'theatrical' revenues abroad were $592 million in 1975 (Table 16). Approximately second equal would be records (including tapes, etc.) and the overseas revenues (commission, not billings) of American advertising agencies. Next would come the roughly $100 million revenue of US television exports; then the overseas revenue of AP and UPI. These five categories together probably earned revenues of between $1,500 and $2,000 million in 1975.

By 1975 British television exports were probably earning about as much as those of the United States, if feature films on television are excluded. This British success depended heavily on the market of the United States itself. But lacking Hollywood's large theatrical film earnings, Britain must have earned a sizeable fraction of her export media revenue through books and EMI records. In video news exports – Britain's strongest single media export field – revenues were extremely small; Visnews in 1975–6 earned revenues of only £3·8 million and no profit at all.

The tendency of the most obviously politically influential media exports to earn the least revenue is consistent with the non-profit goals which often obtain in news, plus the market strength of such major purchasers of news as national news agencies and broadcasting organizations. Over half American export media revenues are earned from the young people who buy pop records or visit cinemas, and from advertisers, around the world. Or to express the same point in media imperialism terms: Media exporters earn monopoly profits by selling entertainment to young consumers of entertainment and young housewife users of advertised products, while the media exporters dump their products at low prices on national broadcasting organizations and news agencies.

IMPORTING NEWS

In retrospect it may seem inexplicable that the governments of certain countries ever allowed media importing to take place on the scale of Hollywood film importing around 1920 or American television series importing after 1960. But governments are more interested in news than any other media form; and international arrangements for controlling the trade in news had been established long before 1920.

The main instrument of news trading was the international news agency; the main exporters of international news around 1870 were Reuters and Havas – and all the other countries were the customers of the British and the French agency. More precisely, the importers were often national news agencies in particular countries; any government could indirectly control the incoming flow of British or French news by controlling or guiding the national agency through which the news was sieved before it reached any domestic newspapers. It was not surprising that the great diplomatic and financial nations, France and Britain, should dominate the world wholesaling of news. Moreover a powerful and rising European nation like Germany was able to get itself included as the third member of the cartel with its own special area in Scandinavia and Russia.

The international dissemination of news thus acquired a strong flavour of free trade – free trade as a doctrine interpreted by Britain and France. One of the contributions of the United States on the world scene was to give this free trade a fresh flavour; the American agencies in the early twentieth century brought an increase in direct competition both amongst themselves and between themselves and the Europeans; the news cartel slowly lost its imperial overtones and incorporated more competition. The American agencies in the inter-war period seemed to be giving a new meaning to the notion of a free trade in news; moreover, the main enemies of this notion in the 1930s – Hitler for instance – by their very opposition must in many countries have increased confidence in the English-language agencies.

At the time of the Hollywood world-wide export dominance of 1920, most of the world's governments were more or less willing to accept the western international news agencies. And this situation has continued ever since. The western agencies have largely maintained their international acceptability despite the emergence of the communist bloc and the independence of ex-colonial nations. Governments in these countries can still control the in-flow of news, and to some extent the out-flow, through the mechanism of their national agency. The world's governments, with almost no exceptions, allow the international agencies to gather news about them for world dissemination. Governments know that it is possible to cover a country from outside – via radio and newspapers, by interviewing plane passengers arriving in neighbouring countries and so on; most governments prefer to have the foreign agency men based in the country, where correspondents often have little alternative to heavy dependence on the local national news agency. International news agencies are partly mere go-betweens for national news agencies. But the two American agencies and the British agency have acquired special international legitimacy. Most governments, politicians and journalists acknowledge that this news – while neither neutral nor always accurate – is at least more neutral and more accurate than any likely alternative. Even though the Anglo-Americans only behave as if neutrality were possible or accuracy meaningful, nevertheless the energy which goes into the 'as if' performance is apparently widely thought to be impressive.

These agencies have largely shaped the presentation of international news in all countries around the world; these agencies do not merely play a major part in establishing the international political agenda, but they have done so now for a hundred years. And for a hundred years they have been the main definers of world 'news values', of what sort of things become news.

This news legitimacy has, of course, been very strongly connected with the agencies' considerable success in being, if not all things to all governments and all newspaper readers, then at least acceptable to most governments and most newspaper readers. This has been done partly by parcelling the world up into regions with regional services;* just as the two American agencies distribute regional services to the main regions of the USA, so also in the world. The 'two sides' style of domestic reporting – 'the Republican said and then the Democrat said' – has led to a two-sided style of international reporting. Even

* In general Reuters' services are more regionalized and Associated Press the least regionalized in most world regions. A common economy measure adopted by the American agency is to reduce the regional news element in regional services.

though an American news agency is in many ways totally American, it is easy to edit the service into a 'one-sided' shape merely by leaving out what the Republicans or the Democrats said, or internationally by leaving out what the capitalists or the communists said. Any newspaper or news agency journalist in the world who wants a ready supply of pointed and critical comments on the American President or the British Prime Minister need go no further than the agency ticker tape already installed across the hall.

The quality of being easy to bend and shape, easy to edit selectively, is also found in Anglo-American feature news material of various kinds. The *New York Times* service in 1972 was taken by 119 foreign newspapers in 46 countries.* The *Los Angeles Times/Washington Post* news service was available in English, French, Spanish or German and was taken by 100 newspapers also in 46 countries.

One of these leading prestige papers in a sizeable country is unlikely to buy a foreign news service lightly; buying such a service implies at least respect, probably admiration. Buying these services from American prestige newspapers (and their British junior partners) amounts to a re-affirmation that the paper buying the service is continuing to follow Anglo-American news values. In all but a few countries in the world (such as Britain) these prestige newspapers are not only the most politically influential but also have the largest or among the largest sales; many are also looked up to as leaders in technological innovation and the practice of journalism.

Time and *Newsweek* are available in most countries in the world; even at the height of the Cold War such American magazines were relatively seldom censored,[7] and in many countries there are now domestic imitations – which often copy the American formats in considerable detail. In western Europe export sales of dailies, weeklies and monthlies are dominated by American and British publications (French and German foreign sales are confined largely to Switzerland, Belgium and Austria).[8] A large number of American technical magazines have significant foreign sales.[9]

'Off-shore' media production, which is especially familiar in the feature film industry, was pioneered in Europe by American tycoon publishers. From 1887 James Gordon Bennett jnr produced a daily edition of the *Herald* in Paris, and since then – apart from 1940–4 –

---

* The leaders in this field are the *New York Times* news service and the *Washington Post/Los Angeles Times* news service. The *New York Times* news service was taken in 1972 by *Al Ahram* (Cairo), *Politika* (Belgrade), *The Times* and *Sunday Times* (London), *Le Figaro* and *L'Express* (Paris), *Der Spiegel* (Germany), *Corriera della Sera* (Milan), *Asahi Shimbun* (Tokyo), *Times of India* (Bombay); it was also taken by a number of leading 'prestige' papers of Latin America – *O Estado de São Paulo* and *Jornal do Brasil*, *El Mercurio* (Santiago, Chile), *Excelsior* (Mexico City), *La Nacion* (Buenos Aires) and *El Nacional* (Caracas).

there has always been at least one American daily newspaper published in Paris. These efforts not only directed European attention towards American newspaper tycoons but also brought to Europe many young American journalists, who often later worked on other publications. Bennett's journalists were the first of many succeeding waves of American communicators – others appeared in films (from about 1910 on), in commercial radio (about 1930 on), in television (especially 1955 on). There were also waves of agency journalists and of advertising men. The off-shore style of production led to overseas editions of various magazines of which *Reader's Digest* is the most famous; women's magazines were another major field later followed by men's magazines. Recently we have seen off-shore American business magazines.*

Even those relatively few of the world's newspapers and other news media which have their own staff correspondents tend to station a high proportion of them in New York, Washington and London. Staff correspondents reporting from the United States tend to rely heavily on the dominant us domestic media. Foreign correspondents subscribe to a special American agency wire for such correspondents; every day they read the *New York Times* and *Washington Post* and perhaps the *Wall Street Journal*; every week they plough through piles of magazines – and they follow the networks.[10] The Editor or foreign editor back home in London or Tokyo has often himself previously been stationed in the USA and he continues to take an active interest in American news – he does this via the London or Tokyo service of the self-same agencies available in the USA, via local editions of the self-same news magazines and so on. Consequently foreign correspondents stationed in the USA tend to receive enthusiastic requests for reports on the latest White House briefing, the

* McGraw-Hill is involved in an international network of business magazines, which has three main elements:
   1. *Business Week* – McGraw-Hill's main US business magazine also has an international edition.
   2. *International Management* – was established by McGraw-Hill in London in 1946; it is a monthly aimed at Britain, the British Commonwealth and the English language world market. This magazine also has a Spanish language edition for Latin America.
   3. McGraw-Hill has established various kinds of editorial, sales, advertising and in some cases, joint ownership, arrangements with business magazines in major countries; these include *Espansione* (Italy), *L'Expansion* (France), *Manager* (West Germany), and *Nikkei Business* (Japan) – the latter for instance, involves a partnership with the Japanese financial daily, *Nihon Keizai Shimbun*.

These arrangements allow economies not only in editorial – but the world chain of McGraw-Hill offices provides economies in selling copies and attracting advertising between countries.

latest dark-horse for the Republican nomination, and requests for
the correspondent's own version of *Newsweek*'s fascinating feature
on the worse-than-ever difficulties of New York's Mayor. Thus the
correspondent finds himself rewriting at source bits and pieces of the
very same American national media which in regional versions are on
sale around the world. Something similar happens for foreign correspondents based in Britain.

With Visnews and UPITN the international news agency tradition is
married to the BBC tradition and the result is world-wide acceptance.
The video news stories which Visnews and UPITN supply to their
customers around the world each day contain (in contrast to CBS)
only natural sound – the thud of rifle butts on heads, perhaps –
thuds alone without spoken commentary. There is a written commentary describing such details as names, time and place, but different television networks can shape the film to their own ideological
and stylistic requirements by adding commentary and by editing.
Richer customers use fewer stories and typically edit down those they
do use to shorter running times. Many stories are supplied to customers only in a single world region; normally a story has to be of interest to several countries to get covered. An item of interest to only one
country – such as an African President visiting Latin America – can
be specially covered. In addition many news background and documentary television stories are compiled by TV network customers
around the world from the archive film libraries of the video
agencies – Visnews has 35 million feet of archive newsreel and TV
news-film.

The Anglo-American video news agencies also provide the core of
the material for the Eurovision daily news exchange. Visnews alone
provided 25·5 per cent of all news material on Eurovision in 1973.
Eurovision has the most significant and long established daily television news exchange in the world and it is now linked to other
regional exchanges; it has a daily exchange with the Soviet and east
European Intervision. Its news goes daily from Madrid via Atlantic
satellite to Latin America. Its exchange links are also spreading
across the Mediterranean into North Africa and the Middle East. In
all cases the flow of news is either entirely, or mainly, 'one-way flow'
out of Eurovision, and in all cases the Anglo-American video news
agencies provide the core of material transmitted. It is thus difficult
to exaggerate either the direct presence or the indirect influence of
Anglo-American materials and styles on television news throughout
the world.

Having shaped the world's print news values, the Anglo-Americans
have largely written the international grammar of television news;
the main television news bulletin in most countries in the world will

normally carry some Visnews material. Why? Audiences in all countries have been taught to expect television news to include an expensive commodity – foreign news film. If you don't buy it cheaply from the Anglo-Americans there is no practical alternative. Morcovcr, as with newspapers, this foreign covcragc is of more visually dramatic material; it is typically of higher technical quality than local material (in most countries) and among television 'professionals' it carries more prestige than does domestic material.

Being dependent upon foreign countries for their information about international politics may have been a difficult pill to swallow. But foreign ministries – faced with the alternative of not having the information, or having to rely entirely on their own diplomats – swallowed the pill. After this, accepting entertainment from abroad was easy; foreign advertising, easier still.

SOME APPEALS OF HOLLYWOOD ENTERTAINMENT*

Many countries failed around 1920 to grasp the near impossibility of shutting out Hollywood films. Later, especially in the 1930s, some countries began to develop coherent policies for such resistance. But having made non-commercial arrangements for broadcasting, most of these same countries then failed to recognize that a state controlled broadcasting system also would face an importing dilemma. State broadcasting systems were in the late 1940s taken somewhat unawares by music imports. The same broadcasting systems were later taken unawares by television imports.

The most successful resistance to Hollywood imports in the 1930s occurred in the Soviet Union, Japan and Germany. These governments all saw Hollywood imports in political as well as cultural terms; all these countries had substantial economic resources – and their governments were willing to pay the price of maintaining major domestic film industries.

Television was invariably established as an off-shoot of radio, a decision which confused and weakened initial resistance to American television imports. Most countries outside Latin America had a public service (or BBC) style of radio. European and other state broadcasting organizations overestimated their ability to resist importing Hollywood materials and styles; and in countries where a domestic mini-Hollywood has been painfully established, broadcasting organizations typically failed to grasp the relevance of this hard-won domestic experience.

The importing of entertainment materials has primarily been of pop music records, feature films, recorded television drama series

* The next chapter will deal with Hollywood and other US entertainment.

and recorded entertainment shows. Much of this material adopts the form of a fictional story – children's programming, in comic strips, in women's magazine fiction and paperback books. In these fictional stories the American media present their characteristic themes of status, success, personal qualities, sex roles, youth and ethnicity. The response of foreign consumers will depend partly upon their own ethnicity, age, and sex. In Europe imported material reaches the entire population, but outside Europe those most heavily exposed to imported media are mainly urban, employed in the modern economy, are relatively youthful and have higher than average incomes. In Latin America, Asia and Africa the typical consumer of imported media will be a young white-collar worker or a factory worker – not an elderly peasant in a remote rural area. Many of these urban consumers will themselves have a personal history of social and geographical mobility, and may respond to these themes in American media. Many will be women – often escaping from traditional views of appropriate women's roles – and the portrayal of women in American media output may be appealing.

People in authority may not like emphasis on upward social mobility, relative freedom for women and support of the young against the old. Hollywood's favourable portrayal of people with white skins and its much less favourable portrayal until recently of people with black skins must have led to very mixed responses. Within many countries in Latin America, the Arab world and Asia, there are people of both lighter and darker skin colour – so the possibilities for racial identification and antagonism even within a single country are quite complex.

The appeal of stylized violence to the frustrated urban youth of many lands cannot be better illustrated than by the many imitations of the American western. Some of the most obvious are the Italian and Spanish, Spaghetti and Paella, westerns. There have also been many Asian imitations of the western including Chinese films made in Shanghai in the interwar period, Japanese historical films, and more recently the Kung-Fu (or Chop Suey) westerns of Hong-Kong.

The various mini-Hollywoods of the world have copied the phenomenon of the star and in many countries the most popular single star performer is a local national. But Hollywood had established the first star system around 1920 and has managed to convince the world that it still has a uniquely large supply of uniquely dazzling stars. Part of the glamour of the Hollywood star lies in his or her stardom itself – fame and fortune not only in the United States, but also around the world. This factor of stardom in many countries as an integral part of star appeal was already evident in 1920 when Douglas Fairbanks and Mary Pickford visited Europe ostensibly on their honeymoon:

The crowds were so thick outside their suite at the Ritz-Carlton in New York before they sailed that they couldn't leave the hotel. Word was called ahead to England, France, Holland, Switzerland and Italy that Doug and Mary were coming. . . .

They first stopped at the Ritz in London and crowds thousands deep waited all night to catch sight of their idols. Doug delighted in carrying Mary through the pressing throngs in London and later in Paris. . . . Doug and Mary escaped to the cottage of Lord Northcliffe on the Isle of Wight only to be discovered surrounded by hundreds of fans at dawn one morning.

These scenes were repeated on the Continent and not really discouraged by Mary and Doug. . . . In Lugano, Switzerland and Venice, Florence and Rome the fans hailed 'Maria e Lampo' (for 'lightning', which is what Douglas was called in Italian). In Paris one afternoon they were afraid to leave their suite at the Hotel Crillon, the crowds were so thick, but they announced their intention of visiting Les Halles one morning and took satisfaction in stopping all traffic. . . .

Only in Germany, the so recent enemy, were they ignored, and neither Doug nor Mary could stand it. . . .

Word of the triumphal tour came back to New York through the newspapers, and America wasn't to be outdone in honoring the pair of cinema artists.[11]

Charlie Chaplin was greeted by equally enormous European crowds. Mary Pickford and Douglas Fairbanks also visited the Soviet Union, where in 1925 their films still dominated local screens, and they were again greeted by huge crowds.

All of this was powerfully encouraged by the Hollywood publicity mills, the result of operating publicity across a continent of daily newspapers; Hollywood also drew on the techniques of 'advancing' Presidential campaigns and theatrical tours. The arrival of famous faces from 6,000 miles away must have seemed more dramatic than any arrival of a star in one European country coming from another. These Hollywood stars also had an excuse for perpetual movement – a continuous succession of photogenic arrivals and departures – just like their film selves.

The Hollywood star arriving on a publicity trip in Europe was the inheritor of an established tradition of exotic American publicity trips to Europe. Increasingly during the latter half of the nineteenth century American minstrels, celebrities, circus freaks, founders of new religions and wild west entertainers had arrived to entertain the staid Europeans with the latest American exotica. Douglas Fairbanks established a pattern by which the indication of success in such a trip was the number of Kings and Queens met in Europe and subsequently invited back for visits to Los Angeles.

The same thing continues still as waves of American singers, dancers, actors, actresses and celebrities come remorselessly fluttering out of the western sky – here today in Europe and gone tomorrow around the world. The same preceding and succeeding waves of publicity operate; now, for the old tradition of shipboard interviews, arrivals and departures for the benefit of the local press, have been substituted the rituals of the airport and the television chat show.

The status themes, the stars' personalities, the intimate career details are put on display. The star modestly admits to the two hundredth interviewer how she was just so lucky to get her latest and best yet part. The media audience is invited to identify with the star who is so dazzlingly successful and yet not much different from you or me – sincerely worried indeed about her next show, film or disc.

Success in the media has long been one of the American media's staple topics. And as the American media have moved out on to the world scene, media success-on-the-world-scene has become a staple media topic: 'Yes, darling, already doing good business in Japan and Sweden, not released here until tomorrow.'

IMPACT ON DOMESTIC MEDIA: A CANADIAN EXAMPLE

'Media industries' in many importing nations are internally divided. In many countries the press is very partisan and competitive while broadcasting is a state monopoly. There is often a small film industry, quite separate from press and broadcasting, and itself internally torn between importing foreign products and domestically producing rivals to them. In contrast, the Anglo-American exporters – whatever their domestic battles – as exporters tend to operate somewhat more as an integrated media industry. A single news agency sells written, spoken and film news. The spread of Hollywood interests across all of the electronic media results in a single company selling feature films and television series and records. American media tycoons whose interests diffuse through the media also add to this industrial definition.

One great advantage of the Americans, then, was that they knew in their own minds what the media were mainly about. Or their uncertainties at least were less than those of the Europeans and other importing nations – who were less able to agree as to what the media were about or for, or even whether the media constituted a single meaningful field of activity.

A study of Canadian responses to the importing of United States magazines is one rare example of a detailed case study of one country's response to a particular media import. Canadian responses are probably more clearly articulated than would be the responses in many other countries. Yet Litvak and Moule's *Cultural Sovereignty: The Time and Reader's Digest Case in Canada*, reveals a situation of great complexity and with quite a chequered history. United States magazines in Canada first became a national Canadian issue around 1920. The issue, as raised by Horatio C. Hocken, a former Mayor of Toronto and an ex-journalist, included these points:

The great bulk of United States magazines consisted of salacious literature that dissipated the morals of Canadian youth.

That American publications were mainly responsible for Canada's 'brain drain' by depicting the United States as a land of unlimited promise, higher wages, better living conditions, and 'good times' . . .

That United States publications, especially those of the Hearst syndicate, often expressed opinions repugnant to British sentiment in Canada.

That United States magazines posed an economic threat because of the substantial volume of advertising they conveyed, which attracted customers that would otherwise buy from Canadian manufacturers.

That the Canadian magazine industry was fighting a losing battle for its very survival and desperately needed protection or assistance. . . .

That magazines are crucial vehicles in the generation and dissemination of national sentiment and therefore deserve special consideration apart from strictly commercial calculations.[12]

These arguments have a familiar ring – all have been used in many other countries. Most of the arguments against American imports are negative ones; they cover a wide range of concerns – moral, cultural, political and commercial – and some seem to be rather contradictory. The main arguments in favour of media imports into Canada – as elsewhere – were projected on a rather general plane; the entry of United States magazines should be allowed to continue – proponents of this case argued – in the interests of freedom of the press, and freedom of citizen choice.

In Canada the most effective and unified lobbyists were the advertisers. Differences within Canada occurred along the lines of the national and central versus the provincial – American magazine publishers found allies in maritime (east coast) and western Canadian publishers against the central Canadian publishers. These differences also overlapped with Quebec v. the rest, and Liberals v. Conservatives – a Canadian government of one party tended deliberately to undo the policy of its predecessor. Finally there was the argument of Canadian cultural identity and autonomy against the argument of employment for Canadians – if the favourable tax position of US subsidiary local Canadian editions was removed, it was argued, the Canadians who produced these editions would become unemployed.

The complexities of this Canadian example are simple compared with the internal conflicts which exist in some other countries, and across the entire range of media. Expensive products at low prices inevitably induce – among media entrepreneurs, relevant government officials, producers and journalists – conflicting responses. Admiration, greed, envy, contempt and fear put together in various combinations, and in various sectors of the media industry, do not always make for well considered and realistic policies.

SKEWING DOMESTIC MEDIA: MADISON AVENUE

The press in many countries – including capitalist and communist ones – is often regarded as an extension of political party and government. On the other hand films, radio and television are frequently seen – while having some political significance – as being mainly a matter of entertainment and leisure. Advertising is often officially regarded – again in capitalist and in some communist countries – as being primarily an area of commerce and trade, only incidentally connected with the media.

This latter view is so common that many governments, which prohibit or severely limit foreign ownership of newspapers or radio/television stations, have no objection to their advertising agencies being heavily foreign owned. This evolved historically, perhaps, because originally the influence of American advertising in other lands was mainly indirect, depending upon imitation. It was not until the 1960s that American ownership of advertising agencies developed in many foreign countries.

By 1973, and with the exception of Japan, in each of the other leading advertising countries – West Germany, France, Canada, Australia and Britain – at least half of the twenty largest advertising agencies had an American name. Countries where at least three of the five largest advertising agencies had American names were: Argentina, Belgium, India, Italy, Mexico, Netherlands, New Zealand, Norway, Spain and Venezuela. In at least another twenty countries which were smaller advertising spenders, the largest single advertising agency was American – including Indonesia, Pakistan, Thailand, Malaysia, Nigeria, Ghana, Kenya, Colombia and Peru.*[13]

By the 1970s the only serious rivals to the American multinational advertising agencies were a few international associations of national European agencies – and some, even of these, included an American partner. A similar pattern exists in European public relations and market research firms. And what the American advertising agencies have done in western Europe they had also done in most of Latin America and much of Asia (minus Japan) and Africa.

The familiar strategy of an entry via London into Europe and the British Empire was one factor in the internationalization of Madison Avenue. The post-1945 period saw an enormous overseas expansion of American consumer goods companies. American prominence in such classic fields for advertising as toiletries and packaged foods had a special 'multiplier effect'; in such fields the proportion of total cost which advertising expenditure makes up is much higher than in industry overall. Thus if incursions of American, mainly consumer goods, companies account for 10 per cent of a Latin American country's national product, the advertising which accompanies those products may account for, say, 30 per cent of total advertising. More-over, this will mainly be *national*, not local, advertising; American companies might thus account for 50 per cent of all advertising in *national* media.

American manufacturers and advertising agencies *tend* to work together. Several American advertising agencies 'went international' specifically to service the multi-national operations of one or two major consumer advertising clients. Some agencies maintain offices in specific foreign cities as a loss-making service to a major domestic client.

American agencies were able to benefit especially from their widely presumed superior expertise in commercial television and in the broader area of 'marketing' – which also was becoming fashionable in many nations in the 1950s. There was a long tradition in Europe and elsewhere of believing that advertising was peculiarly an area of American expertise.

The acceptance of imported infusions of market orientation – of which foreign advertising agencies are a spearhead – tends to become part of a gradual change not only of entire national media systems, but also of those aspects of political, cultural and social life upon

---

* The criterion of 'American name' has been used because the precise details of advertising agency ownerships change rapidly and are often not publicly known. Some agencies with American names – for example Hindustani, Thompson of India – in 1973 involved only a large minority American holding.

which the media most directly impinge. The early impact of foreign advertising agencies is to increase *competition* between, and sometimes within, media at all levels; advertising agencies have acquired within the American system certain tribal rules (such as 'no competing accounts', independence of media and advertisers) which make competition more vigorous between advertising agencies than is competition between, for example, American newspapers. American public relations and market research agencies are similarly competitive.

This American competitive commercial presence usually brings other consequences – such as a downgrading of particularistic 'who knows who' criteria and an upgrading of 'rational' objective criteria such as audited circulations, survey research and cost-per-thousand. Emphasis upon 'neutral' criteria is not really value-free. Advertising agencies always have their own prejudices, which may have some rational basis internal to the operation of advertising agencies. Large American advertising agencies prefer electronic media to print. 'Rational' grounds include these agencies' experience with the very largest US marketing companies (such as Procter & Gamble) which often favour television, and the fact that television requires fewer insertions and may thus be more profitable for agencies. Radio and television typically are more 'measured' than the press, are less politically partisan, require more 'creative' advertising expertise and may be more responsive to rational bargaining over bulk discounts, and favourable scheduling. This preference for the electronic media tends to produce more revenue for these media which in turn allows them to spend more on providing programming and hence to competing still more with the press. Few governments are likely to be worried by such a tendency since governments typically find their electronic media more amenable, in the areas which most interest governments, than their domestic press.

Foreign advertising agencies proclaim a particularly strong line against 'bribes' and 'kickbacks' and by projecting an 'honest' commercial image may encourage both local and 'international' companies to increase their advertising expenditure. Even if much of this increase goes to a limited range of electronic media, the effect nevertheless is to expand the total revenue, and total share of national income, which goes to the media. The appearance on a substantial scale of American advertising agencies has, then, three major consequences. First, the total size of the media industry (in terms of revenue and of audience time) is increased. Secondly, the advertising agencies play a major part in switching revenue towards – and hence expanding the output of – commercial broadcasting. Thirdly these agencies play a decisive part in swinging entire national media systems towards *commercial*, and away from traditional *political*, patterns. This has occurred in most countries of western Europe, Latin America and Asia.

CULTURAL IMPERIALISM V. AUTHENTIC LOCAL CULTURE

The cultural imperialism thesis claims that authentic, traditional and local culture in many parts of the world is being battered out of existence by the indiscriminate dumping of large quantities of slick commercial and media products, mainly from the United States. Those who make this argument most forcibly tend to favour restrictions upon media imports, plus the deliberate preservation of authentic and traditional culture.

This problem of cultural identity is part of a larger problem of national identity. The United States, Britain and France belong to a minority of the world's nations in having a fairly strong national identity. Almost all their citizens speak roughly the same language; but even in these countries there are major internal frictions – regional, ethnic and language, as well as social class, differences. And even this degree of national identity has only been achieved after several centuries of national existence, including civil war often followed by the brutal subjugation of regional and ethnic minorities. Countries which have an unusually strong national identity – such as USA, Britain and France – also happen to be the very same countries which have the longest traditions of the press and other media, conducted primarily in a single national language.

The strength of national identity is less marked in Latin America either despite, or possibly because of, the use of Spanish as the language of all but one of the main countries. In much of eastern, central, and parts of northern, Europe there are two, three or more separate languages, religions and cultural traditions within a single state. The Soviet Union has this pattern on an even larger scale, as does India and some other Asian countries. There are similarly sharp cleavages within many Arab countries; and Africa is the continent where national identity is least strong of all.

The variety of languages within many nation states is at once a major factor in 'cultural imperialism' and in lack of national identity. There are also very big differences between urban and rural areas, a very uneven pattern of development between some backward areas and other areas with exportable resources. Not only peasants' rebellions, guerrilla uprisings and palace revolutions but large-scale civil wars are a recent experience or an immediate realistic prospect in many lands. In the many countries where the prime object of policy is to reduce the threat of armed conflict, the need to strengthen 'authentic culture' may not be seen as primary.

The most authentic and traditional culture often seems, and not only to the ruling élite, to be also the most inappropriate. This is not merely because traditional culture sanctions what would now be called civil war. Traditional culture is also typically archaic, does not fit with contemporary notions of justice or equality, and depends upon religious beliefs which have long been in decline. Many traditional cultures were primarily carried by a small élite of scholars and priests, who often used languages which few other people understood. Not only Arab and Hindu cultures but many others ascribed a fixed subservient position to women, the young and the occupationally less favoured. It is precisely these unpopular characteristics of much authentic culture which make the imported media culture so popular by contrast.

The variety in traditional cultures is clearly enormous but two frequently found types of music can be used as illustration. One is the type of traditional opera found in a number of Asian countries; such traditional opera is musically complex, often having its own specialized acting traditions as well as its own musical instruments. Both its total repertoire and its total audience were often quite small. Such music belongs to a traditional hierarchical society which has long been in decline. Clearly it is unlikely to become a hit parade or television staple; it has to compete, moreover, with Beethoven and Mozart as well as with the Beatles and the movies.

A second common type of traditional music is found in many parts of Africa and some parts of Asia. This music is less complex and depends on simpler instruments; the music both appeals to and is produced by the ordinary people. The music indeed is an integral part of the major individual (birth, marriage, death) and collective (especially harvest) events and symbolism of ordinary life. It was often played for a few days or few weeks on end. It has influenced jazz and all subsequent western popular music; but in its authentic and traditional form it is difficult to adapt to media usage – although many African radio services do broadcast such music, and it is often popular especially in the immediate area from which it originates.

Another difficulty of 'authentic culture' is that one might expect there to be some level of regional culture beyond the tribal or national, but smaller than the international. There is indeed quite a lot of radio listening across national boundaries, but many governments and broadcasting organizations wish to discourage it. Many nations in the world, both 'old' and 'new', have uneasy relations with their neighbours. Subjecting the neighbour's citizens to your media, while protecting your own citizens from his media, is a common purpose of radio policy.

The debate about cultural imperialism and authentic culture is reminiscent of, and related to, another debate about 'mass society', mass culture and indeed the 'mass media'. The term 'mass' has a long intellectual genealogy of its own – and has long been used by both left and right with various shades of meaning and implication.[14] When this debate dealt with Europe and the United States it was confused enough. But the same debate, transposed to Asia and Africa, gets confused even further. It is precisely the highly educated élite in Asian and African countries who are the most active consumers of imported – and presumably 'low, brutal and commercial' – media. It is the rural dwellers – short of land, food, literacy, income, life expectation, birth control devices and so on – who are the main consumers of traditional and 'authentic' culture.

T. W. Adorno at one time claimed that even a symphony concert when broadcast on radio was drained of significance; many mass culture critics also had very harsh things to say about the large audiences which went to western and crime films in the 1930s – films which yet other cultural experts have subsequently decided were masterpieces after all. Even more bizarre, however, is the western intellectual who switches off the baseball game, turns down the hi-fi or pushes aside the Sunday magazine and pens a terse instruction to the developing world to get back to its tribal harvest ceremonials or funeral music.

Such a caricature illustrates that the real choice probably lies with hybrid forms. In many countries there are older cultural forms which continue in vigorous existence, although modified by western influences. Pop music often takes this form; 'eastern westerns' or the Latin American *telenovelas* are other examples. The debate should, then, be about whether such hybrid forms are primarily traditional and 'authentic' or whether they are merely translations or imitations of Anglo-American forms.

POLITICS AND INEQUALITY

How do the Anglo-American media affect politics or inequality within an importing country? Do they, as the Media Imperialism thesis implies, buttress reactionary politicians and solidify inequalities? Or do they have democratic and egalitarian implications?

Among nineteenth-century élites in Europe one of the main anxieties about the American press was its lack of respect for established practices and people. Charles Dickens, returning from the United States in 1842, expressed these anxieties with vigour and clarity:

Among the herd of journals which are published in the States there are some, the reader scarcely need be told, of character and credit.

From personal intercourse with accomplished gentlemen connected with publications of this class, I have derived both pleasure
and profit. But the name of these is Few, and of the other Legion;
and the influence of the good, is powerless to counteract the mortal
poison of the bad.

Among the gentry of America; among the well-informed and
moderate; in the learned professions; at the bar and on the bench:
there is, and there can be, but one opinion, in reference to the
vicious character of these infamous journals. It is sometimes con-
tended – I will not say strangely, for it is natural to seek excuses
for such a disgrace – that their influence is not so great as a visitor
would suppose. I must be pardoned for saying that there is no
warrant for this plea, and that every fact and circumstance tends
directly to the opposite conclusion.

When any man, of any grade of desert in intellect or character,
can climb to any public distinction, no matter what, in America,
without first grovelling down upon the earth, and bending the
knee before this monster of depravity; when any private excellence
is safe from its attacks; when any social confidence is left unbroken
by it, or any tie of social decency and honour is held in the least
regard . . . then, I will believe that its influence is lessening, and
men are returning to their manly senses. But while that Press has
its evil eye in every house, and its black hand in every appointment
in the state, from a president to a postman; while, with ribald
slander for its only stock in trade, it is the standard literature of
an enormous class, who must find their reading in a newspaper,
or they will not read at all; so long must its odium be upon the
country's head, and so long must the evil it works, be plainly visible
in the Republic.

To those who are accustomed to the leading English journals,
or to the respectable journals of the Continent of Europe, to those
who are accustomed to anything else in print and paper; it would
be impossible, without an amount of extract for which I have
neither space nor inclination, to convey an adequate idea of this
frightful engine in America.

Responses to imported American media continue to be related to
attitudes towards currently prevalent inequalities. But it would be
quite misleading to think in terms of media imports always favouring
the poor at the expense of the rich. Even within the United States the
media are primarily aimed at the middle of the population, not at its
very poorest members. In terms of England in 1842, or western Europe
today, imports of American media may quite realistically be seen as
potentially hostile to established élites. But the emphasis of these

media upon success and status favours the new rich more than the old poor. These media also present a heavily *urban* view of life.

In multi-party nations of western Europe, and perhaps to some extent in eastern Europe, imports of American media materials may tend towards democratizing and egalitarian effects. Such commercial infusions will tend to influence, if not the basic substance of political power within importing countries, then at least the *styles* politicians use in presenting themselves to local and national publics. Increased amounts of market oriented media fare – more entertaining entertainment, and more 'neutral' news – will tend to make the more obviously political party fare seem less entertaining and more obviously dull and unattractive. Thus politicians try to dress up their political messages in more entertaining and neutral-looking packages. This in turn implies the use of PR and market research skills – in presenting the chief executive and his supporters, but also in presenting and shaping policies in even the most complex and delicate areas.

In multi-party countries, the rise of commercial or mainly advertising-financed media and the decline of party or government-financed media may become cumulative. Politically or government-controlled media tend to become less attractive to audiences, hence less important to politicians, and so on. More and more politicians use the techniques and the advice of advertising, market research and public relations, while the argument is heard (and heeded) that media which are obviously controlled by government or party constitute bad political strategy. There is a gradual change by which politicians and governments in multi-party countries seek accommodations within an increasingly commercial pattern of media.

But in poorer African and Asian nations infusions of Western media may indeed buttress and extend existing inequalities. Since these imported media are consumed mainly by the urban and relatively affluent, and since importing becomes a substitute for providing cheap domestic media to most areas, inequality may be increased. In many poor countries, also, the media are controlled by the government; the national media may become a key instrument through which a small affluent élite maintains itself in power. This view of the media as prime defenders of the status quo is often shared by politicians in power and illustrated by the heavy military guard found outside many capital city radio stations.

Thus foreign media may in some affluent countries favour more equality, but in other less affluent countries favour more inequality. In yet other countries, such as those of Latin America both sorts of effects may occur at the same time. For example Wells may be right in believing that the imported media tip the scales away from the country and in favour of the city; but within the heavily populated

Latin American cities those same media might have an egalitarian effect.

ONE MEDIA IMPERIALIST, OR A DOZEN?

The media imperialism thesis does not confront the presence of strong regional exporters in various parts of the world. Mexico and Argentina have a tradition of exporting media to their neighbours; Egypt exports to the Arab world, while Indian films and records go to many countries in Africa and Asia. Not only the United States, Britain and France, but also West Germany, Italy, Spain and Japan all export some media. Even Sweden has its own little media empire in Scandinavia. And the Soviet Union has strong media markets in eastern Europe.

This phenomenon can be seen as running counter to the media imperialist thesis – showing that American and British media exports have many substantial rivals. But there are also grounds for seeing Mexican or Egyptian or even Indian exports as an indirect extension of Anglo-American influence. *The countries which are strong regional exporters of media tend themselves to be unusually heavy importers of American media.*

Italy in 1972 was after the USA the second largest exporter of feature films, with considerable strength in every world region. Yet Italy itself took over half of its imports from the USA (Tables 2 and 3); Britain, Mexico and India all took an unusually high proportion of their imports from the USA. Other strong film exporters – Japan, Egypt and West Germany – were strong importers of American films. Only the USSR, among major film exporters, imports virtually nothing from Hollywood (Table 3).

By 1972 the majority of films made in Britain were Hollywood financed and distributed; and a substantial proportion of Italian and French films (including Italian-French co-productions subsidized by both governments) were also American-financed and distributed. And all of the major film exporters in the world (except USSR) take around three-quarters of their film imports from the USA, UK, Italy and France combined. Thus almost all significant film exporters in the world are themselves open to heavy current Hollywood influence.

The strength of Soviet film exports in eastern Europe is noticeably weaker than Hollywood's unassisted export strength in all world regions apart from eastern Europe (Table 2).

These data, incidentally, illustrate that television is not necessarily the best example for the media imperialist thesis. The continuing extent of Hollywood feature film exports around the world is all the more remarkable because Hollywood has here retained its export leadership for 60 years.

The television imperialism thesis cannot be considered merely for television alone. A more historical approach, covering all media, is required. We must also note, for example, both exporters and importers' intentions – as well as recognizing that many social consequences are unintended. Nevertheless the Schiller thesis has a number of strengths. It takes the whole world for its unit of analysis – and Schiller's domino theory of American media influence is one illustration of the benefits of so doing.

In my view the Anglo-American media are connected with imperialism, British imperialism. But these media exports both predate and still run ahead of the general American economic presence overseas or the multi-national company phenomenon. Schiller attributes too many of this world's ills to television. He also has an unrealistic view of returning to cultures many of which although authentic are also dead. In my view a non-American way out of the media box is difficult to discover because it is an American, or Anglo-American, built box. The only way out is to construct a new box, and this, with the possible exception of the Chinese, no nation seems keen to do.

CHAPTER THREE

Entertainment: Occupational and industrial structure

NEW YORK, 1890–1920: MAKING IT

In New York around 1900 the media were for the first time shaped into a comprehensive media industry. The New York media became especially oriented towards poor immigrants from Europe, because New York at the time was packed with poor Europeans. The subsequent enormous appeal of the same media back in Europe is thus no great mystery.

While Paris before the First World War saw a unique flowering of the serious arts, New York saw a unique flowering of the new popular media arts. The press, advertising, popular music and films were all battered into their modern industrial shape in New York City in these years. All of those developments were closely connected with earlier New York traditions in just two fields – the newspaper and the popular live theatre (the Minstrel Show, Vaudeville and Broadway).

Pulitzer's *World* and Hearst's *Journal* fought out in the 1890s the epic sales war of the New York press. But more weighty newspapers in New York were already developing a new American model which was to modify the European notion of a prestige newspaper. New York was also the most important single centre for news agencies, magazines, comics, syndication.

Advertising agencies existed in a simple form in London before anywhere in the USA. But the modern form of the advertising agency was knocked into shape especially in New York City. In the 1890s agencies still usually sold advertising only for particular newspapers or magazines; but the comprehensive agency, handling all media, and including such new trades as the copywriter, was well established by 1910.

Popular music also became an industry for the first time in New York in the 1890s. Tin Pan Alley was some streets on the fringes of the then Broadway Theatre area; song entrepreneurs got songs written, plugged them to singers, published them and hoped to sell them to the public.

The film industry also was based in New York more than in any

Adolph Zukor

Jesse Lasky

FOUNDING FATHERS

The Warner Brothers as children

Louis B. Meyer (*right*) with President Coolidge (*left*)

World Sales Conference at MGM Studios

other single city. D. W. Griffith directed Mary Pickford films in New York – for long the Biograph studio was a brownstone house on East Fourteenth Street. And the greatest single market for the movies was also in lower Manhattan, swarming with immigrants.

Although New York became the dominant centre for each of these media fields, it did not achieve the easy victory of London or Paris over their respective hinterlands. In each case New York had to compete fiercely with other major cities such as Philadelphia and especially with Chicago. Time and again Chicago has been in the forefront of each major media development only to lapse back into relative insignificance on the national scene.

This has happened in the press and in each of the electronic media – films, radio, television – because national American dominance has ultimately always been shared between New York and Hollywood. Film production migrated to California from 1915 onwards, and so did radio after its initial phase, and then so also in 1954–5 did television production. New York remained the business centre for each medium – providing capital and advertising.

New York thus became a switchpoint at first sucking in influences, experience, competition, talent from the American hinterland; then exporting much of this to Hollywood for production. New York continued also to suck in talent and ideas from Europe, while at the same time exporting vigorously to, and being copied by, Europe. In Europe, Britain (and its then Empire) was the best single market but the main countries on the Continent were important markets – for example being heavy importers of American films and songs by 1914.

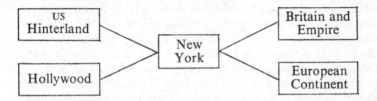

Just as Hollywood drew upon the us hinterland mainly via New York, so also there was relatively little contact between Britain and the rest of Europe; European countries often imported from New York press practices or songs which had earlier British origins.

Both the early film industry and Tin Pan Alley were especially heavily populated with recent Jewish immigrants from the Lower East Side of New York City. Their poor recent immigrant status was at least as important as their being Jewish. The waves of Jewish immigration resulting from persecutions especially in Russia, and eastern Europe, brought these people into the poor areas of New York just in time to get mixed up with the disreputable gutter trades of song plugging and nickel odeon management. Isaac Goldberg, an early historian of Tin Pan Alley, wrote in 1930:

> Tin Pan Alley is forty years old. Beginning as a musical zone of New York City it blazed a trail along Broadway in close pursuit of the theater. The moving picture did not destroy it; the radio poured new life into its veins; the talkies adopted it, until they found that the child was endangering its foster parents; the coming of television can have no adverse effect upon this singing fool; if anything the contrary. . . .
>   . . . the Alley . . . manages, stammeringly yet at times inimitably, to speak the yearnings, the sorrows and the joys of a new, an emergent folk, different from any other people in the world; and it is most gratefully accepted by that folk in the one true way that song may be accepted: it is sung. Tin Pan Alley, in brief, has cradled a new folk song, a song of the city. . . .[1]

The movies also were cheap entertainment especially welcomed by immigrants, the poor and the lonely. Tin Pan Alley provided the song of the city, the movies provided its art, while Hearst and his competitors provided the literature.

All of these media lived off, and were influenced by, each other. Song writers and film makers alike devoured the popular newspapers in search of dramatic phrases and stories. The silent movies were not silent but throbbed with piano noise (to drown the projector), pop Chopin, ragtime – and while the reels were being changed singers plugged their latest Alley songs. Another sound in the nickel odeons was the murmur of immigrant voices translating aloud the titles into the languages of Europe. In New York City at the turn of the century there was no question of Americans not being good at European languages. At least half of the New Yorkers were at least half-European themselves. As the media expanded, the idea of selling films and songs and comics in Europe was as natural as selling them in the midwest.

Above all, these New York media were to do with selling. Of all the New York media booms of the 1890s, the advertising boom was perhaps the most spectacular.

DREAMS: SMALL BATCH PRODUCTION, MASS MARKETING

The industry whose products were to be sold around the world was industrialized in New York City. But the characteristic production pattern was not, and is not, mass production of the car assembly kind. The similarity to car production is only to the very early pattern of cars when a few were built at a time in a small garage or workshop. Tin Pan Alley especially was in many ways a variant of the tailor's business or clothing sweatshop. The boss sat downstairs in a shop dealing with the customers; upstairs instead of a few people leaning over sewing-machines were a few people leaning over pianos. While for sweatshop operatives the task was divided up by parts of the garment, for songshop operatives songs were divided up into words and music and song styles. Songs were turned out in batches of a dozen a week, or if business was brisk perhaps a dozen a day. The early film studios were also in small batch production. A common pattern was one short film a day, six films a week. In well-managed establishments wordsmiths sat up all night writing the next day's script. Often the plot was taken from a newspaper story and often it was written by an ex-newspaper man.

The newspaper was the original small batch production shop. The typical newspaper office in New York in 1890 was still only a small printing shop, with a sweatshop upstairs for reporters and a delivery problem akin to that of a rather successful city bakery. When Pulitzer in 1890 built himself a twenty-storey building for the *World* he was widely thought to be over-reaching himself (which he was); even then most of the storeys were taken up with a gilded dome and offices leased out to other businesses.[2]

But while the production process was, and largely remains, of the small batch variety – the marketing and distribution process was reaching national, and would soon reach international, proportions. Newspapers could be run from small shops because sales were local and much of the news came in from the great news agencies, the precursors of the electronic revolution. But the prime means of *national* distribution was still in 1900 the us Post Office. Advertising agencies based in New York sent their advertisements to papers across the us by mail. Later, electronic distribution was to become more important – radio and television networking. 'Exchanges' of film gave way to circuits of cinemas linked to production studios. New devices like the juke-box enabled enormously large total audiences to be combined with some individual choice.

This combination of large-scale marketing arrangements with quite small-scale batch production reaped scale economies, it provided a high average standard of quality and also flexibility in response to current market demand. At the local level very small and very local output was possible, still linked in various ways to the national market.

Film studios moved on from employing a few dozen to employing by the 1920s a few hundred people; but each studio by now made only a smallish number of features per year. Similar production arrangements still persist in Hollywood today, where television series episodes are produced in small batches. Advertising agencies also developed on this kind of scale – claiming to offer national advertisers individual attention plus wider experience and scale economies.

When a new phenomenon like the animated film appeared, it merely adapted the small batch industrial methods of the film studio and the advertising agency 'creative' department. Walt Disney had – like many media innovators – worked in advertising; he introduced division of labour, with drawing tasks divided up between the more and less skilled. He also developed some star artists whose names he was able for years to keep secret – in the tradition of the early acting stars and their low-paying employers. Disney, however, retained much flexibility and variety – between formats and media – and, like most successful media tycoons, he was first, last and always a salesman.

ELECTRONIC MEDIA FOLLOW THE PRESS

A new medium in America is heavily dependent on the previously existing media. While in 1910 the European lower working class still did little newspaper reading, in the US newspapers already reached the poorest immigrants. Robert Park reports on one group of 312 Russian immigrants; in Russia only sixteen read newspapers regularly – whereas in America all of them were subscribers or readers of Russian-language papers, a quarter also read English-language papers and 'all are visiting the movies'.[3] One reason why the film industry grew faster in America than Europe lay in the popular press – both 'foreign' and English language – which provided the movies with a publicity engine capable of reaching the urban poor on a *daily* basis. Between 1910 and 1914 the advertising of films became common in American daily newspapers, but the papers had given films news coverage even before 1896. The films were always producing new 'events' and later the emergence of the stars fitted the 'personality' news canon on a spectacular scale. The films provided advertising revenue for the press (quickly followed by film reviews) and, by boosting readership, probably contributed to sales revenue as well. Both the early production and the most voracious consumption of films occurred only a few city-blocks away from the great popular newspapers of America in Chicago, New York and Philadelphia. Since the period up to 1914 saw the height of 'muckraking' journalism, the many ex-journalist screen-writers probably helped to provide a dose of informed social criticism which appealed to movie audiences.

The American film industry developed an enormous supporting barrage of publicity – both paid advertising and fan material supplied free to newspapers and magazines. The impact of these publicity practices was all the greater in Europe because American press agentry was there less familiar. By 1910–12 superior American publicity was an important aspect of the British film industry's decreasing ability to compete in its home market.[4]

The famous serial movies such as *The Adventures of Kathlyn*, *Lucile Love* and *Perils of Pauline* all resulted from a Chicago newspaper circulation war in 1913–14;[5] the serials ran both as weekly film episodes and as newspaper serials (in the *Chicago Tribune*, the *Chicago Herald* and the Hearst chain respectively). These film and newspaper serials were forerunners of soap operas for both radio and television. At least four such film serials were circulating in Britain by 1915.[6] Before the blockade of 1918 they were also shown in Russia.[7]

Many of the myths of huge salaries, outlandish behaviour and the inevitable 'romance' (between two stars who just happened to be appearing together in a new film) were invented, or at least exaggerated, by studio press agents. By 1940 there were 400 journalists assigned to cover Hollywood full-time.[8]

American news agencies and the syndicated film gossip columns did much to beam Hollywood stars around the world. The early exporting years of American television were years when the American press was especially much copied on the world scene. Hollywood distributors have also acquired for their films and television series endless column miles of publicity around the world via visits by stars tied into local release dates.

The first major attempt to limit competition – the 'Motion Pictures Patents Company' – lasted from 1909 to 1914;[9] it was defeated primarily by the rivalry of such 'independents' as Carl Laemmle and William Fox, both of whom employed very skilful press publicity and advertising in frontal opposition to the cartel. Had production not moved to California such eastern publicity might have made the 1930s Hollywood cartel impossible – and, without it, American dominance of world media might have been less. With the most spectacular part of industry, studio production, tucked away in California, it was less obvious that the financial guts of the industry lay in the cinema chains. Such competition as existed was heavily focused in Hollywood itself – between stars, and directors and producers. The national and international publicity spotlight was upon Hollywood, sheltered by distance, by friendly Californian laws, and by a star-crazy local press corps, from the more sceptical east coast.

Especially from 1930 – with sound – the Hollywood cartel became more fixed and more under the control of a few New York banks. But in the 1930s, there were more pressing problems for Washington. Many Washington politicians as well as east coast journalists were also probably dazzled by the Hollywood publicity machine.

For the world market Hollywood performed an impressive publicity conjuring trick. Although the American film industry was run by a cartel – which largely kept out foreign competition – on the world scene Hollywood was the apostle of free trade and no-holds-barred competition. Its ability to perform this dazzling conjuring trick was partly dependent on Hollywood's location in Hollywood – remote from New York beyond the shimmering desert, cocooned behind the mountains in a large and growing smog of publicity, stardom and illusion.

The power of the press and the threat of hostile press coverage was one reason why the Hollywood companies did not buy radio stations in the inter-war years. Some of the earliest radio stations were owned by newspapers – intended as a means of collecting news and as a publicity megaphone for the paper itself. Newspapers had an interest in keeping radio out of the two key preserves of news and advertising. It was partly this very press suspicion which drove radio into the arms of Tin Pan Alley. Early American radio was the classic era for live pop music. Not until the talkie revolution of the late 1920s did the link between radio and movies become fully apparent. The dominant part *records* were to play in radio emerged still later.

When television appeared it was not at first realized, in America and elsewhere, how closely television would be allied to films. Around 1945 it was largely taken for granted that American television was to be an offshoot of radio; subsequently it became apparent that, at least on its production side, television is closer to feature film making – this realization accompanied the move of most network television production to Hollywood.

American television is strongly dedicated to localism; the local stations have precedence in both time and law over the networks, which evolved later. But the localism of the system and the high costs (and hence scale economies) of television production make national networking especially essential. A pattern of three networks emerged, very closely related to the radio pattern. The television networks (like the vintage Hollywood film companies and the radio networks) are tied into the local marketing pattern through their own local stations; NBC, CBS, and ABC each predictably have their own local stations in New York and Los Angeles, as well as in Chicago and a few other lucrative 'markets'.

The guts of American television are the 150 network-affiliated stations in the top 50 urban markets of the United States. The 150 stations pull the bulk of the audience for the vital three hours of prime-time network-provided material each evening. Those stations are the television equivalent of the few hundred large downtown cinemas which were the commercial heart of the Hollywood film industry's golden years.

SELLING IS THE NAME OF THE GAME

'BO' – meaning both box office and body odour typifies what the American media system was all about. 'Strong at the BO' is a key term in the special phraseology of *Variety* magazine. BO meaning body odour is equally indicative. Dreams can be good or bad. BO was bad and in selling a product to deal with the bad dream, the advertiser first of all had to sell the bad dream.

The selling origins of American media tycoons have often been remarked upon. Why should men whose previous experience was in selling, say, furs, do so well in constructing a media industry? Various explanations can be given. Furs are dreams, too, just like the movies. Furs are volatile, luxurious, insecure things, of uncertain origin and uncertain value – experience enough for the movies, motivation enough for wanting some cartel security.

There certainly is a remarkable similarity between the early movie magnates and the early Tin Pan Alley entrepreneurs:

> Louis B. Mayer was a movie-theater owner, the Warners were a butcher's sons, Samuel Goldwyn was a glove salesman, the Schenks were drug store owners. . . . Adolph Zukor and Marcus Loew began as furriers, Colonel William Selig was an upholsterer, William Fox and Carl Laemmle were clothing merchants, Lewis J. Selznick was a jeweler.[10]

Many of the early Alley managers had similar backgrounds. Isadore Witmark, Leo Feist, Joe Stern and Ed Marks had selling experience respectively with water filters, corsets, neck-ties and buttons.[11]

There is, however, an even simpler explanation for these selling backgrounds – both Alley men and nickel odeon operators set up in small shops. Once in the song or movie business, they had no option but to be very close to their audiences. The movie exhibitor was close enough to hear what the audience said, doubtless to smell them also, and survival came to depend upon anticipating their tastes. In the song business the difficult task was to get the song sung – and many early song entrepreneurs plugged their own songs, singing them free to movie audiences, in bars and in cheap vaudeville shows. Irving

Berlin, later perhaps the most productive and successful pop song writer of all time, had worked as a singing waiter. Harry Cohn – later the head of Columbia Pictures – had worked in vaudeville and as a song plugger.

Only the newspaper entrepreneurs lacked such selling experience. This suggests that it was simply proximity to, and familiarity with, the audience which was crucial. For newspaper reporters were out among the people looking for the urban melodramas of the day; circulation wars were a crash course in popular psychology and selling, sometimes also in organized violence.

The selling and marketing orientation of the whole media were evident in the dominant position in 1900 of the popular newspaper and its advertising. The requirements of press publicity and advertising were built into the basic commercial practices of the newer media; for example the movie release pattern – starting in the centre of the larger cities and moving outwards – was designed to maximize editorial and advertising, plus word of mouth, publicity. The typical media tycoon had as his right hand man either an ex-journalist or an ex-advertising man.

THE OCCUPATIONAL STRUCTURE OF DREAM PRODUCTION

The American media arrived at the stage of an industrial pattern – comprehensive, nationally spread and still flexible – earlier than did those of Europe; in Europe the media stayed closely linked to political machines for longer. The consequent early specialization in America led to an industrially elaborated division of labour. The occupational role of 'journalist' in the US threw off the overlaps with printer, politician or man-of-letters earlier and more decisively than in Europe. A few basic occupational types emerged – journalist, advertising man, film director – to add to the traditional actor/singer.

These occupational divisions carried basic assumptions about how the media worked. For example the sharp division between journalist and advertising man reflected the ideology of a sharp division between those sections of a newspaper which were for sale to commercial advertisers and those sections which were not. Such ideological divisons, plus simple occupational specialization led to notions of 'professionalism' which were subsequently extremely influential in media occupations in Europe and beyond.

The American film industry quite early developed some distinctive subject matter, and the peculiar mixture of savagery and sentimentality for which Hollywood became famous. Its relatively weak theatrical, high culture or capital city connections enabled the American industry to search more vigorously for material suitable to the new medium. Cowboy films were popular well before the industry moved to Hollywood.

Most of the early actors had some theatrical experience – indeed the American theatrical touring tradition was a major contributor to Hollywood; but few of the earliest actors had been successful in the theatre and few returned to it. In Europe the more volatile film industry conditions meant that actors, producers and directors moved back and forth between films and theatre. Not only did Hollywood go further and faster in developing continuous employment, it also went further in establishing a constellation of new occupational roles and providing them with an ideology of 'professionalism'.

The American advertising agency pioneered a new specialized occupational role – the 'advertising man' who claims to be independent of the media and functionally separate from the advertiser whose advertising is being placed. This role was quickly subdivided into copywriter, artist, account manager, media buyer and so on. Related to the advertising man role a number of other more specialized ones emerged – of which the public relations man and the market researcher are especially important. The development of public relations is connected with advertising in many ways. Once newspaper editorial space was free of political party control, it became possible for outsiders to try to influence it; the larger the number of advertising pages carried, the more space there was to be filled 'to keep the advertisements apart'.

The market research role was given a major boost by the establishment in America of an Audit Bureau of Circulations in 1914. When circulations became more or less known it also became worth while to look at the composition of the audience in a more sophisticated way. Market research grew up mainly in and around advertising agencies and also in and around the major advertising companies in such fields as soap, packaged foods and patent medicines.

CARTEL, COMPETITION, CARTEL

Hollywood's own history resembles the plot of the classic Hollywood crime film. Rival gangs decide to make an arrangement and carve up the territory between them. For a while Mr Big and Mr Bad honour this agreement, engaging in the profitable pursuit of crime while co-operatively managing the guidelines, bribing the police and the politicians. Then, however, something goes wrong. Competition starts up again – Mr Big and Mr Bad are both gunned down by their former partners' hired hands. In Hollywood there was a period of frenzied competition, resulting in a cartel from 1909 to 1914; then there was another frenzied period of competition – escalating star salaries and film budgets – which led to the cartel of the golden period. This was terminated after ten years of legal struggle and – just as post-war television was appearing – the major Hollywood companies were forced to divest themselves of their largely non-competing cinema chains.

New forces in the media invariably became involved in political negotiations, legislation and often in anti-trust agitation or legal action. The monopoly issue first arose in the case of the Associated Press. From 1850 onwards the Associated Press became involved with two great commercial interests – the telegraph and the railways. The Western Union company soon after the Civil War in 1866 was in a monopoly position. The railways needed the telegraph for quick communication and effective operation of the rail network. The railroad provided the telegraph company with a right of way, office space in each station and the cheap part-time help of station masters.

The railroads and the Western Union developed a strict policy of avoiding any actions which would damage each other's interests. The agent of the Associated Press, D. H. Craig, stated that between 1850 and 1867 it was an unwritten rule of the New York Associated Press and the various telegraph companies that neither should do anything to prejudice the other's interests. Craig also demanded that all Associated Press 'member' newspapers should use the same telegraphic companies and should refrain from publishing any news from sources other than AP which might conflict with telegraph company interests.[12] Thus the Associated Press, in reaching its dominant position, agreed to protect, and not to distribute critical news about, the nation's leading private monopoly, the Western Union, and the nation's leading modern industry, the railroad. The Associated Press's relative independence of government and the possibility of a market orientation were, thus, bought at considerable cost in dependence elsewhere.

In both radio and television, involvement with major commercial interests and with the federal government was more direct; major electronics interests were involved in licensing, and the issue of American military requirements was vital to the birth of the leading (RCA–NBC) network.

Through the twentieth century the American media have been involved in an endless series of monopoly cases – some of which have involved legal decisions and legislation aimed at increasing competition, but others of which have led to the apparent legal confirmation of monopoly practices. Even in the American newspaper industry in the late 1960s legislation was introduced (and passed) which allowed 44 competing daily newspapers in 22 two-newspaper cities to merge their business operations, but to carry on 'competing' editorially.[13]

An important consequence of Federal government (FCC) regulation and its discouragement of any signs of collusive behaviour between the television networks is to force the three networks into head-on competition of the most vigorous kind. Much of this vigour goes into a steady escalation of the cost-per-hour of producing network programming. In 1952 it already cost $38,000 to produce half an hour (really 25 minutes) of *I Love Lucy*.[14] By 1976 network shows were costing up to $300,000 an hour, and the three networks were together spending over $2 million each evening during the new programming season. This concentration on producing more and more expensive programming for only three networks, for only three hours per evening has many consequences. Domestically, in the USA, these include shorter seasons of new material and more re-runs; another major consequence is that re-runs, syndication of old once-a-week series on a once-a-day basis, and so on, become more and more important. Also important here are the arrangements for selling old cinema films for television showing, and the practice of made-for-TV 'feature' films.

The characteristic cartel-competition-cartel sequence, or mixture, within American media is often seen as deliberately shutting out European imports from the US market, while at the same time facilitating US exports. There is certainly some truth in this – and of course European governments, and media industries, have tried (less successfully) to pursue the same goals.

But cartel tendencies in the US media have often involved European participation. The late nineteenth-century strength of the AP relied heavily upon its control of the incoming world news service of Reuter. The original film industry cartel around 1910 included two French companies. Many developments in the rather closed US record industry of the inter-war period involved British record company participation and competition.

American media cartels have usually not been absolute enough to shut out all the stimulus of competition; and competition has usually only continued on an all-out ferocious basis for quite short periods – especially during the development of a new medium or technology.

FIRST GET THE TECHNOLOGY, THEN FIX THE FORMAT

The characteristic format of each new medium has normally been fixed within the United States, and the rest of the world has then usually copied the format regardless of how 'appropriate' it may be. A new media format has usually occurred first within the United States because the technological, commercial and political ingredients have been put together there while in Europe the separate ingredients were either not present or had not yet gelled.

As an example, the press has gone through three major periods of technological innovation. The first was the emergence of the large-sale daily press in the early 1800s; the new printing and paper-making technology plus the commercial market, were all available in Europe – but the political will to have a cheap popular daily press as yet was present only in the USA. The second revolution occurred around 1890 with much faster presses, cheaper pulp paper, faster setting and so on. Again the pattern gelled sooner in the USA. The third great press revolution is the electronic printing revolution which began in the 1960s in the USA – and involves photo-composition, computers and so on; the American lead is less obvious here but the technology was originally applied primarily to match the requirements of the main US market – namely smallish sale daily newspapers, containing much advertising and syndicated editorial.

Robert Houlton has suggested the term 'template'[15] to indicate the technological underpinning of any major new medium or media development. While technology alone determines nothing, the new technology is hammered into shape as the result of commercial and political struggles, and it then reflects these forces. Since the commercial and political forces are American ones the established technology is arranged into an American format and carries with it various other American assumptions.

The American style of news agency developed around the technology – in this case the telegraph – plus the commercial and political circumstances of American newspapers in the nineteenth century. The first American film cartel, the Patents Company, also focused heavily upon technology. The standard speed and size of film were fixed in Europe. American struggles centred on the camera patents and the supplies of raw film – Eastman Kodak granting the cartel a monopoly of its supplies.

In the 1920s commercial and political battles were fought for control of the new radio technology and this had to be refereed by a government agency. Subsequently there were further battles between the RCA–NBC and CBS over the standards for television, for VHF radio and also over the standard size and playing speed (33 or 45) of long-playing records.

In this series of commercial battles, refereed more or less passively by the FCC and the Federal government, the big American electronics companies (especially RCA and ATT–Bell Telephone) played a strategic part in fixing the standard technologies of all the electronic media; and it was because they glimpsed the significance of such decisions that the French and Soviet governments were so insistent on not accepting the American *colour* television system. In pure technical terms they had a good case, since the American technology, as in previous American media pioneering, was less satisfactory than that subsequently developed in Europe. One of the oddities of American television is that both the (non-cable) black-and-white and colour picture quality is so poor.

The general point, however, is that the Americans have largely managed to 'fix' the basic format of each medium – as a consequence of being early with the technology, having an affluent enough audience to reach a large scale quickly and having a federal government favourably disposed to encouraging commercial media expansion. Thus the pattern of American newspapers around 1900, of Hollywood films around 1920 and American television around 1950, were widely copied by other countries looking for a model of what the new medium was. Many countries attempted to copy particular media formats without adopting the more comprehensive industry which lay behind them. Such partial copying often had unanticipated consequences.

CHAPTER FOUR

Immigrant dreams, export sales

THE MEDIA TYCOON: AS PROMOTER AND EXPORTER

Such media tycoons as Pulitzer and Hearst in the press, the founders of Hollywood, or the radio network founding fathers, constitute a symbolic and actual link between immigration into America and the exporting of American media to the rest of the world. David Sarnoff, a founder of the NBC networks, was an immigrant, as were most of the early Hollywood tycoons. Having arrived in New York as children in immigrant families, these men by their middle years were already selling their media products to the 'old country' and across Europe.

The press tycoons were in their lifetimes the subjects of many biographies, nearly all adulatory and written by journalists; the biographical pendulum was already starting to swing towards heroes of consumption and the media. Both before and since Orson Welles' movie, *Citizen Kane*, which is loosely based on the life of Hearst, American writers on the press tycoons have become more and more sceptical of the tycoons' significance; a sceptical portrait of the press tycoon type might be as follows:

The tycoon achieves some great circulation success while he is still very young. Most of his techniques have been used before. But the tycoon uses them on a publication or a type of publication to which they were not previously applied. He uses the old tricks with a new brashness and vigour. He is very rich, very young. His mother is the dominant person in his life. He marries, is frequently unfaithful, but continues to live with his wife. In his early days he personally is both editor-in-chief and business manager, surrounded by a dedicated band of young colleagues and relatives. He is fascinated by the many opportunities for small exercises of power which ownership and personal control of newspapers makes possible. He is passionately excited by the news of the day, crusades, fresh challenges. He is a person of enthusiasms – especially for new projects, new publications, new crusades. In time the press tycoon becomes more and more interested in politics, but does not adjust to its different requirements. He is domineering and unpredictable with subordinates – given to impulsive hiring and firing – and is increasingly surrounded by hatchet men and sycophants. In middle age he becomes rather remote from his newspapers and other publications but still insists on exerting detailed control on an irregular basis – this is done from anywhere in the world by inspecting a copy of the paper and dictating terse instructions about particular items and employees. In later years he becomes embittered by the failure of his political ambitions and the declining tendency of his newspapers. He is given to many maladies, and much self-pity, spending his time far removed from thankless politicians and disloyal readers. In some remote palace of extraordinary vulgarity, or on a yacht cruising on a distant sea, he lives surrounded by a small band of followers amongst whom the male secretary is prominent. Sending sharp memos to distant subordinates provides his last remaining pleasure. He dies and the great publishing empire he founded survives, but in rather reduced circumstances.

This sceptical view should not detract from the significance of media tycoons. Some of the mystery about the early tycoons results from a lack of financial detail – and the general failure of journalist-biographers to interpret such detail as is available. The simple economies of scale account for much of the apparent mystery. Media tycoons typically discover some way of very rapidly building a large audience – which leads quickly to new economies of scale.

Pulitzer and Hearst while they scarcely personify genius do indeed represent some very important themes in the American press. In the 1880s and 1890s newspapers could still be dominated by a single individual – while the concurrent development of syndication literally telegraphed their innovations across the United States. Both Pulitzer and Hearst appealed to immigrants; both campaigned against the trusts. Between them they popularized, even if they did not invent, nearly every known trick of modern journalism. Hearst also established the pattern of the diversified multi-media empire. Besides newspapers, he was involved in glossy magazines, a major international news agency (INS), feature film production, newsreels and radio news; with King Features he was a major force in syndication.

When Hearst moved into feature film production he could teach the movie tycoons little about autocratic eccentricity. The movie tycoons' behaviour was similarly based on secure finances and magnified by press agents and sycophantic journalists. Other eccentric tycoons built magazine groups – Luce of Time Inc. was quite a mild case compared with some others. Even the impersonal Associated Press was presided over for some years by its own tycoon figure –

Kent Cooper – who at least credited himself[1] with the achievement of breaking the European news cartel.

All of these tycoons were men of a basically promotional disposition. The same was true of the founding fathers of American radio and television: David Sarnoff, William Paley, and Edward Noble – of the NBC, CBS and ABC networks respectively – would none of them have been out of place as movie magnates. It may be evidence in favour of some oral gratification theory of radio and television that Paley came from the cigar selling business, while Noble was from the candy business – the Lifesaver, no less.

The list of media tycoons runs on yet further to Ivy Lee and Edward Bernays in public relations. Nor was the advertising industry short of self-publicizing tycoons, while the history even of the market research trade is not lacking in self-styled tycoons – varying from the vaguely idealistic George Gallup to more profit-conscious research tycoons like Nielsen. These salesmen just had better opportunities than most businessmen for publicity on a national and international scale. Their publicity usually preceded them in Europe and other parts of the world, where – out of their American context – they were studiously imitated by their European equivalents.

But the international significance of the tycoons was not restricted merely to their publicity façades being copied in other countries; these men had an interest in demonstrating their success and superiority in Europe. The easiest way of paying off Europe for its earlier hard blows was for the tycoon to demonstrate his business pre-eminence to the Europeans on their own turf. Even William Randolph Hearst, the native born son of a millionaire US Senator, seems to have felt such urges. Pulitzer, who was Austrian born, was always returning in splendour to Europe. At least half of the early Hollywood tycoons' families had been driven to America by militant anti-Semitism and/or dire poverty. Lewis J. Selznick, an early movie entrepreneur and father of the Selznick who produced *Gone with the Wind* had been born in Kiev in 1870, one of a Jewish family of 18 children. When in 1917 Selznick heard that the Tsar of Russia had been deposed he amused the American movie industry by cabling the Tsar an offer of employment:

WHEN I WAS A BOY IN RUSSIA YOUR POLICE TREATED MY PEOPLE VERY BADLY. HOWEVER NO HARD FEELINGS. HEAR YOU ARE NOW OUT OF WORK. IF YOU WILL COME TO NEW YORK CAN GIVE YOU FINE POSITION ACTING IN PICTURES. SALARY NO OBJECT. REPLY MY EXPENSE. REGARDS YOU AND FAMILY.[2]

These Hollywood tycoons would have been less than human had

they not been especially satisfied at their ability to reap some commercial revenge for the poverty and persecution their parents had suffered in Europe. There must have been such personal motivations present in the cold and merciless manner with which the Hollywood tycoons exploited the enormous advantages they found themselves with in the European markets from about 1915 onwards. The hard and effective tactics of block booking, sales boycotts and the buying up of budding European stars – all these were gentle tactics compared with those used in the Russian pogroms.

This understandable wish to 'show' Europe, the undoubted scale economies of wider sales, the autocratic managerial style of the first generation tycoon – all these factors combined to perpetuate an active promotional interest in foreign markets among American media tycoons.

A striking example of this 'forward' strategy is provided by David Sarnoff, perhaps the most appealing and most influential of all American media tycoons. Sarnoff, born into a Jewish family in the Minsk area of Russia, became an American national hero in 1912 as the Marconi radio operator during the *Titanic* disaster. Thirty-two years later, by 1944, Sarnoff had long been the leading personality in American radio, and he was near to concluding years of lobbying which would establish him as the key founding father of American television. As the head of RCA, Sarnoff was asked early in 1944 to sort out the technical and diplomatic problems of reporting the imminent invasion of France. Having done all this, Sarnoff might perhaps have been expected to hurry back to New York. But, no, he wanted to see some real action and arrived in Paris a day before de Gaulle's official entry. Sarnoff went straight to Radio France (CTSF) to liberate it, and spent the next two weeks getting the radio station back on the air in the Allied cause. Four weeks after his entry to Paris Sarnoff also submitted to the military authorities a detailed plan for the organization of radio and postal services in Germany, when it had been occupied.[3]

STARS, STATUS, MOBILITY

The American media appeal to the great middle market of the United States by emphasizing personalities, personal celebrity, the individual achievement of success. This is especially true of the video media, and of entertainment, and the view of social inequality thus presented is a status view. This lack of emphasis on class and caste divisions is found not only in Hollywood output, but also in much American literature and social science. The idea is typically American and un-European. Less often noticed is the point that although un-European and somewhat unreal even of the United States, this status view of inequality is still immensely appealing in Europe. Europeans have a long tradition of thinking of America in terms of geographical and social mobility, of the United States as the land where the unreal might become real. Both English and German writers wrote about the American West long before the first cowboy films. And since the beginnings of Hollywood, even the most serious of European writers have been influenced by media portrayals of American social reality. Bertolt Brecht was continually returning to Chicago gang warfare as a metaphor for capitalism, and although Brecht did spend some time in the US his knowledge of Chicago gangs seems to have been derived from press and film coverage. Franz Kafka's gothic novel, *Amerika*, is a parable of social success in the New World and full of visual melodrama straight out of Hollywood.

Even in Hollywood portrayals, traditional forms of social inequality such as class and caste are not entirely absent – clearly upper-class and lower-class people sometimes come on stage, but they usually play minor parts. One's personal qualities matter more than whether one is rich or poor, it is implied. Success has to be earned. Status and personal qualities are vital, too, in being successful as a man or woman, as a child or parent; immigrants and members of minorities can also succeed, but if you are black you may have to try even harder than the rest. This status message is portrayed in news and political coverage, in entertainment and in advertising. Such a status view of inequality accords well with the middle of the market thrust of American media.

This status view of American society is essentially urban – it is a top-50-markets view. The countryside – whether in westerns or in Disney cartoons – is the countryside as seen by urban dwellers. This is also an extremely mobile view of society. People are socially mobile – with sympathetic characters usually moving up the success escalator. Geographical movement is rapid – there are always new guys in town. And media people are also physically mobile – they are for ever arriving and departing via spacecraft, aircraft, cars, trains, ships or horses. Physical mobility provides 'events' in news value terms and something to film in video terms.

In this status view of society there are still some dilemmas to be solved – but in solving them the individual shows his personal qualities, achieves his status. American media output is heavily peopled with professionals and executives – there are three times as many lawyers, police officers, private detectives, doctors and business executives in the television labour force compared with the division of labour revealed by the US Census.*[4]

* Daniel Bell's 'post industrial society' does at least seem to exist on television.

National advertising has long been aimed more at women than men; the woman as consumer has long been a staple editorial topic. Radio invented the daytime radio drama serial, or soap opera. Any television series which is followed by a highish proportion of young affluent married women receives the ultimate commercial accolade – 'good demographics'. A continuing theme in American entertainment has been the American woman's 'dilemma' or 'two roles'. The result was Hollywood's 'good-bad' girl;[5] in 1940s American soap-operas the protagonists were middle-class women who depended upon their personal qualities for solving their dilemmas.[6]

The characteristic dilemmas and ambivalence of American media output aimed at men are highlighted in *Playboy* and its many American and European imitators. The ambivalence of *Playboy* (like the ambivalence of the traditional women's magazines) encourages the reader to dream that somehow it's always possible to solve dilemmas and play two or more apparently contradictory roles. Once again the material stresses *personal* qualities – it is the task of the individual to try to 'have it both ways', to be both housewife and heroine, or to be both Casanova and suburban husband.

American media's stress on reaching young people dates from attempts of the English-language press to wean young immigrants away from foreign-language papers. Certainly Hollywood always recognized that it had a young audience.[7] The preference of advertisers is for reaching the young – regarded as better 'prospects' for new products and for switching their 'brand loyalty'. The part played by juke-box and record purchases in radio hit selection produced an enormous bias towards youthful preferences and the intricacies of teenage love in America. Much American material aimed at children was, like comic strips, also aimed at the children's parents.

All of these themes – status, individual qualities, social and geographical mobility, contradictory roles for women and men, youth against age – all are literally embodied in the star. This is true both of the fictional characters the star portrays and also 'factual' portrayal of the star in other media and publicity material.

Stardom was partly forced upon the early film-makers by the public. Not until 1910 did the promotion of actor's names and the publication of fan magazines begin. But this public demand for stars to worship had been known in the theatre and literature. American society had some special characteristics which predisposed both it and its media system to focus upon personal celebrity. The American political system encouraged voters to see politics in terms of a few individuals – such as the President, the state Governor and the two US Senators from one's own state. The American popular press from its early days stressed personality and celebrity. The Associated

Press, when it appeared, was the perfect mechanism for imprinting a few prominent names upon the minds of all Americans. Press agentry grew up around the promotion of theatrical celebrities.

American magazines long concentrated heavily on biography;[8] the best-selling magazines of the 1890s averaged more than one biographical article per number. By 1940–1 three-quarters of all biographical subjects in *Saturday Evening Post* and *Colliers* came from 'consumption' areas – almost entirely from the movies, entertainment, sport, newspapers and radio. American media have continued to present the media industry itself as one of the main spheres in which 'success' can be earned, and this, too, has been copied in other countries.

Radio helped the same celebrities to appear across the entire range of news, entertainment and advertising. Stars 'endorsed' products and politicians; politicians adopted the styles of entertainment-advertisers. Franklin Roosevelt, a master of the newsreel statement and the radio 'chat', found himself in 1940 confronted in Wendell Wilkie by a Republican opponent whose main claim to fame was the pleasant sound he made on radio. Television has led to yet further overlapping between politics and Hollywood. C. Wright Mills pointed out that the stars always intermingled:

> All the stars of any other sphere of endeavor or position are drawn toward the new star and he toward them. The success, the champion, accordingly is one who intermingles freely with other champions to populate the world of celebrity.[9]

One celebrity meeting another is in news value terms an event; 'guest star' A appearing on star B's television show is a theme for the week; putting six stars into one film is an expensive form of accident insurance; getting a film star to attend a political rally may avoid the embarrassment of empty seats.

Celebrities can bid up their star value by appearing in some suitable setting with other countries' stars. America having more and bigger stars – as well as more and bigger ways of beaming them around the world – has an irresistible attraction for stars from other lands. European and other stars are constantly crossing the Atlantic to confer with, star with, make a show with or cut a disc with, suitable American stars. Hollywood from its earliest days imported both ready-made, and not-yet, stars. Especially prominent amongst these were stars of British origin. In this panoply of Anglo-American celebrities the British royal family appear as the most celebrated of guest star family acts.

Personal qualities can also be negative. And whereas financial success in Hollywood output often correlates with pleasant personal qualities, so also the wicked rich man, the evil personality, recurs again and again in the American media. He appears especially in the western and the crime film; in the western he is the big bad farmer who controls the land, the women and the hired guns, while in the crime film he is the sinister Mr Big hovering in the background. In American fictional coverage of politics – as in the news presentation of politics – we are often confronted with a sinister and corrupt Mr Big. This presentation of sinister wealth and power in terms of a single deviant personality relieves the American media from having to make general statements about social inequality, or class, or wealth, or power. Such a formula for personifying evil maximizes audience appeal, while minimizing offence.

It is not difficult to see that many of these themes, while popular within the United States itself, may be even more appealing in Europe, and to the urban population of Latin America and Asia. The enormous in-flow of population into American cities, the great increases in education and in white-collar employment – these trends have also been experienced in Europe, Latin America and in the great cities of Asia. Stress on personal qualities, social mobility, status, youth, role-conflict for urban women, the tyranny of the boss at work – all of these can be expected to have a strong appeal.

But the appeal of American media in other countries may relate more to the pace or 'grammar' of films or television, comics or advertising. American output emphasizes pace, brevity and terseness. The American media, compared with those of other lands, have bigger production budgets, are more involved with advertising and operate in a more media-saturated society. Pace is a device to seize audience attention. Hollywood horses always seem to set off at a gallop on even the longest journey and under the hottest sun – not because horse or rider ever favoured such lunatic speed but because the audiences did. Outdoor 'action' sequences are obviously more expensive to produce than are studio 'talking heads' (or the talking bodies of sex films). The 'action adventure' style on television derived from the ABC network's pursuit of a more competitive style of television in the late 1950s.

Many devices which stress brevity and speed are simply intended to catch the attention of the jaded American public. Comic strips are an obvious example of material suitable for readers with little time and perhaps not much reading ability. The pyramid style of news agency writing spills the guts of the story into the first sentence, each descending sentence contains less and less essential material. The advertisements, which also assume a short attention span and limited interest, while primarily complementing the other material, to some extent compete with it.

These themes tend to reinforce each other. Their appeal has been so great in other lands that all film industries have tended to adopt or copy the Hollywood themes. The various mini-Hollywoods, out-side the communist world, then start making their own stars, their own status, mobility and action themes. Popular as some of these themes are locally – especially if linked with some local myth or tradition – they cannot easily compete on the world export stage with Hollywood, because Hollywood has chosen ground on which it seems unbeatable. It has more stars, more mobility, more action.

There have been many imitations of the western but these have reinforced as much as they have rivalled the authentic American western. The same point is even clearer with science fiction – whether books, films, television series or comics. When the American astronauts put their footprints on the moon they also – media fact and fiction, as often, blurred – put American footprints on science fiction. The Japanese and others can, and do, make science fiction films, but they lack the 'authenticity' of American ones. Hollywood cornered the media market in space, that ultimate sphere of stars and mobility.

THE ETHNIC MIX: BLACKS, JEWS, LATINS, WASPS

The ethnic composition of the American media industry must reflect the overall character of the American melting pot and presumably must partly account for the popularity of American media around the world. Isaac Goldberg in his book *Tin Pan Alley* (1930) empha-sized the importance of Negroes and Jews in American jazz and related this to their common experience of oppression:

The spiritual is religious; the blues are secular, and, as their words readily prove, sexual. Jazz, then, has a decidedly sexual significance. We touch now the root of the antagonism to it. That antagonism, that dour, symptomatic aversion, was largely non-musical, non-esthetic at bottom. It was the evidence of a caste, and, as we now see, a purity complex. For jazz is the sexual symbol of an inferior race.

Is it merely fanciful if I find, in these selfsame observations, the reasons why the Jewish composers of America have been so im-portant in the development of jazz? Read such a novel as Carl Van Vechten's *Nigger Heaven*, and you may be struck, time and again, by certain traits of character that are quite as Jewish as they are Negro; more, the prejudices which the Harlem intellectual has to contend with have their counterpart in Jewish-American life. The Jew, racially, is also an Oriental and was originally much darker than he is today. He has the sad, the hysterical psychology of the oppressed race. From the cantor grandfather to the grandson who yearns 'mammy' songs is no vaster a stride than from the Negro spiritual to the white 'blues'. The minor-major, what we might call amphibious, mode of the typical blues, with its blue notes, is by no means a stranger to the Jewish ear. The ecstatic songs of the Khassidim – the pietist sect of the Polish Jews – bear striking psychological analogies to the sacred and secular tunes of the Negro. I have heard Jimmy Johnson imitate a singing colored preacher, and the cantillation could have passed – almost – for the roulades of a Jewish precentor. The simple fact is that the Jew responds naturally to the deeper implications of jazz, and that as a Jewish-American he partakes of the impulse at both its Oriental and its Occidental end. The Khassid, too, walks all over God's heaven.[10]

American popular music has played an enormous part not only on radio and records around the world, but also in films and television. American black music has not been entirely Afro-American in origin; English folk music contributed much to most southern USA music upon which both whites and blacks drew. Nevertheless the black origins of American popular music have been greatly muted in its media presentation – Irving Berlin, George Gershwin, Bing Crosby, Frank Sinatra, Elvis Presley and most other leading names in such white music acknowledged having drawn heavily on black material.

And throughout most of the nineteenth century the Minstrel Show – featuring the black man as spectacle and all-purpose object of humour – was the predominant form in popular entertainment. Even here the black part was usually played by a white man.

Minstrelsy's unprecedented success demonstrated the great, almost unlimited, demand for popular entertainment that spoke for and to the great mass of middling Americans. . . .

Lambasting aristocrats and making extensive use of frontier language and lore, minstrels asserted the worth and dignity of the white American common man. They created ludicrous Northern Negro characters that assured audience members that however confused, bewildered or helpless they felt, someone was much worse off then they were. . . .

If Negroes were to share in America's bounty of happiness, minstrels asserted, they needed whites to take care of them. To confirm this, minstrels created and repeatedly portrayed the contrasting caricatures of inept ludicrous Northern blacks and contented, fulfilled Southern Negroes . . .

Beginning with early blackface entertainers who adapted aspects of Afro-American music, dance and humor to suit white audiences, minstrelsy also brought blacks and at least part of their culture into American popular culture for the first time. The enthralling vitality of this material, even as adapted by white performers, accounted in large part for minstrelsy's great initial impact. Although minstrel use of black culture declined in the late 1850s, as white minstrels concentrated on caricatures of blacks, when Negroes themselves became minstrels after the Civil War, they brought a transfusion of their culture with them. Again, Afro-American culture intrigued white Americans. But black minstrels had to work within narrow limits because they performed for audiences that expected them to act out well-established minstrel stereotypes of Negroes. . . .[11]

The minstrel tradition was a major formative influence upon American vaudeville and subsequently all American media entertainment. D. W. Griffith's *Birth of a Nation* (1915) represented southern white stereotypes of blacks. But the most commercially influential of the early sound films, *The Jazz Singer* (1927), explicitly followed the minstrel tradition – Al Jolson, a white American Jew, played the part of a blacked-up minstrel as he had often done with enormous success in vaudeville and on Broadway. The following year another minstrel-derived show, *Amos 'n' Andy*, began on radio and became the first great popular success of networked radio; it featured two simple but lovable southern blacks – played by whites.[12] *Amos 'n' Andy* subsequently appeared on television and was the focus of many early efforts to remove racial caricatures from American television.

In more recent years black faces have appeared on American television in larger numbers – and in less caricatured form. The more recent approach to them has been the familiar one of personal qualities, the individual achieving success – and status. Many blacks, we are told now, are nice people, 100 per cent Americans, with college degrees, holding down fine jobs, doctors, lawyers, policemen and private eyes. Some of them are rotten apples too but there are always a few such in any barrel.

American Jews and American blacks clearly share the historical legacy of oppression. But the Jews have played various go-between, creative, organizing and performing roles which have been denied to blacks. Most obviously Jews have often been the interpreters and transposers of black music for white America and for the world.

Jews also have spanned the gap between the rich and poor – with the first generation Hollywood tycoons being perhaps the most startling example. Jewish immigrants also settled disproportionately in the go-between city of New York.* American Jews have also often spanned between educated and illiterate, between high and low culture and between popular and serious music; George Gershwin, a Jewish boy born in Brooklyn, was a Tin-Pan Alleyman but also wrote the black musical *Porgy and Bess*, the first American music ever performed at La Scala, Milan.

Most important of all – from a world media perspective – American Jews were well suited to a go-between role linking Europe and America. Not only did many first generation Jewish immigrants have psychological scores to pay off in Europe, they also had friends and relatives in Europe and a deep feeling for European culture, aspirations, and prejudices. And although Hitler destroyed the majority of central European Jewry, his regime also drove a further wave of migrants to New York – some of whom returned to Europe after 1945.

How important have Jews been in the overall direction of the American media? Clearly in nearly all aspects of films, radio and television they have played a large part. In the press Jewish influence has been smaller, although the *New York Times* and some other important newspapers are controlled by Jewish families.

In order to decide how powerful the Jews have been in shaping American media one would need to look also at the WASPs, the White Anglo-Saxon Protestants. Undoubtedly people of British and other north European Protestant origin have been the single most powerful ethnic force; for example when the movies switched to sound in the late 1920s they also came much more closely under the direction of Wall Street WASPs. The bulk of American daily newspapers and magazines appear to be WASP controlled, and this also applies to a large extent to the news agencies and top 150 television stations.

The WASP-Jewish alliance involves also a division of labour within the media. For example Edward Jay Epstein in his study of the New York network television news operations found that 58 per cent of (36) network producers and news editors he interviewed were Jewish;[13] however of correspondents who appeared on the television screen the 'predominant' pattern was of Protestant parentage, and there were also some Catholics. A similar division of labour seems to have worked in Hollywood's golden age. While there were many Jewish

* The Jewish population of the United States reached one million in 1898. A generation later the most heavily Jewish area was no longer Manhattan but the Bronx. See Henry S. Linfield (1927).

performers, there was prejudice in favour of Hollywood's having a mainly WASP face. One of the simplest but most important values of the Anglo-American media is the status given to north European physical appearance. The first human faces to become literally known around the world were those of Hollywood stars such as Mary Pickford and Douglas Fairbanks. Their faces and those of a thousand other northern stars, have ever since looked out from the screens and hoardings of the world's cities, establishing a nearly universal notion of physical beauty.

But there is also a fourth important ethnic strain in American media. This Latin strain comes partly from Mexico and Latin America and partly from Italy. Mexico, at least as subject matter, has been incorporated into the Hollywood system. Italy was the original home of the supercolossal film (around 1914) and the Italian industry has been the only one in the world to match Hollywood's carefully flamboyant ways. American film tycoons move to Rome and Italian tycoons to New York with equal ease. Not accidentally the Hollywood off-shore industry has had its biggest foreign base in Rome. Puerto Rican and Mexican Spanish are now the second languages of New York and Los Angeles. The Latin bravura of American films and television accounts in part for their success not only in Latin America and southern Europe but everywhere in the world; these larger than life qualities are, quite simply, suited to the visual media, or to the dominant forms into which these media have been developed.

Latin and Jewish looks tend to merge. This gives the American visual media their three characteristic skin colours: white WASPS, slightly darker Jews and Latins, and black blacks. And along with this ethnic visual typology often goes an ethnic division of labour as simple as heroine, seducer, and slave or policeman, criminal and servant. This ethnic division of labour is capable of endless manipulation – the black man as hero is drama in itself – and it also seems to have been copied by the film industries of other nations, such as Mexico, Egypt and India. The white/light brown/black hierarchy was already deeply embedded in each of these societies, but another appeal of this division must have been that it allowed the stars of these infant film industries to look like Hollywood stars – pale spot-lit figures surrounded by supporting players with darker skins. This WASP-Jewish-Latin-Black ethnic mix could scarcely have been better arranged had its sole purpose been to appeal to Europe, the white British Commonwealth and Latin America. But it is a less obviously appealing ethnic mix for Asia. Most countries, when they import American material, *select* quite heavily. It is therefore possible to select those parts of the ethnic mix which seem most appealing locally.

HOLLYWOOD CONQUERS THE WORLD: ONCE, TWICE, THRICE

During and after the 1914–18 war Hollywood films achieved world dominance with a completeness which astonished people in many countries and which has still not been fully explained. From 1915 to about 1955, this dominance was challenged in only a few countries; even in the 1950s the main blows against it were struck from within the United States – first by anti-trust decisions and secondly by the arrival of television, based on New York.

American television in the early 1950s greatly exceeded the scale of television in the rest of the world; and in the early 1960s a sizeable fraction of screen time in the rest of the world was filled with American materials – Hollywood feature films as well as recorded television programming. Meanwhile the production of nationally networked entertainment had migrated to Hollywood.

Hollywood's first triumph in feature films and its more recent triumph in television series were crucially linked by yet another made-in-Hollywood triumph – in radio and records. From 1930 onwards Hollywood became the world centre not only for making talking films but *sound* radio shows and records. Jack Benny, Bob Hope, Bing Crosby and others stepped from feature films into radio shows into television series. Records carried Hollywood sounds around the world and the American style of commercial radio, already by 1940 established in Hollywood, was, after the Second World War, increasingly adopted in many countries.

After the talkie revolution Hollywood poured out a flood of musicals and movie songs – which could be promoted and preserved on records. The radio industry – both local stations and networks – had already found that music was the staple of radio, and if the music was live, an expensive staple. Thus local radio favoured recorded music, and then there was the juke-box – this American gadget allowed the public to vote with their coins for their preferences; the juke-box was a combined revenue earner, market research and publicity machine, as well as a talent scout. The radio hit parade – which was to become the dominant form in American and, later, world radio – was closely linked to the juke-box. The Wurlitzer revolution was a distinctly American one; in Europe pop music remained linked primarily to sheet music sales much longer.

The rest of the world imported, borrowed and copied various bits and pieces of American popular music from the earliest days of American radio, but it was not until 1945 – well into American radio's third decade – that Europeans finally recognized the various forms of popular music as adding up to a distinctive form of output for the entire medium of radio. American network radio output had more audience appeal and was more expensive to produce.

Most estimates agree that about 80 per cent of all film screenings throughout the world in the early and mid 1920s were of Hollywood products (Table 4). The United States moved more quickly into radio than did other countries and from 1930 to 1950 always had nearly half the world's radio sets; in the 1930s the outpourings of American recorded music on to foreign record players and radio stations was already well established.

Early American dominance of the bulk of the world's screens was even greater in the early days of television. In 1950 the USA had over ten million television sets, while the rest of the world had less than one million (and the majority of these were in Britain). This dominance only dwindled slowly during the 1950s; it was there during the crucial period, when all of the other sizeable nations in the world were establishing their television services.

Preceding the films–radio/records–television triple triumph of Hollywood, was the early leadership of the American press. Throughout most of the late nineteenth century probably over half the world sale of daily newspapers was in the United States. And in one media field this 'more than half the world's' situation continues – more than half of all world advertising expenditure still occurs within the United States.

PART TWO

British Commonwealth, English language . . . Anglo-American cartel?

CHAPTER FIVE

Britain and the white Commonwealth

Britain has been, and is, a lynch-pin in the worldwide spread of American media. Britain first established itself as the principal media power and English as the language of international communication. Britain is still today a major media exporter. But it is also a major media importer – and, more than any other equally important nation in the world, Britain has long drawn its media imports almost entirely from the United States.

The British Empire was unambiguously also a media empire. Just the ex-British territories of South Asia (mainly the former Indian Empire) and the ex-British colonies in Africa today contain about one quarter of the world's population. In these enormous areas the press and broadcasting were quite simply set up by the British, as imitations or offshoots of *The Times*, Reuters and the BBC. Only in films did the British not impose a British pattern; or rather in films the Hollywood domination of the British home market around 1920 was reproduced in the Empire.

British models and British personnel were also important in establishing the press and other media in Canada, Australia, New Zealand and South Africa. These countries were subsequently opened to very strong United States media influence.

DECORUM AND DEFERENCE: THE NINETEENTH-CENTURY BRITISH PRESS

Britain in 1850 had a press marked by decorum, deference and monopoly. Even in the United States newspapers had a chronic tendency to become respectable; but there at least new waves of immigration, the prevalence of popular elections with a strong show business element, and the influence of the frontier – all these were correctives.

In the 1830s the British government was still putting down its popular press with force and penal taxation; but then it was discovered that gentler taxation muted journalists even more effectively. By 1850 the alien notion was being heard that perhaps newspapers should not be taxed at all. This alien idea came from the United States.

And so in 1855 *The Times* lost an effective monopoly conferred by taxation.

American influence was important even before 1850. It was known that printers who had suffered persecution in England could set up untaxed newspapers in the United States. One such was Joseph Gales who was indicted for conspiracy in 1794 because he had advocated radical reform in his weekly *Sheffield Register*; he emigrated and in 1799 founded the *Raleigh Register* in North Carolina. His son Joseph Gales junior was in 1810 one of two partners who took control of the Washington *National Intelligencer*, President Jefferson's semi-official mouthpiece and America's first political newspaper of record.[1] A leading inspiration in the illegal 'Pauper Press' in England in the 1830s[2] was the example of William Cobbett, who had been a pioneer in American journalism as 'Peter Porcupine' in Philadelphia.[3]

1855 saw the founding of the penny *Daily Telegraph* which quickly passed *The Times*'s circulation. J. M. Levy modelled the *Daily Telegraph* on James Gordon Bennett's *New York Herald*.[4]

But forty years later Britain's national popular *daily* press had still not arrived; the halfpenny *Daily Mail* launched by Northcliffe in 1896 went some way towards remedying this lack. Yet even the *Daily Mail* was still hardly a popular paper. Its main news page concentrated on foreign news, its front page was all classified advertising; its most important concession to popularity lay in brevity and terseness – and its main audience were serious-minded office workers. Fleet Street mythology presents Northcliffe as an heroic innovator.

Even before 1850 two-thirds of the English working class were capable of reading, if not of writing;[5] William Cobbett's paper which began in 1816 at twopence had quickly reached a sale of 50,000.[6] The vigour, simplicity and raciness of Cobbett's style was still not used after 1855 by the solemn morning papers but it was imitated by the mildly disreputable Sundays.

Low incomes, lack of popular advertising, lack of women readers, lack of both political and commercial *motivation* among newspaper owners – all these held back the growth of a popular daily press. The vote was extended in 1832 but took another 96 years to become universal. The abolition of taxes on newspapers occurred only gradually also, and led merely to a series of minor alterations in the pattern of newspaper ownership, not to any major incursion of some fresh breed of owners.

The commercial drive of printer-owners who successfully built up papers like *The Times* and *Daily Telegraph* faded in their offspring. New York supplied the Linotypes and Hoe rotary presses used by Northcliffe on the *Daily Mail* in 1896.[7] There were adventurous

Mary Pickford and Douglas Fairbanks, London, 1920

Harry Cohn – 'Tsar of Columbia Pictures' – and underlings

International looks: Bruce Lee and Douglas Fairbanks snr.

Lew Grade, 1955

English newspapermen in the 1880s but they were pioneering papers in Shanghai or Bombay, not England. There was some shock-and-horror popular journalism but it was confined to Sundays like the *News of the World*. In the 1890s *The Times*'s head printer still chose types and designed page layouts – a formula for an unchanging and increasingly unread newspaper.

The 'taxes on knowledge' and the railways enabled London to dominate the morning newspaper field throughout England. Wholesale and retail sales were controlled by a few firms like W. H. Smith. Smith and his book library rival, Mudie, were both men of strong religious, moral and commercial views; Mudie exerted an iron grasp on the three-decker novel and all London book publishing.[8] Smith, like Mudie in the book trade, discouraged all reading matter which was cheap in price or tone. Mudie insisted on three-volume novels at retail prices so high as to discourage any but library sales, while W. H. Smith discouraged magazines and newspapers which lacked decorum:

> Smith quickly earned the title of 'The Northwest Missionary' for his success in eliminating the 'unmitigated rubbish' previously found on the platforms of the London and Northwestern Railway.[9]

This respectable and high-priced distribution system exercised a veto on disreputable national dailies; the only non-respectable dailies to survive were evening papers with their own local distribution networks. The other significant exceptions were a handful of populist Sunday papers which, with early Saturday printing, evolved a separate once-a-week distribution system.

NORTHCLIFFE AS IMPORTER OF AMERICAN METHODS

Northcliffe was able to make his *Daily Mail* in 1896 into Britain's first successful halfpenny national morning, partly because he was known to the distributors as the producer of a number of eminently respectable children's publications (some based on American models). Northcliffe deliberately made the *Mail* look dull and sombre, but it was more lively to read and much more lavishly promoted than its morning rivals. However, Northcliffe's attempt to print a *Sunday Mail* was sabotaged by the distribution trade amidst the outcries of bishops and anti-Semitic mumblings against the Jewish owners of the *Daily Telegraph* (also attempting a Sunday edition).[10] Northcliffe was lucky in the all-time low price of newsprint in 1896–7, itself largely due to new production methods used in Canada and the United

States.[11] He was also lucky with the Boer War which helped double *Daily Mail* sales between 1898 and 1900.[12]

The London evening papers were the first importers of American innovations. The evening *Star* was the most influential under its editor T. P. Connor who, in 1889, was advocating a 'new journalism'[13] which he had learnt in the London office of the *New York Herald*. The key people in the so-called 'Northcliffe revolution' were mostly either protégés of O'Connor or had other American links.* The major news agency event in 1890s London was the appearance of the American-financed Dalziel agency, whose American news methods for a time worried Reuters.[14] London's first halfpenny morning paper was the work of yet another American – Charles Ives, whose brightly presented *The Morning*, launched in 1892, failed because it did not look like a morning paper.[15] Northcliffe is sometimes claimed to have been a pioneer of advertising, but there is little evidence for such an assertion.

Numerous Americans assisted this rebirth of a British popular press, but the most important was William Randolph Hearst. Many British memoirs of the 'Northcliffe Revolution' were written after the First World War and Northcliffe's propaganda role in that war has coloured the recollections of 1896. By 1918 Hearst had become known in Fleet Street (and among Anglophile Americans) as an enemy of England and hurt English national pride subsequently promoted Northcliffe to the role of composer instead of his deserved title of imaginative interpreter. Perhaps the evident triumph of American films and popular music around 1920 made English writers more eager to claim the press 'revolution' for themselves. Certainly the awful examples of Hollywood, Tin Pan Alley and early American radio horrified many tidy British minds.

THE BBC: NO BARBARIC YAWPS HERE

American broadcasting in 1922 was already moving towards advertising finance; so the BBC would be licence financed. American radio began locally and anyone could set up a radio station; the BBC would be national and controlled in the public interest. American radio was competitive; so British radio would be a monopoly. American radio

---

* Northcliffe himself visited America in 1894 just before he bought the London *Evening News*. The man who persuaded him to buy the *News*, and subsequently became his editorial hatchet man, was Kennedy Jones, who had worked under O'Connor. Another O'Connor protégé was Thomas Marlowe, editor of the *Daily Mail* from 1899 to 1926. A number of key figures were American citizens, such as R. D. Blumenfeld who was news editor of the *Daily Mail* and then editor of the *Daily Express* from 1902 to 1929 (by which date it had nearly won the British circulation lead).

was becoming geared to the market; so British radio would be insulated from the market.

A Post Office civil servant, F. J. Brown, has in some respects a stronger claim than Reith to be the father of British broadcasting. When, in October 1922, John Reith saw an advertisement for the first senior posts in the British Broadcasting Company he still scarcely knew what radio was. But during the previous winter F. J. Brown had visited American radio stations, and he didn't like what he saw. Brown so reported to the Postmaster-General, and the result was a meeting between Post Office officials and the radio manufacturers. Monopoly was not at first the idea – merely to do things in a more orderly way than the Americans.

In both Britain and America, radio was shaped by political parties, the central government, the press and the radio hardware manufacturers. The national political parties in Britain favoured a national framework. The Conservative Party naturally favoured a high-minded solution, insulated from working-class tastes and susceptible to government 'guidance' (as the General Strike in 1926 showed the BBC to be). The Labour Party, flushed with early enthusiasm for public corporations, was also in favour. The national newspapers were shrilly opposed to any radio incursions into either advertising or news. The manufacturers wanted any radio service which would sell their sets and hardware. The central government department, the Post Office, could in the BBC satisfy its preference for engineering over commerce and employed an engineer, John Reith, to manage the radio.

By the time the BBC monopoly was broken in television in 1955, the BBC had a worldwide reputation for the accuracy of its news and for its cultural leadership. Yet these BBC 'traditions' were of recent origin. The news reputation derives from 1939–45 and the cultural leadership reputation largely from the Third Programme which began in 1946. Up to 1939 the BBC carefully avoided, for instance in music, both the outright popular and the outright avant-garde.[16] This was consistent with the BBC's own delicate position and Reith's personal background as engineer, soldier and civil servant. Reith's second-in-command was Rear-Admiral Carpendale (recommended by F. J. Brown of the Post Office). When this ex-soldier and ex-Admiral at last decided in 1932 to have a news department they placed in charge of the department (four sub-editors and no reporters) not a journalist but an ex-chief of the Indian Police. The first controller of programmes was a retired colonel.

Almost immediately after Reith left in 1938, the BBC began to respond to the stimulus of impending war; in 1939 new overseas services mushroomed. By 1945 the BBC was regarded throughout Europe and beyond as both the Voice of Britain and the world's leading broadcasting organization. But the BBC in 1945 quickly reverted to its cautious pre-war stance. With a devastated Europe at its doorstep the BBC cut most of its European output; after 1945 it was the American broadcasting influence in Europe which mainly filled the vacuum. Representative of the BBC strategy was William Haley (soon to be Director-General) who was opposed to the BBC 'spawning in Europe'.[17]

Government policy in wartime had forced the BBC to stimulate British public morale, which involved entertainment for the working class. But BBC television (starting again in 1946) appealed to the affluent middle-class early buyers of TV sets. The BBC offered little radio material to match the sort of appetite indicated by the pre-war appeal of Continental commercial radio stations, by the ravenous demand for Hollywood films, or by the huge sales of the popular daily newspapers. In 1950 just three popular British newspapers were together every Sunday selling 18 million copies of papers packed with sport, sexy court cases and lurid crimes of a sort which the BBC had no hesitation in ignoring altogether.

Listeners in German-occupied Europe had admired the BBC's accuracy and modesty. But during the war the British domestic audience showed a marked liking for American music and humour. After 1942, Briggs notes, 'there were to be two distinct strands in war-time Variety, one essentially British provincial and one American'.[18] These two traditions were combined in the most successful entertainment BBC radio show 'ITMA':

> Although it became the most English of English programmes, it had started very differently as an 'attempt to create a British version of the Burns and Allen show' in the United States.

Another of the most popular entertainment shows, *Bebe, Vic and Ben*, simply featured an American showbiz family. Bob Hope and Jack Benny were also immensely popular in Britain.[19]

There was a running debate among senior BBC personnel on the British-American issue:

> A year later (1944) there were complaints of too much 'Americanization' of variety and Haley urged that 'in the entertainment field it is essential that the use of . . . American serial material such as Bob Hope, Jack Benny and other programmes does not become a Frankenstein'. Norman Collins, the Director of the General Overseas Service pointed out realistically that while he had been 'constantly and persistently nagging for straight English Variety',

... 'if any hundred British troops are invited to choose their own records 90 per cent of the choice will be of American stuff'.[20]

The BBC North American Service deliberately adopted American techniques. American ideas also arrived in Canadian clothing; *Radio Newsreel*, subsequently a BBC domestic staple, was originated by Canadians broadcasting from London to North America.[21] Personnel with experience of pre-war offshore commercial radio tended to make popular wartime programming. These people, such as Howard Thomas, were to become prominent again after 1955.

1955: ADVERTISING-FINANCED TELEVISION JUMPS THE ATLANTIC

The arrival of the British commercial television channel in 1955 is a key event in the influence of American media in the world. In London first, and then in the other regions, the advertising-financed channel took the bulk of the audience from the BBC, which soon found itself pleading that the *size* of the majority was somewhat smaller than the commercial TV rating service claimed. The commercial stations, which at first suffered heavy losses, found American imports irresistible; American filmed material already offered the attractive combination of high audience appeal and low price to the importing company. There were soon big proportions of American material in the peak audience hours; much American influence involved the wholesale borrowing of formats – such as audience participation shows – which combined popularity with low production costs. *Double Your Money*, *People are Funny* and *Beat the Clock* were immensely popular programmes of an American style not previously seen in Britain. At this time a popular ITV show could use the same name as the American original, feature some lesser American personality and might be produced by a Canadian. The purchase of American scripts – including American jokes for performance by British comedians – was another form of American influence.

Some imported American formulae have been in Britain so long that they now seem entirely British, while the original shows have long since disappeared from American screens. But the quota arrangements which allow only 14 per cent of American imports mean a much higher proportion at the times when large audiences are viewing. Indirect American influence continually takes new forms. Lew Grade increasingly from the later 1960s used his ATV commercial licence and his own previous American experience to become an 'offshore' production company for American network television – these shows used American stars, American production styles and (as a result of, or in anticipation of, American sales) American-sized budgets. The resulting series forced the main BBC 1 channel into its own expensive 'international' crime and 'action' series. This increasing tendency, by which television companies accustom their audiences to more expensive productions than the audience revenue will finance, inevitably increases the pressure towards co-production deals with American interests, and the making of yet glossier series.

In part such trends merely represent the realization, in Britain also, that television is closer to films than to radio. But in Britain, ever since 1915, the majority of film audiences have been seeing American films; domestic British film-making has long made films aimed at the US market. Alexander Korda, Britain's most commercially successful film producer of the last fifty years, himself had Hollywood experience and was always trying to repeat the success which his *The Private Life of Henry VIII* (1933) had in the American market. And since 1960, domestic British film production has depended heavily on direct American finance. Hence the film influences in British television are inevitably American influences as well.

American influence operates more diffusely through notions of 'professionalism' within each of the communications occupations in Britain. British press journalists, radio and television producers, film-makers, and advertising men, all look towards their opposite numbers in New York, Washington and Los Angeles. The very powerful pull of this influence can be seen in many small ways – for instance the eagerness with which most senior British media people demonstrate their up-to-date knowledge of working conditions in the USA.

THE PRESS IN CANADA, SOUTH AFRICA, AUSTRALIA AND NEW ZEALAND

Canada, South Africa, Australia and New Zealand each historically shared some aspects of the United States media pattern – original dependence on England, and the English language – added, however, to other cultural strains and set down in vast empty expanses of territory. But Canada also shares its status of immediate neighbour to the USA with Mexico and Cuba. South Africa, despite a history of white domination, may, under an African political regime, eventually become the media capital of black Africa. All four countries tried to spread the media over large physical distances using relatively small total national incomes.

England in 1850, still held back by taxes on knowledge, actually had fewer daily newspapers than did Australia. These territories each developed a frontier press similar in some respects to that of

the United States. But with less fertile land and much lower populations than the USA, all of these new countries tended to be dominated
by only a few cities. Canada in 1900 had Montreal and Toronto;
Western Canada was a string of villages linked by a line of rail just
north of the American border. The media in each Australian state
focused on one coastal city – Melbourne, Sydney, Brisbane, Adelaide,
Perth. South African press history was dominated first by Cape Town,
then by Johannesburg.

In Australia, New Zealand and South Africa the press long after
1900 was still actively influenced by London; as political dependence
declined, cultural dependence continued – fed by British emigration
and by movements of journalists in both directions. Two exceptions,
which followed the classic partisan European pattern, were the
Afrikaans press in South Africa and the French-language press in
Quebec. But the Canadian English-language press differed from the
London press mainly in absorbing even more American influence
even earlier.

In radio a brief laissez-faire stage in each country was followed by
a BBC-style public broadcasting authority. Subsequently, South Africa
retained a broadcasting monopoly in government hands; New
Zealand developed a mixed pattern of government control and substantial advertising finance. But Canada and Australia moved much
closer to the American pattern of an all-out commercial system
although both retained some 'public service' element.

While the editors of the Afrikaans press have often been the leading politicians of that language group, the English-language South
African press has developed a distinctive commercial orientation
stressing business efficiency, 'editorial independence', liberal editorial
policies and Anglo-American 'neutral' news. The English-language
press has acquired many Afrikaans readers, for whom English is a
second language, and has also appealed to 'non-white' readers.[22]
But the English-language press in South Africa is a commercial cartel;
the two major press groups limit competition, they control both the
main national news agency and the entire press distribution system,
and they discriminate against the Afrikaans press. This cartel is
directly controlled by the Johannesburg gold industry.[23] The Nationalist party controls broadcasting, and all the force of the state. This
conflict between a cartel-run 'liberal' press and a government which
monopolizes broadcasting gives the South African media a special
character.

In both Canada and Australia family-originated press groupings
date far back into the nineteenth century; they have taken a much
more aggressive approach towards commercial broadcasting than
have their equivalents in London. Both the Canadian and Australian

press acquired major holdings in radio and television.[24] The subsequent multi-channel commercial competition forced the 'public service' Canadian CBC and Australian ABC into beleaguered defensive positions. Both lost the bulk of the audience, lost the support of newspapers with commercial broadcasting interests, and also lost much of their political support. Multi-channel commercial competition opened radio and television in both Canada and Australia to large-scale importing from the USA. New Zealand, with lower domestic resources, has an even higher level of imports, although with a somewhat larger British component.

Hollywood feature films provide the single least ambiguous example of an American media presence. By 1925 Canada, Australia and New Zealand were all importing 95 per cent of their films from the USA; they were providing 13 per cent of Hollywood's export earnings – and combined with the UK almost half of these worldwide earnings.

Even before the First World War, the English-language Canadian press was said to look almost indistinguishable from the newspapers across the United States border. In 1900 Toronto, the principal English-speaking city, had a smaller population than the American border cities of Buffalo and Detroit and daily papers from these cities were on regular sale in Toronto. All across Canada newspapers originating from, usually larger, nearby American cities were available in Canadian cities on the day of publication. In telecommunications, as in transport, Canada was merely part of a larger North American structure – and the Associated Press had its first major foreign market in Canada. At the end of the nineteenth century the great wave of American syndicated materials was used by Canadian newspapers to appeal cheaply to readers; there was an upsurge in Canada of American originated advertising and in the sales of American magazines. By 1900 Canadians read mainly American books, Canadian printers belonged to a New York based printing union and so on.[25] An American writing on the Canadian press at the time observed: 'It has been intensely Canadian in sentiment, but in everything else it has been American.'[26]

Canadian 'sentiment' remains important in the media and has grown rapidly in recent years. Fresh waves of American media influence since 1900 have led to fresh defensive responses – such as subsidized cable rates, a Canadian news agency, the Film Board of Canada and the governmental media agency, CRTC. The enormous penetration of American magazines into Canada has been restrained by penalties against their advertising – while the exemption from these penalties of *Time* and *Reader's Digest* was a long major issue in the 'Canadian' debate. But the big economic and population expansion after 1945 helped to make the Canadian newspaper press one of the most prosperous in the world and allowed profits big enough to leave room for increased doses of Ottawa-encouraged Canadian 'sentiment'.

In the other three countries it is more difficult to distinguish between British influence, American influence and spontaneous local evolution. Australia and New Zealand participate in the ownership of Reuters (and Visnews) and Reuters has a special position in those countries. On the American influence side there is a very substantial penetration of American syndication services and American-owned magazines.

THE ARRIVAL OF COMMERCIAL TELEVISION IN THE WHITE COMMONWEALTH

Was it inevitable that Canada, Australia and New Zealand should all by the 1960s have a pattern of television so heavily influenced by American material and examples? Substantial American influence probably was inevitable but some of it was accidental. The white Commonwealth countries, faced with their great physical areas, were cautious in starting television. Canada finally began in 1952 and Australia in 1956, while Britain in 1954–5 added an advertising channel to the previous BBC one. These three decisions were too close in time for any of the three countries to learn much from the others' experiences. Policy-makers in Canada, Australia and Britain seem only to have been aware of the 'invasion' threat in a general way; in all three countries the full financial burden of competitive domestic production was under-estimated, as were the political pressures which would build up to extend the service to remoter areas, and the consequent urge to raise revenue by providing yet more competitive fare. Also insufficiently anticipated was the full commercial appeal of American television exports – the attractive ratio to importers of the high cost of the original American production against the low cost of importing a film copy. In the early 1950s the subsequent export pattern of American TV had not fully developed. Indeed in 1952 most American TV was not yet being recorded on film[27] and thus was not yet available for export.

In Canada the proximity of US cities meant that people living in Toronto, Hamilton, Windsor or Vancouver were able to receive American TV stations across the border. Even before any domestic Canadian TV transmissions began, more than 100,000 Canadian-owned sets were being tuned to American programming.[28] The public service CBC was at first deliberately given monopoly situations and – in contrast to the previous radio pattern – these early CBC stations were in all the most commercially attractive large urban centres. The CBC stations tried to produce most of their own material – but their few hours* of well-intended material meant that many Canadian viewers switched their sets to American stations; soon CBC itself began to carry much American material. Had Canadian television planners acknowledged that a fairly high proportion of Canadian television fare must inevitably be American, it might have been possible to maintain a larger level of Canadian programming than resulted. It was totally inconsistent with these 'Canadian' goals not to challenge the United States FCC's decisions to license some American stations near the Canadian border which intended to beam programming and advertising into a nearby Canadian city.†

In Australia, despite its geographical remoteness, there was a very similar outcome. Australia began in 1956 with both 'public service' ABC stations and also private commercial TV stations. Within a few months Sydney and Melbourne each acquired one 'national' station and two commercial stations. This situation, of a city which one month has no TV and a few months later has three channels, creates a sudden demand for a very large number of hours of programming per week. Thinly populated Australia, with few TV sets and low revenue, was forced from the start into massive imports of TV programming. Four years later, in 1960, when Australia had nearly one million TV sets, a pattern was already established of huge imports of American programming. Australia, like Canada, has established minimum quotas for locally produced programming. In 1972–3 Australian commercial stations were showing 46 hours per week of 'Australian programmes', and nearly 4,000 hours of imported programming were passed by the Australian censor – enough to fill an Australian TV screen for eleven hours a day. 73 per cent of imports came from USA, 24 per cent from Britain and 3 per cent from other countries.[29] Sydney and Melbourne, each now with two national and three commercial channels (the latter transmitting 17 hours a day) had a large output of Australian quota material – large enough to be very under-financed. Australians are perhaps the only national population outside North America substantial proportions of whom actually see more American television programming than do millions of light viewers of television in the USA itself. With eleven minutes of advertising allowed in peak hours, Australians are also perhaps ex-

* In 1952 Toronto and Montreal CBC stations were each transmitting 23½ hours a week, while two New York City stations were each transmitting over 100 hours per week. Unesco (1953), pp. 43, 76.

† The main population centres within reach of KVOS in Bellingham, Washington, are Vancouver and Victoria (both in Canada); the main centre within reach of KCND in Pembina, North Dakota (population 600) is Winnipeg (also in Canada).

posed to greater quantities of American advertising* than any people outside North and South America.

AUSTRALIA, CANADA AND BRITAIN: SPECIAL RELATIONSHIP WITH AMERICAN MEDIA

Both Australian and Canadian policy-makers probably thought that as a result of their greater commercial radio experience they knew more than Britain about the prospects for *commercial* television. (If so, they ignored the already established weight of American pop music on their radio and the domination of their record markets by American and British companies.) Both Canada in 1952 and Australia in 1956 drew quite different conclusions.

Canadians when considering the experience of British TV around 1950 could see only the BBC, apparently unchallenged. Although already well behind the US diffusion of sets, Britain was far ahead of the third country, which in 1950 was Canada itself.[30] The BBC was still pursuing a programme policy fatally lacking in competitive audience appeal; but in 1950 this was not widely understood and the BBC example probably 'misled' Canadian policymakers into their initial exaggerated 'public service' approach – the early CBC monopoly in Canadian television.

Australians, contemplating the British situation in 1954 and 1955, were confronted with a new quite different example. In 1954 the British Parliament decided to introduce in 1955 an advertising-financed TV channel to compete with the BBC; this decision, taken by a British Conservative government, was naturally seen by the Menzies government in Australia as implying that the British themselves thought the BBC-style concept could be retained within a 'mixed system' (of which Australia already had experience in radio).

The special relationship of the Australian and Canadian media with those of both Britain and the United States is further discussed in Chapter 7.

---

* 'American' in the sense of either being for goods produced by American owned companies or advertising placed by American owned advertising agencies based in Australia. Eight of the ten largest Australian advertising agencies in 1974 were wholly or partly American-owned (according to *Advertising Age*).

CHAPTER SIX

Ex-British Africa and India

THE LONDON MODEL: MEDIA FOR A QUARTER OF MANKIND

The ex-British black African nations and India had imposed upon them British-style media. The press was established for the use of British businessmen, settlers, teachers, government officials and soldiers; small newspapers scattered across the world in sea ports and colonial capitals were linked by Reuters. The newspapers, like many in provincial England, tended to model themselves on *The Times*. When broadcasting arrived in these countries it was an off-shoot of the BBC in London and modelled after the BBC – strategically dependent, therefore, on the colonial government, although at least notionally independent in programming; as with the press, broadcasting was set up by and designed to appeal mainly to the British themselves. Inevitably, then, the media were set up to appeal to a foreign élite; inevitably also not only equipment such as transmitters and printing presses were imported, but so also were media models such as the serious daily newspaper. So also was material – news, entertainment and advertising.

There are some major differences, however, in the patterns established in Africa and India. India was more populous, was colonized much earlier and had very elaborate cultural traditions of its own; the British press started much earlier in India and a modern Indian press grew up in the nineteenth century, so that by independence in 1947 the Indianization of the press had largely already occurred. The much shorter colonial history in Africa meant a shorter history of British newspapers; by 1947 the Africanization of the press had not gone far and even around 1960, when those countries became independent, most newspapers were still conducted almost as if they were in the provinces of England or in Scotland. In India radio broadcasting became established earlier than in Africa, although this gap was of only a few years. But the cinema provides the greatest contrast. By 1960 each black African nation had at most a few dozen cinemas showing imported American and British films. India, on the other hand, had one of the world's largest film industries even by 1930.

Nevertheless India shares with these African countries many similarities which it also shares with most other Asian and African countries – and to a lesser extent with the whole of Latin America. Despite their media systems being more developed than many of their neighbours', there is still a common general lack of media. Both income per head and national income are low; such media as exist are confined mainly to the cities. The press reaches relatively few people, television even less. If the rural bulk of the population are exposed to media at all, this is likely to be radio or very occasional cinema shows. While the majority rarely encounter any media, a tiny urban élite has a pattern of media consumption not much different from the middle class in Britain – indeed much of the matter is imported from Britain and the United States.

India, like most black African countries, has enormous problems with language. Literacy itself is low; there is a great diversity of languages – and in order to be able to understand both one's neighbours and the available media it is often necessary to be tri-lingual, in a local language, a national language and in English. Even where both local and national language competence exists, the available media in these languages may still be in the 'wrong' version of the language or in some other way difficult to comprehend. Behind these language differences, lie broader ethnic differences – which have ramifications in religion, education, employment, politics and way of life. Given these formidable obstacles it is perhaps not the poverty of media which is remarkable, but the existence of the media which do appear in English or any other language.

MEDIA INEQUALITY AND MEDIA IMPORTS

In Africa and India ethnic differences do not eradicate class differences; both ethnic and class differences are great and greatly affect the media. This can be illustrated by a very rough sketch of the relevant differences between the top 1 per cent, the next 10 per cent, and the rest – in terms of income, education and media use (all of which tend to correlate very strongly in Africa and Asia).

The 90 per cent or so majority

These live in the country or in urban shanty towns without electricity and with very low cash income. They never see television; even those who can read cannot afford regular reading matter. There are many children, some of whom get some schooling. A mobile cinema may come occasionally, but many adults have never seen a film show. The radio is more familiar, although many only hear the radio in a neighbour's house or in a village shop; even then the radio may lack a battery, or may need repairing, or reception from the distant transmitter may be bad. And even if the programming can be heard it may only be in the right language for an hour or two a day; much of what is spoken cannot, for one reason or another, be understood. What these people hear on the radio, then, is mainly music, commercials and short news bulletins.

The 10 per cent or so middle class
They mainly live in or near a city, and are likely to have an electricity supply. They may or may not see television – but the cinema will be relatively familiar. The children go to school. The adults work in clerical jobs for the government or government agencies, in transport, in retail shops or in factories. In India they may well be graduates, but their cash income is low and families large. These people are likely to speak some English or one of the major national languages or both. The adults may read a daily newspaper; if not, they will read *weekly* newspapers, film magazines, paperback books or comics. The household will contain a working radio set, the family will listen to the radio for many hours a week; they will probably hear programmes in two or three languages, including English, and they will comprehend what they hear. Music will still be the most popular radio fare – and at least some of it will be American or British in origin or influence.

The top 1 per cent or so
In India this amounts to six million people, but in an African country a much smaller number. They will live in or near cities in comfortable houses, with servants, just like the remaining expatriate Britons and other Europeans. They have the best jobs – in the government, the big nationalized commercial enterprises, or they may be businessmen or professionals; journalists on the main publications and broadcasters are in this group. These people are educated – in India they will not only be graduates but will have been to the better schools and universities. They will speak and read English – using it even at home, perhaps mixed with another language. They may have television. They can attend films easily if they so wish. They read a daily newspaper, probably in English (or in India perhaps in a major regional language). They read imported publications – including serious British and American weeklies; they also read local magazines – often again in English. They listen to the radio – often again to foreign stations, including the BBC World Service. They buy books and records which are either imported or produced locally by a subsidiary of a British company. They have bookshelves, and hi-fi

sets and expensive radios. They are exposed to quite a lot of sophisticated advertising.

AFRICAN MEDIA: COLONIAL HERITAGE

The 1930s saw the first sizeable indigenous African press, mainly in west Africa. The leading figure of this movement was Azikiwe – who returned from nine years in the United States and quickly began to establish a well-managed chain of African nationalist newspapers. Then came the new white press around 1950; three separate London newspaper managements set up a number of pro-African newspapers in west, east and central Africa. An interesting mixture of political liberalism, missionary zeal, romanticism, profit-seeking and business and political naïveté lay behind this wave. The post-independence press involved only a modification of the new 'white-press' phase. The Lagos *Daily Times* had easily the largest sale in black Africa before the Nigerian Civil War began in 1967, and during the years between independence and the civil war largely followed its pre-independence policy. Even before 1960 the London *Daily Mirror* owners wanted their west African papers to reduce political tensions, to avoid attacking those in power in general or individual leaders in particular.[1]

Reuters trained journalists for the first African national news agencies such as the Ghana news agency set up in 1957.[2] The international news agencies usually distribute in Africa through the national agency. This gives African national news agency journalists daily exposure to the incoming news wire from London.

Hollywood has always dominated cinema screens in Africa. Although films do not require literacy and mobile film units also exist, the total annual audience remains small.* This inevitably means very low total revenue, and if black African feature film industries do expand beyond the token level now found in certain countries, they will have to cater to audiences long attuned to Hollywood products.

Radio, the other 'popular' electronic medium, is in some ways the most African. But the radio services of all ex-British African nations began as off-shoots of the BBC. Kenya, with its large settler population, was ahead of the others. Zambia (Northern Rhodesia) in 1950 had three hours of radio a day – about one hour in English, with the

---

* Graham Mytton in his major national sample survey found in 1971 that less than half of all Zambians had seen even one film show in the previous year. Unesco (1975) figures indicate that in the early 1970s annual cinema visits were well below one per caput in Ghana, Kenya, Tanzania and Uganda. The Nigerian figure was just above one visit per caput.

other two hours distributed among six local languages – Bemba, Nyanja, Lozi, Tonga, Sindebele, Shona.[3]*

The BBC also played an important role in the birth of television in ex-British territories. In Zambia television began in 1961, before independence – ten years later only 17 per cent even of urban Zambians saw TV as often as once a week.† In Nigeria the proportion was probably much lower, although Nigeria had been the first black African country to have television – the West Nigerian station 'WNTV – First in Africa'. This 'First in Africa' challenge was taken up by Nigeria's other regional governments and by the federal government – leading to four completely separate television services each set up with a different combination of Anglo-American assistance – mainly commercial and British.[4] The competitive urge seems to have been felt alike in independent and not-yet-independent countries, as well as in both 'white settler' and non-settler countries. But the cost of imported television sets was so high as to ensure that most of the early customers were Europeans. A year after Kenyan television began there were 5,800 licensed sets – only 1 per cent owned by Africans.[5]

Advertising, even more than television, was introduced to Africa by the colonizers. Under their rule, advertising was run by Englishmen, and after 1960 – as many British advertising agencies became American-owned – the frontiers of Madison Avenue began to spread, if not into the African bush, then at least to Lusaka, Lagos, Accra, Blantyre, Freetown and to Nairobi.

Advertising men were probably the last wave of British communicators to establish a new communications occupation in Africa. Journalism in these ex-British colonies had to a great extent been established by British journalists; the African journalists who campaigned for independence largely left journalism after independence for political office and/or prison. The remaining British journalists then gradually handed over to Africans. A similar pattern occurred with radio producers, and then was repeated in television. Recently also Africans have been taking over the senior advertising jobs.

GOVERNMENT AND MEDIA IN EX-BRITISH AFRICA

The typical British colonial government had a loose but reasonably effective control over its small commercial press and its hastily thrown together local outpost of the BBC. African nationalist newspapers

* In 1972 English still had 38 per cent of radio air time, Bemba 14 per cent, Nyanja 12 per cent, Lozi and Tonga 10 per cent each.

† The operation of the extended family system in the towns means that quite a number of young Africans (especially men) with lowish incomes see television in the homes of wealthier relatives. Mytton (1972), pp. 31–4.

could be, and were, knocked into line by fines, temporary suspensions, or the arrest of editors; other useful weapons were colonial government advertising and the ability to stop newsprint supplies. The local mini-BBC was also unlikely to flout the colonial government in any major way.

For newly independent African governments it was quite difficult to decide what the former colonial power had intended as the purpose of the media. The mini-BBC shared the parent BBC's goals of information, education and entertainment – but what did such terms mean in Africa? The commercial press was there historically as an offshoot of commerce, settlers and the colonial government. As the settlers tended to leave, as commerce came more directly under the new independent government's control, and as the trend towards one party systems advanced, the place of an independently owned press became less and less clear. These new governments did not all actively set out to nationalize the media. They had no need to do so, because however the media are formally owned in black Africa, the government inevitably controls them. This has been quite clear even in a country like Kenya where private ownership of the press was allowed to continue for a decade after the one-party principle was established.

The media did come into direct government control, certainly. But they drifted into government control rather than being ruthlessly seized as a high initial priority.

A common pattern in ex-British African countries now consists of a central government Ministry of Information, within which the national radio and television form one section – the Director-General (the old BBC term) is thus a civil servant who reports to the Minister of Information. The news agency which also is a section in the Ministry, will normally have the only elaborate news-gathering service – and hence it largely shapes what the newspapers can say; the newspapers often are government, or government party, owned as well.

One consequence of this Ministry of Information pattern of control is that all broadcast producers, and at least some journalists, are civil servants. Usually they are on ordinary civil service salary grades and subject to promotion by seniority. Radio scripts are – civil-service-wise – vetted in advance by higher authority. This does not favour scintillating journalism or riveting radio broadcasts. The Government's senior public relations personnel are superior civil servants within the same Ministry as the journalists and producers. The senior public relations jobs are thus the journalistic jobs which have not only the highest pay and status, but also have the greatest potential for independence and initiative. It is commonly said that in Africa all the best journalists and producers are in PR. Another consequence of the civil service pattern is that the media become the subject of wrangles and conflicts between the Ministry of Information and other ministries – such as those dealing with education, finance, economic planning, and rural development.

In African countries the media eat up scarce foreign exchange. Newsprint is usually imported as is all hardware – printing presses, transmitters, cameras, studio equipment. The production even of radio sets is a recent phenomenon in black Africa. Consequently media goals and plans require Finance Ministry approval. Usually the colonial government had only just begun an elaborate telecommunications investment programme, which means that even radio coverage is still not adequate. In view of other claims on public investment and foreign exchange, plans for television transmitters, new studios, micro-wave links, new cinema construction, photo-offset printing plants and domestic TV set manufacture are all cut back.

The typical African government has been through a series of re-appraisals of the goals of its media. Their aim is to use the media to contribute to national development plans, to inform citizens of relevant government policies, to 'educate' (both broadly and narrowly) and to maintain and propagate traditional culture and music. They admit that the media should also entertain, and some role is seen for commercial advertising – both in helping with finance and in encouraging the widespread use of products such as soap, batteries, simple cooking products and medicines.

These goals are no more or less vague or absurd than the supposed goals and claimed purposes of the media in the United States or Britain. But their vagueness means that someone has to interpret such goals in the light of today's news story or radio schedule. Since the media are government controlled, the politicians in practice decide these things – and, like politicians anywhere, they approach the media with their own political problems and preferences in mind. Indeed this is probably one of not many policy areas where African politicians can decide something at the stroke of a pen. If the programme controller of national television is told to stop using a particular imported series, or to send a camera crew to cover the President's speech, such orders will immediately be carried out. Partly for this reason, television in African countries tends to be used as the President's personal public address system to the local élite.

'Education' is a difficult goal for the public media anywhere. Within the formal educational system it requires the active co-operation of teachers as well as a combination of several other things (which probably don't in practice all happen) – receiving sets have to be available and in working order, there must be accompanying written material for teachers and taught, well planned and scheduled programming, and the correct language must be used.

Internal and external political rivalries pose challenges to the media and result in politically directed output. Special government 'news-papers' (perhaps monthly) and related radio programming are aimed in the appropriate language at particular ethnic groups. Often there are border disputes, ethnic groups which spread across frontiers, and also media which cross frontiers. Consequently priority in setting up new transmitters may be given to remote frontier areas, while more populated and accessible rural areas go without. Most African countries engage in radio transmissions aimed at neighbouring countries in their languages – despite the lack of programming in some home areas and languages.

The maintenance and propagation of 'traditional culture' also poses enormous problems and inevitably produces political solutions. The fear of civil war is a desperately real and urgent fear in several African countries. In practice the easiest positive solution here is to record local music for radio transmission and to broadcast news and talks in the main local languages. But much of this may have a rather neutered sound, since so many aspects of traditional culture are too violent or inegalitarian or unhealthy to fit with any kind of modern development goal.

The rural–urban divide is the classic problem for African governments in most policy areas, including the media. To take the full panoply of modern media to rural areas is enormously expensive – it requires not only rural electrification, elaborate telecommunications facilities, and many language channels, but the press needs hugely improved roads (for distribution), and massive imports of newsprint, quite apart from a much higher standard of education and literacy. The revenue to finance such developments is just not there; in the relative absence of advertising, the realistic sales price of a daily newspaper widely sold in every African village would be forbiddingly high even by the standards of rich countries. Television in every rural home is an even more remote goal. Large thinly populated African countries also present climatic and atmospheric hazards not experienced in Europe. The enormous expense of taking conventional television transmitters to the remoter areas of European countries is multiplied in Africa. Domestic space satellites are an alternative, but scarcely a cheap one. Consequently the concentration on radio as the rural mass medium – with some cinema support – does have obvious merits.

In the cities everything is the other way about. The great bulk of the cash income is here; these are the people advertisers want to reach. and the problems of distribution are minimal. There are cheap sites for cinemas; daily newspapers are easily distributed over good suburban roads. Radio presents few problems. And even television is quite practicable if confined to 20,000 or 30,000 urban sets; these sets are already expensive to import – and the government adds a massive luxury tax – but the wealthy can still afford a set costing perhaps three times as much as in Europe. Advertisers find a nice audience for luxury goods, imported cigarettes and the like. Moreover, television programming is cheap – a captive élite audience for the President, some educational material aimed as much at teachers as at children, a certain amount of local entertainment and talk shows, and plenty of Hollywood feature films, Anglo-American entertainment series and Visnews film clips – all cheaply imported from London.

INDIAN PRESS AND BRITISH EMPIRE

India's daily newspaper sale in 1970 was twice that of the entire African continent. The number and variety of Indian publications reflects India's enormous language and cultural diversity; eleven separate languages are each spoken by at least 10 million people as their mother tongue. The Indian press has a history in several ways comparable to that of central and eastern Europe. By 1870 Bombay alone had 22 newspapers, mostly weeklies, appearing in three different Indian languages.[6]

India's nearest thing to an effective national language is 'Hindustani' – a flexible colloquial mixture of Hindi (the official national language) and Urdu, plus English words and phrases to fill gaps in these two ancient tongues. But fewer Hindi speakers are literate than is the case with some other major Indian languages. Hindi's official recognition has been countered by the affirmation in South India and elsewhere of other official languages at the state level and a reshuffling of state boundaries around dominant regional languages. Thus at the state level one finds media in the official state language, other India-wide media in English and perhaps Hindi, and yet other media in the minority Indian languages of the state. In a state with about 30 million people, typically only a small minority are literate in any single language. All India Radio broadcasts daily news bulletins in some 70 separate languages and dialects. India has mainly illiterate villages but the cities are overflowing with large numbers of students,*

* In 1946–7 at Independence there were 266,000 students enrolled in higher education and 1,528,000 in 1964–5. Only 3 per cent of these students were studying agriculture; B. Kuppuswamy (1972), p. 251. Six years later this figure had doubled again to three million students.

most of whom have dismal employment prospects. The top-heavy nature of the educational system is reflected in the Indian media – which tend to be either highly escapist or very serious, even sombre.

India's media are mainly urban. There were some 700 daily papers in the early 1970s, but almost all of these were based in towns of over 100,000 population.* Very few Indian daily papers reach more than a short distance out into the country. Radio is still heavily biased towards the urban centres.† Seeing a film on an occasional visit to a local town is the only exposure to the media many Indian peasants get. The daily press confines its readership to the urban middle class – which maximizes the favourable ratio of advertising revenue against low distribution costs. The weekly press was highly politically partisan; there is a low total sale of women's magazines in India.‡

The largest and most established commercial media organizations are in the press; these groups are tied to big industry and party politics. The film industry lacks large business groupings – one result of the Indian government's pressure on large industry seems to have been to push 'black' (untaxed) money into many small film production companies. Radio has always been under government control; during most of the years since 1947 it has had a low priority in the Five Year Plans.

The leading Indian newspapers 25 years after independence (indeed until press censorship was introduced in June 1975) remained much more critical of the government than those in any black African country. Even government control of radio has mainly been used in an astonishingly high-minded manner; one of All India Radio's main goals during the 1950s was to spread classical Hindi by using it over the radio – a project akin to adopting Chaucerian English as the standard language of BBC radio, or of reverting to early Renaissance Italian on RAI radio in Rome.

The Indian government's stated media goals – furthering education, enlightenment, economic growth and agricultural production – would have been difficult enough to achieve even with big financial investment and imaginative execution of policies. Among those farmers who are exposed to any media the increments in agricultural

* India in 1971 had 142 towns above this size.
† Even by 1971, 35 years after the start of Indian radio, medium-wave transmitters covered only a little more than half of India's land area and just under three-quarters of the population.
‡ The largest women's magazine in India in 1972 was *Femina*, a Bombay English-language fortnightly with a circulation of 146,000. The next largest was *Stee*, an Ahmadabad Gujarati-language weekly selling 35,000.

knowledge are very modest.[7] In 1970 All India Radio was devoting 50 hours a day to external broadcasting in 24 languages while most Indians still seldom heard radio; the Indian government's willingness to succumb to middle-class urban pressures for more and more university education also contrasted with its extremely modest efforts in using radio to combat rural illiteracy. After years of beaming 'experimental' television programmes from one low-power transmitter to peasants just beyond the suburbs of New Delhi, a new television policy quickly followed the 1965 war with Pakistan; special priority was given to a station in Amritsar, because its wealthier citizens could receive Pakistan TV across the border from Lahore.

But the gentleness of government controls over the media (at least until 1975) has certainly contributed to the substantial growth of all the Indian media since 1947 – which contrasts sharply with the pattern of government control and stunted media growth in both Pakistan and Burma. The Pakistan media received a severe jolt at the time of partition in 1947 – many Pakistani newspapers were owned by Hindus – and subsequent military rule further inhibited growth.

English-language papers in the early 1970s accounted for only about a quarter of daily Indian sales, but these papers sat at the top of a steep-sided pyramid. The leading English-language dailies have a dominant position in the four metropolitan cities of Bombay, Calcutta, Madras and Delhi. The second step on the pyramid is occupied by smaller English-language dailies, and by the leading Indian-language dailies (some of which are owned by the same groups as the major English-language dailies). The third step is occupied by the many small Indian-language dailies and weeklies in the smaller cities. The fourth step consists of various rural one-page weeklies, handouts, astrology sheets and the like.[8]* At the bottom end of this pyramid an astrology sheet in a local small Indian language may seem to have no connection at all with any English influences. But the English influence is a commanding one at the top end of the pyramid. There are differences of opinion as to how much material in India's leading circulation Hindi paper, *Navbharat Times*, is merely translated from its sister English-language paper, *The Times of India*, but certainly the latter paper is recognized as the senior paper in the company.

The paper for which Rudyard Kipling worked in the 1880s, the *Civil and Military Gazette* of Lahore[9] was a typical child of the Empire. But in addition to English-language commercial and military papers there were already many Indian-language papers – started

* Weeklies have about the same total circulation as dailies.

both by European missionaries and by educated Indians. Even these had strong 'English' overtones; those in Bombay around 1870 focused their attention on such issues as the employment of English-educated Indians and the demand that Indians should elect members to sit in the British Parliament.[10]

The main Indian news agency, PTI, is historically an off-shoot of Reuters. The Press Trust of India is co-operatively owned by the Indian newspaper press, on the Anglo-American model. Foreign international news agency correspondents in Delhi in 1972 had a high opinion of PTI's 'professionalism' – meaning, perhaps, that they saw it as maintaining Anglo-American traditions. PTI's staff of some 200 full-time journalists was the backbone of daily journalism in India; PTI had separate wires for Indian news and for world news which went to the four metropolitan cities – and both these and its regional wires (within each of the 17 states) went out in English. Until 1975 the Indian government's easiest method of exerting pressure on PTI was presumably via All India Radio – PTI's biggest single customer.

THE INDIAN FILM INDUSTRY: STEP-CHILD OF HOLLYWOOD

But American films, not British, provided the predominant influence on the Indian film market and its infant film industry. The first Indian feature film was made in 1912. The early Indian films were devoted mainly to mythical and traditional subjects. In 1924–5 India made 70 feature films and the next year made 111.[11] But in 1926–7 still only 15 per cent of all films released in India were Indian-made (while about 75 per cent were American). The Madan chain which owned 65 of the most luxurious cinemas preferred American films; apart from occasional spectaculars, most of these cost a small Indian cinema less than half the cost of booking an Indian film.* The Cinematograph Committee of 1927–8 found some evidence of Hollywood block-booking tactics but recognized that the Indian market yielded below 1 per cent of total Hollywood revenue.[12]

Another Committee found 20 years later that Hollywood imports into India had stayed more or less stable, but were now vastly out-weighed by a massive increase in the production of the domestic Indian film industry.[13] The arrival of sound around 1930 posed a special problem; the variety of Indian languages threatened to frag-ment India's otherwise potentially vast market. Separate film produc-

---

* The 1927–8 Committee (p. 24) quotes small 'mofussil' cinemas as being able to rent imported films for 100 rupees a week, but Indian films seldom cost less than 40 rupees a *day*.

tion centres emerged for the larger languages; these centres were linked by elaborate dubbing and re-shooting practices and by concentration on visual spectacle strongly garnished with dance and song and yet more song.

475 feature films in 13 Indian languages were made in 1975. Hollywood imports are now low. The Indian film industry's combination of sexual suggestiveness and puritanism has both classical Indian and 1930s Hollywood origins. Indian film music may sound oriental to western ears, but traditionally-minded Indians regret its use of western styles and some western instruments. The chaotic cottage industry character of Indian film-making may seem un-western, but the current dominance of stars and music directors has many similarities to 1930s Hollywood. The film industry contrasts sharply with most of the press and with All India Radio, because the film industry alone among the Indian media has faced the full onslaught of American competition.

The Indian film industry for some 40 years after its birth in 1912 was forced and battered into adopting a commercial market approach. Its enormous success in doing this is undoubted; despite government restrictions on cinema building, the compulsion to show government documentaries with every feature film* and a high level of taxation, Indian films undoubtedly have immense popular appeal. Indian film music dominates the record market and provides the most popular radio fare; film magazines are the only really buoyant part of the magazine industry. 'Film Hindi' – a market-tested, colloquial spoken version – may slowly become the effective popular language of India.

Unattached youth, drink, romantic love, night clubs, cars and palaces constitute the standard obsessions of Indian films. In a land of poverty, prohibition, arranged marriages and with hundreds of people sleeping on the streets outside the cinema, the demand for film realism has been limited. In the main film production cities (Bombay, Madras, Calcutta) there was still in 1972 a wide choice of American-made and distributed films on show; and this was during a complete halt on new imports from Hollywood. New Hollywood fashions – such as James Bond films – are shamelessly copied by the Indian film industry.† But few Indians have visited either America or

* The Indian government took over and retained the old British practice of inserting government 'information' films in this way.

† One study of Hindi films produced in 1954–9 found that purely urban settings outnumbered purely rural settings by 52 per cent to 28 per cent. 67 per cent showed homes of the rich against 18 per cent showing homes of the poor; love at first sight, drinking and murder (or attempted murder) each appeared in about 60 per cent: Rikhab Dass Jain (1960), p. 27.

Britain and the Indian film industry in drawing upon American films rather than upon American life, becomes not mererly a dream factory, but one dream factory locally assembling dreams originally designed in a dream factory 10,000 miles away.

ALL INDIA RADIO: THE BBC REBORN

All India Radio is a child not of 1930s Hollywood but of the 1930s BBC. 'All India Radio' was a name invented by Lionel Fielden, a young BBC man who was sent out to India by John Reith in 1935. Fielden seems to have quite enjoyed his four years in India, setting up transmitters, selecting artistically inclined Indians and training them with the help of the BBC training school; yet he summarized his achievement up to 1939: 'Four years of hard labour had produced fourteen transmitters and a competent staff – and in four years the 400,000,000 people of India had bought exactly 85,000 wireless sets. It was enough to make a cat laugh. It was the biggest flop of all time.'[14]

Radio expanded at a still leisurely pace both before and after Indian independence. The one million radio licence mark was not reached until 1955, and two millions only in 1960. Nehru was vulnerable to charges of being too English and of speaking Hindi poorly; some Hindi-speaking politicians saw the radio as a key means for introducing classical Hindi and traditional Indian music to the Indian masses. The Reithian tradition, reinforced with 1950 BBC Third Programme cultural thinking and then translated into classical Hindi, resulted in perhaps the least market-oriented national radio service ever operated in a sizeable nation. This traditional authenticity in word and music had fairly little appeal – few Indians being familiar with traditional Indian music or literary Hindi. The inevitable foreign challenge came from a foreign commercial station, Radio Ceylon – and its chief resource was recorded Indian film music. During the mid-1950s with the Hindi purity policy at its height on AIR, Radio Ceylon was attracting much of the radio audience in South India. The usual response in such a situation is to play the same music in reply and eventually AIR began a pop (largely film) music service called Vividh Bharati* – which in 1967 also followed Radio Ceylon in accepting advertising.

Throughout the 1960s Indian television existed only in the token form of one small station in New Delhi. AIR officials long prided

---

* A key event in the change was the defeat in the 1962 elections of Dr B. V. Keskar who had been the Indian Minister for Information and Broadcasting since 1952.

themselves on having evaded the sad television experiences of most other Afro-Asian nations. When the decision to expand television was taken – largely due to Indira Gandhi's initiative (as Minister of Information and Broadcasting) and to military anxiety during the 1965 India–Pakistan war – the official rhetoric carried familiar claims about public service, agricultural extension and mass literacy campaigns.

Television sets were largely confined to 50,000 homes of members of the New Delhi élite when in 1972 India's second station began transmission in Bombay; the new plan was to place production studios in all of India's state capitals, with a total of 100 main and relay stations. In 1972 the BBC (monopoly era) philosophy was still prevalent; there was careful avoidance of either all-out education or all-out entertainment. The Delhi station compromised also between English and Hindi. But cynical observers of Indian television thought that this was only the phoney war period before the real battle. The estimate of costs made by a Unesco working party for the Indian government was (as usual) unrealistically low. The initial licence-based system would be inadequate and the gap could only be met by advertising revenue. The claims about mass education via AIR television were unreal.

Domestic manufacture of telecommunications hardware was intended to boost the Indian electronics industry; and the production of TV sets by many small firms was encouraged. Another goal was to give primacy to all the state capitals as sites for studios and transmitters. Thus politicians seemed likely to want to expand the audience for their own regional political offerings; this would require nationally distributed entertainment programming in order to draw in viewers for locally made news and talk programmes.

But India, unlike most Afro-Asian nations, had a major alternative to large-scale direct importing of Anglo-American serials and films. The enormous backlog and current production of Indian feature films would make it possible to show feature films each night on television as a permanent programming policy.

In 1973 the two largest advertising agencies in India were the old J. Walter Thompson and McCann-Erickson agencies – now with only a minority American ownership element. Agencies of American origin typically had offices in all four of India's 'metropolitan' cities. They also played, with their clients, a major part in Indian market research. A key event in the history of modern Indian advertising was the arrival of J. Walter Thompson in 1929. Another early arrival, in 1931, was National Advertising, which for some years took only American accounts.[15]

All the Indian media – despite big expansion – have remained remarkably fixed into the basic patterns which prevailed when the British departed in 1947. In what other country would a visitor be told that the 1951 report of the film industry committee was still the standard account twenty years later? Or in what other country would a working journalist want to discuss the British *Picture Post* nearly twenty years after its death? In what other country would one be able to hear radio announcers speaking with the English girls' public-school intonation of a quarter-century ago?*

The communications occupations are still very small in India. The film industry employs over 10,000 people but is dominated by a small élite of stars, music directors, playback artists, directors and producers who for long have led a basically western style of life.† One study of Indian daily journalists showed that almost half were either Brahmins or Christians.[16] A more limited study of an élite group of '29 leading journalists and political writers' showed that two-thirds were Brahmins and all the rest came from upper castes, or were Catholics or Parsis.[17] Since All India Radio is part of the Indian Information Service some ambitious producers move on into government public relations work[18] – but both jobs are extremely elevated by general Indian standards. It was also noticeable, in talking to senior people in various branches of the Indian media in 1972, how many of them had gone to one of a few exclusive schools, which were modelled on English public schools and from which the leaders of the federal Indian civil service are disproportionately drawn. American and German visitors notice among the Indian communications élite a continuing obsession with the British metropolis.[19]

Is there then no alternative between the modern western media on the one hand, or on the other hand traditional culture which is so authentically traditional as to be unsuitable for the goals which present-day African and Asian societies want to pursue? India indicates a number of possible middle ways – of which those with the strongest popular appeal are India's version of Hollywood films and their hybrid film music. Africa offers other varieties of part-traditional, part-western, hybrid music. High Life (in west African cities),

---

* This strange sense of listening to a recording from the BBC archives is heightened by the practice of reading the English language news at a deliberately slow pace (in order to aid understanding) or at dictation speed (as a news service for small newspapers).

† One study of 377 film people (including 145 stars) showed that the majority owned a car, had some financial stake in film production, were smokers, drank and 'are found interested in gambling and are habitual of making Race-Course engagements'. Rikhab Dass Jain (1960), pp. 141–2.

Chachacha (Zaire) and Kwela (South Africa) are all popular not only in the country of origin but in neighbouring countries as well. Radio hit parades made up of such hybrid music are likely to be the most popular African and Indian media output for some years to come.

CHAPTER SEVEN

English language, British invasion, Anglo-American media

THE COMMONWEALTH: BRITISH PRESERVE, AMERICAN ENTRY POINT

Mutual use of the English language was crucial in American entry to the British and Commonwealth markets. This entry both consolidated English as the world media language and gave the American media a flying start into the world market.

The first Commonwealth markets to be entered in strength by American media were Canada and Britain itself. The 'loss' of Canada to the American media before 1900 encouraged Britain to concentrate on its dominance in world telecommunications. British dominance of the world's cable system was successfully exploited during the 1914–18 war. In 1930 Britain had over half of the world's ocean cable mileage,[1] but the United States challenge was growing in both cable and radio – and with it the challenge of American news agencies. In 1945, British and American civilian cable-and-radio communications were still about equal on the world scale, although Britain's strength was in a cable system now becoming obsolete, contrasted with the greater US strength in radio-based telecommunications.[2] London only unambiguously ceased to be the telecommunications hub of the world in the 1960s, while the Cable and Wireless group remains active in telecommunications in some fifty nations and territories.

The most sudden capture of British Commonwealth markets occurred around 1915 to 1920 when Hollywood triumphed throughout the world. Probably the book business will be the last Commonwealth media field in which American exports will push those from Britain into second place. The Australian market has long been protected from the full flood of American competition, but as a result of anti-trust action in the USA this situation is changing. The deep involvement of American book publishing firms in Britain itself, and the strength of some British imprints in the United States will, however, make this a relatively gradual transition. Britain is certain to stay in second place, and no other exporting nation is likely to get much of a chance of serious entry.

ENGLISH AS THE WORLD LANGUAGE AND THE MEDIA LANGUAGE

English is the world language because of its position in the USA, Britain and the white Commonwealth; in ex-British Africa and Asia; in western Europe and Latin America; and as the most used language of international organizations. But it is also the language most suitable for, and most shaped by, media use.

The survival of English as the major national language of the African and Asian Commonwealth countries is by no means automatic. However the unusually strong emphasis placed by the Tanzanian government on Swahili illustrates – despite Swahili's being very widely understood – the formidable problems involved in dropping English even in the most 'favourable' of African situations. The adoption of Swahili even as the school language presents enormous difficulties; the cultural associations of Swahili are coastal Arab ones – unfamiliar to most Tanzanians. A detailed account of the position of Swahili in east Africa[3] illustrates the reasons for the general continuing preference for English of governments in 'Anglophone' Africa.

In India the case for retaining English lies partly in the unpopularity among other language groups of the decision to make Hindi an official language. The effect of this decision has been, while strengthening Hindi to some extent, also to increase regional consciousness and the strength of other major regional languages. After the government's decision the number of South Indians voluntarily learning Hindi declined very sharply.[4] In this situation English seems likely to continue as the common language of the national élite. Over half of all Indian government publications in 1969 were in English. English remains the dominant language in higher education and science and technology. The problems of translation into Indian languages – with their archaic vocabularies, difficult scripts and their number – remain daunting. And translations into Indian languages are overwhelmingly *from* English – whether in daily journalism or in book publishing.[5] The likelihood, then, is that English-language and Anglo-American media influences will continue to be poured into the apex of the Indian media pyramid.

Those Indians and Africans who favour retaining English point out that English has now become the leading second language of Europe. This is confirmed by survey evidence (Table 5). Both the Germans and the French have decisively chosen to teach and learn English rather than each other's languages. This switch towards English is illustrated by the much higher proportions of young adults who speak English as opposed to older adults. A similar strong switch to English as a widely understood foreign language seems to have occurred in eastern Europe. And in Latin America English is now widely taught and understood among educated people.

English is probably the major language most shaped by and most attuned to media use. English not only has a long and stable cultural history in Britain, but the United States is also one of the world's older nation states and has always used English as its sole official language. English has, however, benefited from the interplay of the British and American versions as well as from the refreshing effects of the American frontier and melting-pot.

The English language is relatively free of separate scholarly 'high' and vulgar 'low' forms – compared for example even with German. Until recently most languages of central and eastern Europe were spoken quite differently by educated urban people as against uneducated rural people; the same phenomenon was especially common in Asia, and in China the term Mandarin referred both to high social position and the educated version of the language spoken by people occupying such positions. Similar caste-related language differences prevailed throughout the Indian subcontinent and throughout the Arab world.

English also has an unusually small gap between its written and spoken forms. Some of the reasons for this may lie in the importance of spoken literary forms – drama and poetry – in English, the Protestant religious tradition of using the native language in worship and the centrality of the authorized version of the Bible plus the book of Common Prayer; presumably the vigour of the English tradition of public political debate since the sixteenth century is also relevant.

Many of these features, already present in English and in the language of the American founding fathers, were carried further in nineteenth-century America. The great national vehicle of American English was the newspaper press. These trends have continued – and, perhaps rather importantly – continued steadily, without any dramatic changes of direction. English as a language has not been subject to any language reform, alphabet reform, grammatical reform; no official Academy, as in France, has laid down official forms for English. No governmental policy has, as in Norway, tried to push forward a shotgun marriage between 'high' and 'low' language.

English has evolved as a language with and through the media, especially the press. All of the great popular American journalists understood the significance of using simple *spoken* English in the press. But even late twentieth century English is also a language still closely tied to its own history. The march of the British Empire around the world and the westward continental march of the United States have meant that, in becoming a world language, English has also deposited a number of archaic dialects in remote localities behind the advance of empire and frontier. In the Alleghenies, the American deep south, and in the West Indies, examples of such archaic dialects exist, and they feed back into the English language mainstream through music and the media – once in New Orleans, later in Nashville, or in Reggae music from the West Indies exported to Britain. In the twentieth century obviously the electronic media have been an enormously powerful force in the evolution of English; but almost all American pop music has drawn directly or indirectly both on nineteenth-century American and on eighteenth-century English ballads and folk songs.

The leading current makers and shapers of the English language are, then, journalists – both print and electronic. The newspaper and the news bulletin are the new authorized version. Journalists, in the USA especially, have long been especially prominent in literature – Mark Twain, Theodore Dreiser, Stephen Crane, Ernest Hemingway are examples; many American writers have moved easily between literature and the media and (in contrast to Europe) they have usually worked not for prestige newspapers but for the popular press. Various forms of documentary writing down to the latest 'New Journalism' (of many) are in this tradition and both reflect and help to maintain the absence of contrasted high and low forms of English.

These influences retain the brevity, terseness, pace and precision of the English language. English contains a greater variety of pithy phrases and simple words from which to choose (compared with French for example) and the English-language version is usually shorter than the version in any other language. And English has simpler grammar than possible rival languages such as Russian. English is the language best suited to comic strips, headlines, riveting first sentences, photo captions, dubbing, sub-titling, pop songs, hoardings, disc-jockey banter, news flashes, sung commercials.

BRITISH MEDIA IN THE US MARKET

Although most of the latest slang crossing the Atlantic comes from the USA, some new British terms still take root there. Such terms partly reflect the substantial flow of British influences upon the American media in recent years.

Nineteenth-century book publishing provides one of the earliest and most vigorous examples of interchange. In the second half of the century American writers were enormously popular in Britain, partly

Soviet Picture Palace

TV Centre, Cairo

Winston Churchill and
Charlie Chaplin,
Chartwell, 1932

Japanese Prime Minister
Tanaka suffers western
ritual with beauty queen,
1972

because they tended to write in racier language than English authors. But this fact in turn was partly caused by the influx of British books into the USA. In the absence of an Anglo-American copyright agreement, American publishers simply printed the works of the most popular English writers.[6] British publishers similarly pirated American literature. Not having to pay royalties to English writers such as Dickens, American publishers made them available to the American public at such low prices as effectively to retard the emergence of a separate American literary profession. This was one reason among others for American novelists and literature being so closely linked to journalism and newspapers.

After the Second World War, as after the first, Britain imported media almost exclusively from America – but starting in the mid-1960s there began a powerful new wave of British media influences, in fields as varied as news agencies and pop music. Reuters, following the termination by Associated Press of the previous exchange agreement decided to enter the domestic US news agency market; and it is the third force in the international news agency field in the United States.* In pop music the British invasion was led by the Beatles and from 1964 to 1966 nearly a third of all domestic US top ten hits were British.† The Beatles, the Rolling Stones and subsequent British groups were doing what so many successful pop musicians had done in America before – they were white boys singing black American music, or drawing on black music to appeal to white America.

Television was the other main area of influence. Lew Grade pioneered off-shore television series production by which American network television series were packaged in London and in Birmingham, England, instead of Hollywood, USA. Grade's British-made *Space: 1999* set several new precedents in the US market in 1975. The expansion of Public Television has drawn heavily on mainly BBC drama series. Some of these series would not be made at all, or would not be made with such a large production budget, did the American market not exist. But other British programming imported into the USA makes few allowances for American tastes. There has also been the more diffuse influence of the borrowing of formats. This was true not only of shows like *All in the Family* and *Sanford and Family* (based on *Till Death* . . . and *Steptoe* . . . respectively) but also includes the adoption of the British mini-series concept.

The Economist is about the only foreign publication quite widely read in Washington and New York and whose news service is syndicated in American newspapers. The ownership of the Capitol record

* Of the 12 largest sale daily newspapers in the US in 1973, 12 took AP, 10 took UPI, 7 took Dow Jones and 6 took Reuters. Michael Singletary (1975), pp. 750–1.
† In these three years 98 out of 334 according to Charlie Gillett (1971), p. 341.

label by the British company EMI is also well known; less familiar perhaps is the point that all of the major national press groups in Britain also have press interests in the USA.*

BRITISH MEDIA IN EUROPE AND THE WORLD

In the 1960s British pop music was also enormously popular in Europe and beyond. This was part of a longer tradition by which British pop music has imported American influences and then exported them to Europe. Britain was exceptionally heavily influenced by American Tin Pan Alley from the 1890s onwards. Many famous 'traditional' music-hall English songs are in fact of American origin. But all through the interwar period British pop music was very successful in Europe.[7]

The British press and Reuters were influential in Europe right through the later nineteenth century. *The Times* was widely acknowledged as Europe's premier newspaper and the prestige newspapers of several countries copied it closely. In the inter-war period this leadership was continued – especially since the press in Italy, Germany and France was first commercially corrupt and then politically controlled. British popular newspapers were used as models also – for instance by *Paris-Soir*, the French 1930s circulation leader, and by *Bild-Zeitung* the dominant German post-war popular newspaper.

The immediate post-1945 period saw the height of American media influence (as the next chapter argues) but Britain was, by a long way, the second most potent media influence during this period. In occupying the northern zone of Germany the British forces cast Hamburg in the role of London, and Hamburg has remained the German media capital. And even though the BBC declined to 'spawn' in Europe, there was quite a lot of spawning of British military radio stations in various parts of the world.

The BBC's enormous prestige in 1945 led to its being carefully copied by most of the media systems of western Europe. One example of such influence is the late 1940s BBC pattern of Home, Light and Third radio channels. The BBC's external services have also continued to attract sizeable audiences in eastern Europe and the Soviet Union, in the Arab world, and in some non-Commonwealth Asian countries. British television programming sells throughout western Europe, Scandinavia and other areas never colonized by Britain. The British were influential in setting up the presses of Japan, China and

---

* The most obvious is the Thomson chain of newspapers. Rupert Murdoch's News International owns several American publications including the *New York Post*. The Pearson-Longman interests own the *Oil Daily* and Viking Books.

Argentina among other important non-Commonwealth nations.

Much of this only needs saying because with the British media now overshadowed by those of the United States it is easy to forget that were it not for the worldwide strength of US media, the continuing strength of British media in the world would seem more obviously remarkable.

ANGLO-AMERICAN MEDIA CARTEL?

The American and British media are to a considerable extent integrated into a single industry which gives them an enormous advantage in white Commonwealth nations and in ex-British Asia and Africa. If ease of entry is a criterion of cartel, then clearly this English-language club must look very like a cartel to the media exporters of non-English-speaking nations.

Clearly also the success of the Anglo-Americans in marketing their media elsewhere has relied heavily on their very emphasis on *marketing*. The American media just have gone further in the commercial, advertising-financed, market-oriented direction, than have the media of any other nations. The American media sell well partly because, unlike some other nations' media, they are intended for just that – to be sold. But their British connection also prevents the American media from getting so far down the commercial path as to lose some of the advantages of not always being completely commercial. Of course, some American media – especially the great newspapers and the news agencies – are not profit-oriented in the conventional profit-earning sense. But, also, the existence of non-commercial British media – notably the BBC – gives the Anglo-American media on the world scene a vital non-commercial ingredient.

Canada and Australia also have for some time played an important part in the Anglo-American media. Canada has been a test market for American media entering both the English-speaking and the French-speaking worlds. Canadians and Australians are free of the taint of being either British or American imperialists, and yet they are on the Anglo-American team. Canada is a substantial external broadcaster to western and eastern Europe, while Australia broadcasts heavily to Indonesia and south-east Asia.

Canada and Australia have long been regarded both in New York and London as especially attractive markets for media exports. Both do a lot of media importing, and both are unusual in the world in retaining head-on broadcast competition which means that higher prices are paid for imports in Canada and Australia than in most countries. Indeed Canada and Australia are (with Britain, West Germany, Japan and France) among the countries which pay the highest prices for US television series and films (Table 17). In both Canada and Australia the resentment of the 1960s against excessive media imports has quickened in the 1970s. However, policies designed to reduce imports and to encourage home-produced media (including feature films and pop records) predictably contain elements of goal conflict and paradox. The enormous growth of cable television in Canada, for example, seems to indicate a demand for yet further supplies of US programming. Increasing the numbers of hours of domestic programming in Australia has the result of spreading limited budgets over even more hours of output – a dilemma recognized by the Australian Labour government's unfulfilled hope of cutting out one commercial network. Both Canada and Australia are also beguiled by the possibility of media exports, especially to the English-speaking world. The probable compromise consequence of such resentments and ambitions is that Australia and Canada will be more closely incorporated into the Anglo-American team – perhaps by various co-production and off-shore agreements and quota deals.

Canada and Australia also now have substantial numbers of recent European immigrants. They are thus following in the United States' melting-pot tradition and absorbing influences conducive to successful media exporting. In this ethnic connection it is noticeable that Britain also retains Jewish and African elements in its media – which although smaller than those of the United States – are probably conducive to media exporting as well. Jewish press pioneers, like the early owner of the *Daily Telegraph*, have had their later electronic equivalents. Alexander Korda, the nearest the British film industry came to having a Hollywood tycoon, had not only worked in Hollywood but was of Jewish-Hungarian origin and had also worked in both the German and French film industries. Several of the key pioneering figures in British commercial television (who thus also influenced BBC television) were Jews, who tended to be more aware of both American and European developments than were most British media men; examples include Richard Meyer (a Radios Luxembourg and Normandie pioneer, later active in ATV), Lord Sydney Bernstein (of Granada) and Lord Lew Grade (of ATV).

The ability of British pop singers to talk with a cockney or Liverpool accent but to sing with an authentic black American accent has often been noted by American commentators. Less often noted is the point that the 1960s British singers grew up in a world where black musicians were part of the local scenery; since the 1950s West Indian Calypso and West African High Life music has been provided in Britain by strong contingents of black musicians. This British combination of resident black musicians plus some Jewish media entrepreneurs may seem rather unremarkable to American eyes. But it is different from the contemporary situation in most other European countries; its mini-melting-pot, and its black citizens have, then, helped to keep Britain – compared with its European neighbours – on a cosmopolitan and export-oriented path. To take this point a little further, one could argue that Britain's most spectacular media export success was the 1939–45 external performance of the BBC – staffed very heavily with foreign-born personnel broadcasting back to their home countries.

Undoubtedly London has a special place in the worldwide spread of American media. It is the entrepôt through which much American media exporting reaches both Europe and the British Commonwealth. In many electronic media fields London offers high quality at low price. The principal foreign bureaux of a number of American news organizations are in London.

But London also has another significance, as the base city of several large British multi-media organizations each of which tends to have some secure domestic British areas of media monopoly or semi-monopoly, each of which has Australian or Canadian connections, each of which sharpens its competitive edge by operating inside the US domestic market, and each of which has substantial media exports throughout the British Commonwealth and beyond.

PART THREE

1945: American media conquest

CHAPTER EIGHT

The high tide of American media, 1943–53

American media leadership had been steadily growing for over 100 years, but only at the end of the Second World War did it emerge on a scale which few could any longer fail to notice. It was closely connected with the status of the United States as the dominant military power, but the American media ran beyond – for instance, even into eastern Europe, despite Soviet military control there.

The decade of greatest American dominance ran from 1943 to 1953. In 1943 Sicily became the first area of Europe to have 'free' (mainly American-style) media forced upon it. Italy, West Germany and Japan all later underwent the same process. 1953 marks a declining point in American media dominance. Stalin died that year and his passive approach to Soviet media was slowly altered. By 1953 the conquered nations were starting to go their own way again. And by 1953 the chronic shortages of media materials of all kinds were beginning to ease. 1953 marks a shift from direct to more indirect American media influence on the world.

This period provides the most unambiguous examples of American military force and political strength being used to impose media on other countries. Generals did quite literally set up newspapers, license radio stations, select certain senior personnel, and veto everyone else.

But it would be inaccurate to describe this period as one in which the American Imperial Presidency used its military and industrial might to attack communism and subvert the poor nations of the world by forcing upon them American commercial media culture. Despite American military power, President Truman throughout most of his period of office was in serious difficulty with the American electorate, with Congress, and the American media. The war-time governmental media apparatus was largely disbanded. Nor was there a great struggle between rival American and Soviet media imperialism in the late 1940s. The American military triumph had been gained against the Axis powers; the Soviet Union during the late 1940s was still weak in both domestic and foreign media. In 1950, Britain was still the world's leading external broadcaster, with the United States in third place.* Moreover there were examples – notably in West Germany – of the American military trying hard to resist Hollywood attempts to dominate foreign markets. In this latter case Hollywood won and the American military relented. Hollywood's success in once again dominating the German market was, however, only made possible by the American (and British and French) military presence there.

American media dominance after the Second World War was, then, very clearly connected with American military strength. But the main thrust of American media was not itself military or governmental; it was, as always, primarily *commercial*. Military strength provided a very favourable environment. American governmental agencies did some restrictive licensing and controlling, but primarily worked for, and through, the commercial media.

In this immediate post-war period of rationing, controls, quotas and military dominance, the foundations were laid of a new post-war doctrine and system of free trade in the media. The 'free flow of communication', a basically American notion, was built into the structure of Unesco. Moreover GATT (1947), and the whole American-led movement to limit tariffs, outlawed discriminatory tariffs against any particular country. Media import quotas and the like had to be across-the-board. In a field such as the media, characterized by extreme economies of scale and one dominant exporter, across-the-board restrictions tended to limit the efforts of smaller media exporters rather than those of the largest single exporter.

WORLD MEDIA AND WORLD WAR

The emergence of the American media during the Second World War into an unambiguous position of world dominance relied quite heavily on foundations laid during and after the First World War. During both world wars there was very active co-operation between American and British media, followed immediately after the war by an American bid for dominance.

1917 and 1918 marked the triumph of Hollywood films and Tin Pan Alley songs in Europe, including Britain. American daily journalism came to Europe in strength and was to remain. The United States also mounted at home and abroad an enormous

* 1. BBC – 643 hours per week   5. Australia – 181 hours
  2. USSR – 533   6. Italy – 170
  3. USA (VOA) – 497   7. Poland – 131
  4. France – 198   8. Netherlands – 127

BBC Handbook 1975, p. 71.

publicity campaign. Under the direction of George Creel, who had written a 1916 Election campaign biography of Woodrow Wilson, the Presidental election campaign was switched on to a global scale – selling America replaced selling Woodrow Wilson. The British since 1914 had been no less active at selling Britain in the United States. Not only did the British cut the German Atlantic cables, but Reuters during 1914–18 became the 'independent' front behind which the British government successfully orchestrated a war-long and world-wide flow of anti-German propaganda.

It did not escape the attention of the United States Navy that British dominance in cables was a major strategic asset. The us Navy set about challenging this British cable dominance, through the new medium of radio. And thus the us Navy was initially responsible for a train of events leading to RCA and its present position as a multi-national telecommunications– electronics– television– radio– records colossus.[1]

During the inter-war period the American news agencies, also, benefited from us Navy assistance, especially in extending their news services to Japan and China. Even after 1945 Britain was still the dominant power in cables,* and the United States needed space satellites to become in the 1960s unambiguously the hub of world telecommunications. But United States foreign expansion in the interwar period was not confined to radio; for instance in central and south America ITT became a dominant force in cable and telephone services, which tended to make New York the telecommunications capital of both south and north America.

In the Second World War there was again close co-operation be-tween the United States and Britain. American radio broadcasting to Europe used BBC facilities and adopted many BBC external broad-casting practices. Since Havas sided with Vichy, the American news agencies shared with Reuters the main control of the worldwide flow of news. The British, of course, continued to control the media throughout their Empire.

Latin America became, in its turn, an area which the British and the Russians left to the United States. Latin Americans, with their European connections, were obviously avid for news of Europe and the Anglo-Americans had little difficulty in channelling nearly all this news of Europe via London and New York. Hollywood had an established dominance. Canada had the supplies of paper. But even despite these strong cards, the United States managed by 1945 to achieve an extraordinary ascendancy in Latin-American media.

---

* In 1945 Britain had 190,000 nautical miles of cables and 63,000 miles of point-to-point wireless circuits; the USA in 1945 had 94,000 miles of cables and 236,000 miles of point-to-point wireless. White and Leigh (1946), p. 19.

Edward Jay Epstein describes Nelson Rockefeller's 1940–5 stint as Co-ordinator of Inter-American Affairs:

> To gain control over the media of Latin America during the war, Rockefeller obtained a ruling from the US Treasury Department which exempted the cost of advertisements placed by American corporations that were co-operating with the Rockefeller Office from taxation. This tax-exempt advertising eventually constituted more than 40 per cent of all radio and newspaper revenues in Latin America. By selectively directing this advertising towards newspapers and media stations that accepted guidance from his office – and simultaneously denying it to media which he deemed uncooperative or pro-Nazi – he skilfully managed to gain economic leverage over the major sources of news throughout South America. Moreover, as the newsprint shortage became critical in South America, his office made sure that the indispensable newsprint licences were allocated only to friendly newspapers. With a staff of some 1,200 in the United States, including mobilized journalists, advertising experts and public opinion analysts, and some $140 million in government funds (expended over five years), the Rockefeller Office mounted a propaganda effort virtually unprecedented in the annals of American history. . . .
>
> . . . The Rockefeller Office provided not only 'canned' editorials, photographs, exclusives, feature stories and other such news material, but manufactured its own mass circulation magazines, supplements, pamphlets and newsreels. To ensure understanding of the 'issues' being advanced in Latin America, the Office sent 13,000 carefully selected 'opinion leaders' a weekly newsletter which was to help them 'clarify' the issues of the day. The CIAA also arranged trips to the United States for the most influential editors in Latin America (and later scholarships for their children). More than 1,200 newspapers and 200 radio stations, which survived the economic warfare, were fed a daily diet of some 30,000 words of 'news' in Spanish and Portuguese, which were disseminated by co-operating news agencies and radio networks in the United States to their clients in Latin America. By the end of the War, the CIAA estimated that more than 75 per cent of the news of the world that reached Latin America originated from Washington where it was tightly controlled and monitored by the Rockefeller Office and State Department.[2]

Reader's Digest was one of several publications which used the 'encouragement' provided by Rockefeller's Office to vault from Latin America into other foreign markets. Its first foreign edition was launched in Britain in 1938. The idea of a Latin American edition, already rejected, was revived in 1940. *Reader's Digest* halved its price and accepted advertising for the first time for its Latin American editions. By 1941 there were sales of 150,000 in Argentina, Mexico, Chile and Peru. By 1944 a Portuguese edition was selling 300,000 copies mostly in Brazil. After Office of War Information prompting, *Reader's Digest* launched a Swedish edition in 1942, and an Arabic edition in 1943 (which ceased in 1947 and re-started in 1956).[3]

1947–8: THE HIGHEST TIDE

In 1947–8 American media reached their highest point in terms of direct dominance of the media in other countries. Both China and eastern Europe were still open to Hollywood films; and American media were all-powerful in western Europe.

Control of raw materials was one basis of this dominance. In much of Europe and Asia not only had many radio stations, film studios, and newspaper plants not yet been re-built but the dominant supplier of printing presses, radio transmission and film equipment was the USA. There was a chronic world shortage of raw film stock and also of paper, even though by 1948 newsprint production was already showing signs of recovery. Canada and the United States taken together (and there was heavy US ownership of Canadian paper companies) produced 62 per cent of world newsprint. But the United States alone consumed over half of all world newsprint production.

Hollywood feature films were the most obvious field of American dominance; there was the backlog of war-time production, not yet seen in many countries. These Hollywood films were much more expensive products than those of the other larger producing countries of the time – such as India, Japan and Mexico. While in 1948 Hollywood made 432 feature films, the Soviet Union made under 20 and even Italy, at the height of its neo-realism boom, made only 54.

In radio also the USA had a commanding position – with over twice as many sets per population as Britain, three times France, and thirteen times the Soviet Union (Table 6). Along with this radio predominance went manufacturing capacity and leadership in all other aspects of radio – except perhaps serious programming.

Ninety-two per cent of the world's television sets in 1948 were in the United States, and 6 per cent in the United Kingdom. The remaining 2 per cent were in the Soviet Union and France. The United States probably provided an even higher proportion of television revenue and, needless to say, was the dominant manufacturer of production equipment – with 98 transmitters already in place. It was also the only country which had broken out of the television vicious circle of low revenue, weak programming and low sales of expensive receiving sets.

In newspapers the United States now had only a quarter of the world's daily sale, but it was unique among the world's larger nations in having both fat newspapers and a high rate of sale per population (Table 8). The other nations with high total daily sales – Soviet Union, Britain, Japan, Germany and France – were all reading daily papers with between two and eight pages against the United States' normal daily paper of 24 pages or more. This was also the golden age of large circulation and fat American magazines. Magazines were still the major national advertising medium in the United States. And as for advertising itself . . . American pre-eminence was in this period even more marked than usual.

So much for American domestic production. How much of this reached other countries? Some countries were having their media forcibly reshaped; in other countries there were United States military forces and consequently AFN radio stations. The most widely available American media products were Hollywood feature films. Ravenous demand, lack of domestic output, official Washington encouragement – all these meant that by 1948 in many countries the great bulk of films for which audiences queued were Hollywood products. Countries in which, according to Unesco data, US films had 70 per cent or more of the market included: Ethiopia, South Africa, Mozambique, Canada, Cuba, Dominican Republic, Haiti, Honduras, Nicaragua, Panama, Brazil, Ecuador, Paraguay, Peru, Venezuela, South Korea, Persia, Thailand, Turkey, Belgium, Denmark, Greece, Iceland, Ireland, Luxembourg, Portugal, Australia, New Zealand and Fiji (Table 9).

In 1946–7 Hollywood still had the bulk of the film market in China and was also still strong in eastern Europe. In 1947 the Hungarian market, for example, was still dominated by films from Hollywood, France and Britain. In 1948 the proportion of Hollywood films fell below that from the Soviet Union (presumably including old films), but the western nations were still supplying more than half the Hungarian market.

No reliable figures are available for records, but in 1948 radio listeners around the world heard a great many American records – some of them perhaps supplied free by thoughtful record executives in New York. American magazines and print advertising were relatively little seen by the public in the rest of the world; but probably few of the many new magazines launched around the world in this period escaped American influence.

Reuters seems still to have been the leading international news agency. Reuters was equal to or ahead of the American agencies in western and eastern Europe, Africa and Asia and only clearly behind in Latin America.[4] On the other hand the United States had two of what were in 1948 clearly the three strongest agencies – Reuters, AP and UP. Agence France-Presse was in fourth place, with its position in Latin America still weak after the war. The Soviet TASS was fairly clearly behind these four – being the leading world agency in only one region, eastern Europe; in some other areas of the world TASS was clearly well behind even the third US agency, INS. At this period many countries and territories in the world lacked domestic news agencies. The stronger looking national agencies in 1948 included ANA (Egypt), ANA (Argentina), CNA (China), PTI (India), Kyodo (Japan), DPA (West Germany), ANSA (Italy), TT (Sweden) and AAP (Australia) – but every single one of these was heavily dependent (in terms of ownership, recent origin, political control, or news exchange) upon one or more of the three dominant English-language agencies.

Around 1947–8 the United States reached its pinnacle of political, military and media supremacy. At this time for audiences in most parts of the world there was a magic quality, if not in the United States as a society, certainly in the standard and style of living portrayed in American media. The cars, food, clothes and houses looked even to European eyes like something on the moon. Hollywood films, AFN radio, the international editions of *Life* magazine had for those exposed to them an almost hypnotic attraction. One of the many exotic American fads and fashions which fascinated Europeans, and Latin Americans, was television. And this portrayal of American television as the latest in the long line of all-American all-conquering media helped to ensure that the rest of the world accepted without question the key American definition – that television would be a *domestic* medium, an off-shoot of radio rather than a new kind of *public* cinema.

TELEVISION, ADVERTISING AND THE NEW NATIONS

The first Hollywood export peak was in the early 1920s; subsequent decline was reversed by the appearance of sound, which gave Hollywood a second peak in the early 1930s, followed by another decline. The late 1940s peak was thus Hollywood's third peak and it too was followed by a decline in the 1950s.

Hollywood's fourth peak, in the early 1960s, was in *television* exports. Although most European, Latin American and some Asian nations had television services well before this, the Hollywood export boom did not begin in the early 1950s partly because Hollywood was not yet even supplying US domestic television.

In the early 1950s the Hollywood majors still regarded television as a rival and jealously guarded the bulk of their backlog of feature films. In 1953 most US television programming was still being made in places like New York and Chicago. *I Love Lucy* was a lonely pioneer – a TV series made on film by an independent production company in Hollywood. By late 1954 about a third of ABC and NBC night-time programming was being made on film in Hollywood.[5] It was only in the late 1950s that American television took on its 'mature' shape – Hollywood production companies selling old feature films and freshly packaged made-for-TV filmed series to the New York networks. Hollywood had not fully absorbed this new TV pattern until then, and only then did it begin to export seriously. Around 1961–2 was a period of really big growth; revenue for Hollywood TV exports reached a peak in the late 1960s, according to *Variety*, and in the early 1970s remained at around $100 million a year – meaning a real decline against inflation.

Several factors on the buying side contributed to this pattern. In the early 1960s television in Europe was becoming a little more competitive. Monopoly single channels were being joined by second channels. Television was starting to attract sizeable amounts of advertising revenue, not only in Latin America – but increasingly in Europe and Asia. Sales of sets were booming – leading to lower prices, more sales of sets and more programming hours. And all this led to a demand for more elaborate programming.

Also around 1960 the wave of newly independent nations in Africa was followed by new national television services. The result was common enough: a need for more and more popular and expensive programming and a lack of revenue with which to pay for it. The supply of expensively made Hollywood telefilm series available at low prices was thus around 1960 the answer to a TV schedule planner's prayers.

But each of Hollywood's export peaks tends to be slightly lower than the previous one. And each time the political objections in receiving countries tend to be stronger and articulated more quickly. The Soviet Union, China, Bulgaria and Cuba – of countries which had significant TV services – were about the only non-participants in the early 1960s Hollywood export boom. But then a number of other countries – led by eastern and western Europe – began to have second thoughts, and reduced their imports.

CHAPTER NINE

Forced to be free: Italy, Germany and Japan

Italy, West Germany and Japan immediately after their defeat had their media forcibly reshaped along Anglo-American lines. The media of all three of these conquered nations have since been partially incorporated into the wider Anglo-American pattern, and all three are also significant media exporters. Italy is the most striking example – the Italian film industry is heavily entwined with Hollywood and in the early 1970s was, undoubtedly, after the American domestic industry, the world's second largest exporter of feature films. Japan is the only major media power which has in some respects taken further than the United States such typically American things as the advertising agency, and head-on competition between large newspapers and in commercial television. West Germany is the leading media power on the continent of western Europe – influencing some ten neighbouring nations in western and eastern Europe.

The media of these nations were not entirely re-invented along Anglo-American lines; rather they were forcibly jerked back into patterns of influence which in all three cases derive from the nineteenth century – influences which all three nations had then rejected before and during the Second World War.

1900 AND 1930: IMITATING, IMPORTING AND
EXCLUDING THE ANGLO-AMERICAN MEDIA

Despite a long history, the German press in 1900 still consisted mainly of small and very local newspapers. In 1900, when the daily circulation lead was taken from Scherl's *Berliner Lokalanzeiger* by Ullstein's *Berliner Morgenpost*, the latter's sale was only 250,000. The largest Italian sales, although growing fast, were well below these Berlin figures. In Japan the leading sales were comparable to the German ones; the four leading dailies in Osaka and Tokyo in 1905 together sold about one million copies.[1]

In Germany the rise of the popular press was, as in many countries, associated with strident xenophobia, and with some continuing political control and censorship,* but there were also unmistakable traces of American influence. August Scherl founded one of the three major pre-1914 German newspaper chains – the other two, Mosse and Ullstein, largely following his lead. Scherl's most famous paper, the *Berliner Lokalanzeiger* (Local Advertiser), became a daily in 1885 and was the German circulation leader for the next fifteen years. Scherl, who visited London several times as a young man, was an enthusiastic reader of English and American newspapers. His first newspaper, launched in Hamburg, was for emigrants and was associated with a travel agency; thus he must have been familiar with the American German-language press, such as the *New Yorker Staats-Zeitung* which at the time (1880) had a bigger daily sale than almost any paper in Germany itself.† Scherl was the first German publisher to use an American Linotype machine. His promotional methods had a distinctly American ring. Hugo von Kupffer, Scherl's chief editor, had worked for Reuters in London and Madrid and for the *New York Herald* in New York.[2] Similar American influences are found in the career of Mosse who was an advertising agent both before and while he was a newspaper owner. The Ullstein family was much more willing openly to acknowledge its debt to various American examples – for instance, Ullstein's *Blatt der Hausfrau* was modelled on the *Ladies' Home Journal*,[3] and the first of the 'boulevard press', Ullstein's *BZ am Mittag* (1904) was modelled on the New York populars.[4]

In Italy the *Corriere della sera* was in 1900 just taking over the daily circulation lead – and it, too, followed Anglo-American examples. Luigi Albertini, who built up the *Corriere* on the model of the Anglo-American prestige paper, had studied in London, where he took a special interest in the operations of *The Times*.[5] As editor of the *Corriere* he imported not only English styles and American equipment but also American syndicated comic strips for the *Corriere dei piccoli*.[6] Another Italian journalist who worked in London (1899–1910) and advocated British models was Mario Borsa, editor of the important radical paper *Il Secolo* from 1910 until it came under Fascist control in 1923.[7]

Between 1890 and 1910 some five million European migrants returned from the United States. Of two million Italians who migrated to the United States between 1902 and 1921, over half returned to Italy.[8] This enormous return flow of migrants undoubtedly

* Between 1890 and 1914 Social Democrat (SPD) newspapers and editors were continually harassed by legal actions, fines and terms of imprisonment. See Alex Hall (1974 a and b).

† In 1889 German-language dailies in the USA had a total sale of about 400,000. See Wittke (1957), p. 209.

also brought to Europe a flood of American immigrant
newspapers, whose influence on the European press needs its
historian.

In Japan the modern press was created originally as an off-shoot
of the English language China coast press. *The Nagasaki Shipping
List and Advertiser* was launched by Albert W. Hansard, the British
agent in Nagasaki of the *London and China Telegraph*. British edited
publications predominated among early Japanese newspapers and
the first modern Japanese magazine was *Japan Punch* (1862).
American journalists were also extremely active in early Japanese
journalism and Joseph Hiko, often referred to as the father of Japanese journalism, was a naturalized American citizen. The first Japanese
language newspapers were straight translations of English language
ones. A historian of British–Japanese relations in this period comments:

British editors dominated the English press in Japan from 1861
until 1883. Through their newspapers and magazines they introduced to the Japanese people the ideals, the skills, the values, and
the abuses which two hundred years of experience with a press had
taught them at home. . . . With the exception of Howell, all were
primarily interested in the growth of English commerce and the
welfare of the merchant class. This made them fearless critics of
their own officials and brutal in attacking leading personalities. . . .
A desire to prevent the abolition of extra-territoriality led these
journals, during the latter part of the period, to indulge in un-
warranted criticism of the Japanese people and government with
a view to proving them incapable of assuming the responsibilities
which such a revision of treaties would entail. . . .

No western institution appealed more quickly or more generally
to the awakening Japanese nation than the popular press. Within
less than fifteen years after the publication of the *Nagasaki Shipping
List and Advertiser*, the Japanese people had a powerful widespread
press of their own. Young Japanese journalists seized upon all the
traditional British freedoms as goals for Japan, and courageously
attacked the new Meiji government in their efforts to attain them.
. . . The clamour of the *Herald* and the *Gazette* urged them on. The
Meiji government's attempt to control them by a series of *Press
Regulations* was inevitable in view of the existing political in-
stability. But the punishments they meted out had little effect on
the growth of newspapers, nor did these punishments blur the
aims of the journalists for the free institutions which their contacts
with the West engendered.[9]

During the 1880s the Japanese press already had its specialized advertising and news agencies, and was using price-cutting tactics and serial stories to boost sales. In the 1890s the high sales of the French *'Petit'* press seem to have attracted attention, and rotary presses were imported from France. But by 1900 the business practices of the American press were becoming a predominant foreign influence, although well into the twentieth century the high Pacific cable charges ensured that the Japanese press relied mainly on Reuters, drawing its foreign news mostly from Europe, especially Britain. By 1915 the total daily newspaper sale was 4·5 million[10] making the Japanese press already the fifth largest in the world (after USA, Britain, France and Germany).

By 1930 Anglo-American influence on the media of other countries was both more obvious than in 1900 and also more widespread. It included not only newspapers, but also films, radio, advertising and news agencies. In 1925, American films made up 60 per cent of all films shown in Germany, 65 per cent in Italy and 30 per cent in Japan (Table 4). Even Japan had until recently a higher level of Hollywood imports. Several Japanese directors had American training; the Japanese film industry had deliberately chosen a Hollywood-like site on the edge of Tokyo bay – where it was destroyed in the earthquake of 1923.[11]

In radio the influence of Britain was stronger. Policy-makers in all three countries recoiled from the American example of the early 1920s. The success with which the British government used the BBC during the general strike in 1926 helped persuade the Japanese government to maintain control over their radio system[12] which in 1930 accounted for nearly all the radio sets in Asia.[13] In Italy and Germany the governments – despite some advertising – were firmly in control of radio. The amount of new American influence here seemed small. Moreover, during the 1930s with Japan at war with China, Italy fighting in Abyssinia, and Germany making war preparations, all three governments tightened their grip on the national media.

But this increasing government control was also a defence against penetration by foreign media interests, especially American. It was generally believed that during 1914–18 the western allies had won the propaganda war – and, starting with German legislation in 1920, all three countries adopted increasingly severe restrictions on Hollywood imports.

In Italy government domination of the media came earliest – Mussolini eventually gained control of the *Corriere della sera* and *La Stampa* early in 1925[14] but in some ways the control was remarkably gentle. Mussolini, himself an ex-journalist, retained considerable respect for the American press. His relatively gentle gagging of the Italian press involved such subtleties as giving journalists special privileges. He also successfully used flattery and the PR approach on the United States press. His 'autobiography', serialized in 1928 by the *Saturday Evening Post*, was 'edited' by a former United States ambassador in Rome and probably ghosted by him in collaboration with Mussolini's brother. The *New York Times* also gave him consistently favourable coverage; a Hollywood publicity man, responding to a request from Il Duce, proposed him in 1929 for membership of the National Press Club in Washington. The opposition of such trouble-makers as Marquis Childs and Drew Pearson narrowly resulted in Mussolini being blackballed.[15] Presumably because of his considerable success at taming both the domestic and foreign press, Mussolini was relatively gentle with Hollywood films. As late as 1937 Hollywood had 75 per cent of the Italian market (Table 4).

In Japan the more commercial newspapers survived the Depression better than did the Liberal papers. Increasingly, during the 1930s the Japanese film industry's cartel arrangements shut out Hollywood imports – the Japanese cartel was itself deliberately modelled on the Hollywood one.* The large Japanese newspapers similarly formed a cartel alliance with government. The main newspaper innovation in 1930s Japan was the *Yomiuri*, a brash Tokyo evening paper which quadrupled its circulation between 1931 and 1938,[16] partly by using New York tabloid tactics.

In Germany immediately before 1933 some major media interests adopted similar cartel defensive arrangements, also primarily against American incursions. The victorious allies of 1918 placed some restrictions on the early development of German radio – which contributed to the subsequent central position of the Postal Ministry in German radio and radio advertising. The German film industry in the early 1920s was the European leader in both quantity and quality: yet this golden period of the German cinema was already fading by the mid-1920s. Germans could blame not only Hollywood's direct competition but other Hollywood machinations – including the seduction of leading directors and actors away from the low-paying German industry to Hollywood, and the incursions of Hollywood finance into the German industry. UFA, the first important production and cinema combine in the German industry, was formed in 1917. UFA became involved in financial deals with American interests. FANAMET (involving Famous Players, First National and MGM) and

---

* In 1909 there had been an attempt to set up a Japanese copy of the US Motion Pictures Patents Company: J. Anderson and D. Richie (1960), p. 30.

PARUFAMET (Paramount, UFA, MGM) were two linked combines through which Hollywood interests provided production finance in return for guaranteed exhibition of Hollywood films in German cinemas.[17]

German deals with Hollywood interests are part of a chain of events leading by 1933 to the Hugenberg media empire – a private enterprise media cartel on a scale which has probably never been surpassed in any major nation; the existence of this Hugenberg media empire greatly facilitated Hitler's rapid seizure of the entire media apparatus in Germany. Hugenberg was a Ruhr industrialist. The motivations behind his private media empire were anti-socialist, anti-Semitic, anti-American and pro-nationalist. Almost certainly, Hugenberg was also inspired by the examples of Hearst, Pulitzer and Northcliffe. The first component of the Hugenberg empire was the old Scherl newspaper group; unlike the Mosse and Ullstein groups, Scherl's was neither Jewish nor under efficient financial management. The Mosse and Ullstein newspaper groups were accused of favouring mid-1920s American policy (such as the Dawes plan) and being in league with American press and film interests.[18]

Hugenberg's antipathy towards cosmopolitan, western, Jewish and socialist elements in German life was shared by many Germans at the time:

> A bitterness towards the West, its political institutions and modes of life had taken root in German thought after the Napoleonic invasion ... the so-called Westerner among German intellectuals easily passed for a subversive. A very high percentage of the Weimar left-wing intellectuals combined all the characteristics repugnant to Germanic ideologists: Francophile, Jewish, Western, rebellious, progressive, democratic, rationalist, socialist, liberal, and cosmopolitan. ...
>
> ... Jews were responsible for a great part of German culture. The owners of three of Germany's greatest newspaper publishing houses; the editors of *Vossische Zeitung* and the *Berliner Tageblatt*; most book publishers ... were all Jews. Jews played a major part in theater and in the film industry as producers, directors and actors. Many of Germany's best composers, musicians, artists, sculptors, and architects were Jews. Their participation in literary criticism and in literature was enormous. ...
>
> The left-wing intellectuals did not simply 'happen to be mostly Jews' as some pious historiography would have us believe. ... The extraordinary Jewish participation in German culture is to be explained by the peculiarities of the Central European Jewish intellectual tradition and by the Jews' historic exclusion from the

more 'respectable' professions [such] as the civil service, the army, the judiciary, or university teaching.[19]*

Hugenberg was first called in to help to reorganize the Scherl newspaper, magazine and book interests and by 1916 he had managerial control. In 1914 he launched his Ausland agency to handle German commercial advertising abroad; this agency later turned into ALA, which by 1920 was Mosse's main rival – a financial holding company controlling newspaper interests and advertising agencies. In 1917 Hugenberg launched Vera Verlagsanstalt – which offered advice and finance for industrialists and others who wished to buy newspapers; Vera later also engaged in news, feature and photograph agency services – and seems increasingly to have been used by Hugenberg as an intelligence gathering agency which enabled him to buy, influence, and subsidize more and more newspapers.[20] In 1918 a number of German newspapers were temporarily taken over by socialist journalists, which strengthened Hugenberg's opposition to foreign, socialist and Jewish forces. In 1922 he founded WIPRO,† a news agency designed to funnel nationalist-slanted news into small provincial newspapers; WIPRO provided moulds ready for casting and ultimately 350 papers relied entirely on this service.[21] It was only after this deep involvement that Hugenberg became interested in rescuing UFA – he acquired a controlling interest in 1927.

In the late 1920s Germany had some 4,000 daily newspapers – most inevitably with negligible sales. Berlin alone had daily newspapers owing allegiance to 50 separate political persuasions. But most of the bigger dailies in the main cities were owned by newspaper groups, which also operated as advertising agents (selling their own and other papers' advertising); Mosse, indeed, was an advertising firm first and a newspaper firm only second. The big press groups also had news agency interests; they operated as public relations agencies (distributing publicity material for a fee); they promoted their own group's other services shamelessly; and they were involved with political party and industrial alliances and subsidies. Within this chaotic jungle there was being fought out a newspaper war to the death – quite literally for some participants. Few Anglo-American niceties were observed – no 'neutral' news, little 'professional objectivity' among

* Deak comments: '. . . Western liberal historians generally underplay the cultural significance of the German Jews, while the Communist historians do not mention it at all. Yet there is no reason why it should not be acknowledged that, in twentieth-century Germany where the Jews formed less than one per cent of the nation's population, Jews were responsible for a great part of German culture.'

† WIPRO – Wirtschaftsstelle für die Provinzpresse. ALA – Allgemeine Anzeigen. UFA – Universum Film A.G.

journalists, no audited circulation figures, no advertising agents independent of both media and advertisers, no independent news agencies; nor was any single publication, news organization or personality accorded general respect. To any Anglo-American advertising man or to any British or American journalist, the German media in the late 1920s must have looked like a jungle – with no objective facts and where everything was tainted with political and financial corruption.

Anglo-American involvement quickened rather than decreased in the late 1920s. Hollywood, with the coming of sound, became an even bigger force in the badly floundering German film industry. Some American businessmen, appalled by German advertising conditions, favoured familiar Anglo-American advertising agencies. When J. Walter Thompson opened a branch in Berlin in 1927* it joined several other Anglo-American agencies; the American McCann-Erickson, the British Dorland and Unilever's Lintas followed in 1927 and 1928. Such agencies insisted on the Anglo-American level of 15 per cent commission.[22] This Anglo-American invasion may have seemed innocent to some people but hardly to an anti-Semitic, anti-American, German nationalist like Hugenberg. He had already suffered the indignity of employing Jewish journalists and of making unfavourable deals with Hollywood businessmen – indignities, indeed, for the man who became chairman of the German National Party, shortly before he formed his alliance with Hitler in 1929. Now he had to witness American advertising agencies coming to Germany to compete with his own advertising agencies. He probably saw an even more sinister threat in the Anglo-American news agencies. Reuters and the American agencies wanted reliable news of the dramatic course of German politics. Competition between domestic German news agencies inevitably involved competition to obtain the most favourable exchange agreements with the international agencies.

In the late 1920s Hugenberg moved more deeply into news agency activities. His Telegraphen-Union took over the family-owned Dammert Verlag and two other news agencies and became a serious threat to Wolff, the traditional German international agency. Another Hugenberg news agency became increasingly strong in economic news services, enabling him to undermine Wolff's mon-

---

* The office opened in February 1927 and was a full service agency on the New York pattern (art, mechanical, traffic, media, research, and copy departments). Its clients included General Motors, Horlicks Malted Milk Co., Sun Maid Raisin Growers, Quaker Oats, Royal Baking Powder, Ponds and Coca-Cola. There were also German clients. The office closed in 1933. Information kindly supplied by the librarian in the JWT London Office.

opoly of official news. The Depression brought many bankruptcies which aided Hugenberg's expansion. By 1932 he controlled Germany's major film company and its nationally exhibited newsreel, and elaborate advertising and press interests:

> A rough estimate would be that Hugenberg enjoyed some form of control or influence over close to one half of the German press by 1930. Almost without exception newspapers which professed a right-wing nationalist political orientation – in 1932 about 1,200 papers – and much of the so-called non-partisan press – 2,029 *parteilose* papers existed in 1932 – had contracts with one or more of Hugenberg's operations. There were 1,600 papers that subscribed to the TU alone. . . .
>
> . . . Without asserting that Hugenberg's press dominion destroyed the Weimar Republic, one can say that it presented a major obstacle to the implementation of democratic, republican ideas amongst the German public.[23]

The main press opposition to Hugenberg came from the Mosse and Ullstein groups, and from Sonnemann's *Frankfurter Zeitung*. Ullstein's newspaper, magazine and book combine claimed to be the largest in Europe; about half the Ullstein journalists were Jewish and the company had many Anglo-American overtones – including the joint sponsorship of car and plane races with New York and London papers.[24] There were similar Jewish and Anglo-American overtones in the *Frankfurter Zeitung*, Germany's leading prestige newspaper. Its editor and dominant personality in the 1920s, Bernhard Guttmann, had been the paper's London correspondent before the First World War.

As early as 1930 Hugenberg had shown himself willing to use his media cartel in the Nazi interest. The first German showing of the American-made pacifist film *All Quiet on the Western Front*, on 5th December 1930, led to demonstrators organized by Goebbels preventing the second evening screening of this film in Berlin. Further rioting followed and the subject was debated in the Reichstag. The Scherl Verlag (Hugenberg controlled) film trade paper gave the American film a favourable review on the morning previous to the first rioting; a week later, however, the same paper called for the banning of the film. The film was indeed banned from public exhibition.[25] The *All Quiet on the Western Front* episode is a celebrated event in the decline of Weimar and the rise of Nazism. The Nazis in 1930 also bitterly objected to *The Blue Angel* for which UFA had employed a Hollywood director.

ITALY, 1943–5, AND AFTER

Anglo-American military occupation policy towards the media involved the establishment of a market-oriented and 'democratic' media system in each country. The intention was to strengthen such local 'democratic' traditions as had existed in the past – for instance in the 1920s; this meant different policies in each country. Another intention was to facilitate the 'free flow' of information from outside. Favouring the opponents of the wartime regime, the allies initially found themselves favouring communists. By encouraging 'free flow' the Americans were in practice encouraging long-term dependence upon American imports. In trying to downgrade government influence the Anglo-Americans adopted a somewhat unrealistic and sentimental view of their own media and especially of the BBC.

The first Anglo-American controlled newspaper, *Corriere di Siracusa*, began publication in Sicily on 13th July 1943. In Italy a polite fiction was maintained that the people had never really been Fascist. The cleansing operation in Italy was largely confined to 1943–5; in northern Italy it was very brief indeed. The Italian mass media were less sharply jerked in a 'democratic' and market direction than the German or Japanese media. The military authorities in Italy used their control of newsprint to do two main things. First, newspapers run by the military authorities were set up in the main cities; but secondly democratic (anti-Fascist) Italians were encouraged to become the new élite of journalism. In Italy, also, the existing approved political parties were allowed their own newspapers – at first mainly weeklies, then dailies. The Psychological Warfare Branch's official daily paper in Milan was installed at the *Corriere della sera* with a circulation soon fixed at 300,000; but the five authorized Italian political parties were also allowed to start one daily paper each – with a total circulation initially of 150,000. The 'democratizing' of the Italian press later led – with the resumption of party politics – to a largely party based newspaper press; soon only indirect allied control was retained through the American and British news agencies. There was a rapid mushrooming of weak partisan newspapers. Thirty Italian daily newspapers ceased publication in 1948 alone.[26]

Italy emerged from the war with a strong film industry (as a result of Mussolini's subsidies) which made possible the post-war neo-realist Italian cinema of De Sica, Rosselini and others. But the longer-term position of Rome as the major foreign bastion of Hollywood was soon foreshadowed by the enormous strength of American films in the Italian market. In 1948 only 11 per cent of all films exhibited in Italy were Italian products, while 73 per cent were American or

British products (Table 9). The BBC was used, with some minor variations, as the model for Italian broadcasting; there were even three radio channels on the then BBC pattern stratified into one 'popular', one optimistically middle-brow and one unambiguously highbrow.

Thirty years after the war most major Italian newspapers were still owned by such organizations as Fiat, the Bank of Naples, the Christian Democrats, the Communist Party, the Roman Catholic Church, the ENI nationalized power group and the employers' organization 'Confindustria' (which also provides various free news services for small provincial newspapers). These groupings are primarily concerned to use their newspapers as prestige flagships or as weapons in their wider political and industrial struggles. The general commercial weakness of Italian newspapers is also illustrated by the predominance in sales, as well as in prestige, of such papers as *Corriere della sera* of Milan and *La Stampa* of Turin. Italian newspapers retain a secretive, somewhat conspiratorial character – more like the newspapers of South America than of northern Europe. Despite some attempts, no audited circulation information of an Anglo-American type exists. Italian newspaper owners do not trust other people's accountants. Advertising agencies do not encourage clients to advertise in such newspapers. Italian industrialists are reluctant to place advertising in newspapers many of which belong to their commercial and political enemies. The Italian public are in turn much less avid newspaper readers than those of the other wealthier European countries.*

Long accustomed to Christian Democrat controlled television and these highly politicized newspapers, the Italian public has favoured feature films, magazines and sports newspapers. The top circulations include not only Italy's main prestige papers but also daily newspapers devoted entirely to sport.[27] The magazines really constitute Italy's popular press and they also attract the bulk of press advertising expenditure. There is a rich assortment of women's magazines, picture weeklies, news magazines, sports weeklies, and scandal magazines. In these magazine types the Anglo-American influences are fairly obvious, and when these magazines struggled into existence after the war they relied heavily on using American syndicated features and picture services.† *Selezione del Reader's Digest* has long

---

* In the early 1970s only 142 daily newspapers were sold per 1,000 Italians – compared with 330 in West Germany, 515 in Sweden and 99 in Spain. See Unesco (1975).

† An interesting anonymous article (*Belfagor*, July 1952) claimed that *Epoca* obtained much of its material from *Life*, and *Tempo* (then selling only 10,000 copies) from *Picture Post*. Other Italian magazines 'are composed of material of exclusively American origin, translated and adapted to suit Italian readers:

had one of the leading circulations and there are also the inevitable 'men's' magazines with English-language titles. Only one type of Italian publication looks unfamiliar to Anglo-American eyes. These are the very widely read photograph romance and crime comics, but these were based on American comic formulae and then crudely photographed (as in Latin America); indeed, their stories were often set in American cities.[28]

Italian television has gradually accepted more and more advertising. In the 1950s there was little advertising expenditure on TV or in the press, and Italian advertising was regarded as very backward. But several British agencies moved in and during the 1960s Italy had its own Madison Avenue invasion. By 1970 most of the leading advertising agencies in Italy were American; characteristically, also, most of the advertising placed by these agencies went into magazines and television, not newspapers.*

FORCED TO BE FREE: WEST GERMANY, 1945–9

American policy in Germany sought to incorporate some lessons from the occupation of Italy and also to prevent any new Hugenberg cartel. In Germany American policy favoured a non-central broadcasting system and city-region newspapers to match; the political parties in the American zone were at first kept out of the press. The German case is also marked by some interesting contrasts between British and American policy which led to some results (such as the Springer empire) intended by neither. But only in the film industry did American military policy fail – and here it was defeated not by German resistance but by Hollywood.

The American attempt to impose 'free' German mass media ran from October 1945 to June 1949. The American authorities published one major newspaper, deliberately presented as an example of what a responsible paper should be. This paper *Die Neue Zeitung* began publication on 18th October 1945 in Munich with a message from General Eisenhower on the front page; the paper was privileged –

This is true of *Intimita, Selezione Femminile, Confessioni Storie Vere*, and of several well-known film magazines such as *Cine Illustrato, Novelle Film Hollywood* . . .' The article also claimed that a glossy magazine called *Lavoro Illustrato* was subsidized with American Marshall Aid funds. Jean Louis Servan-Schreiber (1974) says (p. 71) that *Panorama* was based on *Time* and *Grazia* on *Elle. Elle* itself used US models.

* In 1973 no less than four of the largest five and thirteen of the largest twenty Italian advertising agencies had American names. For example, Young and Rubicam Italia, the third largest agency in Italy in 1973 placed billings as follows: Newspapers 3 per cent; magazines 41 per cent; radio 17 per cent; television 32 per cent. *Advertising Age*, 25th March 1974.

with a subsidy, a generous newsprint allowance, good printing and distribution facilities and a circulation of about 2 million copies (daily from 1948). Hans Habe and Hans Wallenberg, two European-born journalists who edited the paper over the first ten years, each managed to maintain some element of independence from American policy.

Hitler's subjugation of the German press had been so thorough, and its independence so wasted even by 1933, that the allied authorities had considerably difficulty in discovering senior press personnel sufficiently free of the Nazi taint. The Germans who were granted the first licences to produce newspapers in the American zone, were a rather motley collection: 'Some had frequently suffered arrests and long periods of confinement in concentration camps. Many were of advanced age. . . . The younger members of the group, on the whole, were inexperienced in writing and editing as well as in the financial and management aspects of publishing. . . .'[29]

The American occupying authorities (but not the British) set out to build a system of strong city-region newspapers such as one could find in 1945 in, say, Indiana or Illinois. Each newspaper was given a specific format and market: 'When a license was granted, the frequency of issue, the size of format, the number of pages, and also the size of the edition was specified. In addition each newspaper was assigned a specific circulation area in which it had a monopoly but beyond which it could not be delivered. The American licensing program anticipated one copy of a newspaper for five inhabitants of a circulation area.'[30]

In this interpretation of a free press, 'freedom' somehow seemed to rest upon monopoly. It was also an optimistic view of the press, a hope that all newspapers in Germany should be like the most liberal and serious newspapers in the us hinterland. It was above all an attempt to avoid a fragmented weak provincial press vulnerable to subversion by some new Hugenberg.

The motley collection of people who ran the licensed press had an initial monopoly of the legal right, the paper, the equipment. The licensing period ran for nearly four years, until June 1949, when the floodgates were opened and almost anyone could start up a paper. Two years after the end of licensing the former licensed papers still had over 70 per cent of total daily sales.[31] This was in line with a substantial number of sample surveys conducted from 1945 onwards by the American authorities, which had revealed the American licensed newspapers, magazines and radio to be fairly well liked by the German public[32] (in contrast presumably to the offerings of the Hitler-controlled media).

The Americans sought also to avoid the centralized radio system under Postal Ministry control which Hitler had so easily taken over in 1933. The Americans (and the French in their zone) deliberately organized radio at the *Land* (regional government) level and then embedded it into the power structure – by including representatives of all the political parties and the main religious, economic, social and cultural pressure groups in the region.

German politicians inevitably wanted to take over the control which the 'democratic' military authorities were relinquishing; the Americans in particular had insisted upon writing the 'regionalized and free' media structure into the legal framework of the new federal state – making it impossible to unscramble the media without unscrambling the entire federal constitution. But the Adenauer government wanted to commence this unscrambling process; the German press was still weak in revenue, experience and manpower. The Federal capital was covered by only a tiny handful of German journalists and Adenauer's proposal to set up a Ministry of Information was only prevented by vocal criticisms of foreign correspondents and news organizations based in Germany.[33] Adenauer also attempted in 1960 to set up a new television channel under Federal government control; this was forbidden by the Federal Constitutional Court in 1961.

Well into the 1950s a pattern of local media continued, leaving a vacuum at national level. This was partly filled by networking arrangements in broadcasting. The nationally significant press consisted at first almost entirely of large news agencies; the western international agencies, operating as national agencies within West Germany, provided not merely a strong Anglo-American news presence but for some years provided much of the effective political opposition to the Adenauer government.

The British in their large northern zone imposed a centralized media pattern in which Hamburg played the role of London. Their one-big-station policy was justified with the traditional BBC argument of engineering convenience. American insistence that German broadcasting should operate at the *Land* level had the consequence that the British zone, as much the largest single broadcasting unit, played a predominant role in shaping the ultimate arrangements. The Americans set up four broadcasting corporations in their zone, the French two, and the British only one – Nordwestdeutscher Rundfunk; the original NWDR was broken up into smaller units in 1953–4 but not before it had strongly influenced what was to become the prevalent style of both radio and television programming. NWDR began daily television transmissions in 1952 along BBC lines subsequently largely copied in the other West German regions. NWDR also took the lead in establishing the original ARD radio (subsequently also TV) network.

In the British zone the new German press, as well, was constructed on a more British model; the Italian precedent of allowing newspapers to political parties was repeated and the British – with their own national press in mind – allowed each paper to circulate throughout north-west Germany. Hamburg thus became the most important press centre in Germany. Axel Springer built what by British standards was only a moderately large press combine in Hamburg – closely following the model of the London *Daily Mirror* and *Daily Express*. Springer, like many newspaper tycoons, built the foundations of his press combine in magazines – in particular the radio guide *Hör zu* which amassed large profits. In contrast to the cosy monopolistic start given to licensed papers by the Americans, Hamburg was a newspaper centre of a more competitive and earthy character. The good, grey, correctly democratic, ex-licensed papers of the American zone left a gap for more partisan and extreme journalism. From the Hamburg circulation war there emerged a clear sales leader, *Bild Zeitung*, which by 1970 had sales of almost 4 million against the next largest German daily *Westdeutsche Allgemeine* with only a little over half a million sale. In 1970 Hamburg was the home of three of West Germany's six largest selling newspapers; from Hamburg also came the majority of the largest selling magazines.

Springer himself, like many other press tycoons, had no firm political loyalties in his first days of growth. In the early 1960s however, Springer moved strongly to the right – and to many people the largest newspaper group's right-wing partisanship seemed a threat to the entire political system. But perhaps equally significant was the German version of the news magazine, and specially *Der Spiegel*. The 'Spiegel Affair', which began on 26th October 1962 with police raids on *Spiegel* offices and the arrest of senior personnel, clearly established the significance of the press as an independent force in West German politics. Many German newspapers, including papers normally favourable to the Christian Democrat government, attacked the arbitrary police actions; the press took the initiative in events which led to major ministerial resignations.

Rudolph Augstein had been 22 years old when recruited by British Press Control personnel in Hanover in 1946 to work on a German news magazine. Four years later, as editor of *Der Spiegel*, he accused one hundred *Bundestag* deputies of accepting bribes in connection with the establishment of the federal capital in Bonn.[34] Augstein symbolized the new generation of young German journalists, who drawing very heavily upon both British and American influences, helped to produce a press pattern somewhat different from what either the British or the American zone authorities intended.

Nevertheless, in 1970 the pattern of West German media was one in which both the British and the Americans could clearly see pieces of their own systems transplanted. DPA, the German news agency (which also started in Hamburg), is a true child of the Anglo-American agencies; German market research largely grew out of the numerous sample surveys commissioned by the Americans between 1945 and 1955 – and on which German personnel worked for all but the first two months.[35] German public relations derives from the elaborate public relations machine built up by the American authorities to 'help' the new unlicensed papers after 1949;[36] the German Audit Bureau of Circulations was set up in 1950 on the ABC American model. The broadcast networks, ARD and ZDF are a federalized version of the BBC and closer to the British BBC and ITV than to any other two networks in the world. And the majority of the largest German advertising agencies are wholly or partly owned from New York.[37] A more general sign of continuing influence is the large post-1945 increase in the use of English terms throughout the German media, including the prestige press.

JAPAN, 1945–50: A NEW MEDIA COLOSSUS EMERGES

In Japan only one media organization, the Domei news agency, was closed down (while Kyodo and Jiji were created in its place). In contrast to Italy and Germany the American policy in Japan was to work through the existing organizations, using stick and carrot methods and encouraging various 'democratic' currents, such as the setting up of trade unions within organizations. In Japan, unlike Italy and Germany, the British occupation presence was minimal and had no significant effect on the pattern of post-war media.

When in late 1945 some American journalists interviewed the Emperor, the Japanese Home Ministry, shocked at such a blasphemy, banned distribution of newspapers carrying the interview. The American authorities, noting that when the Deity can be interviewed his Godly days are numbered, insisted that newspapers containing the interview should be distributed. General MacArthur in a series of policy statements decreed the forms which Japanese democracy should take. As early as March 1946 he was already commending Japanese journalists on their quick learning of American neutral news values: 'Editorials are becoming soundly based. . . . Both sides of controversial issues are presented and reporting is showing a greater responsibility. The mixing of editorial and news material has diminished.'[38]

Just as Japanese journalists were quick to learn the 'two sides' approach and the division of news and editorial, film producers were eager to adopt American feature film values. The period film genre

British stars – US media

Indian advertisement, 1976

was almost completely forbidden as reflecting Japan's undemocratic past. More 'democratic' film genres such as the crime thriller were encouraged: 'Thus some of the period-hero types were given business suits instead of armor, pistols instead of swords, and put to work as detectives since the occupation did not mind modern murder-thrillers at all.'[39]

In radio, also, lessons were being learnt. Japanese radio had not previously had programming scheduled at regular, announced times; an American style regular round-the-clock schedule was introduced, plus amateur talent shows, quiz programmes and all the standard formulae of American 1945-vintage commercial radio – although NHK was still a BBC-style monopoly corporation. By March 1946 87 per cent of Japanese interviewed in an audience survey at least claimed that they preferred the new style of radio.[40]

The Americans had in Japan at first shown a preference for a broadcasting structure more British than American. However, as they were preparing to cease the occupation they made two important decisions: to introduce TV and also to introduce multi-channel *commercial* TV to compete with NHK. This was not to be like the Italian and German models, a basically 'public service' system, but a nearly all-out commercial system – with American style commercial channels destined inevitably to pull most of the audience away from the public service alternative. NHK's television and the first commercial TV station both began in 1953.

Since then the Japanese have developed a national media pattern unique in the world, dwarfing in scale the domestic media of all other nations except the United States and the USSR. On few conceivable measures of media scale does Japan come lower than in third place in the world, and in several media league tables Japan is clearly in first place. In some respects the Japanese media are ahead of the United States, while in others they are reminiscent of the US media of the late 1940s.

The Japanese media are exceptionally highly centralized in Tokyo; there is an unusually high degree of press ownership in television. In some respects both the major newspapers and the television exhibit more fierce head-on competition than is found elsewhere; but this fierce competition also takes place within a framework of some cartel-like restraints. In 1951 the three largest Japanese newspapers and the largest advertising agency combined together to form Radio Tokyo, which soon became the leading force in commercial television (TBS). Cross ownership has recently been re-shuffled to allow each commercial TV channel to be linked to a single newspaper.

Moscow is the only city with a trio of newspapers conceivably comparable in sales to Tokyo's *Asahi*, *Yomiuri* and *Mainichi*. In addition to having satellite provincial papers these three have taken the daily newspaper to its logical conclusion – morning and evening editions seven days a week. The Japanese newspapers long ago adopted the American practice of home delivery and now have home delivery rates around 90 per cent. Kyodo is, by a long way, the largest non-international news agency in the world – with a total revenue which exceeds that of Agence France-Presse. Japan is equally clearly the world's second most voracious user of newsprint.

This heavy use of newsprint follows partly from the volume of advertising. In 1973 Dentsu became the world's largest advertising agency – it had for some years previously been handling about a quarter of all advertising in the Japanese media. Its advertising placements in 1973 were worth 922 million US dollars and it employed 5,194 people.[41] In keeping with the practices of American late-1940s radio advertising, Japanese advertising agencies still play an active part in constructing television programming. Japanese commercial television is extremely competitive – there being four 'quasi-networks' which compete with two NHK channels in Tokyo. NHK can claim to be a world leader in educational broadcasting; the Japanese media are, after the United States, probably the greatest users of survey research.* The Japanese are clearly, also, leaders in many aspects of media technology – including photo, colour and multi-centre printing and in the production of radio and television receivers. For the first time in this century American leadership in media technology (and its sale) has been seriously challenged.

In several respects, also, the Japanese have managed both to learn from the Americans and to minimize the importing of American media. In no other important capitalist country are American advertising agencies so far down the league table as in Japan (Table 13). Japan shares with China, alone of major nations lacking an international news agency, the honour of being nevertheless nearly self-sufficient in gathering world news. But despite such substantial media independence, even Japan in many ways is still dependent on the American media. And Japan's existing degree of independence results largely from being more American than the Americans. In no other nation (apart from those neighbouring the USA) does television carry so much baseball. Few other nations manufacture at home so many war comics, television commercials, rock songs, westerns, horror epics and so much science fiction of all kinds. In few other nations was it possible to see in 1975 the latest Hollywood disaster movies – and also the locally produced imitations of this current Hollywood fashion already playing across the street. In 1975 *Gone*

---

* As long ago as 1964–5 the Japanese media commissioned 781 large-scale (sample of 300+) surveys in a single year. NSK, *The Japanese Press '67*, p. 51.

with the Wind was shown in two parts on television, the second part receiving the highest ever audience rating for Japanese television.[42]

MEDIA EXPORTS AND IMPORTS: THE FORMER
AXIS POWERS

Despite its enormous media strength and its phenomenal success in selling hardware, Japan is only a minor exporter of media materials* and is still a substantial importer of entertainment. Germany is both a substantial importer and exporter, while Italy is a substantial media importer and a large exporter of feature films.

In news West Germany has been the most active trader of the three. The Anglo-American news agencies continued to operate as domestic agencies inside Germany long after the end of the occupation; now there is a moderate amount of exporting through DPA, and to neighbouring German-speaking populations especially in magazines. Kyodo, lacking such natural news export markets, believes that there is no significant demand in Asia or elsewhere for a Japanese international news agency. A similar self-denying ordinance has been operated by Dentsu – which became the world's largest advertising agency entirely on domestic Japanese business.

In entertainment all three nations have continued as substantial importers of Hollywood films and TV series and American and British pop music.† In 1971 Italy imported 13 per cent of its TV programming, West Germany 23 per cent and 30 per cent (ARD and ZDF) and Japan 4 per cent and 10 per cent (NHK General and commercial); in all three cases the main source was the United States followed by Britain. All three countries still import substantial quantities of Hollywood feature films, and German cinema owners for example still complain of strong-arm cartel practices by American distributors.

The only world-wide media export performance by any of these

---

* In each of the years 1971 to 1974 Japanese feature film exports earned between $3m and $4m. *Variety*, 11th June 1975.

† Statistics on the Japanese record market for 1975 illustrate this. As elsewhere the very highest selling records are mainly made by national stars; The Carpenters were the fourth highest earning record artists in Japan in 1975. The bulk of single record sales were Japanese, but of 8,700 record albums issued, 4,100 were imports pressed and published in Japan. Leading gross sales and record market shares were:

Polydor $36·98m. 15·8 per cent of market.
Victor, 32·91m. 14·1 per cent of market.
CBS/Sony, 31·58m. 13·5 per cent of market.
Toshiba/EMI, 27·97m. 12.0 per cent of market.
Warner Pioneer, 15·8m. 6·8 per cent of market.
King, 13·6m. 5·8 per cent of market.   *Variety*, 11th February 1976.

three nations was by the Italian film industry. This was in 1972 responsible for an average of about 13 per cent of all film imports in all regions of the world and was clearly, after Hollywood, the world's second largest feature film exporter. West German film exports were small except to German-speaking neighbours. Japan had no single strong film export market in the world – and accounted for only about one per cent of world-wide film imports (Table 2). The one exception, Italy's film industry, had also established itself as Hollywood's leading European base, a substantial proportion of all Italian films using American finance, distribution and stars.

The Second World War itself, of course, is a major reason for these countries' continuing dependence upon American media. Not only did they lose foreign markets and control even of their post-war domestic markets, but they lost legitimacy. Few neighbouring countries would have wanted to buy news from Germany or Japan in the 1950s. These countries also lacked the imperial media springboards of the British and French. But, perhaps as important, all three nations lacked any distinctive media traditions which fitted with their post-1945 democratic politics. All three countries after 1945 revived an older tradition – importing Anglo-American media products and styles – a tradition which in all three cases had nineteenth-century origins.

CHAPTER TEN

The other America

Latin America might seem to have been a leading candidate for establishing some authentic regional pattern of media separate from that of the United States.

The populations are large – Brazil, Mexico, Argentina and Colombia together have as many people as the United States. Linguistic differences amongst these mainly Spanish and Portuguese populations are minimal compared with Asia or Africa. Moreover Latin American nations have been pioneers in the press and then in the electronic media. They have a number of prestige newspapers founded well back in the nineteenth century – more venerable than any to be found in most European countries. They were also prominent in the early development of film industries, radio and television. Argentina for several decades was a world leader in all aspects of the media.

Yet this eagerness to embrace new media has been a major contributor to their media's dependence on the United States. The very scale and formidable geography of these countries led to uneven development. Despite Brazil's being the size of the United States, most of its population has been spread along the Atlantic coastline. In Argentina the bulk of the population has sprawled outwards from Buenos Aires. Mexico shares with the United States a long border over which people and media have poured. Even Colombia, much the smallest of these four countries, is twice the size of France, and dominated by mountains higher than the Alps and by tropical rain forest; Colombia also has a Caribbean coastline – easily open to US influence. All of these large populations huddled into small corners of their vast territories tend to turn towards north American influences rather than to their own hinterlands or to their neighbours. They have, like European countries, long histories of rivalry with their neighbours – and considerable reluctance to import media from each other. As far as the media are concerned, Brazil, the largest, has until recently been a sleeping giant; media rivalry between Argentina and Brazil is long standing; Argentina, once the leader of Latin America, continues a policy of nationalism; Cuba, both before and since the arrival of Castro, has been a media leader and rival to the larger Latin American nations.

This chapter will concentrate mainly on Argentina, Colombia and Mexico (the three most populous Spanish-speaking countries) and to a lesser extent on Brazil. These are the critical cases, because the less populated countries in Latin America, as elsewhere, are in general even more dependent on media importing.

POLARIZED SOCIETIES AND MUSHROOM MEDIA

Not only has there been chronic rivalry between the major nations of Latin America, each of the nations has been internally polarized. The media have existed in Latin America mainly among the affluent and literate, who are mostly of European origin and live in European-style cities with moderate climates. In contrast there has been little or no media outside the main cities, among the illiterate, and for those with little or no cash income, who are often partly or wholly of Indian origin and who live in countrysides dominated by extremes of temperature, rainfall and altitude.

Each Latin American country is something like one European country bolted on to an African country – Portugal (with Lisbon) bolted on to Morocco, or Belgium bolted on to Zaire. These countries are polarized especially between large cities and the countryside and this enormously affects the media. But it is not simply a matter of the single dominant city. Mexico City, Buenos Aires, Rio de Janeiro – and even Bogota – are all mammoth cities, but these countries have numerous important provincial cities as well, each typically equipped with several daily newspapers, several radio stations, and at least one television station. While media grow like mushrooms in the cities and towns, out in the vast stretches of the countryside the media are relatively silent. If mountains don't get in the way, radio may reach; but few newspapers are read and television is rarest of all. In Colombia in 1973, 65 per cent of all Bogota homes had television – which included many shanty dwellings* – while only 5 per cent of rural homes had television.†

Latin America society is also polarized by income – especially between those who have a regular cash income and those who do not. 'Revolutions' in Latin America often turn out to favour not all the people but the bulk of the urban population – the large affluent middle class, the white-collar workers and the organized manual workers.

---

* Television has been available sufficiently long in Latin America for black and white TV sets to be relatively cheap and also to be available second-hand. 'Shanty dwellings' in Bogota would not necessarily be so regarded in Bombay or Calcutta.

† The figure for all 'urban' homes was 53·6 per cent. Figures derived from audience research data and supplied by an advertising agency source in Bogota, May 1973. Unesco (1975) indicates 1·2 million TV sets among Colombia's 22·5 million people.

These people consume the media on a more or less European, or southern European, basis. The rest of the population, lacking income, obviously will also lack the media; in some Latin American countries about half the population is largely outside the cash income modern economy and thus beyond the media as well. In some countries, like Argentina, the proportion is lower. In one of the poorest countries, Peru, more than half the population has been and, despite a supposedly left-wing revolution, still is largely without income and without media.

Peru is also a clear example of ethnic polarization – Peru's poor are mostly Indian. But Argentina has few Indians, having slaughtered them a hundred years ago. In Mexico most people are of mixed Spanish and Indian blood. Nevertheless a very broad generalization holds true in Latin America as elsewhere: the person who reads a daily newspaper or owns a television set is likely to have a pale complexion – and this is even truer of someone who owns a newspaper company or TV station. The person who makes no use of the media is likely to have a dark complexion and to speak Spanish (or Portuguese) imperfectly or not at all.

Despite four centuries of European rule and religion, illiteracy is extremely common in Latin America; it is still so widespread in the two most populous countries, Brazil and Mexico, that the governments are too embarrassed to publish reliable figures. In both Brazil and Mexico the *proportion* of illiterates may be falling, while the actual number of illiterates still increases with very rapid population growth. Argentina is again an exception, with a tradition of high literacy. In many Latin American cities you can buy a daily newspaper which has been in continual publication for 100 years, and yet the man who sells you the paper on the street may be unable to read much beyond the title.

Latin American countries are also typically polarized in political terms. On the right is often an oligarchy of old families who at most times in most Latin American countries have run both national politics and the national media. On the left are some trade unions, tens of thousands of Marxist university students and assorted others – but despite their substantial numbers these people usually find little media expression for their political views. If, as is sometimes said, Latin American is like southern Italy two decades earlier, then it is like Italy with the left-wing views but without the communist party newspapers.

This is hardly the place to summarize the enormous complexities of Latin American political history. But a basic point about the media and politics is that these societies do have recent experience of large-scale civil strife, of military coups, of insurgents in the mountains and kidnappings in the cities. And the media have been deeply involved in all of these events – in Mexico's savage revolution leading to one-party rule, in Argentina's remorseless descent from its relative prosperity of the 1940s, in Brazil's extraordinary recent history and not least in Colombia's unique rituals of two-party democracy and political assassination. These are dangerous times and dangerous places for the media.

The powderkeg nature of Latin American politics leads to yet one more form of media polarization. The media are polarized on the one hand between an obsessive, all-embracing concern with politics, and on the other hand an equally obsessive concern to avoid anything remotely connected with politics. The first concern is most prevalent in newspapers, the second in radio and television.

This seems to induce an overwhelming claustrophobia, the favourite solution for which is to rely on cheap imported materials. Cheapness is, above all, crucial. The Latin American media are poverty stricken. They are poorer than the societies to which they belong because of their mushroom growth, their excessive concern with either politics or profit, and their vulnerability to political upheaval or military seizure. The Latin American media could never have reached their present shape without dependence on United States models and cheaply imported materials; and having been constructed astride this pipeline of imported material, they cannot easily move without collapsing.

THE PRESS: FROM EUROPEAN TO UNITED STATES MODELS

American or British accounts of the press of Latin American countries strike a characteristic note of exasperation. Here is an account of the Revolutionary (but conservative) and Democratic (but one party) press of the major Mexico City daily newspapers in 1965–6:

First, there were the enthusiastic descriptions of the country's material and cultural progress. Emphasis was on benefits to be realized at some distant date. Present and future were confused, and vague plans appeared as faits accomplis. . . .

The second category of published material was centered on the cult of glorification of the President of the nation. Even his most inconsequential remarks were quoted, repeated, and glossed by newspaper editors and columnists and television and radio commentators until they acquired the inviolability of sacred texts. . . .

The last note in the triad of preferred subjects noted in the period under study concerned national history. Biographies of national

heroes and villains were printed and reprinted at great length. . . .
In the major newspapers, datelines on stories about foreign affairs
usually carry the names of the principal United States news
agencies. . . .

. . . much space in newspapers and magazines is filled with
classified and display advertising, social news (weddings, showers,
christenings, obituaries, receptions and parties), comic strips and
other 'boiler-plate' material purchased principally from United
States syndicates, sports and entertainment papers, and paid publicity disguised as news. Some of this publicity is commercial, pro-
moting products or services of certain firms. The bulk, however,
consists of direct or indirect government publicity. . . .

. . . Many reporters and columnists are employed only part-time
in their editorial capacity; the rest of the time they either direct or
are employed by the very firms which prepare and disseminate the
publicity releases.[1]

External influences on the Latin American press were for many
years overwhelmingly Spanish.[2] The first Mexican daily paper appeared in 1805 and the active part played by the press during the
1810–21 independence struggle led to a long-term appreciation of its
general political importance. After independence the Spanish-language press proceeded on a highly partisan course, somewhat similar
to United States press partisanship of the time. But the Latin
American societies lacked the steady march westwards; Latin
American societies retained dominant capital cities; adult literacy and
public education were less widespread; voting for public office,
although prevalent, was less meaningful than in the USA; the land-
holding system evolved upon a radically different basis. In contrast
to North America, the Spanish American press throughout the nineteenth century remained polemical, factional and urban.

Many early Latin American newspapers were in languages other
than Spanish, especially in English. By the later nineteenth century
Texan and Californian newspapers, in both English and Spanish,
crossed the border into Mexico on a daily basis. But perhaps the
most dynamic foreign influence on the nineteenth-century Latin
American press were the European immigrants who after 1870
flooded into Argentina. Argentina's two most famous dailies, *La
Prensa* and *La Nacion*, both date from 1869–70. This period saw a
flowering of Argentinian newspapers, and the Italian-language
Argentinian press played a part similar to the United States immigrant press by 'training' immigrants in newspaper readership.

The *Daily Mail* in London was paralleled by the appearance in 1896
of *El Imparcial* in Mexico City, using American linotype machines and

price-cutting tactics (one centavo). The owner of *El Imparcial*, Reyes
Spindola, became Mexico's first modern press tycoon – although he
was supported by a government subsidy. In the next decade American and British investment in Mexico increased sharply. During the
Mexican Revolution there was a substantial Mexican exile press
based in Texas and California, involving many of the leading figures
of the post-Revolution press,* some of whom also came from northern Mexican areas where American papers circulated; indeed the
Constitutionalist movement which ultimately triumphed in the revolution was based on northern Mexico. Mexican journalists returning
from exile played a part in introducing picture journalism to Mexico
in the 1920s.†

American influence was dominant in the Latin American birth of
popular magazines. By 1938 Mexico had its own news magazines and
movie fan magazines, while Argentina had 383 daily newspapers and
1,216 magazines and reviews; these Argentinian magazines represented the first really major Latin American example of a press firmly
aimed at both the middle, and the lower half, of the national population. Many magazines sold at the equivalent of 3 or 4 American cents,
used cheap paper, and were clearly pirated translations of American
fan magazines and comics.‡[3]

Latin America at the turn of the century 'belonged', in foreign
news terms, to the French agency Havas; the challenge to this French
monopoly came entirely from the North American agencies. Rivalry
between Latin American countries assisted both the French and
American agencies. The typical domestic national press of a Latin
American nation failed to combine into one or more co-operative
agencies on the European and Anglo-American pattern. Latin
American newspaper owners typically saw each other, not as sharing
commercial interests, but as political-commercial enemies. Meanwhile the international agencies were already supplying nearly all the
foreign news in each Latin American country; daily papers in provincial cities also provided a ready supply of journalists eager for

* Manuel Becerra Acosta in 1914 edited a Spanish-language newspaper in Los
Angeles. He later became editor-in-chief of *Excelsior*, the Mexico City prestige
daily, and from 1963 its director-general.

† An example is Felix Fulgencio Palavicini, who was prominent in the Madero
(elected President of Mexico in 1911) Movement during 1909–10 and editor of
its newspaper, *Anti-Reelectionista*. He founded the important Mexico City daily,
El Universal, in 1916. In April 1918 he left Mexico for New York because he dis-
agreed with the pro-German stance of the Carranza government. On returning
from New York he became a leading figure in the introduction of tabloid newspapers to Mexico.

‡ These publications were defended by the Argentinian delegation at the 1939
Montevideo International Law Codification Conference; the delegation opposed
international recognition of copyright on the ground that piracy spreads culture.

extra income as agency 'stringers'. Thus the international agencies began to operate also as domestic national agencies, and were as late as 1970 still collecting and distributing domestic news within Chile and Brazil. In Argentina the Saporiti agency, since its birth in 1900, had close ties with the European agencies;[4] another Argentinian national agency, ANA, from its birth in 1908 until 1948 was a wholly owned subsidiary of the Associated Press of New York; United Press, which began in Argentina in 1910, was still in 1948 easily the largest agency in Argentina – distributing at that time 60,000 words daily of both foreign and domestic news; the other long established Argentinian news agency, TELAM, was involved with the American INS agency.[*5]

During the Second World War many Latin American newspapers were dependent on the United States for world news, for advertising revenue and for newsprint supplies. This was certainly not the first time most Latin American papers learnt to bend with the wind. But this wartime experience may, paradoxically, have made the Latin American press seem especially corrupt in American eyes. Certainly J. Walter Thompson, McCann-Erickson and other US-owned leading advertising agencies in Latin America do not encourage their clients to advertise in newspapers; they favour radio, magazines and television.[†] All of Mexico City's 20 daily newspapers, including *Excelsior*, sell editorial space and openly publish the rates they charge per line for such editorial coverage.[‡] In Mexico, advertising agency executives are sceptical of all claimed sales figures, once again including those of the leading prestige daily, *Excelsior*. Newspaper display advertising is limited, which underlines the importance of *classified* advertising upon which a few prestige papers rely; even so, some papers probably lose money on their advertising. Newspaper pictures of the latest arrivals at Mexico City routinely include the airline's name in the photo caption. Most of a newspaper's editorial space is for sale. It is difficult to escape the suspicion that some

* In 1948 Saporiti was distributing 8,000 words a day, ANA 15,000 words and TELAM 5,000 words – a total of 28,000 words a day. In contrast, the international agencies were in total distributing 132,000 words daily in Argentina.

† For example J. Walter Thompson in 1973 was the largest advertising agency in Argentina, and placed 15 per cent of its billings in newspapers against 61 per cent in TV and radio; in Brazil JWT was the second agency, placing 8 per cent in newspapers and 45 per cent in radio and TV; in Mexico, JWT was third, placing 8 per cent in newspapers and 74 per cent in radio and TV. (*Advertising Age*, March 25th, 1974.)

‡ Such paid-for editorial is known as *Gacetillas*. The quoted rates vary according to position, page and section. In 1972 the rates published in *Medios Publicitarios Mexicanos* were about one US dollar per agate line in the larger Mexico City dailies; ordinary classified rates were about one-half or one-third of this.

Latin American newspapers carry many pages of advertising, not because this makes money, but because it conforms with the image of the fat US newspaper.

The prestige papers of Latin America have typically devoted large proportions of their total space and of their front pages to foreign news.[6] Heavy use of agency foreign news is easier, safer, and cheaper than detailed coverage of domestic politics; if powerful politicians complain, the blame can be placed on the foreign agency; the readers of prestige papers are interested in such news; Latin American journalists have a genuinely high regard for the international agencies; heavy foreign coverage fits the image of seriousness and independence which the Anglo-American model of the prestige newspaper requires.

Five of Colombia's six largest selling magazines in 1973 were North American either in ownership or origin: *Selecciones* (Reader's Digest), *Vanidades** and *Buenhogar* (both owned by Good Housekeeping), *Vision* and *Diner's Club. Reader's Digest*'s 1970 Mexican sales were 460,000 – a formidable figure by Latin American standards – and many of the innumerable Mexican picture, news, fan and comic magazines undoubtedly buy or take pictures from American sources.

COMMERCIAL RADIO: IN AT THE BEGINNING

Latin American countries, and Argentina in particular, played a key part in the spread of the United States style of commercial radio around the world. In 1930 Argentina had as many radio sets per population as France and the eighth highest national total in the world (Table 6). Latin American countries were by 1930 major importers of United States radio equipment.† A United States trade commissioner described 1931 Argentine radio as follows:

Of 29 principal broadcasting stations in Argentina, 19 are located in Buenos Aires. . . .

The management of a good proportion of the Argentine broadcasting stations is divided into three principal groups. . . . The first group is called the 'Primera Cadena Argentina de Broadcastings', and from time to time it broadcasts 'chain' programs. . . .

* *Vanidades Continental* in 1970 was a bi-weekly women's magazine with 8 editions (Chile, USA, Mexico, Puerto Rico, Central America, Colombia, Venezuela, Peru). Published in Panama, editorial office in Miami, publicity and advertising in New York. Estimated circulation: 400,829. See *Ayer Directory*, 1971.

† In 1929 Argentina was second only to Canada as an importer of US radio equipment; Mexico was fifth, Cuba seventh and Brazil ninth. See Batson and Schrutrumpf, eds, *Radio Markets of the World* (1930), p. 39.

The relative amount of time spent on advertisements as compared with that devoted to entertainment may be as low as 20 per cent in the best stations and as high as 50 per cent in the stations of minor importance. . . .

Phonograph records are used considerably by the broadcasting stations, and all of them have extensive record libraries. . . . Standard records as made by the well-known American and European manufacturers are used. . . . Arrangements are now under way by which some stations will offer broadcasting time through accredited agents in the United States.[7]

The Mexican radio pioneers were mostly natives of the northern part of the republic who had studied in the United States. The Mexican Revolution delayed the start of Mexican radio, but Mexican enthusiasts were keen to catch up with both their northern and southern neighbours. The first Mexican radio station was jointly owned by a radio retail sales agency and the *El Universal* newspaper and was managed by two brothers, Luis and Raul Azcarraga, whose brother Emilio later became the dominant personality in Mexican radio and television. The second station was established by a cigarette company, El Buen Tono, and later became the key Mexico City station, XEB. The third, in March 1924, was owned by the prestige newspaper *Excelsior* and the Parker radio receiver sales agency. In 1923 commentary on a boxing contest in New York was broadcast on radio in Mexico City; the Mexican champion, symbolically perhaps, was defeated in this fight in New York by the American heavy-weight, Jack Dempsey. The first full-time news department in a Mexican radio station was introduced by Felix Palavicini in 1930 on a station called Radio General Electric (after its previous owners).[8] A United States trade commissioner in Mexico City in 1931 commented:

As late as 1929 Mexico could boast of no more than a mere handful of commercial stations, but the last 18 months have seen the number jump with phenomenal rapidity until now no less than 30 stations are broadcasting commercial programs. . . .

All broadcasting equipment is of American manufacture. . . .

Some dealers state that an average of seven or more persons can be reached by each receiver. It is estimated that there are 100,000 sets in use. . . .

The large department stores have taken great interest in radio possibilities, and they are continually advertising their sales, bargains, and staples over this medium. The radio audience in Mexico now learns of the qualities of an American radio; that an American insecticide will free their kitchens of roaches; that the Centro

Mercantil has the best bargains in ladies' hats; that a talking-machine hour is sponsored by the Mexico Music Co.; that Aguila or Buen Tono cigarettes are as good as any imported brand; that a well-known light six is the car of their dreams. . . .[9]

Already, then, in 1930 Latin American countries were establishing a pattern of many small radio stations, short of revenue and serving out a diet of recorded music and much advertising. During the 1930s these stations continued to multiply; they also increasingly became dependent on advertising from United States advertisers or agencies, and upon records supplied by North American record companies. Low revenue and even lower costs constituted a profitable formula, and attracted yet more stations on to the air.

Commercial radio has continued in Latin America. Mexico City in the early 1970s had more commercial radio stations than New York City; Brazil had over 1,000 radio transmitters. Some of the stations are linked into networks, but even these are modest affairs. One of the major commercial networks in Mexico City involves several stations housed in one quite small building – each station putting out a specialized brand of Mexican pop music; this network used entirely American equipment and with both disc-jockey chatter and commercials pre-recorded the network constituted in effect several automatic juke-boxes linked to the transmitters. Information on the output of this chaotic jumble of stations is itself patchy and chaotic; the superfluity of stations is a research nightmare – one per cent of the total potential audience is quite a high, but also a highly unreliable, figure. Hale estimates that 40 per cent of all radio stations in 17 Spanish-speaking Latin American countries use free material provided by the US Information Agency.[10] Many records are supplied free by record companies among which in Latin America, as elsewhere, the 'international' companies are prominent. It is not surprising, then, that some estimates place the proportion of foreign (mainly US) music at over half. Advertising takes up much time and much of it is also for US consumer products and/or placed by US advertising agencies. The foreign news may also come from American agencies.

Educational radio exists on a substantial scale but with some notable exceptions – especially in Colombia – Latin American educational radio tends to fall into the many traps which await the unwary and ill-organized in this field.

COMMERCIAL TELEVISION: WHERE FILMS AND RADIO LED

Latin American nations, like all others in the world, began their national television services as an off-shoot of radio. In Latin America both television and feature films were especially clearly established on United States models. In 1925 Latin American countries were taking nearly all of their feature films from Hollywood; by 1937 this dependence had been reduced a little – especially in Argentina, which now took only 70 per cent of its feature films from Hollywood. Argentina had established a special 20 per cent tax from which European film industries, but not Hollywood, were exempt. By 1937 Argentina was producing 30 feature films a year and although Hollywood products were most popular in the big Buenos Aires theatres, Argentinian films were already more popular in smaller cinemas and rural areas. By 1938, also, Mexico had established one of the world's larger film industries.*

During the Second World War Latin America was the only large world region which continued to receive the full weight of current Hollywood film output. Nevertheless the Latin American domestic industries continued to make feature films: in 1945, consequently, Argentina and Mexico had two of the world's more viable film industries. Both were building up their own modest export feature film markets throughout Latin America (Table 9), while Brazil and even Chile were making some features. This relative success of their own feature films may have been one reason why Latin American countries entered so optimistically and early into the television age.

The prominent position of several Latin American countries in the early days of world television probably played its part in encouraging other countries to go into commercial TV. In 1954, Britain decided upon a commercial channel; at that time the world's fourth TV nation (in sets per population) was Cuba, fifth was Venezuela, and seventh equal with France were the Dominican Republic and Mexico. Nor were Argentina and Brazil far behind (Table 10). The Mexican, Brazilian and Cuban TV services all went on the air within a few weeks of each other in 1950. For the next three years Latin America had more TV sets than did continental western Europe. Whether or not this helped to persuade the Europeans to accept TV advertising – as all the Latin American services already had – is unclear; but this early, and advertising-financed, entry to television shaped the whole subsequent pattern of Latin American television. Television was set up in the image of, or as an offshoot of, radio – and it had the same weaknesses, such as too many stations, too many hours of programming, too many minutes of advertising and too few sets, too little revenue, too little money to spend on programming.

A flood of United States TV series doubtless would have occurred,

---

* Latin America made 56 features in 1936 and 90 in 1937. In 1937 Mexico made 52, Argentina 30, Brazil 4, Peru 2, Uruguay and Cuba 1 each. See US Department of Commerce (1937), pp. 4–5, 12.

had they been available, but in the early 1950s they were not yet ready. Consequently Latin American television floundered about, trying to fill up the enormous slabs of airtime. An account of Mexican television in 1953 describes this phoney war period, when Mexico City already had three channels:

> The primary concern of programme directors is to create a series of broadcasts which shall be commercially successful at a low cost. The two largest television stations are closely linked to important radio stations and many programmes are little more than televised radio shows . . . frequently productions are broadcast simultaneously on a radio and a television station. The second source of programming is films, most of them produced some years ago for cinema exhibition. . . . A third source is baseball games and other sports events. Lastly, types of programmes successful in the United States are reproduced in Mexico, while Mexican stations broadcast kinescopes of the United States productions.[11]

It was this last category which increased slowly during the 1950s and then accelerated into a flood at the end of the decade. By 1960 enormous quantities of made-in-Hollywood series were appearing on Latin American television screens, and it was this flood of cheap material which fuelled the subsequent sales boom for TV sets.

During the 1950s a number of US companies became deeply involved in Latin American television, including the ownership of stations. This pattern of ownership was sharply reduced and then eliminated when television subsequently became profitable; although US television capitalists thus failed to make large profits, US styles and influence played a commanding role during the formative 1950s. The earliest adopters were countries like Cuba and Mexico, parts of which could receive US domestic television direct; indeed two of the first Mexican stations were located on the United States border and beamed US material into American homes in south-east Texas and southern California. The founding tycoons of Latin American television (like Mestre of Cuba and Argentina and Azcarraga of Mexico) typically had substantial selling experience working for United States consumer goods companies.

Before the flood of US television imports began, what did the Latin American TV services develop in the way of authentic local programming? Two answers are usually given – one is the marathon variety show, the other the *telenovela*. Both of these forms, and especially the *telenovela*, contain strong US strains. Some say that the *telenovela* is merely the US radio soap-opera transposed. But not only had Latin American radio long used the serial story format, so also had Latin

American newspapers. Any search for cheap programming to build audience loyalty could scarcely fail to arrive at the formula of a serial drama with a tiny cast and minimal studio set. The key point about the *telenovela* is that it originates from a need to fill time (including daytime) cheaply – and this in turn arises from transposing multi-channel all-day commercial television from a rich country to a much poorer one. Had this latter decision not been taken, Latin American television would have been different. It would have been even more different, at least in Mexico and Argentina, if originally television had been married to the domestic film industry. But the Latin American film tycoons – like everyone else – looked at what was happening in the United States and accepted the contemporary Hollywood view of television as an upstart enemy.

Since the early 1960s the importing of Hollywood series into Latin America has somewhat declined. Varis found proportions of imports varying from 10 per cent to 84 per cent of all programming in various Latin American countries in 1971 (Table 1).

In Mexico City in 1973, Channel 2, the most popular and widely networked channel, did carry mainly Mexican programming – partly in order to draw the audience into watching the 90 minutes late evening political show on which members of the government received much friendly coverage. But two other Mexico City TV channels devoted the bulk of peak evening time to American imports plus a few local imitations. One channel was showing between 9 and 10 on successive weekday evenings: *FBI*, *El Gran Premio de los 64,000 pesos*; *Los Intocables*; *El Show de los Polivoces*, and *La Hora Macabra*.[12] The Colombia national channel carried the more popular Colombian shows, but the local Bogota channel relied heavily on American series like *Peyton Place* which was running at 10.30 each night and called *La Caldera del Diablo*.[13] Counting the quantity of imports is difficult; in Mexico both 'Futbol' and 'Beisbol' can be either local or piped in from the United States, while variety and magazine programmes may contain imported inserts. In Mexico, especially, TV documentaries about Australian surf-riding, French châteaux and Canadian Eskimos are supplied free by those countries but not identified as such. Much Anglo-American news-film is routed on to Latin American TV screens via the news-film agencies, Euro-vision, and Atlantic satellite subsidized by the Spanish government. This latter is one of several efforts of the Spanish government to renew the traditional Spanish influence on Latin American media – an influence that has remained strong in book publishing.

UNITED STATES NEWS AGENCIES: PERON, PINILLA AND ALLENDE AS VILLAINS

Peron and Pinilla of the right (or centre) and Allende of the left were three Latin American politicians that the United States news agencies disliked. The news coverage of these men as political villains depended partly upon the sharing of values between north and south American journalists and publics – especially the tendency to present politics in terms of personalities. These examples illustrate the journalistic idealism as well as the commercial self-interest of the US agencies. They show how news agencies based in New York can be the means through which a political campaign is orchestrated against a Latin American politician from neighbouring countries – countries which take the self-same news agency services and transmit them across borders on radio broadcasts. These cases also illustrate a dilemma for journalists in Latin America: should the famous, and usually conservative, prestige newspapers be supported as the bastions of independent thought and journalism or should they be opposed as bastions of domestic oligarchy and foreign commercial interests?

From his election as President of Argentina in February 1946, Peron used various measures against hostile newspapers. By late 1947 only two Argentinian papers, *La Prensa* and *La Nacion*, were still pursuing a vigorously independent line; in early 1951 *La Prensa* was formally seized by the government. The paper only re-appeared under its old ownership five years later. But, in view of the more summary measures against newspapers by many governments both before and since 1950, why did Peron take at least five years to seize *La Prensa*? Peron used the methods of intimidation – such as reducing the supply of newsprint, accusations of unpatriotic behaviour and waste of newsprint on advertisements – leading finally to the mobilization of key trade unions against *La Prensa*'s management.

Peron was clearly anxious about the consequences of a quick seizure. *La Prensa* had a world reputation. With the press of most of Europe and Asia in ruins, as seen from New York or London, *La Prensa* looked in 1945 the most vigorous and independent of all newspapers outside the English-speaking world. Senior journalists in New York and London, quite sincerely, saw Peron's attack on *La Prensa* as something to be resisted. As Peron's measures against *La Prensa* reached a climax in 1950, so also the Anglo-American press criticism reached a crescendo. Prominent in this international press campaign was the Inter-American Press Association. The 1950 IAPA meeting took place in New York; the United States members were instrumental in getting the IAPA constitution changed so that it was no longer partly dependent on subscriptions from Latin American governments of the right and, more significantly in 1950, of the left. Thenceforth IAPA was to be dependent entirely on the dues of its member news- papers – which in the case of Latin America obviously meant the wealthier newspapers. From 1950 IAPA developed into a vocal alliance between major Latin American newspaper owners and some less prominent, but equally wealthy, United States ones. IAPA's new found vigour focused largely upon a bitter campaign against Peron. After the seizure of *La Prensa*, IAPA held its next annual meeting across the river from Buenos Aires in Montevideo; pro-Peronist Argentinians tried to take control of this meeting, but were repelled, and the IAPA campaign against Peron continued.

In several American accounts of these events, the titles convey the flavour: Joseph Kane, 'The Totalitarian Pattern in Peron's Press Campaign'; Donald Easum, '*La Prensa* and Freedom of the Press in Argentina'; and Mary Gardiner's '*The Inter American Press Associa- tion: Its Fight for Freedom of the Press, 1926–1960*'. But no explana- tion is given as to how the campaign against Peron was mounted. The sentiments of IAPA acquired teeth through the international news agencies. The United States news agencies were completely dominant in Latin America, since AFP was only starting its comeback; and they will have needed little prompting. *La Prensa* in 1950 was sinking fast and with it were sinking the news values and professional indepen- dence dear to United States journalists. The story also had a colourful villain (Peron) and a personable hero, '*La Prensa*'s editor and principal owner, handsome, scholarly Alberto Gainza Paz'.[14]

At least five separate US accounts ignore the business interest of the American news agencies. *La Prensa* had been a key in United Press (later UPI) growth in Latin America. By 1950 a few newspapers in each of a number of Latin American countries had become known for using large quantities of foreign news. The great bulk of this foreign news in 1950 was supplied by American news agencies, and these prestige newspapers were able to pay a good price for the internation- al news agencies' services. From 1920 onwards *La Prensa* had handed over its entire foreign news operation to United Press for an excep- tionally high fee (ultimately of around $500,000 a year). The Europ- ean news in which *La Prensa* was especially interested became during the 1920s the basis of UP's expanding world-wide news services.[15] A major common interest thus developed between a few dozen Latin American prestige papers, led by *La Prensa*, and the American news agencies, AP, UP and INS.

The *La Prensa* affair brought President Peron much press hostility in the United States – with whose government he was already in serious conflict over nationalization compensation and other economic issues. Through the international agencies he also received much criticism in prestige newspapers in neighbouring countries, and by 1950 hostile coverage on foreign Latin American radio stations which could also be heard within Argentina. However one chooses to regard 'patriotism', it is undeniable that a prestige newspaper like *La Prensa* in this situation was dependent mainly on foreign news agencies for its large ration of foreign news and was pursuing a brand of independent and high-minded journalism which had been invented and propagated by the Anglo-Americans.

A somewhat similar situation occurred in 1955 in Colombia; *El Tiempo*, the leading prestige paper of Bogota and one of the best known papers in Latin America, was closed down by the Colombian President Rojas Pinilla – another populist military 'extremist of the centre'. Again there was a campaign of protest carried on by the international news agencies and by major newspapers and radio stations in neighbouring countries. Again the theme was: 'Military dictator closes internationally famous liberal newspapers.' But there was another view:

> Colombian newspapers and periodicals are primarily party organs
> . . . *El Espectador* and *El Tiempo* of Bogota established Liberal
> doctrine, strategy and tactics throughout the nation. It is by no
> means accidental or coincidental that owners and editors of the
> leading dailies have always been presidents of Colombia, candi-
> dates or party chiefs. . . . Partisan first, informative incidentally,
> the Colombian press has always enjoyed a maximum political free-
> dom with a minimum of public responsibility. . . . In a society
> where politics always runs along the margin of violence, such a
> 'free press' can easily incite public disorder, even though such is
> not its intention.[16]

El Tiempo was closed for its reporting of several violent outbreaks in early 1955, in one of which 28 people were killed. Pinilla denounced the reporting as deliberately inflammatory and partisan on behalf of the Liberals, the traditional party of *El Tiempo* and *El Espectador*. This occurred during Colombia's 'La Violencia', a long period of sporadic peasant guerrilla fighting, brigandage and political assassination which killed between 100,000 and 300,000 Colombians. 'La Violencia' is agreed to have been the most lethal outburst of domestic violence anywhere in Latin America since the Mexican Revolution. Pinilla's uneasiness about rural violence was thus a real one, and the interpretation put upon the events by the international agencies along the lines of 'denial of press freedom' was at best incomplete.

After getting rid of Pinilla, the two dominant Colombian parties, Liberal and Conservative, agreed to take alternate turns at the Presidency. This unusual arrangement played some part in eliminating the worst forms of violence throughout the 1960s. However, in 1970 General Pinilla put himself forward as a Presidential candidate against the coalition candidate; officially Pinilla lost by a small margin, while he himself claimed to have won. In 1973 *El Tiempo* still had a fixed policy of refusing to mention Pinilla by name, although he was still alive and still Colombia's most remarkable political personality. Even a proud paper like *El Tiempo* – which claimed the largest newspaper circulation in Latin America – thus interpreted Anglo-American neutral news values with a spice of Colombian venom.

The confrontation in Chile between *El Mercurio* and Allende during his 1970–3 Presidency contains some similarities, although Allende, of course, was a non-communist Marxist. *El Mercurio* followed the usual Latin American pattern of the prestige paper owned by one of the country's wealthiest families; the Edwards family, owners of *El Mercurio*, also owned Chile's dominant brewery. *El Mercurio* was for a brief period closed down by the Allende regime; inevitably a Marxist President clashed with such a newspaper. Inevitably, also, there were payments to journalists and subsidies to newspapers; the CIA in trying to influence events in Chile could scarcely have failed to use, among others, this traditional Latin American method. However, in some respects foreign news coverage of Chile in 1970–3 differed from the earlier coverage of Peron and Pinilla. The American agencies played a big part in this coverage, but in contrast especially to the Peron case, the French news agency was a real force in coverage of Allende and ensured that much anti-USA Chilean news went around the world.*

Presidents Peron, Pinilla and Allende are all portrayed as villains, and in each case a complex political situation was presented to the world's press simplistically. Each President threatened newspapers which in turn was a threat to revenue (of the news agencies) and to newspapers which were used by Anglo-American journalists as news sources. Peron, Pinilla and Allende all suffered from being somewhat threatening to Anglo-American media interests without having the power or the will fully to restrict their activities. By contrast the Presidents of many African and Asian countries who keep their domestic press on a much tighter leash have received less unfavourable coverage.

A footnote to this story is that a fair proportion of the correspond-

---

* The liberal concern in the USA about 'biased' coverage of Allende may partly reflect AFP's lack of USA clients.

ents (and bureau chiefs) of US news agencies in Latin America are themselves Latin Americans.* This point can be regarded as ambiguous. But it is clearly further evidence of the interweaving of Latin American and US media.

EXPORTING, IMPORTING AND MEDIA NATIONALISM

Most Latin American countries contain examples of large diversified media companies which play a major part in the national media and also have strong links with United States companies.

In Chile when Allende became President he found himself in opposition to two linked media combines; one (already mentioned) was the wealthy Edwards group which owned two daily papers in Santiago in addition to *El Mercurio*, plus two dailies in Valparaiso, several magazines and a popular radio station. The second large Chilean grouping, Zig-Zag, controlled most of Chile's major magazines – and was bought by the Christian Democrat party shortly before Allende became President. Both groups published Spanish-language editions of American comics; Ziz-Zag printed Walt Disney comics and the local edition of *Selecciones del Reader's Digest*.

The most remarkable examples of such organizations are provided by Brazil and Mexico. In Brazil the Chateaubriand group owned the prestige daily, *O Jornal do Rio de Janeiro*, and 30 other newspapers, a chain of 18 television and 30 radio stations, its own news agency, advertising agency and public relations firms and several of Brazil's leading magazines – including *O Cruzeiro* (modelled on *Life*) which, until 1967 was Latin America's biggest selling magazine.

However, the Chateaubriand group disintegrated with the death of its founder and another media group, Globo, had by the early 1970s achieved an even more dominant position in the Brazilian media. Globo Television was set up with United States Time-Life money and personnel.[17] The direct United States involvement was subsequently removed, but not before Globo had taken advantage of US money and management experience to achieve an extraordinary ascendancy for a single commercial company in the television of a nation the size of Brazil.

Perhaps even more dominant in Mexico is the Televisa group. In Mexico in 1972 the Azcarraga–O'Farrill partnership controlled Televisa, with about two-thirds of Mexico's television stations;

---

* In 1971 of 15 Associated Press 'gatekeepers' (in practice bureau chiefs) only 7 were US citizens and of these 7 two had Spanish surnames and native fluency in Spanish. Of the remaining 8 the nationalities were Argentinian, Bolivian, Cuban, Mexican. See Hester (1974), p. 94.

Romulo O'Farrill junior also owned three Mexico City dailies, including *Novedades* and *The News*, and radio interests. Emilio Azcarraga, who died in 1972, was, besides being the leading figure in both Mexican radio and television, the owner of a cinema chain, the Aztec stadium, and some hotels. Azcarraga and O'Farrill were linked in Televisa (another merger following competition) with a leading Mexican heavy industry and financial combine, the 'Monterrey Group', and also were part-owners of the main Spanish-language television group within the United States.

While Argentinian media exports and protectionism continue, Mexico has become the leading Latin American exporter especially of films and television programming. Mexico is well placed in relation to the small Central American states and to Colombia and Venezuela. Mexico also has some highly distinctive popular music – which can be heard direct on radio in these countries. The Mexican film industry regularly makes off-shore productions in Colombia – with the usual double motive of appealing to a strong export market while using its cheaper production facilities. Mexico is also the main centre in which American magazines and comics are translated for Spanish editions. Mexico's biggest entrepôt and export role is in television. Imported United States television programming is dubbed into Mexican Spanish both for Mexico and for much of Latin America. American television characters in much of Latin America speak Mexican-accented Spanish, which may have helped to open export markets for Mexico's own television output.

The two early Mexican television stations deliberately sited just across the United States border acquired advertising aimed at Californians and Texans, and these us advertising dollars played a decisive role in Mexican television because both border stations were controlled by the Azcarraga and O'Farrill families.[18] Mexican interests are now involved in domestic us television in New York, San Antonio and Los Angeles and in numerous radio stations, while some 400 United States cinemas show Mexican feature films.*

These incursions of Spanish-language material are small as a proportion of the total domestic United States media. But as seen from Mexico City the balance of media imports and exports looks much more even. Mexican media exports, to Latin America and North America combined, are not negligible in quantity. Moreover, the fairly modest quantities of Mexican media exports into the domestic us market receive higher prices than the floods of us material earn in the Mexican market; thus the Mexican government (which largely controls the film industry) like the major Mexican media entrepren-

---

* Although these 400 cinemas are only 3 per cent or so of the us cinema total, this number is equal to about 23 per cent of the Mexican cinema total.

eurs, will be well aware that, whatever the imbalance in quantity, the peso–dollar imbalance is less marked.

This special position of Mexico in Latin American media – and the special position within Mexico of Televisa – can, as usual, be read in more than one way. Mexico can be seen as a new media imperialist in its own right; it can be seen as balancing imports and exports and thus sustaining its independence; or the Mexican government and Mexican media tycoons can be regarded as a peripheral élite carrying out within Latin America a divide-and-rule policy on behalf of the metropolitan élite in New York. What seems incontrovertible is that the Mexican media have a special relationship with those of the United States.

CHAPTER ELEVEN

Communist nations, defensive posture

China and the Soviet Union and their immediate communist neighbouring countries contain over one-third of the world's population – and constitute the most obvious exception to the general thesis of this book. But all of the major communist-governed nations previously had media systems based on Anglo-American models. All had an Anglo-American-style press, all were invaded by Hollywood silent films, and all, except the USSR, established their radio systems under strong western influence.

When the communist governments came to power in each of these countries they inherited a heavily western-influenced media pattern, which has been a fundamental problem in subsequent attempts to shut out foreign media influences. All communist governments have adopted *nationalist* solutions, and most have had to contend with internal ethnic and regional problems. The Soviet Union has not only been unable to market or distribute its media on a world-wide basis; it has had difficulties in getting the east European governments to import more than token amounts.

Moscow has been faced with enormous dilemmas within the non-Russian speaking regions of the USSR. But also in eastern Europe there is a long tradition of looking to the west and regarding New York, London, Paris and Berlin as both cultural and entertainment centres of a sort which Moscow has difficulty in matching. The communist tradition gives more media emphasis to education and information and less to entertainment than does the west. Thus the Anglo-American media – with their entertainment and commercial emphasis – have, at least in attracting audience attention, competitive advantages. The communist media, with a much lower stress on market-place competition are, not surprisingly, weak at competing in the world market with western media.

The communist countries largely or wholly place the media in the keeping of the State and the Party. This gives communist media systems a central characteristic common to most one-party states. In communist countries the *national news agency* is the backbone of the whole media system.

THE MEDIA IN COMMUNIST NATIONS, 1947-8

The general weakness, and inevitably defensive posture, of the communist nations' media can be illustrated by considering the position they were in during 1947-8, the high tide of American world media dominance. The USSR, China and eastern Europe alike had less developed media systems than had the main western nations; and, from the late 1940s well on into the 1950s, their main media concern was to repair the enormous war-time destruction and to carry the media to their own populations.

The Soviet Union had a fairly well-developed newspaper press but in other respects its media – 30 years after 1917 – were still thinly spread. Even the Soviet press in 1948 used less newsprint than Britain (whose newspapers at that time were skinny, but numerous). Soviet magazines were few. The Soviet film industry was still suffering badly from war-time destruction and peace-time shortages. In 1948 the Soviet industry made less than 20 feature films – less not only than India, Japan and China, but less than Mexico, Argentina, Burma, Egypt or the Philippines. In the world league table for radio sets per population the USSR came 38th equal with Colombia – behind seven other Latin American countries.

Nor were the media in a much better state in eastern Europe. Poland, for example, was almost bereft of any media except newspapers. Czechoslovakia – at the time of the 1948 coup – had more widely spread national media than did the USSR; it was even making a comparable number of feature films – and in Czechoslovakia radio sets were four times as common as in the Soviet Union.

The media acquired by the communist forces in China were heavily focused on the cities but nevertheless larger in total than the media of all west European countries except Britain, France and Germany. A 1947 Unesco report claims a total daily newspaper sale of 4·5 million – which put China seventh equal in the world, with Canada; half of this sale was in Shanghai and Nanking. China was also making about 50 feature films a year and had both a network of state radio stations, and 29 private commercial stations carrying advertising. Imports of American feature films were in 1947 still substantial. English-language newspapers still flourished. It was common to find Chinese journalists who had been to American schools of journalism. The US Information Service operated a news service in 12 Chinese cities;[1] and American soldiers were still on the streets, scattering chewing-gum and comic books.

Stalin in 1947-8 preferred to go without rather than import western media, but that was not yet the position in eastern Europe. In 1948

Czechoslovakia and Hungary got half their films from the US, Britain and France (Table 9). The post-1945 radio word war was still in its phoney war phase. The American military radio effort was still directed at its own homesick boys in Germany and elsewhere; the BBC was still the leader in external broadcasting hours.

While Stalin, the Red Army and their friends in eastern Europe were establishing new communist regimes they seem to have had neither the motive, nor the resources, for a big effort in the media. When that effort did come, there was little alternative in international terms to making it a defensive one.

THE SOVIET UNION, 1917–56: SHUTTING OUT FOREIGN MEDIA

Until 1917 Russia had been part of the European and American media system in two respects. Its main news agency was linked to the world cartel, and its film industry was dominated from France. The Russian press was backward and politically repressed by the standards of Britain or France, but in scale it was probably one of the largest in eastern or southern Europe. St Petersburg in 1900 had about a dozen daily newspapers and a total sale of 300,000.[2] There had also been an exile press and an underground press inside Russia. Although Tsarist control of the press was soon replaced with communist party control, it took much longer to establish complete control of the film industry.

The great bulk of screen time eight years after the Revolution of 1917 was still occupied by Hollywood films. This comment is from an American visitor to Moscow in 1925:

> For American films dominate, inundate, glut, overwhelm the Russian motion picture houses today. Clara Kimball Young has a theater devoted solely to her in Moscow. In the Arbat, center of the workers' quarter of the Russian capital, a new building celebrates the glory of Douglas Fairbanks in electric letters three feet high. In the leading workers' club and a dozen other places Mary Pickford holds forth. And so on throughout the list of American stars, from one end of Soviet Russia to the other.[3]

In Leninist tradition the main medium (in support of oral agitation) is the press. This view in practice turns the national news agency into the core of the entire media system. TASS now feeds home and foreign news plus pictures to newspapers and radio/TV; it links the centre with regional news agencies; it provides special secret news services to party, government and foreign policy élites; TASS is also the Soviet international agency – engaged in exchange agreements with all the world agencies.

Stalin's media policies involved heavy concentration on newspapers and films. The press was, and is still, arranged in the form of an enormous official pyramid; at the top of the pyramid are *Pravda* (the party paper), *Izvestia* (the government paper) and the young communist paper – all three reach all parts of the USSR. Other important papers cover individual Soviet republics or particular interest areas. At the bottom of the pyramid are non-daily local or factory papers. The top of the pyramid provides a political lead for all below, and the entire press is tied into the communist party because editors normally sit on the appropriate party committee, while many other journalists are party members. The new wine of a communist underground *Party* press was poured into the old bottles of the authoritarian Tsarist *government* press. In the resulting party-cum-government press, marketing policies were heavily subordinate to political goals. The leading papers were widely distributed and subsidized, print-runs were set irrespective of consumer demand, and sugaring of the political pill was minimal; the press was systematically deployed for political agitation and political education at each level of Soviet society.

In the early 1920s literacy levels were still low, and perhaps as few as a quarter of all adults were literate in Russian (as opposed to other languages). Posters and the silent cinema at first were especially appropriate media, but the continuing preference for visual media, rather than radio, seems to have been mistaken. Heavy emphasis on radio, after about 1930, would have been more effective than talkie films in the multi-lingual USSR. But the top leadership favoured films – although during the 1930s purges the production of new Soviet films slowed to a trickle. The films were the only Soviet medium to have 'repelled' a substantial American invasion; the film medium seems to have acquired a special aura of national success, political virtue and artistic achievement.

The Soviet Union in 1930 had 500,000 radio sets – about the same as Sweden or Argentina and on a population basis only a tiny fraction of their levels. Throughout the Stalin era the media were given fairly low priority in Soviet planning.

Up to the death of Stalin the Soviet Union was not in a position to export much media influence to the rest of the world – indeed it still had a long way to go in providing a basic media coverage for its own people. During the mid-1950s the Soviet press and film industry grew quite rapidly; and there was a steady growth of Soviet television – although through the 1950s it only roughly kept pace with Mexico's.[4]

Soviet external broadcasting hours actually declined between 1952 and 1955; it was only the Hungarian uprising of 1956 which led to a sustained increase in Soviet external broadcasting and a doubling in hours in the next decade.

EASTERN EUROPE

The media of eastern Europe are the source of numerous anxieties both for the communist authorities in each particular country, and for the Soviet leaders. There are three logical possibilities. Each east European country could depend upon the Soviet Union and its east European neighbours for media; it could become self-sufficient; or it could depend heavily upon the west. What has tended to emerge is a series of shifting compromises between these alternatives, with a good deal of stress on self-sufficiency.

Yugoslavia has since 1950 switched fairly decisively to dependence on the west for its media imports.* Two east European countries – Bulgaria and East Germany have relied heavily for imports on the Soviet Union. The flexible compromise path has been largely followed by Poland, Czechoslovakia, Hungary and Romania.

This compromise between the east, self-sufficiency, and the west, also involves a different balance in different media. In the press substantial self-sufficiency can be exercised through a strong national news agency which can choose its foreign news from both western and eastern agencies. National radio output is heavily domestic but has to compete with foreign radio, notably the siren sound of the western pop-and-politics stations. One way of partly drowning out foreign radio has been to boost television and to make the bulk of programming at home; for imports on TV there has been a tendency in the less strongly 'committed' central countries to draw imports quite heavily from both east and west. Only in feature films have these nations not tried to make the bulk of their material at home – and here there is again a mix of east and west; but eastern Europe makes a fair proportion of its own films – once more stressing the powerful national self-sufficiency drive even in this expensive medium.†

Newspapers throughout eastern Europe grew up on the same pattern as in western, or at least southern, Europe. Poland and Czechoslovakia have proud press histories in the western tradition.

* Tanjug, the Yugoslav national news agency, has long been much more dependent upon the Anglo-American than upon the communist news agencies. See Robinson (1971). According to Varis (1973, p. 127) Yugoslavia in 1970 took 84 per cent of her TV imports from the capitalist camp. Yugoslavia has also been a site for Hollywood off-shore film-making.

† In 1971–2 Bulgaria was making 17 features a year, the Czechs 36, Poland 25, Romania 15, Hungary 19, and Jugoslavia 26. See Unesco (1975).

Eastern Europe also used to get most of its world news sieved through the west European agency cartel.

With German interludes during the two world wars, Hollywood films supplied much of the east European film market from 1910 to 1949. In the early 'fifties these imports fell, but there was a fresh flurry of importing of Hollywood TV series around 1960, which then also reduced. American and British pop music has long strongly appealed to young people in eastern Europe. The Polish or Hungarian pop fan has been able to listen to the western propaganda radios, AFN in West Germany and the domestic radios of Austria, Sweden, Yugoslavia, Greece and Turkey. He can also choose among such western pop music as is available on the radios of east European neighbours. Jazz, once frowned on, is now respectable and Poland has a well-known annual international jazz festival. Official anxiety in eastern Europe has shifted towards the great popularity of rock music – equally strong, some reports say, among schoolchildren as among young communist party officials.

The western radios have been relatively little jammed in eastern Europe (compared with USSR). Especially clear evidence of both the appeal of western radio, and official Soviet anxiety about it, was provided during the Hungarian uprising of 1956 and the Czechoslovak events of 1968. A summary of public opinion polls conducted by Czechoslovak research organizations during the Prague Spring suggests that most members of the public did like the new pattern of media; one poll indicated that only communist party officials thought the Czech media had gone too far.[5]

The notion that Polish audiences should be allowed only a carefully controlled ration of the all-too-seductive western media fare is made in this early 1960s statement of the official view:

Between 1949–55 all entertainment was treated by cultural policy as predominantly instrumental, fulfilling strictly a propagandistic and manipulatory function. . . . With 1956 came the recognition of the autonomous entertainment function of mass culture. And formerly banished media such as: detective stories, sentimental pulp-novels, radio family serials, Wild West films, now make their appearance in Polish mass culture.

. . . Crime stories, for instance, no matter how profitable from a commercial viewpoint, are published in editions trailing far behind demand. . . . The sensational material a regular magazine may carry is always accompanied by informational and educational articles. . . . There is no such thing either as Comics for young people, and only a few popular dailies carry some comic strips.

An analysis of the content of the serials covered by most Polish dailies shows that many of them are of the detective story type. Of the 82 serials published in 1962, 41 were of this type and 3 acts of violence were noted per novel. . . . This is not a high percentage in comparison with the frequency of acts of violence on US television. . . .

. . . episodes of violence on Polish television are under strict control. A special sensational programme is presented at night once in two weeks. . . .

The method of sublimating sensational trends characteristic of Polish mass culture consists in the substitution of mass episodes of the last war . . . for crime programmes . . . Polish magazines try not to fall below the level defined as middle brow by exacting critics. . . .

The specific tone of mass culture in Poland is not that it lacks any elements strongly resembling the content of Western mass culture. . . . In the exploitation of domestic material the law of supply and demand has no free operation (despite certain commercial temptations). . . .

No one reads brutal and vulgar comics since the prevailing mass culture supplies no such material. Fans of American Westerns see the better kind of such films since only such are shown on the screens. Those addicted to sensational literature get it in the newspapers and magazines in small doses, always in the company of other, proportionately greater features. . . .

It is possible to attain the above owing to the monopoly character of the system of mass culture, subjected to administrative control. . . .

This method probably does not guarantee the continuous moulding of public taste. It consists of elimination of the temptation of worse choice, not the inculcation of the infallible habit to choose higher values.[6]

The result, as in many compromises, was ambiguous. In 1960 Poland was importing films approximately equally from west and east.*[7]

Although eastern and western imports roughly balanced in 1972, when the Polish films were added the eastern proportion became 58 per cent. But 40 per cent of all films were from capitalist countries; the east European films came mainly from the more doubtful countries in Soviet eyes, and only 16 per cent of all films shown in the most populous country in eastern Europe came from the USSR.

Hungary's pattern of both film and television imports was similarly

* In 1972 all feature films shown in Poland came from these sources: Poland 14 per cent; USSR 16 per cent; other east European countries 28 per cent; USA 12 per cent; west Europe and Japan 28 per cent; other 2 per cent. Total = 100 per cent. Total number = 179. See Unesco (1975).

ambiguous. Hungary in 1971 was importing about 40 per cent of its television. Of hours identified, Varis found 44 per cent of TV imports from the west (UK, France, W. Germany, Italy, USA) and 39 per cent from the east (USSR, GDR, Poland, Czechoslovakia, Yugoslavia) and 17 per cent from 'other countries'.[8] The bulk of educational and information programming came from the east while the bulk of entertainment imports came from the west. While the west thus probably pulls the larger audience, ideological honour is presumably satisfied.

CHINA: CAPITALIST MEDIA

The Chinese media, even more than the Russian, have western and Anglo-American origins. The first modern newspapers in China were the work of Americans, Britons and west Europeans – these were either missionary papers or the traditional Anglo-American seaport newsheets. The *China Mail*, launched in 1845 from Hong-Kong, was the best known.[9] In 1870 Shanghai had two English-language dailies and several weeklies. The first major Chinese newspaper, *Shun Pao*, was founded in Shanghai in 1872 – by a British merchant, Frederick Major. But from this time onwards a Chinese-owned press developed rapidly. The China Coast press seeded the modern Japanese press, but also continued for longer under western and especially British leadership. For many years what the world heard of China was controlled from London by *The Times* and Reuters.[10]

By 1930 a substantial foreign-language daily press – primarily in English – continued on the China coast but there were by now perhaps one thousand Chinese dailies. Amongst these numerous small Chinese publications there were many signs of influence from the English-language press. An American commentator noted a swing towards American style 'affirmative' headlines (rather than former British models); a publisher back from the Columbia School of Journalism was trying to adapt the pyramid make-up style to Chinese characters; there were Chinese magazines based on many American formats including *Time*,[11] and enormous quantities of news about Britain and Europe. The agencies filled up much space:

> Not infrequently on days of tense struggles diplomatic and military, the chief newspapers have virtually been given over entirely to cable and telegraph news.
>   . . . It is not uncommon to see on one page or at least one issue of a paper dispatches from six or eight news agencies, all dealing with the same event and all carried in full . . . in addition to the professional services of United Press and Reuters, dispatches are available at little or no cost from the Japanese Rengo, the French

Havas, the German Trans-Ocean, the Russian TASS, and a lot of other lightly camouflaged propaganda press agencies, masquerading as news associations.[12]

The Kuomintang founded in 1925 what was to be for twenty years the dominant force in Chinese journalism – the Central News Agency. It had special government support and access; it alone had a China-wide network of correspondents. It drove major financial news agencies out of business[13] and became Chiang Kai-shek's chosen instrument for dominating the press. Foreign-language papers were allowed some leeway, although they also were threatened by increasingly severe censorship during the 1930s. The only other licensed deviant after 1937 was the communist *New China Daily* which was established in KMT-held areas as one of the terms of the communist–KMT coalition of 1937. The paper was under the direct supervision of Chou En-lai until its removal from Chungking to Yenan in 1947.[14]

The Chinese film industry was heavily influenced by Hollywood throughout much of its history. By 1920 a domestic Chinese feature film industry already existed, but in Shanghai – the centre of this Chinese industry – western businessmen had complete control of the main cinemas and American films predominated. Many early Chinese film-makers had European or American training. In the four years 1928–31 the Shanghai industry made 400 feature films of which 250, and nearly all the financial successes, were 'a Chinese version of the most popular of all American film forms, the "western" '. And despite this sizeable Chinese industry, 90 per cent of the films shown in China in 1929 were American made.[15] The arrival of the talkies produced new American influences; the 1930s Chinese film industry was firmly tied to the 'star' system. In 1937 85 per cent of all films shown in China came from Hollywood.[16] During the Japanese occupation the Chinese film studios continued their production; many directors prominent in the post-1948 Chinese film industry made films under Japanese tutelage – thus involving further infusions of foreign, and indirectly American, influence.[17]

In 1931 Chinese commercial radio was just getting under way, as this description of one of Shanghai's then three radio stations indicates:

China Broadcast (Ltd.) is sponsored by Reuters (Ltd.), worldwide news service, and Millington (Ltd.), an established British firm of advertising agents. . . . The actual operation and management of the station is under the direction of an American. . . . The method of handling programs will be patterned after that of American chains. Reuters (Ltd.) will supply foreign news and a commercial service. . . . A band of 12 instrumentalists has been engaged to provide musical selections. . . .

It has been unofficially estimated that there are approximately 5,000 radio sets in use in Shanghai. . . .

There are two other broadcasting stations operating in Shanghai, which have facilities for advertising by radio. . . .

Programs are broadcast in both English and Chinese, and announcements are made in both languages. Records prepared in the English language may be used effectively in Shanghai.[18]

Many of the people prominent in the Chinese media after 1948 must have been quite familiar with certain basic approaches of radio advertising – simplicity, the emotional appeal, repetition – approaches which after 1948 were again used, although with different messages.

MEDIA IN COMMUNIST CHINA

The media of China are said to have solved most of the classic media dilemmas of poor nations. The Chinese are claimed to have carried the media to the people and to have avoided media importing.

But this ability by the 1960s to achieve media self-sufficiency clearly follows a long history of importing media styles and products. Press, films and radio were all founded by westerners on western models. The pattern of a far-flung newspaper press orchestrated by a national news agency was one which the communist regime inherited from its predecessors. It was a pattern also used by the Japanese in the regions they occupied; many of the radio sets in China in 1948 had been distributed by the Japanese to allow listening to their broadcasts. After 1948 the strong central media pattern was further consolidated during the period of active Soviet involvement in the Chinese economy (when, of course, the media in Soviet Asia were still fairly rudimentary). But despite these ensuing waves of foreign influence, traditional popular Chinese elements were also strengthened.

The new communist regime at first set out to expand the Chinese mass media on the Soviet model. Later they modified the hierarchical Soviet procedures and put more emphasis on mobilizing the peasants. A major effort was aimed at getting at least *some* mass media into all the villages of China – not into private homes, but to get radio loudspeakers, wall newspapers and occasional film shows into every village street; as many as 10,000 copies are made of a single film for showing in villages.[19]

Communist China has never been entirely cut off from western mass media influence. Hong-Kong is an especially favourable listening post from which to tune in to western media offerings – such as commercial television or news agency operations. Throughout the period 1950–70 Peking also imported samples of the Hong-Kong film industry's output (mainly from its communist studios). Nor should it be thought that the pre-1948 influences of American media had all disappeared by the 1960s. This is an observation of Jay Leyda who lived in Peking from 1959 to 1964:

> The clearest lessons taught by films to another medium (and vice versa!) appeared in the picture-story books – a child of ancient illustrated literature and the comic books introduced to China by American soldiers. Chinese picture-story books of the 1960s still show stylistic traces of Harold Foster's *Tarzan* and *Prince Valiant* and (even!) Milton Caniff's *Terry and the Pirates*. . . . By the 1960s it was not unusual to see adults depending on the pictorial supports of this dubious literature that seemed to increase the dangers of simplification. And children read little else.[20]

Nor was Hollywood's influence absent from the Chinese film industry according to this author who has, from the inside, written books on both the Soviet and Chinese communist film industries. Here is his account of one of the first Chinese films he saw in Peking in 1959:

> *Song of Youth* was an enormously successful novel, recommended for every young Chinese to read for its treatment of the student movement of the 'thirties. . . . My first shock was to see its heroine treated as the starring actress of a typical American film. No Hollywood star has been more isolated and artificially illuminated than this unreal central figure. . . . While looking at the film I imagined that it must have been directed by an old director who had seen too many American films, but I have since learned that it is a first film by the actor Tsui Wei. . . . The influence of Hollywood, and in one of its worst aspects, was a shock. First, it contradicted everything that I heard and read here about the poisons and falsehoods of Hollywood being discarded by a revolutionary, bold, new Chinese cinema.[21]

China has relatively little internal language and cultural variation – very much less than the Soviet Union or India; the aggressive approach to the domestic media is probably in less danger of stirring up separatist and regional conflict than such a policy would have elsewhere. China also possessed in 1948 a more elaborate media industry than did any other nation in Africa or Asia (except Japan).

Although China did have large cities where the media were concentrated, there were major provincial media as well. China has also been somewhat unusual in the extent to which it has closed the doors to media imports and has been able largely to shut out foreign governmental radio. Considerable United States radio efforts have been aimed at China, but they appear to have been less determined and less successful than those aimed at the USSR and eastern Europe. One very simple reason is that China borrowed from the Soviet Union the idea of the wired receiver which provides a limited choice of domestic stations only. China also does not have the problem of the more industrially and educationally advanced USSR where it is practically impossible to prevent, for example, engineering graduates listening to foreign broadcasts if they are determined to do so. China not only has fewer radio sets (as opposed to wired receivers) than does the USSR but it has less widely diffused electronic and photographic apparatus capable of reproducing foreign materials.

In accounting for the success or otherwise of the Chinese media, the obvious case for comparison is India. The Chinese were more fortunate than the Indians. The scale of the Chinese media in 1948 was already larger and the subsequent Soviet infusions made for a still larger base. The Chinese language and cultural problems were simpler; the Chinese were confronted with high and low forms, with at least two major languages or distinct versions of Chinese, and with some important minority languages – but all of these problems were small compared with India's. The relative cultural and linguistic unity of China thus allowed a vigorous national policy towards further integration without the clear danger in India of cultural nationalism and separatist conflict.

Their different experiences in coming to power inevitably gave the Chinese communists and the Indian Congress different views of the media. The Indian Congress adopted a basically western pamphleteering non-violent approach, which led to strong intellectual strains in the post-independence media – both British Fabian and traditional Hindu; in China the experience was of foreign war, civil war and insurgency – and the media were seen as playing a supporting role in the main military, political and word-of-mouth struggle to win the countryside. Mao himself acquired an anti-intellectual streak which was helpful for establishing popular media.

Both India and China in 1948 had, by the then standards of most countries, a large press and a large radio sector. The Chinese clearly were more effective at stretching these existing media out of the provincial cities and into the countryside. The contrast is especially great in films. Whereas the Indian film industry carried on along its immensely popular path, it remained largely independent of government direction and separate from the other media. But in China the equally large and equally Hollywood-influenced film industry was geared to ideological purposes in line with press and radio.

While the Chinese media have reached the villages more effectively this has happened in a fairly crude form. There are still enormous rural–urban differences in Chinese media. And China has a separate élite pattern of media, more clearly demarcated than anything in India. Although quite cautious in expanding television, China – unlike India – expanded TV to the dozen largest cities in the 1960s, and did so on the effective basis of a closed circuit medium for the élite. China also has its *People's Daily* for the ideological instruction of national and regional administrators. China has given an even more commanding position to the New China News Agency (Hsinhua), because it provides the basic national and international news service even to the élite ideological press; the agency also provides for the élite a separate daily gazette, which is not on public sale – this is again on the TASS model, but with wider distribution. There is no similarly centralized or élite equivalent in India, which (at least until 1975) had considerable competition among its serious political publications.

At present China is more or less self-sufficient in media. Unlike the USSR, China has a 'natural' foreign market among the overseas Chinese of south-east Asia – currently catered for by regional mini-Hollywoods, especially in Hong-Kong. But while potential importers in the Third World might admire China in general, they might still object to the strong ideological colouring of Chinese films when subtitled or dubbed into a language understood locally.

Meanwhile China's main exporting and importing of media since 1960 has been in its radio war with the Soviet Union. Here, as elsewhere, the Chinese media have been vigorously aimed at the provinces and countryside – the objective has been no less than to foster non-Russian nationalism and to encourage separatist tendencies in Soviet Asia. A BBC source described this Soviet–Chinese confrontation as 'probably the most hostile and extensive radio confrontation of its kind in the history of international broadcasting'.[22]

SINCE 1956: SOVIET UNION'S DEFENSIVE MEDIA POSTURE

Since 1956 when the Soviet Union's media were still quite thinly spread there has been an enormous expansion in all media fields. Most Soviet households now contain a TV set, have one or two radio sets and take one or two daily newspapers plus weekly publications. The USSR also has one of the world's largest film industries and an annual cinema attendance several times that of the USA. While Soviet publications are still thinner than American ones, and Soviet TV sets offer fewer channels, nevertheless this is the only country which rivals the USA on several media league tables.

This enormous media apparatus has been built up in the last two decades as a result of enormous official Soviet anxiety. The not fully complete success in shutting out all foreign media has been achieved at the cost of adopting a wide range of American practices and dropping or downplaying traditional Marxist-Leninist notions of the media. To beat the capitalists, the Soviet Union has had to join in many of their entertainment formulae.

The contagion of foreign media now comes from east and west. It comes not only from the USA, Britain, West Germany and their friends, but also from China and eastern Europe. Hungary, Czechoslovakia, Romania and Poland are all not only rather western in orientation but they also share land borders with the Soviet Union. Their media are inevitably appealing to the non-Russian-speaking minorities inside this sensitive Soviet border. But although at certain points – such as 1956 and 1968 – these neighbouring media have been the most worrying, over the whole period the Anglo-American radios have been even more disturbing.

The enormous size of the Soviet Union made the use of short-wave radio receivers commonplace, especially after the mid-1950s. But short-wave radios allow listening to foreign stations. Both internal Soviet surveys and external American surveys of Soviet travellers indicate that at least occasional listening to these stations is very widespread.[23] (A later chapter considers this effort from the western side.) The Soviet authorities have taken the Anglo-American radio threat extremely seriously. Jamming, which ceased for some five years, began again in August 1968, and is unambiguous evidence of very serious concern. Jamming is much more expensive than the broadcast it seeks to jam. Jamming as a policy indicates a long-term attitude beyond mere defensiveness, closer perhaps to permanent desperation; it is virtually an admission of defeat.

An attempt to drown out these foreign broadcasts was one major motive behind the great 1960s media expansion. More attractive western-style radio formulae were adopted, and in some cases broadcast on frequencies used by foreign stations. Newspapers and magazines became more available and readable. The cinema industry was given a high priority; and for those who insisted on staying at home, television was vastly expanded – throughout all the regions, languages and time zones of the Soviet Union. Television was largely relieved of ideological duties and let loose to *entertain* the Soviet masses. The most popular fare on Soviet TV are the many films, quizzes, and variety shows; news and actuality programming is less popular; economic, educational and ideological programming is least popular of all.[24] Apart from a distinct lack of imported entertainment series, Soviet television does not greatly differ from television in western Europe.

The main ideological burden has been left to the press and radio. News poses the greatest problems. 'News' is an Anglo-American market-based concept. It does not fit comfortably into a Soviet system. There was no problem so long as the Soviet media avoided this alien notion, and used the press as an extension of oral agitation. But competition from foreign radio stations became increasingly embarrassing in the late 1950s and early 1960s. If Soviet citizens could not get adequate and rapid supplies of bad news from the Soviet media, they naturally listened to the foreign broadcasts – thus went the revisionist argument. The solution was cautiously to adopt some western news practices – radio news on the hour for example; attempts were made to avoid lengthy delays while events were allotted an official interpretation. Disasters were opened up for immediate off-the-cuff coverage.

But an example of the difficulty of teaching Soviet journalists capitalist tricks is provided by the Tashkent earthquake of April 1966. The earthquake destroyed much of the city, thousands of homes collapsed, hundreds of people were killed, and over one million people were directly affected. On the day after the disaster two journalists – from All-Union Radio and *Pravda Vostoka* (chief paper of the Uzbek communist party) had visited the area, interviewed the local seismic station manager and assessed the extent of the devastation. But the radio from Moscow merely reported the earthquake as having caused little damage. Journalists on the scene accepted the apparent decision to play down the disaster, not to inflame passions (in a sensitive border region), not to create a sensation. But it was then announced by central radio in Moscow that a major disaster had in fact occurred, and that Comrades Brezhnev and Kosygin were flying to Tashkent to assess the damage and to launch a major relief effort. Journalists now felt free to tell the Soviet public for the first time the extent of the disaster.[25] An enquiry was later mounted as to how such important news had not been instantly reported.

This media system constructed on a classic German–Tsarist–Stalinist bureaucratic pattern was designed to have instructions poured in at the top end. Such an apparatus cannot suddenly be re-programmed to take in news at the opposite end. The same difficulty arises in the Soviet adoption of media audience research. Predictably the Soviet media, like media elsewhere, only got interested in research-ing the audience when there was serious competition for that audi-ence's attention. American sociology and survey methods were quickly pressed into action. Names such as Paul Lazarsfeld were heard in the corridors of Soviet media power; and the survey results started to emerge. Like other survey results these ones did not please the people who commissioned the work. The Soviet media were none too popular, and foreign radio was too seductive. Some results were published, others were leaked to the west, others remained secret. Predictably not only did the findings then become even more sensitive, but the propriety of adopting this capitalist pseudo-scientific approach, this asking people what they liked, was challenged.

Faced by such appalling dilemmas, it is hardly surprising that the Soviet Union is a weak media exporter – with the partial exception of eastern Europe. No nation can more than marginally separate its domestic from its export media. The American trick is always to assume that if they go for it in Iowa and Illinois, they'll go for it worldwide. The Soviet media controllers have no such illusions; they're not at all sure that what's offered will go down at home, let alone abroad.

This is not merely a problem of the Soviet system lacking a place for Anglo-American concepts of news or audience research. The dilemma goes deeper still. The muted version of the American media which prevails in the Soviet Union has not merely muted – so far as possible – American commercial media values; the Soviet media system also mutes communist values. This all-embracing entertainment machine, with communist trappings pinned on, deviates from and is a threat to traditional Marxist-Leninist interpretations of the media. Under Marxist-Leninist principles the media are an appendage of the communist party, its organization, its oral agitation and political education. The American-style media system, towards which the Soviet Union has reluctantly lurched, makes different political assumptions – one of which is that the media perform many of the functions which the party performs in a traditional communist state. The thought that the modern media may indeed be intrinsically American is one which haunts, and will continue to haunt, the Soviet leaders.

CHAPTER TWELVE

Media knowledge, professionalism and value neutrality

VALUE NEUTRALITY AS IDEOLOGY

The Anglo-American media – operating in the fields of politics, entertainment, culture and commerce on a world scale – cannot possibly be 'value neutral'; but these media do stick, or are widely believed to stick, to the convention of value neutrality. They operate on an 'as if' basis – as if it were possible to be value neutral. This contributes powerfully to the 'least worst' reputation of the Anglo-American media. If you have to import news, entertainment and advertising at all – as most nations in practice do – then your least unpleasant choice may be to use the Anglo-American material and styles.

In these transactions many small forms of deception and self-deception are common. Nevertheless, the Anglo-American media are in general more open, more capable of inspection and assessment, more capable of being selected from and altered, than are most other media. Their enormous world presence alone makes them highly visible; and the conventions of neutrality upon which they operate are more-or-less well understood.

The political basis of neutrality derives from a political character-istic of the United States and Britain, shared by fairly few other countries; whereas most other countries either have only one party or have many parties, the Anglo-American tradition is of just *two* dominant parties – hence such phrases as '*both sides*', and 'playing it down the middle'. Within this usually two-party system both the British and American media have been detached from the two parties, and from the government, to an extent generally unknown elsewhere. Steering between Republicans and Democrats or steering between Conservative and Liberal (or Labour) is a characteristic especially strong in those Anglo-American media which operate on the world stage; this may seem a flimsy basis for steering between the vastly more complex political currents on the world scene. But it is a stronger one – or is widely thought to be a stronger basis for political neutrality – than is the case with media originating in Moscow or Peking, in Buenos Aires or Madrid, in Havana or Cairo, in Accra or New Delhi, in Paris or Bonn.

The scientific basis for neutrality derives mainly from technology but also from social science. Technology is indeed neutral in that technology alone determines nothing. Space satellites and talkie films and printing presses can support capitalism or communism. But the configuration into which various pieces of technology are arranged and made internationally available reflects the values – political, social and commercial – of the nation where the system was first established. Social science 'neutrality' is also far from unimportant here; 'objective fact', whether in market research or in policy recommendations derived from academic social science, is not utterly fictional, although, of course, far also from value free. Social science neutrality can tie itself into some peculiar knots. One school of American social scientists who study the 'diffusion of innovations' implicitly assume that any innovation – be it birth control, new crop varieties, radio listening, toothpaste, or land reform – can be studied in the same way; such scientific neutrality towards the particular message may seem unreal or bizarre. But most regimes find it more acceptable to be told implicitly that 'innovations' (defined as anything which is new in some way and measurable in some way) is a good thing, than to be told that Ghanaian nationalism or Moscow communism is a good thing.

There is also a commercial aspect to value neutrality. This is the 'we'll do business with anyone' syndrome. If they pay they can have it. Commercial motives are relatively uncomplicated and unthreatening, compared with overt political motives.

All of these value neutral elements fit together and are more or less consistent. Having media detached from party and government and having media basically commercially organized seems more or less consistent. The resulting media are not really value free; they are urban rather than rural; they present WASP culture with some Jewish, Latin and Black support; they are supported by closely interwoven commercial and social science research; Anglo-American media neutrality forms a marriage of convenience with Unesco media neutrality. Neutrality carries with it the notion of 'professional' autonomy for communicators which makes it flattering to and acceptable to most journalists and producers in most countries. This media value neutrality involves some choice and flexibility between British and American alternatives; and it is carried around the world through the vehicle of the English language. Language is important to value neutrality and not least in the establishment of phrases like 'free flow of communication' as meaningful. The possibility of establishing such terminology internationally itself derives from the prominence of value neutral American writing on the media, and the propulsion of this knowledge around the world through the value neutral Anglo-American media.

KNOWLEDGE: THE AMERICAN MEDIA RESEARCH INDUSTRY

The production of media knowledge and the production of trained 'professional' communicators are two further fields in which the United States has long accounted for over half the world's total output.[1] The two are connected especially through American universities, and in turn they are closely linked to the business conduct of the American media. The Journalism Professor who trains future journalists may also conduct research financed by the media. This alliance contains some internal conflict; but there is a shared ideology – value neutrality.

The production of knowledge about the American media spans social science, market research, law, history, and many other fields of enquiry. It appears in commercially sponsored research reports, academic journals, books. On any count and any definition the quantity is vast. The field is characterized by numerous bibliographies each containing thousands of items, each bibliography often overlapping very little with the next.

But nearly all empirical efforts implicitly accept the main characteristics of the American media industry. The kinds of changes typically advocated – such as somewhat more 'public' television – often seem to European eyes extremely modest.

American media literature when it floods on to the world market may appear diverse, unco-ordinated, idealistic, empirical, and a-theoretical. Virtually all of this American literature does assume an American commercial media system; the highly empirical and somewhat conflicting character of the research is in line with the predominant 'value free' ideology. The great quantity and variety of the evidence means that when anyone anywhere in the world wishes to consider some new media approach or policy, much of the available research tends to be American.

American media knowledge has emerged from several different academic traditions. The oldest of these traditions, the university Journalism School, dates from the early twentieth century. By the early 1970s there were at any one time about 50,000 American undergraduate students 'majoring' in journalism, broadcasting, speech, film, advertising, public relations or some mixture of these. About two-thirds of this number were majoring in journalism although often in a School of Communications or under some other more general (and less narrowly vocational) label. The professors who teach in these journalism and communication schools produce a large quantity of Ph.D. theses, articles and books. And, as is the way in some other academic fields, while American universities are responsible for some of the lowest quality material produced anywhere on these topics, they also produce much of the best literature on the mass media; moreover these findings are in English, they appear in *Journalism Quarterly* and a score of other journals which are widely (and once again, cheaply) available around the world. There is also a flood of books, many of them cheap paperbacks.

The other most internationally significant strand to emerge in American media research is associated with a single individual – Paul Lazarsfeld – and the Bureau of Applied Social Research at Columbia University. This Bureau established the model for the mixed academic and commercial research organization devoted primarily to sample surveys; Lazarsfeld contributed much to the development of the random sample interview survey, the favourite digging tool of both academic social research and commercial market research. Lazarsfeld drew upon both these areas for research funds. The media, and especially radio, happened to be a major common concern of both academic and market research, and radio also was agreed to be a particularly suitable area for sample survey research. Lazarsfeld's radio research occupies a special place in the histories of media research, commercial market research and modern quantitative social science.

Like many of the people who became prominent both in American market research and in academically based survey research, Paul Lazarsfeld was a Jewish refugee from central Europe. In 1937 with a Rockefeller Foundation grant he set up a small research centre at the University of Newark where his associate directors were Frank Stanton (a young CBS research man) and Hadley Cantril (subsequently a pioneer figure in the use of quantitative social science research for American foreign policy purposes). In 1939 Lazarsfeld's 'Office of Radio Research' moved to Columbia University, and in 1945 finally turned into the Bureau of Applied Social Research with this policy remit:

> Emphasis will be on research and training for research. Conducting work under contracts with commercial or other organizations will not be considered inconsistent with this condition provided the research emphasis be maintained.[2]

Lazarsfeld was first attracted to radio and media research by the availability of commercial funds for his quantitative research methods.

In the late 1930s he showed a remarkable ability to attract both research funds and a wide variety of talented young social scientists to carry out the research. Not only did Frank Stanton, subsequently the leading spokesman for the American TV networks, work with Lazarsfeld but so also did T. W. Adorno, subsequently author of *The Authoritarian Personality* and a founding father of the Frankfurt School of Marxist sociology. Lazarsfeld also worked closely with Samuel Stouffer, who was in charge of the US Army studies resulting in the *American Soldier* volumes. Another close collaborator was Robert Merton, the advocate of 'middle range theory' in sociology. Lazarsfeld himself became a founding father of modern political science by designing the first sophisticated voting study – published as *The People's Choice*; it was typical of Lazarsfeld's greater interest in methods than subject matter that this 'panel' research design was at first intended for studying Department of Agriculture radio programmes, but shortly before the November 1940 election was changed into the first panel study of voting behaviour. Throughout the 1940s Paul Lazarsfeld and his colleagues at Columbia were world leaders in the development of survey methods and other forms of quantified data gathering. Gradually, in the late 'forties and early 'fifties the core interest shifted away from mass communications.

Often academics from Lazarsfeld's Bureau designed or conducted all or part of a straight piece of market research but managed to draw on the market research study for an article to be published in an academic journal.[3] Lazarsfeld's connection with American market research had begun before he left Vienna. He was influenced in Vienna by an assistant who had done market research interviewing – on soap – for 'one of the earliest American market research experts' in Vienna.

Commercial radio was the easiest source of research funds because the radio networks needed evidence for use in competition against the entrenched press media. *Radio Research 1941* was the first of three books Lazarsfeld edited with Frank Stanton. Stanton, whose subsequent task as President of CBS was to be its spokesman in the world of news and political public relations, evidently quickly saw the public relations benefits. Frank Stanton supplied CBS finance to two studies of radio; one is reported in Hadley Cantril's *Invasion from Mars* (about the Orson Welles broadcast), the other in Robert Merton's *Mass Persuasion* (a study of how Katie Smith, the radio star, sold $39 million worth of war bonds during a single marathon broadcast). Both studies originated in phone calls from Lazarsfeld to Stanton and both studies, with their rather pedestrian findings and asides of liberal concern, were helpful for CBS radio generally in disarming more sweeping criticisms, whilst exhibiting responsible concern.

Much of the academically most respected media research in the post-war period was financed by, or closely connected with, CBS and other large media organizations. Joseph Klapper's CBS-financed standard work, *The Effects of Mass Communication* (1960), concluded that the media do not create, but mainly reinforce, opinions – a comfortable conclusion for the radio/TV networks. Klapper later became Director of the Office of Social Research at CBS. Frank Stanton financed another Bureau of Applied Social Research study of television, which is reported in Gary Steiner's *The People Look at Television* (1963). This study again tended to deflate criticism – it indicated, for example, that the television-viewing patterns of highly educated Americans were quite similar to those of the lowly educated. This study was replicated by Robert T. Bower's *Television and the Public* (1973). Once again CBS financed the study, the chosen social scientist was not exactly hostile to American television, and the findings broadly favoured the status quo.*

Press media also financed some research classics. *The People's Choice* was partly financed by *Life* magazine which published two feature articles based on the first tabulations. Robert Merton's study of 'Local and Cosmopolitan Influentials' is really about newspaper readers (local influentials) versus news magazine readers (cosmopolitan influentials) and it was financed by *Time* magazine. Elihu Katz and Paul Lazarsfeld's *Personal Influence*, was financed by another magazine company, Macfadden Publications.

The other two main sources of finance used in communications research by Lazarsfeld and his successors were the government and the foundations. Commercial and 'policy' sources of finance enabled Lazarsfeld and his colleagues (who included many of the future leaders of American social science) rapidly to develop a basis of quantitative techniques and hard data – which impressed not only the academic world, but also the worlds of advertising and government.

American mass communications research for many years focused largely on two centres – the Bureau of Applied Research at Columbia, and, from the late 1940s onwards, the Center for International Studies at the Massachusetts Institute of Technology; the latter centre engaged in projects about US media in the world, funded with Washington foreign policy finance. The key intellectual figure in this new style of research was to be Daniel Lerner. Lerner, as a young man, became, during the Second World War, Chief Editor of the Intelligence branch of the Psychological Warfare Division of SHAEF.

---

* For example Bower's study again documented that even the majority of college educated Americans did not watch educational TV even once a week; the study also used questions which, from long experience, are known to produce answers favourable to TV and unfavourable to newspapers.

He wrote a book about this called *Sykewar*, but his most important contribution was *The Passing of Traditional Society* (1958). Based on surveys in Egypt, Iran, Jordan, Lebanon, Syria and Turkey, his book deals with the process of modernization – in which process mass communications is claimed to play a central part. Lerner's book has been one of the most influential in the whole literature on Third World 'development'. This research originally began as six separate studies based on the Bureau of Applied Social Research; the main field work was conducted in 1950–1 (at the height of the Korean war). Lerner, who had originally worked only on the Turkish study, re-analysed all the research reports and finally produced the book in 1958. Not only did this involve re-coding the data, Lerner's book also sharply de-emphasized the overwhelming concern in the original questionnaire with how well American mass media were doing in the contest against Soviet media in the Middle East around 1950 (the western media turned out to be winning easily).

This change of direction, between the USIA Cold War financing of the research and the scholarly final publication, partly explains the uneasy fit between the vague findings and the hard data upon which they are supposedly based. Lerner suggests that there is some vital but unclear connection between urbanization, media development and 'development' generally. His own book had an important media effect – it encouraged unrealistic faith in the potential contribution of the media to economic development. One remarkable aspect of this school of research was the readiness of these American social scientists, often of Jewish origin, to venture forth into a very unstable* Arab world at the height of the Cold War, armed with anti-Soviet research funds; moreover, despite the research's shortcomings, the liberal concern for the Arabs' plight is clearly genuine, and the intellectual quality of the research high.

Another influential book which spans the Colombia Bureau and the MIT Center is *Communications and Political Development* edited in 1963 by Lucian Pye. Pye's and Lerner's books illustrated just how many leading social science figures were involved in these Cold War concerns with mass communications in developing nations.† The research conducted from MIT was following Lazarsfeld in developing

---

* In 1951 alone, for example, political assassinations removed King Abdullah of Jordan, General Ali Razmara (the Prime Minister of Iran) and Ali Khan (Prime Minister of Pakistan). British troops also occupied the Canal Zone of Egypt in 1951.

† Among those acknowledged by Lerner as having provided some help or guidance to *The Passing of Traditional Society* are: Charles Glock, Paul Lazarsfeld, Robert Merton, David Riesman, Ithiel De Sola Pool, William McPhee, David Sills and Herbert Gans. Contributors to Pye's edited volume include: Herbert Hyman, David McClelland and Ed Shils.

a style of research which only those extremely well endowed with research funds could possibly contemplate. Even the study of Soviet or Chinese media from afar obviously involves resources for acquiring huge quantities of Soviet or Chinese newspapers and other publications and long spans of research time in which to study them. The MIT people were active in spreading the results of their research, and they have been much given to conferences. One volume edited by Lerner and Schramm (and complete with a gushing foreword by the then President Lyndon B. Johnson) commemorates such a conference held in Hawaii at the East–West Center and financed by US government funds.

Daniel Lerner, Ithiel de Sola Pool and Wilbur Schramm in the 1960s became a sort of travelling circus – jetting back and forth across the world, advising first this Asian government and then that US federal agency. Daniel Lerner was the intellectual leader of the circus. Ithiel de Sola Pool was the commissar of the group – one of the US Department of Defense's most vigorous academic spokesmen, and a vigorous anti-communist (with not a little admiration for the Chinese and their dedication to efficient propaganda). The third member of the circus was Wilbur Schramm; although the other two were regular travellers, Wilbur Schramm was the travelling salesman. Based at Stanford, Schramm in the 1960s became Unesco's favourite mass media 'expert'.

UNESCO AND THE FREE FLOW OF ANGLO-AMERICAN 'EXPERTS'

The triumph of the 'value-free' American ideology of the media was nowhere more remarkable than in Unesco, the United Nations agency whose areas of activity include the media. Unesco has propagated such American notions as the 'free flow of information', which inevitably favour the major media exporting nation. The most active architects and proponents of Unesco media doctrines have been Americans; they have openly based these doctrines upon American research – despite the commercial advertising and Washington foreign policy strains in the financing of this research.

One should not exaggerate the importance of Unesco. But if some concerted challenge to Anglo-American media were to have emerged in the 1950s or 1960s it would probably have needed at least the support of Unesco.* The likelihood of such a challenge was not increased

* In the mid-1970s there are some signs of a belated challenge from certain elements in Unesco. Whether Unesco will evolve new media policies, which are any more realistically based or soundly planned than those of the past, remains to be seen.

by the early history of the organization and its media policies – which unfolded in the post-1945 period when American world-wide media dominance was at its height, and while the Soviet government under Stalin had still not awoken to the political significance of this policy area. Until 1954 the Soviet Union boycotted Unesco altogether, and even during the next decade the Soviet contributions consisted largely of desultory criticisms and empty rhetoric.[4]

The Anglo-Americans had two of the three first Director-Generals, the other being a Mexican. The British scientist, Julian Huxley, was the first Director-General, and it was during these early years that some remarkably informative media research was done by a Commission on Technical Needs. At this stage Unesco reports were not yet written in deliberately ambiguous prose.

Under Luther H. Evans, an American, and the third Director-General, Unesco took on its characteristic form. Evans favoured the use of outside funds, from the World Bank and other such sources. He introduced an American business management approach – selected 'major projects', decentralization, limited goals and the 'realistic' evaluation of projects on the basis of measurable indicators.

During Evans' reign of 1953–8 none of this had much impact on world media, but his style carried over into the first serious Unesco media effort, which coincided with the great wave of newly independent nations around 1960. In 1958 the General Assembly of the United Nations voted for a programme of action for developing national media systems. A major conference on Asian media was held in Bangkok in 1961; another conference followed on Latin American media in Santiago in 1961; the African conference was held in Paris in 1962. The stern realism of this conference about African media, taking place in the rather civilized Unesco headquarters in Paris, may be savoured in a brief quotation from the report:

> 195. The meeting observed that although television was only in its infancy in Africa, both internal and external factors favoured its development in a region abounding in visual, oral and ritual tradition but with a population containing only a fairly small proportion of persons able to read and write.[5]

All of this zany logic and all of this conferring was to culminate in one big comprehensive report. This book, Wilbur Schramm's *Mass Media and National Development* (1964), immediately became the Unesco bible on the topic. Schramm's book was an eminently clear popularization of existing, mainly American, research – angled with considerable skill at its intended Third World audience. It concluded with a lengthy list of recommendations for expanding the media in developing countries.

Most of the typical characteristics of Unesco advice and publications on the media, both before and since 1964, are to be found in Schramm's book. Schramm argued for an all-round expansion of the developing countries' mass media. The optimistic hope behind this argument was that such expansion would trigger economic growth and encourage popular participation. Presumably Schramm did sincerely hope to expand Asian, African and Latin American media systems, but he and others failed to acknowledge that such broad expansion was likely to lead to continuing, and perhaps increased, dependence on Anglo-American imports.

Like other Unesco mass media 'experts', Schramm was an enthusiast for public service broadcasting and had even written a book on educational television; but educational broadcasting in developed countries is normally conducted on small budgets and often (as in the BBC) in effect is heavily subsidized by the entertainment programming. Recommendations for general TV services made by people with such interests tend to be wildly over-optimistic; many Unesco reports quote cost figures for television which would be more realistic with an extra nought on the end. An unreal approach to money was further encouraged by offers of free equipment from foreign manufacturers, by the hopes of some TV enthusiasts that when TV did begin the government would be forced to supply extra funds. Many of the expectations about educational television, which Schramm's book did little to discourage, were, on the basis of already existing experience, totally unreal. In particular, the notion was encouraged that educational television can be a viable alternative to an existing weak school system; there was, and there is, little evidence from any country to support this assertion. The opposite generalization has more validity – educational television has only operated successfully alongside, and as a minor support to, an existing school system.

But Schramm's book showed a great capacity to give advice which many Asians, Africans and Latin Americans would find acceptable; as such Schramm's book was a public relations *tour de force*. Moreover, Schramm does usually make a passing reference to some of the more obvious practical 'difficulties'. But despite these saving clauses in the small print, Schramm's book urged the developing nations to move towards a full-scale modern media system. There should be more expenditure, more training, more professionalism, more audience research. Developing nations, such advice implies, must have nothing but the best. Not only is there a financial and moral vacuum in this advice, there is also a historical vacuum. The point is ignored that 'developed' nations did not develop newspapers, magazines, films, radio, television and satellites all at the same time: presumably Schramm sensed that telling developing nations that they should stay out of television and satellites would be unpopular advice. If so, public relations skills triumphed. No sharp statement emerges from the Schramm book of the kind of choices which must be confronted. Consequently there are no real policy recommendations – just that more and more media are a good thing, because they speed up modernization as Lerner (quoted extensively by Schramm) had 'shown' (which he had not) in his Cold War Middle-East research.

Schramm also accepted the existing Unesco minimum standards for mass media development:

> 10 copies of a daily newspaper per 100 population
> 5 radio receivers
> 2 cinema seats
> 2 television receivers

These targets were in line with the Luther H. Evans belief in specific measurable targets; in the nature of an organization like Unesco they were compromises. By the early 1970s very few Afro-Asian nations and only some Latin American nations had reached this stage of media development.*

These targets were likely to be acceptable to urban élites and to educated people who themselves wish to follow Anglo-American styles; but concern for such targets is likely actually to retard media development outside the cities. Typically only *daily* newspapers were mentioned, although their relevance in rural areas of many poor countries is small, since a daily paper may in any case take several days to arrive from the nearest big city. For anyone other than the urban élite, *weekly* (or bi-weekly) newspapers and magazines are much more viable; such papers would do more to encourage – and equally important, maintain – widespread literacy and would make better use of the newsprint which most countries import with scarce foreign currency. (In some developing nations one day's copy of a big city newspaper uses enough newsprint to print a full-length paperback book; thus 10 daily newspapers in newsprint terms would equal 3,500 books in a year.)

Unesco's targets for the electronic media were even more dubious.

---

* For example these figures were reported for the early 1970s by Unesco (1975).

	Unesco target	Brazil	India	Tanzania
Copies of daily newspaper per 100 population	10	3·5	?	·4
Radio receivers per 100 population	5	5·8	2·1	1·1
Cinema seats per 100 population	2	1·9	·5	·1
Television receivers per 100 population	2	6·6	·01	—

The 2 cinema seats and 2 TV sets per 100 population would obviously be concentrated in urban areas, whereas the 5 radio sets per 100 was too low to emphasize the possibility (already evident in 1960) of making radio available to almost the entire population.* Nor did these targets say anything about advertising – although recommending developing nations to adopt the Anglo-American model, but apparently without its main source of finance, represents a somewhat odd conception of responsible and 'expert' advice.

For at least some nations in Africa and Asia an alternative set of targets might have stressed a high ratio of *weekly* papers and magazines per population,† a complete halt on cinema and TV expansion, and a high ratio of radio sets to population; advertising might be heavily encouraged on radio which it could help to finance in a major way and where it would not waste scarce foreign exchange on importing newsprint. (This was approximately the media policy being pursued around 1970 in Tanzania.) These are only some possibilities among many – but the failure of Unesco to state such simple alternatives was a serious weakness.

Unesco's series of *Reports and Papers on Mass Communication* have concentrated overwhelmingly on the educational uses of the media in general and the educational uses of the electronic media in rural areas of developing countries in particular.[6] The more rigorous of these studies – such as an account of Ghana's use of the rural radio forum[7] – typically found that such projects were fairly ineffective. But in their strategic concern for the 'free flow of information' the Unesco media experts can hardly be said to have failed; Unesco has succeeded remarkably in encouraging people to go on talking about 'free flow of information' and not to use such alternative phraseology as free trade (or laissez-faire) for media products.

However, in trying to encourage 'developing' nations to use the media to trigger economic growth, there is little evidence of Unesco's success. The failure of these efforts seems to have been largely at a political level. In most African and Asian countries, governments have tended to use the media as a sedative rather than a stimulant; brave notions of using the media to arouse previously subject people and to achieve economic growth have tended to fade away when it has been realized that the media are as likely to stir up conflict and to exacerbate existing ethnic, language, cultural and religious differences as to make a major contribution to economic growth.

* This possibility was recognized by Unesco on the basis of 1962 data which showed Latin America as already past the 5 sets per 100 population: Unesco (1964), pp. 27–8.

† This policy could easily have been pursued through newsprint allocation, designed to penalize dailies, while encouraging weeklies.

A crippling weakness of Unesco's advice on the media is that all givers and nearly all receivers of the advice tend to be suspicious of the cruder forms of the media; the foreign experts are invariably expert in something other than entertainment or advertising – and the Afro-Asian governmental policy-makers are members of the national élite. These two groups of people in the early days of independence found it easy to agree that the media should not be exploited for mere entertainment or mere commerce, but should be devoted to 'educational' and 'cultural', 'community' and 'national development' goals. It was, naturally, easier to get agreement for these goals – for instance in the Unesco conferences around 1960 – if the notorious vagueness of such hopeful terms was left undisturbed. The foreign experts were the prisoners of their own ignorance as well as of their past experience; American (and French) experts who tended to favour public service broadcasting on some vaguely BBC model, often knew remarkably little about that highly complex organization. Even most experts who offered to conduct sample surveys managed to bungle the research design.

The recipients of this advice were themselves no less the prisoners of their particular past experience. In India and in many African countries those who came to power had themselves had first-hand experience of radical political journalism – and not surprisingly were interested in the political uses of the press. Many African and Asian policymakers had been educated in the west where their own interests had largely been in the *national* media, which carry most foreign news, and not in things like local weekly newspapers, or radio programmes for semi-literate farmers.

Unesco advice-givers, in short, seem to have ignored the expectations that the governing élites of newly independent countries would have of the media. Firstly these élite members had themselves experienced the media as political weapons. Secondly, these educated people while living in the west as students or political exiles had usually become addicted to Anglo-American entertainment; it should not be too surprising that they tended to favour media policies which allowed them still to indulge their own personal addictions.

Many newly independent nations went through an early phase of official enthusiasm for the media – and during this period they decided to have a television service. But quite soon, they changed their minds – the media, and television in particular, were given a lower priority in economic planning. Radio and television stations, as a result of their central role in many political coups, were surrounded with barbed wire and guns. The result of such early enthusiasm as there had been was to extend urban media; subsequent cut-backs were of plans to take media out into rural areas. Thus enthusiasm for the sort of goals Unesco was putting forward around 1960 led to an expansion of urban but not of rural media in many countries. The cities got a western, Anglo-American, media pattern; many countrysides got very little media at all.

Unesco advisers – and Schramm more than most – were aware of the enormous strength of Anglo-American media around 1960. Nevertheless, the policies advocated by Unesco contained no realistic approach to the basic fact of dependence; these policies, if pursued at all, were likely to increase dependence on Anglo-American media. Insofar as any coherent body of knowledge was brought to bear upon establishing the media policies of most newly independent nations, that knowledge was American. Insofar as this knowledge had any practical impact it tended to expand the world-wide market for Anglo-American media.

COMMUNICATORS AS PROFESSIONALS? TRAINING AS IMPERIALISM?

A potent Anglo-American influence in other countries has been the notion of professionalism among journalists, broadcasters and in other communicator occupations. 'Professionalism' in these occupations typically stresses presentation techniques, the ability to select, to balance, to give 'both sides' of the story; it implies autonomy – independence from either political or commercial direction – with the communicator depending upon his 'professional' judgement to make decisions. Claims for 'professional' status in any occupation involve both technical and ideological elements. As compared with, say, doctors of medicine, the technical skills of professional communicators are uncertain and unstandardized; the ideological element is especially salient, then, in the communicator's 'professional' claim – although this ideology is expressed as value neutrality.

Occupations which make professional claims for autonomy tend to pursue this goal partly through suitable professional training establishments. American schools of journalism and communication are dedicated to such goals, and a major example of Unesco's espousal of American values in the media is its support for international communication schools of an American type. Unesco played a central part in establishing such international training centres in France (Strasbourg), Ecuador, the Philippines and in Senegal. Unesco has also helped to set up communication schools and institutes in several countries including Turkey, Lebanon and India.

CIESPAL, the partly Unesco-supported centre in Ecuador, was seen from the perspective of American journalism educators as the lynchpin of a new structure of 'professional' journalism education in Latin

America. North American assistance to Latin American journalism education began in the 1930s. By 1970 there were 68 university level journalism schools in Latin America. CIESPAL was conceived of as a school for training the journalism professors who would teach at these schools. It has used many visiting American lecturers and translated texts by Wilbur Schramm and other American authors. Financial aid to journalism education in Latin America has come not only from Unesco, but from the Ford Foundation, the USIA, and the Inter American Press Association. Another body which assisted in such journalism education was the Inter American Federation of Working Newspapermen's Organizations – until it became known that this body was receiving CIA funds.[8]

A similar pattern in the spread of American styles of journalism education – and American media knowledge – is to be found in Africa, Asia and western Europe. The International Press Institute's pioneering journalism training programme in Nairobi (later part of the University of Nairobi) was at its inception in 1963 financed by the Ford Foundation and directed by a British journalist.[9] In certain areas of Asia, such as Formosa, the Philippines and South Korea where American influence has been especially strong, American styles of journalism education are also very strong. In the Philippines such education has Unesco support and in South Korea it appears to have had CIA (Asia Foundation) support.[10]

In nearly all western European nations, in Japan, and in the white British Commonwealth, American academic media research, journalism training and commercial media 'knowledge' are also influential. Certain countries such as West Germany and Italy have a more literary and artistic tradition of university study of the communications media. But with the onward march of American-style social science in these countries' universities, and the strength of American influence in their domestic media systems, it is scarcely surprising that serious thinking and writing about the media in such countries also are heavily influenced by United States literature, ideas and examples.[11]*

Schools of journalism and communication are far from universally accepted within United States universities and communicator occupations. One of the many criticisms made of such schools is that you cannot teach someone to be a journalist (film director, or TV producer), and that anyhow most graduates of such schools in practice enter quite other occupations. Certainly, many journalism graduates go into public relations or advertising or something outside the media.

* Writing about West German academic research on the media, Kurt Lang comments that American research is well-known and closely followed in Germany, while German research is little known in the USA.

But such patterns ensure that 'professional' values and attitudes become widely diffused and widely accepted throughout the American media. And although many 'j-graduates' do not go into journalism, quite a lot do. A survey of 96 correspondents covering the United States Congress in 1972–3 found that one-third had first degrees in journalism; of those who had done graduate work, two-thirds had done so in journalism.[12] Johnstone found in 1971 that 20 per cent of all journalists in a national US sample had graduated in journalism.[13]*

Unesco in the 1950s and 1960s, even had it wanted to, would have had difficulty in breaking away from this American tradition – because already in the 1930s American journalism education had been exported to other lands. A Unesco document claimed in 1952–3 that the world contained 645 journalism training programmes, of which only 95 were outside the United States.[14] Probably the majority even of these 95 had been set up along US lines. Apart from the clear example of Latin America, China in the 1930s had journalism courses in some ten universities, including Shanghai, Peking and Nanking – some of which were to continue after 1948.

The American University in Cairo launched in 1937 the first journalism course in the Middle East. Australia, Canada, India and the larger Commonwealth countries of Africa and Asia have all launched such courses and – in the absence of British models – have usually copied the United States. The Institute of Mass Communications at Nigeria's University of Lagos was largely planned by an American professor.

American companies, such as RCA, have been active in supplying technical and vocational training, especially for new television services in the Middle East and elsewhere. The British contribution has largely taken this form. The tendency of British universities to frown on vocational training, and the peculiar polarization between the provincial and cosmopolitan in the British media resulted between 1945 and 1970 in a total lack of university communication education and training. One consequence has been the popularity in Nigeria, for example, of London-based correspondence courses in journalism.[15] But many people, especially from African and Asian Commonwealth countries, have followed non-university communications-oriented educational courses in Britain. There have also been in-house courses put on by British press groups (which at the time owned papers in recent ex-colonies). By 1970, over 2,000 broadcasting personnel from Africa alone had spent periods of training and working with the BBC in Britain. Some of these trainees are paid for with British government funds – funds which have also gone, with some from Unesco,

---

* And 34 per cent of the journalists who were college graduates had majored in journalism either in college or at graduate level.

to a major broadcast training centre in Malaysia. The Thomson Foundation has given press and television training courses, entirely concerned with practical skills, to large numbers of mainly Commonwealth personnel; these courses take place in Cardiff and Glasgow.

There has been a notorious highly competitive element in providing courses, especially for Africans and Asians. The British have sought – with their intensive practical courses and characteristic low profile – to retain the loyalty of Commonwealth countries. The Australian, Canadian and Japanese 'public service' broadcast networks are also active trainers. The French, too, have their extremely vigorous training scheme. The United States has striven to dominate the prevalent pattern in Latin America and to enter in force the Middle East and south-east Asia especially, as well as to retain its world-wide leadership. Some other nations – notably West Germany – have tried to break into this media education business. But although in this context the Germans as a non-imperial power are on the whole 'good Germans', nevertheless the language is a major hurdle. There is clearly more point in most English-speaking African journalists learning French (or French-speakers learning English) than German. The Soviet Union (and some east European nations) are also in the game; the Soviet Union in 1970 had 24 universities with journalism faculties or departments – but inevitably both the Russian language and the unfamiliar Soviet system pose problems. There is little doubt that competition to get students has often been detrimental to the interests of the media in the countries concerned; many key personnel have been away on courses, and the training has often been of an unsuitable kind. Nevertheless as the smoke clears, the almost inevitable result is that the Anglo-Americans are still far in the lead.

This applies not merely to practical training for technicians and journalists. It applies equally to social science research and the training of personnel for advertising and market research. The large advertising agencies send selected personnel from smaller offices around the world to larger ones – especially to New York and London. By 1963–4 a one-year international course was under way at Stanford University for teachers of market research from 17 foreign countries.[16]

But training is only one means by which professionalism and value neutrality are demonstrated and inculcated. 'Professionalism' is also built into the Anglo-American media structure which has been copied by, or deliberately transplanted to, most countries in the world. The very conception of what a journalist or a producer (or a PR man or a market researcher) is, carries with it notions of professionalism. Nor is communicator professionalism irrelevant in a single-party African state. One must not forget just how flexible 'professionalism' can be;

Africans receiving training in, or working in, the BBC will normally be attached to its External Services[17] – which are directly financed by the British Foreign Office and thus cannot convincingly claim to be free of government influence.

In an experiment, sample headlines and stories were presented to 30 Indian and 30 American journalists. The differences in their news judgements were quite minor, the similarities very strong.[18] Anglo-American professional values are also absorbed by the many communicators who are in continuing contact with media produced in London, New York and Los Angeles. The greatest readers of the press are journalists, the most enthusiastic consumers of films are film-makers, and so on. Journalists in Africa or Asia tend to read as many American news magazines and British equivalents (Sunday papers, political weeklies) as they can; Anglo-American news agency material is available in newspapers around the world from hour to hour; Indian film-makers in Bombay and Madras have long been enthusiastic followers of Hollywood films; television news editors in virtually every country in the world edit Visnews or UPITN news-film – not just occasionally but on a daily basis. And this material usually carries much higher prestige than the great bulk of locally produced material. The technical quality tends to be better; the level of political independence seems greater than is the case locally – the 'professional' prestige of this material is thus high.

Technical quality and autonomy are related to basic financial and organizational arrangements in the Anglo-American media. An African journalist or producer who re-uses such material may also be staking an autonomy claim for himself. Communicators around the world in practice see these claims for professional autonomy as internationally linked. Journalists and producers are quite sincere, then, in playing up the jailing of a journalist, or the censoring of political TV coverage in another country, as a blow to freedom everywhere. Such actions in another country will make that country more difficult to cover and more difficult to visit safely; from a marketing point of view such actions may mean the loss of a customer. For the communicators in one African country the playing up by the Anglo-American media of the jailing of a journalist in another African country may be reassuring for the future. Such complaints also support the belief widely held by communicators around the world that the media are neither an extension of politics nor simply a matter of consumer marketing. If the media are 'not just' politics and 'not just' entertainment, a role is left for communicators to decide just what they shall be, then, and to do this they rely on their 'professionalism'.

It is easy to make fun of the claimed professional neutrality of American or British[19] journalists. But just because it is an ideology which masks interests, 'professional neutrality' does not completely lack substance. Neutrality and autonomy may indeed be logical impossibilities. But American and British communicators act as if neutrality were possible and as if autonomy were potentially unlimited. And this 'as if' performance, when performed by American and British communicators, is a very different performance from those played out by communicators in some other countries. A journalist behaving on television as if he were equal to, and neutral towards, a US Senator may be acting a charade – but it is a charade which enormously impresses journalists in other lands.

INTERNATIONAL MEDIA ORGANIZATIONS

An illustration of how Anglo-American media values – and notions of knowledge, professionalism and neutrality – are diffused around the world is provided by a batch of six international media organizations.* These organizations seem to share common goals, such as the development of strong media within individual countries and especially within the weaker countries, the international exchange of help and advice in the relevant media fields, and the encouragement of media autonomy and freedom both within and between individual countries. These may sound vague, or even contradictory, but that is perhaps not unusual in the goals of international organizations.

The Inter-American Press Association – which we have already discussed in relation to the Peron regime in Argentina – is an organization of newspaper owners from the entire American continent. It has an opposite number in broadcasting, the Inter-American Association of Broadcasters. Then there are two organizations dealing with the British Commonwealth. The Commonwealth Broadcasting Association was founded in 1945 – its members are national broadcasting organizations in the Commonwealth. Its founder members were the public service broadcasting organizations of the white Commonwealth, plus All India Radio. By 1974, it had broadcasting organization members from 41 nations. The equivalent organization in the press is the CPU.

Finally there are two other organizations open to the entire world, the International Press Institute (founded 1951) and the International Broadcast Institute. Both IPI and IBI, like the Inter-American and British Commonwealth bodies, engage in conferences, seek to foster personal contacts between nations and focus on the encouragement of training and 'professionalism'. Both the IPI and IBI were brought into existence largely by the Anglo-Americans and their friends. In

* There are many more than six international organizations dealing with regional programme exchanges and other specialized activities.

both cases United States finance was instrumental – but in the formal arrangements the United States remains somewhat in the background. Both IBI and IPI are based in London (having moved from Rome and Zürich respectively).

The International Press Institute came into existence at the height of the Cold War. One of its first publications, *The News From Russia*, permanently antagonized the Soviet Union. The IPI has devoted itself to the 'freedom of the press' in general and to the autonomy of editors (primarily in relation to governments). The IPI has been effective in encouraging and supplying information for international campaigns against political regimes (of left, right and centre) which have attempted to nationalize newspapers, jail editors or evict correspondents. In more recent years the IPI has become rather less effective – as many newly independent regimes have incorporated their media into the official apparatus of government.

The International Broadcast Institute, coming into existence after these IPI difficulties were already evident, naturally sought to avoid some of them. It offers membership to *individuals*. It also has chosen to focus upon new technology – such as cable TV and space satellites – presumably in the hope that technology would be less ideological and build a bridge between the resources of rich nations and the requirements of poor ones.

Nevertheless, the IBI merely emphasizes slightly different aspects of the familiar Anglo-American media tradition. The emphasis on new technology conforms to 'value neutrality', but of course the practical configurations of applied technology are not neutral. American (foundation) money was instrumental in bringing IBI to birth. The only internationally prominent personality to have held a senior office in IBI was the former Prime Minister of Canada, Lester Pearson, who was chairman of IBI's board of trustees. At the time of Pearson's election a majority of IBI's officers and trustees came from the United States, Britain, the British Commonwealth. Canadians, Australians and Nigerians have been especially prominent.

That international media organizations of this kind should be dominated by American and British Commonwealth values and personnel is, if not inevitable, then at least extremely probable. Any *international* organization in the field of the media can hardly be expected to favour media nationalism. And while the IBI's search for some relatively non-ideological focus of interest has settled upon technology which is not, and cannot be, value-free – technology is nearer to being value-free (or is ideologically more flexible) than the IPI's central notion of editorial autonomy.

A dilemma for all of these non-governmental media organizations – as for Unesco – is that if you want to 'help' the poorer countries to develop their media, this involves some element of international trade in the media, some infusions of advice, training, technology and also media material from outside. But once the media of poorer nations are exposed to international market forces, they must be exposed to those Anglo American media materials and styles which dominate the international market.

International organizations which seek to assist the expansion of the media in poorer countries are likely also to assist Anglo-American media products and influences in those same countries. That many people both in rich and poor nations do not recognize this 'dilemma' as a dilemma at all is evidence of the very widespread acceptance of Anglo-American value neutral ideology, professionalism and objective knowledge.

CHAPTER THIRTEEN

US government media and
media policy

WASHINGTON: THE MEDIA INDUSTRY AT HOME
AND ABROAD

Any government's domestic and external media policies are closely related. United States governmental policy is shaped by the tradition of minimal interference. Both at home and abroad this means primarily regulating and smoothing the way for the existing commercial media. Especially in the electronic media this minimal level of interference is quite crucial in the patterns which emerge. Nevertheless it remains true that compared with most other nations – in the broadcasting media, as well as press – the American government's intervention is *comparatively* small. On the whole in external media there is an inverse correlation between effectiveness and the extent of government involvement. American government involvement is effective precisely because it only operates to support the commercial media or to fill gaps where there is no revenue inducement for the commercial media.

Substantial governmental media are operated by the United States, not only Radio Free Europe, Radio Liberty (the two former covert radios) but the United States Information Agency – an all-purpose press relations, cultural relations and broadcasting organization which operates the Voice of America (VOA) radio network. Some foreigners see these organizations as potent forces for either good or ill. In Washington, however, these overseas efforts have often been presented in Congress as bungling and incompetent. Behind such accusations has been the Congressional anxiety that the USIA might be used as an indirect propaganda arm of the President in domestic politics.

In the eyes of most Congressmen the most important thing about the media has always been that the media back in the Congressman's home state can sway votes. From the earliest days of the United States there was a tendency for the local Congressman to work in league with local newspapers. In return for support at elections the

Congressman might manage to get the newspaper a federal printing contract. The same pursuit of mutual interests continues today. Incumbent Congressmen tend to get re-elected partly because they get so much home-state publicity *between* elections; Congressmen send enormous quantities of material – speeches, statements, columns – to their local papers. There are special studio facilities for Congressmen and Senators to record brief statements and 'interviews' which are sent to constituency radio and TV stations and inserted into the local news. In return, Congressmen release their best news stories to suit the convenience of the local media's deadlines. They protect television and radio stations from federal interference – reducing the Federal Communications Commission to an agency which cannot decisively alter the *status quo* because it lacks political support. Congressmen protect newspapers and broadcasting stations against hostile legislation especially in the monopoly field, but also over a wide range of other issues such as advertising and employment practices.

While the local media – newspapers and stations – maintain a pipeline to 'their' Congressmen and Senators, the *national* media engage in the customary Washington game of political lobbying with executive and legislature. The media do not always win, because politicians like to attack the national media – accusing them of corrupting youth, destroying culture and appropriating power – the media in the particular politician's constituency being, of course, a rare exception. The Hollywood film industry – after receiving some bad frights in the early 1920s – has been especially committed to having a strong political spokesman in Washington, who knows his way round Congress and the White House. The radio and television national networks fell into the same pattern and some of their most effective leaders – such as David Sarnoff of NBC and Frank Stanton of CBS – have been specialists in political public relations and Washington lobbying.

Particular committee chairmen have continued to call for – and get – the biggest yet investigation of how violence on the media corrupts American youth. Particular Presidents, Vice Presidents or candidates, have continued to accuse sections of the media of the most unfair political coverage of all time, but on the whole everyone in Washington accepts the media.

The Washington government apparatus has long been especially favourable to the notion of media exports. In 1920 the United States still had rather few sophisticated exports. Films and radio were quickly seen as presenting an ideal way for the United States to develop exports in all things electronic. Films, in the eyes of the Commerce Department, had the additional bonus of providing a shop window for other goods – cars, kitchen equipment, indeed almost everything made in America. Radio had the additional bonus of encouraging advertising and spreading American commerce that way. Documents prepared by the Commerce Department during the inter-war period illustrate how trade commissioners in US Embassies were pressed into service to provide media market intelligence; the documents also reveal considerable Commerce Department pride in the success of American media exports.

Washington support for the exporting of American media equipment and materials was also evidenced in various pieces of legislation, which provided useful commercial assistance or exempted the media from anti-trust provisions which obtained at home. The major Hollywood companies in the inter-war period acted abroad in an even more overtly cartel manner than they displayed at home. In the post-1945 period Hollywood companies were allowed to continue to act abroad as a legal cartel – officially registered as the Motion Picture Export Association (MPEA), later followed by a TV equivalent. There was also special legislation – such as the Media Garanty Program – which helped media exporters with finance. And throughout the Marshall Aid period it was made clear that recipients of aid would not be regarded as wasting aid by spending it on movies, rather the contrary – any nation which accepted aid should accept films as well.

Inevitably during both world wars the US media were driven into close collaboration with Washington and the military. But 1945 marked a dramatic reversal of this trend. Congress decided that radio propaganda was alien to the American way and should be left to the USSR and Britain. While Congress was thus taking away some of President Truman's overseas media resources, the media managers were keen to show that with peace-time their total independence of government was reinstated. The American news agencies – which had become closely involved with the military in Europe and Asia and with the Rockefeller office in Latin America – sought to re-establish their independence. One symbolic act was a decision by AP and UP no longer to supply their services to any US government agency. The State Department was naturally annoyed not to be able to buy an American service available to newspapers around the world. But no American President – least of all Harry Truman – can dictate to the big news agencies inside the United States. And probably some foreign customers were impressed – especially since the American agencies were loudly claiming that both the British and French agencies were servants of imperial interests.

A less symbolic post-1945 example of independence was the conduct of Hollywood in dealing with the American occupation authorities

Cinemas in Baroda City, India, 1947

Stars in Indian film magazine, 1975

hie-rich Chintu
ws-off his new
e' —a recently
ight 1973
evrolet
.Vega!

A 'balika's' delight! Moushumi doesn't drive
herself, but why should she, when hubby
Ritesh and good friend and stand-in chauffeur
Vinod M. are only too happy to take over the
wheels of her blue Mercedes Benz?

Indian newspapers and magazines

in Germany. Hollywood wanted to dominate Germany again – and wanted to be involved in production, distribution and exhibition inside Germany. The American military authorities refused – and Hollywood played its old card of the trade boycott. Only an enticing trickle of Hollywood films entered Germany – 25 a year for the first two years. The military authorities badly wanted films for public re-education policies and there were no other adequately large supplies. An agreement was finally reached and in 1950–1 no less than 202 Hollywood films entered Germany. Hollywood won most of its points – including the main objective of crippling German domestic production and (even more important in the long haul) German film distribution.[1] This was the only major defeat suffered by Occupation media policy and it was a defeat handed out by Hollywood using its traditional pitiless tactics in pursuit of its own commercial goals.

Since 1950 there has been a general tendency for American commercial media and US government agencies to help each other. This is intimacy but not marriage. The description used of non-household kin in modern societies – 'intimacy at a distance' – is appropriate.

OVERT AND COVERT US GOVERNMENT MEDIA

It is against this background, then, that one must consider the efforts of Anglo-American government media. It is easy to scoff at the efforts of 'American Libraries', and the various radio offerings which are let loose over the communist heartlands. If anyone still expects such efforts to 'liberate' the enslaved masses, then scepticism is in order. But if the objective is to worry the communist governments and to keep them on the defensive, such Anglo-American media efforts appear to be quite successful. If another intention is to give modest support to the Anglo-American commercial media in the non-communist world – and with these commercial media to prevent the communist government media from getting a serious exporting foothold – then these government media efforts can hardly be shown to have failed.

The Americans became the senior partners in an Anglo-American governmental media alliance which turned from anti-Nazi to anti-communist propaganda. In 1945 the American government (like the Soviet government) reduced its propaganda activities. However, after a series of policy changes a new Cold War pattern of American propaganda evolved. There were two main agencies deriving from the 'overt' and 'covert' distinction of the Second World War. The overt agency was the United States Information Agency.

The covert media operations of the United States government

were carried on primarily by the Central Intelligence Agency. The CIA, in its media activities, drew upon the experience and often the old personnel of two war-time agencies – the Office of Strategic Services (OSS) which was the forerunner of the CIA itself, and upon the experience of the Psychological Warfare Division (PWD) of SHAEF. PWD, which had an integrated American and British staff, engaged in all kinds of 'grey' and 'black' media activities – leaflets, air-dropped newspapers, and radio stations – some of which purported to come from inside Germany, some of which concealed their origins, and all of which were intended to break German morale. The CIA drew upon this tradition in setting up Radio Free Europe and Radio Liberation (later Liberty), aimed at eastern Europe and the Soviet Union respectively. These stations purported to be run by groups of private American citizens through funds raised by appeals within the United States. This 'cover story' both absolved the State Department of public responsibility for what the stations said, and protected the 'private' stations from Congressional committee scrutiny.

The Voice of America has transmitters which can reach all areas of the world, including Soviet Central Asia and western China; RIAS (Radio in the American Sector) broadcasts from West Berlin to East Germany; Radio Free Europe broadcasts to Poland, Hungary, Czechoslovakia, Romania and Bulgaria in their main languages; Radio Liberty broadcasts in Russian and the larger minority languages of the USSR. The American Forces Network, too, broadcasts in many parts of the world. And there are some powerful American-financed religious stations broadcasting in Russian, Chinese and other languages spoken in communist countries.* Britain, France, West Germany, Italy, Sweden, Yugoslavia, Egypt, Iraq and South Korea also broadcast to the USSR in Russian, while Britain, West Germany, Ethiopia, Taiwan, India, Indonesia, South Korea and Australia give Chinese-language broadcasts to China. There have certainly been from time to time yet other covert stations.

Nor is it difficult to broadcast radio news into communist countries which is at least as convincing as the home product. Radio Free

---

* In 1971 such stations included:

Trans World Radio of Monte-Carlo, which broadcast on shortwave in Albanian, Armenian, Bulgarian, Chinese, Czech, Estonian, Hungarian, Latvian, Lithuanian, Polish, Romanian, Russian, Serbo-Croat, Slovak and Ukrainian. It also broadcast on medium wave in Czech, Hungarian, Russian and Serbo-Croat.

Team Radio, HLKX, in South Korea which broadcast in Russian and Chinese.

Far East Broadcasting in the Ryukyu Islands broadcast in Chinese.

La Voz de Los Andes, in Quito, Ecuador, broadcast in Romanian, Russian and Armenian.

International Broadcast Station, KGEI, in Belmont, California broadcast in Russian and Ukrainian. See *World Radio TV-Handbook 1972.*

Europe, in its early days, began to 'intercept' (pirate electronically) the domestic news services transmitted by national news agencies within each east European nation – meaning that it thus received the same basic national service as stations and newspapers within those countries.* Disputes between and within communist nations provide endless possibilities for spicy 'bad news'. Changes in party policy and personnel also provide RFE (which has a very elaborate filing system) with equally endless opportunities to make unflattering comparisons between past and present party policies, personnel and pronouncements. The communist media play down many kinds of 'bad' news items precisely because people have such an 'unhealthy' interest in them – not only disasters, fires and crashes, but comparisons of citizens' incomes and retail prices, reports on increased living standards in non-communist countries, the salaries of communist party and government workers, food shortages and the jamming of foreign radios.[2] Western stations also broadcast popular music not available in the relevant countries. The effectiveness of such broadcasts does not rely solely upon their immediate audience. The foreign radios and domestic Soviet *Samizdat* (illegal publishing) have become reinforcing. Material from broadcasts is typed and passed from person to person, but the foreign stations have also taken to broadcasting *Samizdat* material smuggled out to them. Moreover, not only typewriters but also tape-recorders and cameras are fairly common within the Soviet Union – making the reproduction of both radio broadcasts and *Samizdat* material relatively easy.

The unmasking of the CIA backing of Radio Liberty and Radio Free Europe caused great political excitement in the United States and western Europe. But it is doubtful whether this seriously damaged the stations in the eyes of their audiences. Reading between the lines of American public statements on them it had long been possible to guess that the stations were CIA-financed; this must have been known at least by senior members of the relevant Congressional committees. It was well known to the communist authorities who repeatedly denounced the stations as CIA mouthpieces. The stations themselves have even claimed that their research showed that their credibility increased when it became known that they had been CIA-financed.

The CIA's forerunner – OSS – itself illustrated the overlapping between the media and the intelligence services in forming American foreign policy. During the Second World War, OSS recruits included State Department diplomats, Wall Street lawyers, journalists and

* This presumably was one of several reasons for the adoption by the east European news agencies of the TASS practice of special restricted bulletins for foreign policy and political élites.

advertising men, east coast academics, and refugee intellectuals. An oss man might equally well be a Harvard-educated Protestant Republican or a left-wing Jewish émigré scholar. At least 20 former oss men later became us Ambassadors; oss provided much of the CIA's subsequent senior staff, including two CIA Directors – Dulles and Helms. It provided a number of American Cabinet Officers, senior White House advisers and Assistant Secretaries of State and Defense. A number of oss personnel subsequently became famous politician-academics: Arthur Schlesinger jnr., Paul Sweezy, Stuart Hughes, Herbert Marcuse, Paul Baran, Walt Rostow. But in the present context the most interesting point is that the oss – which in retrospect seems to have provided some of the most powerful makers as well as bitterest critics of post-1945 us foreign policy – included so many men connected with the media. Most were foreign correspondents (for New York or Chicago newspapers or the news agencies) or 'international' advertising men, connected either with such advertising agencies as J. Walter Thompson or with Hollywood overseas publicity.

This prominent part of media men in the oss meant that a former oss journalist like Joseph Alsop at any time between 1950 and 1970 would find oss colleagues in any major American Embassy abroad. But it also meant that a man like Richard Helms (a United Press correspondent in Berlin in the 1930s) – long before he became Director of the CIA in 1966 – would have regarded media activities as part of the forward strategy of American diplomacy. This mixture of diplomatic-business-academic-media personnel probably also ensured that the American foreign policy élite had a fairly realistic grasp of the limitations of government media efforts and the strength of the American commercial media both in American diplomacy and in the world market.

ANGLO-AMERICAN DOUBLE ACT: GENTLEMEN AND PLAYERS

American evidence illustrates that it is not American government media alone which operate in this field. For example Radio Free Europe's own data – based on interviewing east Europeans travelling in the west – report that the size of the western radios' audience in RFE's target countries*[3] descend in the following order: RFE itself first; BBC second; VOA; Radio Luxembourg; Deutsche Welle and Deutschlandfunk; Radio Vienna.

---

* RFE does not broadcast to Yugoslavia or East Germany. These figures (averaged for the five countries with equal weighting) might show the German stations in a higher placing if East Germany were included.

American foreign radio practice built heavily on BBC precedent. But since then there has developed a rough division of labour between Britain and the USA (with Deutsche Welle in practice also playing an important, but smaller part). The division of labour is such that the American foreign media are the tougher, tend to aim at the middle audience and are also willing to engage in covert activities and various dirty tricks. The British stick to the more élite audience, adopt a much softer sell, and try to keep clear of any suspicion of dirty tricks.

The most obvious example is the contrast between the BBC and the American VOA, RFE and RL. A quite different example would be the division of labour which exists in India. Britain has retained a strong and public influence over the style of radio and newspapers; British book publishing firms are active through subsidiaries. What is less obvious in India is that quite a lot of books translated from English into Indian languages just happen to be American books whose translation has been subsidized by the USIA; the subsidy may merely take the form of a guarantee to buy 5,000 copies of, for example, an American political biography if it is translated. These copies are then given away. The only underhand element in this example – as in many similar ones – is that the reader will not know that but for American dollars the book would not have been translated.

Another – slightly more delicate – example would be the issue of whether American Embassies ever subsidize commercial sales of media services. The smaller countries, according to *Variety* – the well-informed New York showbiz trade paper – pay very low prices for television series. In 1975–6 an American company selling a half-hour TV episode to the national television services of Kenya, Uganda, Zambia and Nigeria would be paid only about $135 or $150 by the four countries combined (Table 17). This sum seems inadequate to cover the postal and packing costs plus the clerical and managerial overheads – let alone to produce a profit. Another example is the extremely small sums charged by AP and UPI in some small countries; in the case of one small Asian country an experienced AFP correspondent in the larger neighbouring country quoted prices charged by Associated Press which were so low that, said the French correspondent, the US Embassy must be paying the difference. Whether or not subsidies did occur in these two cases, it seems highly probable that the State Department does provide financial or other recompense in some such circumstances, either directly or indirectly.

The CIA and other agencies have used various kinds of traditional media to carry anti-communist themes. In central and northern Thailand there is a tradition of migrant *mau lum* singers who present musical and dramatic performances in the villages:

The village *mau lum* singer informed us that in Udorn she had recently bought *mau lum* texts for about 100 *baht*, put out by the government in cooperation with certain American agencies. These new texts have as their themes rural development, animal husbandry, government slogans for various development drives, anti-communist propaganda, nuclear rockets (*iarnad nuclear*!), psychological warfare (*songram chittavitya*) and provincial reorganization in the north east.[4]

Other ways of reacting to the local media have been described by Philip Agee, who served with the CIA in Latin America, mainly Ecuador. This involved various sorts of manipulation of the local press and media – paying retainers to prominent pro-American journalists on leading newspapers, planting false stories unfavourable to the local Marxists in other publications, organizing student protests and leaflet campaigns against politicians hostile to the United States – and so on.[5]

The British in contrast deliberately project an exaggerated probity. One commentator, for instance, criticizes the BBC for not giving material free to radio stations in Latin America, on the grounds that the smaller stations cannot afford to pay and BBC integrity would not thus be compromised.[6]

Inevitably it is impossible to know just how widespread or just how dirty all the American governmental dirty tricks are. One view is that they are everywhere subverting free media. Another view is that they are merely doing what everyone else – especially the locals – does in the particular country. Historically certainly, most of these kinds of tricks have been used in American domestic elections and domestic commercial public relations.

A more general point is that this kind of underhand dirty trickery is widely believed not to be the sole, or even the main, way in which American media as a whole operate abroad. More common than the criticism that programming and news services are too cheap is the criticism that they are too expensive. In the case of traditional *mau lum* singing there is no question of subverting modern media – although paying for new songs could be seen either as subverting or subsidizing 'authentic culture'. In Latin America it would be a cause for surprise if American Embassies had no local journalists on their payroll.

Such accusations of dirty dealing imply that most American media match higher standards. The British are always available as an alternative Anglo-American voice – with their traditional awkwardly honest presentation of themselves. The height of the Vietnam war, when the American governmental media clung tightest to the State Department's current line, was also the time when AP and UPI were day after day sending around the world often unflattering accounts and gory photographs of American behaviour in South Vietnam. It was possible also to imagine many things about President Nixon, but scarcely that he had bought off the CBS network news or the *Washington Post*.

PART FOUR

The end of Empire?

CHAPTER FOURTEEN

Arabs, Moslems, Middle East

LANGUAGE, RELIGION, REGION: DIVIDED WORLDS,
FOREIGN MEDIA

President Nasser tried to make Cairo the media capital of three overlapping worlds – the Arabs, the Moslems and the Middle East. To
some limited extent he succeeded. But while Egyptian media were
consumed in neighbouring and more distant lands, Cairo was not
merely a capital in media exporting – it was also a centre of media
importing from the Anglo-Americans.

The Arab–Moslem–Middle East worlds seem to have many advantages in the media field not possessed by most African or Asian
countries. The Middle East contains a group of countries which all
have in common not only Arabic but also the Moslem faith and way
of life. Arabic speakers stretch from Morocco on the Atlantic to the
oil states on the Persian Gulf. The Moslem faith stretches yet further
– encompassing much of the northern half of Africa, right across to
south-east Asia. Yet none of these seeming advantages has prevented
enormous media imports.

Arabic has been less of an advantage than might appear. It has
high classical forms which differ radically from spoken dialects, which
in turn differ greatly between different nations and cities. Nor do all
'Arab' nations have entirely Arabic-speaking populations – there are
important minorities who speak other languages. Different areas were
colonized formally or informally by different European nations –
French, Dutch and British; consequently many 'Arab' countries have
media in at least three main languages – Arabic, an important minority
language and a European language. Outside the ex-French territories
of north-west and west Africa (discussed in the next chapter) this
European language is most often English. A number of these
countries' national news agencies actually distribute news domestically in English – news taken in English from the international
agencies and then made available for translation at the local level.
Several countries devote a substantial fraction of domestic radio
time to the English language. Both oil and non-oil states tend to have
substantial expatriate minorities and often the government owns an
English-language paper with which to address them.

Nor does the Moslem religion seem to be a more effective barrier to media imports than is, say, Christianity in Latin America. Indeed the Moslem faith in some ways is especially unsuitable for modern media; Saudi-Arabia is one of the few nations which have not been substantial importers of Hollywood films – because in the official Saudi view the Moslem restriction on portraying the human form rules out public cinemas altogether.

Religious differences are one component of political differences, both within and between most Arab and Moslem countries, which inhibit any co-ordinated response to foreign media. National frontiers tend to be lines drawn across the desert. In several cases minority non-Arab groups straddle militarily disputed frontiers. Anxieties about such frontiers lead to media priority being given to reaching one's own and the neighbouring state's border areas. Internally the media are used as a resource to bolster the strength of the central state and chief executive. Such motivation leads to concern for expanding the media and the avoidance of importing media from one's neighbours; this is a classic dilemma and the Anglo-American media provide the classic solution of cheap, entertaining and a-political (or not locally political) materials.

The Moslem and Arab world combines many recently formed states and many states which were colonized only partly or even not formally at all. These nation states also have only a brief press history. Illiteracy, distance, deserts and mountains, unevenly spread populations, colonial and/or 'traditional' regimes – all these discouraged and still discourage the growth of the press. Apart from Israel, Turkey is almost alone in having a well-developed press. There are several important national news agencies – notably MENA (Egypt), Anatolia (Turkey), and Antara (Indonesia); but the Moslem-Arab world's press typically uses large quantities of foreign news – nearly all supplied by the western international agencies.

Hollywood films swept all before them throughout the Arab-Moslem world generally. However, in competition with American films a number of important mini-Hollywoods grew up – especially in Egypt, Turkey, Lebanon and Pakistan; Iran and Indonesia are now following suit. Nevertheless those countries remain heavy importers of films from Hollywood and its west European partners.

In radio and television there has been very dramatic growth. Unesco figures for the early 1970s suggest that Israel was surpassed by Bahrain, Iran, Kuwait and Syria in radio sets per population and several other states had nearly as many. Arab and Moslem nations have tended to rush into television also and have become substantial importers. Varis found in eight Middle Eastern countries television

importing levels in 1971 which averaged about half of all programming (Table 1); with a few exceptions (such as Iraq and Syria) most
countries rely heavily on the US, with Britain often in second place.
Television, especially, had a very American-influenced birth in the
Middle East. One factor was the early presence of television stations
on the Persian Gulf used by the USAF and American oil companies.
There was also much activity by RCA, with whom the United States
government was directly involved in establishing television in both
Syria and Egypt (as a balance to Soviet financing of the Aswan dam).
In several cases enthusiastic local entrepreneurs (usually with an
American selling or educational background) set up their own television stations as a do-it-yourself operation to sell receivers. But the
amount of advertising remains very low. Only Lebanon of all these
countries has had a history of sophisticated advertising. Radio and
television are usually directly government controlled, on the African
model, by a Ministry of Information – or, as in Kuwait, a 'Ministry
of Guidance and Information'.

An unusual aspect of the Arab-Moslem world is that the weak press
tradition, combined with government enthusiasm for television, leads
to several countries having television set ownership more widely
diffused than daily newspaper sales. This is true not only of oil states
like Saudi-Arabia, Iran, Bahrain and Kuwait but also of Jordan and
Syria.

EGYPT: VOICE OF THE ARABS OR MOSLEM MEXICO?

The Egyptian media have a long history by the standards of the Arab
world. French media influence there was substantial but has now
diminished; combined Anglo-American influence in Egypt, which
was once less than the French, is now much greater.

Literacy has been very low and when the 'New Egypt' was being
created in the early 1950s there was already both a surplus of university graduates and a shortage of school teachers.[1] Egypt was also
similar to India in the importance of Civil Service employment and
in having a long history of both an expatriate and a nationalist press.
In 1948 Egypt had 24 foreign-language daily papers – 13 in French,
7 in Greek, 2 in Armenian and 2 in English.[2] There were also 26 dailies
in Arabic.

Egypt had an especially sharp distinction between poor countryside and the two large cities, Cairo and Alexandria, where much of
the cash income and almost all the media were concentrated. In 1961,
after nearly a decade of 'new radio', a study in six Nile Delta villages
found among 14,000 people only 135 radio sets, nearly all owned by
shopkeepers. Almost the only readers of daily newspapers were the

local civil servant administrators.[3] Despite the substantial spread of radio since 1961, Egypt is an extremely hierarchical society, and the traditional role of women in Arab societies scarcely encourages a market orientation. Even among the highly educated it remained unusual for a woman actually to buy a newspaper.*

In Egypt, as elsewhere in the Middle East, the media have always had strong political overtones. In the press the modest proportion of market-oriented material aimed at European expatriates and their families declined in the 1950s when most of these people returned to France, Britain and Greece. Subsequently the Egyptian press was taken over by the governing party. But like India, Egypt has a film industry which has grown up in head-on competition with Hollywood; some of this film industry commercialism has spread into radio and television. These market-oriented elements have been deliberately encouraged within a basic political strategy entirely determined by the government. President Nasser, in the common pattern of the 'Father of the new nation' set his personal stamp on radio and especially on television in Egypt. This was a political, Arab nationalist stamp but Nasser also encouraged imports of some Anglo-American material; at Nasser's personal directive during much of the 1960s an entire television channel was aimed at expatriates resident in Egypt and was filled with mainly Anglo-American programming.

The first printing press in Egypt was set up by Napoleon. In the second half of the nineteenth century many papers were launched by Turks, Armenians, Greeks and Lebanese, as well as by Frenchmen and Englishmen. *Al Ahram* was founded in 1876 by two Lebanese Christians. During the early twentieth century the press took on a more nationalist tone, playing an active part in the events leading to the Revolution of 1952. Egypt also had a substantial news agency, the Arab News Agency (ANA), which was a subsidiary of Hulton's in London; ANA had offices throughout the Middle East. No less than three Egyptian universities gave courses for journalists; and the daily sale of 350,000 copies in 1948 dwarfed the press of neighbouring countries.† After the Revolution, the Egyptian press went through a series of upheavals which involved slimming down the number of titles; but the paradoxical legacy of a colonial Egyptian press which was itself somewhat imperialistic seems to have marked all post-1952 media developments in Egypt.

Egyptian newspaper sales are dominated by serious and heavily

---

* A promotional pamphlet called *When It's Middle East It's Al Ahram* based on a 1967 readership survey, reports that only 2·2 per cent of *Al Ahram* buyers were women – in contrast to 43 per cent of readers being women.

† Unesco (1950) estimated daily sales of newspapers in 1948 as follows: Egypt: 350,000; Israel: 136,000; Lebanon: 100,000; Jordan: 15,300.

political newspapers like *Al Ahram* and *Al Akhbar*; these papers –
still influenced by the prestige papers of the west – leave the main
burden of market orientation to a few popular magazines (mainly
based on standard Anglo-American formulae) and the electronic
media. Arabic-language magazines already provided in 1931 an example of the strength of American syndication operations:

A close examination in May, 1929, of *al-Lata'if, Kull Shai, al-
Siyasa, Al-Musawwar*, and *al-Sabah*, five of the weekly periodicals
was a revelation of the important place of the United States in the
eyes of Egyptian editors. American manufacturers had a large
share of the foreign advertising. In one week's issue of these five
magazines there were articles on Byrd in the Antarctic, the rivalry
between Ford and General Motors, the Monroe Doctrine and
Coolidge's Five Years in the White House. The moving picture
industry occupied considerable space. There was a discussion of
the process of making 'talkies', a young Egyptian contributed an
account of a visit to Hollywood and an interview with Harold
Lloyd and Douglas Fairbanks, and Pola Negri in two different
papers told at length why she didn't marry Charlie Chaplin. The
ever-present problem in America was referred to in an article
headed, 'New Ways of Avoiding the Prohibition Law', while a
study of the divorce problem in the United States revealed that a
Los Angeles judge suggested a renewal of the marriage contract
every five years to make it valid. This last fact proved to the writer's
satisfaction that in the great republic across the ocean the bonds of
wedlock are practically nil.

The same weeklies in their issues for the third week of December,
1930, in addition to pages given over to pictures of American actors
and actresses, present in illustrated articles the following subjects
dealing with America: 'Why was Sinclair Lewis awarded the Nobel
Prize?' 'Life at Vassar College', 'Germany bans the film ALL QUIET
ON THE WESTERN FRONT', 'Al Capone, the Head of Chicago's
Racketeers', 'The Dancing Negress, Josephine Baker, talks about
herself'.

During the year 1930 the *Hilal*, probably the most popular
monthly of the whole Arabic-speaking world, published among its
wealth of material on the United States, a review of the Personal
Papers of Colonel House, a study of the life and success of Wool-
worth the millionaire merchant, a paper with pictures and maps
of Byrd's expedition to Antarctica, an interview with the former
Minister of Egypt at Washington concerning the wonders of
America, an article on religious films, a discussion translated from
World's Work of the possible cure of the criminal and insane by

treating their glands, and a symposium in which prominent Americans gave personal views on the secret of success. . . .

The press of Egypt leads a precarious existence. A strict censorship on political activities has produced a new record in the number of daily newspapers banned. But a few days as a rule are sufficient for the invention of a new name, the securing of a new permit and the appearance from the same office of a new paper that differs from the old only in its more guarded statements regarding the ministry in power. The illustrated weeklies and the monthly reviews as a rule escape much of this closing and opening of doors, because they depend for much of their material on foreign sources. Though there are fifty-seven Greeks, thirty-nine Italians and twenty-six British subjects to every American in Egypt, the United States furnishes literary material far in excess of this proportion.[4]

The American magazine articles were widely used, it seems, in Egypt as elsewhere because they were politically safe – and doubtless fairly cheap. Typical American magazine themes are mentioned – biography, success, marriage and divorce, Hollywood stars.

Egypt, like most of the world's more highly populated countries, has had a substantial film industry for several decades. The first major imports of films into Egypt occurred in 1914–18 for the entertainment of Allied soldiers. From then on, as elsewhere, Hollywood exports long reigned supreme. Early efforts at Egyptian production in 1925 were guided by mainly American experts.[5] The plot of the first Egyptian film, involved a 'handsome Bedouin interpreter Ahmed who falls in love with an American woman whom he followed to the United States'.[6] Since then the Egyptian film industry has developed its own vigorous commercial orientation and – as with 'film Hindi' – Egyptian 'film Arabic' has gone some way to becoming the spoken *lingua franca* of the Arab world. These star-dominated films are cheaply made, and have stuck doggedly to commercially successful formulae – such as the comedy and the 'tear-jerking social film of a musical character'.[7] Naturally they appeal especially to less sophisticated Egyptians, and thus may superficially seem totally non-western. But Egyptian films have, like those of India, been beaten and knocked into this market orientation through decades of competition with Hollywood films. In 1937 of all films shown in Egypt 76 per cent were American and 7 per cent British.[8] Egypt still imported 275 American and British films in 1950, and 265 in 1960; in 1971 Egypt imported 234 features from Hollywood and Italy combined.

Egyptian radio had a similarly Anglo-American (and Anglo-French) birth. In 1931 Egypt had two radio stations – one each owned by an Englishman and a Frenchman; both stations took advertising and regular advertisers included American toothpaste, razor, car, radio and tyre companies plus a German piano company. Announcers used Arabic and French, but 'English' concert and dance records were in daily use.[9] Apart from the French settler colonies and Turkey, Egypt in 1930 was the leading radio power of the Arab-Moslem world.* In 1931 one of the Egyptian stations increased its power, enabling it to be heard in the Sudan and Syria.

The 4,000 radio sets of 1930 had by 1948 grown to 183,000 – with broadcasting occurring in Arabic, English and French. Thus there was a background of some 25 years of strongly Anglo-American and French influenced radio when the Voice of the Arabs began in July 1953. Between 1952 and 1971 Egypt expanded her radio transmission power seventy-fold.[10] In the early 1970s Egypt was the sixth largest external broadcaster – ahead of both France and Japan in hours broadcast.

When Egyptian television was born in 1960 there were again strong American influences – in the form of RCA–NBC. In 1971 Egypt had more TV sets than any other African or Arab country.† But most Arab states by 1970 were far ahead of most African states in terms of TV sets per population. Egypt was the pacesetter in this growth of television which had much Anglo-American support – not only in Egypt and Syria, but also in Saudi-Arabia (NBC and the Aramco Oil Company) and in Lebanon (the French ORTF, American ABC and Thomson). American influence has been especially strong in the birth of television in the small oil states of the Persian Gulf. In the mid-1960s Israel was the only country in the eastern Mediterranean which did not have television – partly because another 'Father of the new nation', Ben-Gurion, was against it. But Israel eventually succumbed and went to the American CBS for help.

As in Africa and India the enormous importance of Anglo-American instruction, advice, and help – especially in the early stages of each new medium – has resulted in the communications occupations in Egypt looking towards New York, London and Paris. Nor is this respect purely a one-way matter. For example, Anglo-American international news agency correspondents stationed in Cairo and Beirut have considerable respect for the Middle East News Agency (MENA – successor to ANA) which collects and distributes news throughout the Middle East. One basis for mutual respect is that a number of senior MENA men previously worked for the Anglo-American agencies.[11]

---

* According to the US Department of Commerce Algeria in 1930 had 9,500 radio sets; Turkey 5,200; Egypt 4,000; French Morocco 2,500; Tunisia 1,000; Persia 300; Palestine 150; Syria 150.

† Unesco (1975), but Iran had more.

Egypt's traditional media exports have been films, which she has long exported to most of the Arab world.* In the 1950s Egypt became a major overseas broadcaster and has remained an 'exporter' of radio throughout the Middle East and beyond. Some Egyptian publications go abroad in substantial quantities; for instance *Al Ahram* claims substantial daily export sales – especially to Iraq, Yemen, Kuwait, Sudan and Syria. Through its Middle East News Agency Egypt exports a subsidized news service. Egypt has also gone into the television export business; some Middle East countries are suspicious of the political overtones of Egyptian TV, but in at least one country – The People's Republic of Yemen – Egypt was in 1970–1 the leading source of television imports, mainly feature films and series.[12]

The Egyptian media are mostly owned by the state or the ruling party – there are state publishing houses, state film studios and, of course, state radio and television; the government and various state-owned industries are also the main advertisers. But, although Arab nationalism is a major theme of Egyptian media, the Egyptian communications élite remains strongly oriented towards the Anglo-American world and France. Attempts have been made to 'balance' these influences – for instance the Middle East News Agency has exchanged staff with some east European news agencies. But few senior Egyptian journalists or broadcasters speak Russian, whereas many speak English or French.

TURKEY, PAKISTAN, INDONESIA: TOWARDS MEDIA
SELF-SUFFICIENCY

Turkey, Pakistan and Indonesia are three populous and predominantly Moslem nations which to some extent are heading towards media self-sufficiency. Certainly none of the three has media exports on the scale of Egypt, but all three are probably also less dependent than Egypt on media imports. Nevertheless none of the three avoids substantial Anglo-American media influence – all three import agency news, films and television programming.

Turkey's media are remarkable first for an elaborate and highly partisan newspaper press of a southern European or Latin American kind; secondly Turkey has long had one of the largest of all mini-Hollywoods, making a peak of 300 feature films in 1972. Nevertheless Turkey is a substantial importer of Hollywood films and television; it is also tied into European pop music patterns with the British EMI a powerful force.

Pakistan until 1947, of course, shared its media history with India.

* Egypt in 1971–2 was exporting films to Bahrain, Sudan, Algeria, Tunisia, Iraq, Lebanon, Syria, Israel and USSR.

After Urdu, English is the main newspaper and radio language, but in other respects Pakistan has tried to downplay the influence of British media (partly in deliberate contrast to India). This means a switch towards American (and to a lesser extent German and French) products. American media appear to predominate in Pakistan's imports of news, films and television. Pakistan – like most populous Asian nations – also has a sizeable film industry, which historically is an offshoot of India and Hollywood. Pakistan is, of course, uniquely provided with giant neighbours – China, USSR and India, as well as Afghanistan and Iran. Its media response is hostility to India especially; this is expressed in external radio warfare and a refusal to import Indian films. Pakistan, like a number of other Asian nations, deliberately avoids importing media from any of its neighbours. Instead it seeks partial self-sufficiency with substantial imports from USA and western Europe.

Indonesia's media are clearly very thinly spread[13] – much more thinly than in some nearby nations; Sukarno banned most western media imports as degenerate. Only in radio would Indonesia be ahead of many African nations; it is behind Egypt and most other Moslem countries. As the world's fifth most populous nation Indonesia is extremely unusual in only very recently having started seriously making feature films. But as the Indonesian film industry expands it does so against the familiar Hollywood background. In 1948 85 per cent of films shown were American or British. Indonesian film imports in 1970 came primarily from USA, Hong-Kong, Italy and India. Antara, the national news agency, distributes foreign news within Indonesia in English, with Reuters perhaps the leading foreign agency. Indonesia appears to engage in little media traffic with the rest of the Moslem world. Television has existed since the Asian Games of 1962, but growth has been extremely slow – a situation which decisions to adopt colour TV and to acquire a space satellite may or may not transform.

SAUDI-ARABIA AND IRAN: OIL EXPORTS, MEDIA IMPORTS

Saudi-Arabia's enormous oil wealth contrasts with its very brief history of modernization. While behind its more northerly Arab neighbours in terms of development, it is still ahead of the small Gulf states. Saudi-Arabia also illustrates the dilemmas of the politically conservative regimes in the Arab world, which seek to maintain Arab traditions – while the centre of traditional Arabic learning is Egypt, which has been politically radical. The Saudi regime has tended to favour the United States – and to prefer importing media from the USA, or from Lebanon, which made Arabic media products on a more purely commercial basis than Egypt. But these Lebanese influences were in some ways more alien to Arab and Muslim tradition than were those of Egypt.

The media in Saudi-Arabia have a short history. During the Second World War its minimal newspaper production virtually ceased due to an inability to secure newsprint. The first Saudi *daily* newspaper appeared only in 1952; domestic radio broadcasting began in 1949. When domestic television began in 1965 the law was modified to allow private film showings. Despite its wealth, Saudi-Arabia had no domestic news agency until 1971.

There were two television services in Saudi-Arabia at much earlier dates – both American. A television station was set up by, and for, United States military personnel in Dhahran in 1955; the Arabian American Oil Company (ARAMCO) built a television station for its personnel in 1957 in the same area – on the Persian Gulf opposite Bahrain and Qatar. The USAF station was the first television service in the Middle East – Iraq's television started in 1957, while Lebanon and Egypt began in 1959 and 1960. Probably then, these American stations had the 'demonstration effect' seen elsewhere of encouraging some neighbouring countries to adopt television against their better judgement.

Saudi-Arabia in 1955 was still very far from having its own domestic television. After the first radio station (constructed by an ITT subsidiary) was set up in 1949, the programming policy was on the cautious side:

> In 1950, one year after the station was established, its General Manager, Mr Mohammed Shata, tried to introduce limited items of music, religious songs and folksongs. As soon as the items were heard, King Ibn Saud was angered and ordered the station to stop all singing, limiting broadcasts to regular religious schedules, with a minimum amount of march music (which is performed by the army marching band). . . . It was not until the mid 1950s that the station, cautiously and gradually scheduled programs with folksongs and music, all of which were performed by male vocalists from Saudi-Arabia or from other Arab countries.[14]

Domestic television did not begin in Saudi-Arabia until 1965. An agreement between the US and Saudi governments led to the installation work being undertaken by the United States Army and RCA–NCB. Technical staff were trained in the USA but programme personnel, as in radio, drew mainly on Egyptian education and experience.

Despite the attempt to confine American influence to engineering, despite a very cautious television programming policy, and despite also the continuing absence of Hollywood films in cinemas, the rapid media expansion of the 1960s led by 1970 to major Saudi-Arabian dependence on Anglo-American media for its materials and styles, and on their news agencies for its view of the world. Radio news depended on UPI, AP and Reuters with Reuters Arabic service getting especially heavy use. *Al Riyadh*, the leading Saudi newspaper, subscribed to the Associated Press and its coverage of news outside Saudi-Arabia carried rather little about the rest of the Arab world, but much more about the United States, Britain and France. Saudi-Arabian television was heavily dependent on Anglo-American news-film. In 1970 Saudi television was receiving an average of 34 minutes per day of news-film from Visnews and UPITN and transmitting 20 minutes per day of this; Middle East coverage accounted for only 10–15 per cent of news-film received.[15]* Indeed, Saudi television imported about 40 per cent of its entire programming – mostly entertainment material – from the United States and Britain.

The other main source of imported programming was Lebanon – the Middle East television production centre which most closely conformed to Anglo-American styles. Lebanese television with a relatively small export market (and a very small domestic market) was charging prices between ten and twenty times those charged by the Anglo-American companies.† These relatively expensive Lebanese imports accounted for only about 3 per cent of Saudi television time. Saudi-Arabia also had a substantial domestic radio output in English aimed at foreigners living and working in the country.

Thus, in evading Egyptian media influence – or in restricting it to the inevitable minimum of some Saudis listening to Egyptian radio – the Saudi-Arabian government allowed strong influence by Anglo-American media. And a country which in 1950 had almost no media at all, only twenty years later was transmitting to the citizens of Riyadh, Jidda and Mecca such materials as *Dr Kildare*, *Perry Mason*, *The Virginian*, *Wagon Train* and *The Fugitive*.

Although Saudi-Arabia could not possibly match Egypt's media exports, it nevertheless did have some media influence over the small Gulf states such as Kuwait, Bahrain, Qatar, Oman and the United Arab Emirates. In 1969 the Saudi government built at Dammam its own television antenna, some 1,327 feet high and producing a

---

* Saudi television was receiving 6,173 ft (2 hrs 45 m) from Visnews each week, and 2,925 ft (1 hr 15 m) of news-film from UPITN. These figures included daily news and non-daily special film feature stories. The three Saudi stations were together paying Visnews $2,500 a month and UPITN $2,000 – a total of $54,000 a year in 1970.

† For example the normal price for Anglo-American series in 1970 was $110 an hour against $1,350 an hour for Lebanese programming. A. S. Shobaili (1971), p. 249.

northerly radiated signal (towards Kuwait) which was at the time probably the most powerful television signal in the world.[16]

Iran's media are some ten years or so ahead of Saudi-Arabia's, and Iran provides perhaps the world's most extreme example of an attempt to expand the media rapidly – or at least the electronic media. Iran has a much bigger population than Saudi-Arabia, but Iran similarly has a large area, difficult terrain (mountainous in Iran's case), a backward and illiterate people, a dominant language (Persian) but some important language-ethnic differences, a monarchy – and enormous oil revenues.

By the early 1970s the press was still confined largely to the capital, Tehran, but radio had probably reached most families and the regime was determined to follow this with a television set in every household. Most of the radio growth occurred in the 1960s. Television was launched in Iran by a local entrepreneur who had studied business administration at Harvard. On returning to Tehran – where his family represented RCA and Pepsi-Cola – he started transmitting imported US television programming. Advertising agents handled the importing, RCA trained the technical staff, and this commercial TV operation had a monopoly from 1958 to 1966. Then the Shah decided to have state-controlled TV; this was launched on a high-minded Paris–London model and failed to provide the commercial channel with effective competition. Further decisions were taken to merge all broadcasting – including radio (run since 1964 by the Ministry of Information) – into a single super public corporation called NIRT. It is modelled on pre-advertising French and British television and radio, but NIRT also has wider cultural goals:

> Since its establishment in 1966, NIRT has grown in size and the extent of its activities by leaps and bounds. It employs nearly 7,000 people, of whom 2,000 are stationed in Tehran. Radio covers about 90% of the population, and 100% of the urban centres. . . . There are about 8 million radio sets in the country.
>
> NIRT has a total of 14 *television* production and transmission regional centres with 153 transmitters. . . . The Fifth Plan includes projections for a 70% coverage of the population by the First Programme (currently broadcasting 41 hours a week), devoted to lighter programming, and a 50% coverage by the Second Programme (35 hours) with more exclusively cultural programming. There are about 1·7 million TV sets in the country. . . .

The Asian Games of 1974 were broadcast in colour, but the introduction of full colour programmes was delayed for four years in accordance with the domestic manufacturers' projected ability to fulfil the anticipated demand for colour TV sets. The purchase of a satellite for use in educational as well as general broadcasting is under negotiation.[17]

Iran is an extreme case of a chief executive (the Shah) trying to use television as a weapon to consolidate power, confer prestige, divide the bureaucracy, to project a single national culture – and generally to identify his personality and office with national plans and prestige. Although the intended beneficiaries are the people, those who already have power and cash are the immediate audience – and general considerations of prestige seem to predominate. As far as TV is concerned, the most backward rural areas have been given low priority except where they are sensitive border territory. Despite the great concern with cultural elevation there is heavy importing of American TV series and films. Imports accounted for about 70 per cent of programming in 1972 and 40 per cent in 1974. Early use of the Atlantic space satellite concentrated on moonshots, sporting events and the Shah's visit to the USA.

Television in Iran is also used to stress dynastic continuity. NIRT specializes in lavish television coverage of ceremonies and festivals in which the Shah plays a central part. The television conception of Iranian tradition appears to resemble a Cecil B. DeMille movie in which the part of the Shah is played by the Shah.

Iran also has what is intended to be a major film festival and is rapidly expanding its own sizeable feature-film industry; financial links have been established with Italian producers. All of which stands in remarkable contrast to the anaemic state of the press, daily and weekly. This seems scarcely consistent either with the goal of eradicating illiteracy or with economic development generally. If Iran continues on its present path it will be the first nation in the world to have nationally spread television before a nationally spread press. Politically motivated as the emphasis on the electronic media clearly is, it will be interesting to see if Iran can industrialize without the political intelligence system and infrastructure of an elaborate press which has so far characterized all 'developed' nations whether capitalist or communist.

But in one way neither Saudi-Arabia nor Iran is exceptional. Their policies of forced-draught media growth have been fuelled with Anglo-American imports.

CHAPTER FIFTEEN

France: The perils of imperialism

HOW TO EXPORT FRENCH CULTURE WITHOUT IMPORTING ANGLO-AMERICAN MEDIA?

In many ways France can, or could, claim to be the great exception to the general western media pattern. Indeed, France could claim to be itself a clearer case of media imperialism than either the British or the Americans. Some twenty ex-French colonial territories, from Tunisia round the west African coast to the equator, are still much more closely locked into French culture and French media than the ex-British colonial territories are locked into London.

The period around 1900 was a golden age for the French media. Paris had the world's largest newspaper circulations. French culture and language, supported by Havas news, held sway throughout much of Europe and the Mediterranean. France in 1900 dominated the exciting new medium of the cinema; between 1896 and 1910 the French film industry colonized the entire world including the Far East, Russia and, for a brief period, even the United States. Paris seemed to dominate not only the serious arts, but the popular arts as well.

This golden age was somewhat illusory. The sway of French culture and language was confined mainly to the smaller southern European countries. The French popular press – despite a few large circulations – was commercially less well founded than the American or British. Havas was too dominant a force in the French media – too close to government and too dependent on commercial monopoly. The French film industry was too centralized and became too closely aligned to Parisian high culture to survive serious commercially based competition.

Centralization, Parisian dominance, governmental involvement, commercial monopolies and lack of market strength, the pursuit of some ill-defined cultural glory, a concern with literary elegance – these were the strengths, and these remain the weaknesses, of the French media.

The French were brilliant innovators in most aspects of media technology and output. Havas was the original news agency; the Parisian *Petit* press pioneered the mammoth daily-sale newspaper;

the early French cinema industry was an extraordinary mixture of technical innovation, artistic panache, and world-wide salesmanship. Yet such innovation always ran out of steam. The French media were always fundamentally about something else. The cinema was seen as an extension of the art gallery, of the Comédie française, of the novel, even of film criticism. The mammoth early newspaper sales were also about something else – and not merely votes, but about the raising of money by financiers from small investors through advertising and sometimes news columns. And Havas, the grand-daddy of the news agencies, it was also about something else – and not just stock-exchange information; Havas was also the great advertising agency of France. The lack of clear commercial goals, the pursuit of cultural objectives, the drive towards monopoly (rather than cartel) were caused by, and led to, government involvement. Lack of commercial strength led to government support. The French media tended to depend on governmental (or party, or other interest group) commercial assistance, more than on the French public. The French media were based on Paris; the larger organizations tended to acquire government support at cost of being unpopular with sizeable sections of the French public. Aligned against the centre there developed powerful regional and apolitical media which were to be a Trojan horse for the Anglo-Americans.

As often happens with official governmental media and cultural policy, no single agency in the French government was responsible. Media policy was established by a shifting alliance of several governmental agencies and several commercial companies. Their coalition goal was a French culture and media independent clearly of Germany and other continental powers on the one hand and independent of Britain and the United States on the other. In practice, of course, opposition to Germany was often more pressing – and some Anglo-American media influences could apparently be swallowed without threatening the overall policy. Opposition to continental enemies was also something upon which literary intellectuals could agree with government officials and commercial monopolists.

The French media thus tended to become proponents of French culture, consisting of an official version of French history, the great tradition of French literature and a determination to make the world speak French. If not the world, then at least the world's diplomats must speak French, and if not all the colonized then at least the educated élite of the colonies would speak French. Thus authors of books, auteurs of films, the commercial monopolies such as Havas and Hachette, and French finance and foreign ministers could all agree that French literary culture should be beamed into the classrooms, cinemas and homes of the colonies. The considerable success of this policy locked the over-centralized French media into a Napoleonic myth of French culture and international success which had one lethal weakness. It lacked a secure popular and commercial base at home.

This French media tradition also encouraged a tendency to accept myths and to avoid reality – to accept a mythical view of a French media tradition which never quite existed.

RESISTANCE: TO 1939

In 1900 France was the only country (apart from the United States) which had a daily newspaper press on a scale comparable to, and perhaps larger than, Britain's. While in 1900 the *Daily Mail* briefly became the first British paper to sell a million copies, *Le Petit Journal* had sold a million in 1890.

France developed a diverse and highly political press – but these political papers were taxed until 1881; the paper taxes ended in 1886. A few newspapers were deliberately apolitical to evade taxation; some papers used serial stories to entice votes, others to attract the savings of small investors. *Le Petit Journal* surged forward to a daily sale of 350,000 in 1873 and 583,000 in 1880. The *Petit Journal* cost five centimes – equivalent to the halfpenny *Daily Mail* which only appeared in London a generation later. Most French newspapers remained political and of small circulation but the success of the *Petit Journal* led to other '*Petit*' papers at a sou.

Le Petit Journal and *Le Petit Parisien* prospered and were joined by *Le Journal* and *Le Matin*. These four were the dominant French popular newspapers of the First World War and well into the inter-war period. Some aspects of these papers – the fiction stories, the advice columns and gossip, the rotary presses, the coverage of sport and crime rather than politics – were completely French and without any foreign influence. But some of the key innovations in this 'golden age' of French journalism were direct imports from America. Women's fashion pages, the news interview and promotional guessing competitions – these were all established in New York a generation before their regular appearance in France.

Mergenthaler Linotype machines were imported from the USA by the *Petit* press of Paris in order to combat the advantages which the telegraph gave to provincial papers in covering late news. James Gordon Bennett, jnr, owner of the *New York Herald*, who lived in Paris most of his life, launched a Paris edition in 1887. Charles Ives, the American who later started *The Morning* in London, also launched in Paris, in partnership with an Englishman, an English-language *Morning News* and the French *Le Matin*; the latter was transformed into a limited company in 1884 with 8 shareholders, all English and American. The first editor of *Le Matin* was a French-educated Englishman, Alfred Edwards. Another Anglo-American presence was that of Dalziel's news agency; its Paris branch hurt Havas between 1891 and 1893 even more than its London branch hurt Reuters. Dalziel quickly showed that its American news-gathering techniques were far superior to those of Havas; this may have led to a measure of anti-Americanism increased by Havas's financial difficulties following a decline in its advertising revenue. *Le Petit Journal*'s accusation that Clemenceau's shady alliances involved the receipt of British government funds was an example of anti-British feeling.

The First World War marked the end of the golden age of the French media. Whereas in the early years of the century French films had predominated in world film exports, by 1925 some 70 per cent of all films shown in France came from Hollywood (Table 4). This decline was not caused solely by the war; the French industry was starting to lose its foreign markets several years before 1914.

During the 1920s the French media were on the defensive, but more or less successfully. Film imports were slowly reduced. The large newspaper circulations continued – upon a seemingly French path not influenced by foreign models. It was not until around 1930 that the steady increase of Anglo-American influences within the French press became more and more evident.

In the 1930s *Paris-Soir* was the main French newspaper innovator, and became the circulation leader. *Paris-Soir* drew quite openly on such Anglo-American examples as the New York tabloids, *Time* magazine and the London *Daily Express* – and its editor, Pierre Lazareff, was a vocal advocate in Paris of these and other Anglo-American models. *Paris-Soir* (like *Yomiuri* in Tokyo), using flamboyant American-style promotion and motor transport, showed that a capital city evening paper could no longer be vetoed by the existing distribution cartel. The strength of this cartel in France was amply illustrated by the history of Coty's paper *Ami du Peuple*. Havas played the key role in the French press cartel because its dominant position as the leading news agency and the leading advertising agency in France meant that the cartel could, and did, cut Coty off from basic supplies of both news and advertising. Hachette, with its dominant position in Paris retail sales and national press distribution could, and did, cut Coty off from the orthodox means of selling *Ami du Peuple*. Most leading newspapers – such as *Le Journal*, *Le Petit Journal* and *Le Matin* – had, during and after the First World War, handed over their entire distribution to Hachette. Another leading paper of this period, *L'Echo de Paris*, refused to print Coty's paper.

François Coty, the perfume millionaire, overcame all of these difficulties but only after getting alternative services at onerous terms, and only through drawing on his quite exceptional reserves of determination and cash.

Much has been made by historians of inter-war France of the right-wing slide of the major French papers and the prevalence of subsidies from French and foreign political sources. Few commentators have recognized the substantial element in the cartel of a defensive strategy against American media incursions. The strength of Hollywood in the French market was obvious. But the combined defensive interests of the newspapers, the Havas news-and-advertising-agency and the government, were perhaps most threatened by the blows which Havas had been dealt by the Anglo-American news agencies; this was so not only on the world scene, but also within France itself where United Press in particular made serious inroads in the 1930s.

Many aspects of 1930s French media are ambiguous as far as foreign influence was concerned. Hollywood could be regarded as in decline – in 1937 the typical French cinema show was of a French-American double feature. In 1937 only 45 per cent of films shown were American – a sign perhaps of decline; but only 40 per cent were French.[1] The success of commercial radio in 1930s France was also ambiguous – in 1939 *Le Petit Parisien* earned the same advertising revenue as its radio station, 'Le Poste Parisien', whereas in 1933 the radio station had only one-sixth of the newspaper's advertising revenue; but was this an example of American commercial radio influence or merely of intelligent press diversification? The decline of the popular press cartel was also somewhat ambiguous. True, the Anglo-American style *Paris-Soir* was successful; but the bulk of the French press continued on more traditional and political paths. Not only were many of the leading newspapers in the 1930s controlled by Steel, Oil, and similar industrial interests, some of the smaller French papers – several political scandals of the 1930s revealed – had developed another effective form of press subsidy; this was the blackmail tactic – the newspaper threatens to publish certain information in its possession about a prominent individual unless ... The continuing weakness of advertising, which lay behind the failure of the French press to establish independent viability on the Anglo-American pattern, could be read also as a sign of the French press having chosen a separate Gallic road.

LA GUERRE EST FINIE: FRENCH MEDIA REBORN (1944)

1944, so the present-day orthodoxy has it, was the date when everything in the French media began. The Germans departed, the resistance and the Free French founded the French media afresh. A new golden age occurred in the French press; novelists and resistance fighters emerged from the underground to edit newspapers. Agence France-Presse was launched as the new world-wide press voice of France, in place of Havas which had collaborated; radio was reborn – modelled on and staffed from the French service of the wartime BBC, rather than 1930s French radio. The film industry was reborn in terms of artistic excellence and in export capability. In 1948 the French film industry was re-established in its home market and also in exports; not only in western Europe, but also in Czechoslovakia and Hungary, French films were prominent (Table 9).

But much of this golden age was as mythical as the previous one around 1900. There was a serious lack of fit between the ideological aspirations and the market-place realities. The French media had indeed been reborn in 1944 – but, rather than a completely new birth, the clock had been put back to 1920; while the French media of the 1950s repeated the 1920s, the 1960s were to repeat the 1930s.

The biggest component of the 1944 myth concerned collaboration with the Germans, in which the bulk of French media and media personnel had participated. This was especially noticeable in the film industry; 'new' films and directors were catapulted into the post-war era in France, as in Italy (and China) because they had collaborated – Bresson and Clouzot for example first made their names as film directors under German tutelage. The advertising wing of Havas lived on as a key component of the French media – only the news side had any claims to rebirth. In AFP, and in the new radio arrangements, what happened as much as a rebirth was a mere changing of the guard. Even the brilliant post-war period of the press – involving France's most eminent writers as journalists and editors – was a phase which passed quickly. The literary and political ex-underground papers bloomed and withered; waiting in the wings were the collaborationist Vichy press and the provincial commercial newspapers which had gained so markedly in the 1930s. And as for film exports – most were to French colonies, France's culturally close neighbours (such as Belgium) and to east European nations looking for a temporary solution to the Hollywood glut and communist film famine of the late 1940s.

THE FRENCH MEDIA AMERICANIZED (1960s)

For the French media the 1960s were a repetition of the 1930s in at least three respects. The French media fatally lacked market appeal; the public simply switched off. Secondly, the French media operated in a financial vacuum – advertising revenue was still weak, as in Italy and Latin America, and no adequate alternative was discovered. Thirdly, the French government's vigorous pursuit of a nationalist media policy was unpopular both with domestic and with foreign audiences.

These weaknesses were first, and most, apparent in the press. The ex-underground papers lacked commercial viability; so long as they appeared on a single sheet of paper this was not clear, but as commercial normality returned, the brilliant blossoms quickly withered. Agence France-Presse, born afresh, could claim neither the foreign nor the domestic dominance of Havas; the Anglo-American agencies prospered and found willing allies in competing national news agencies which have remained more significant in France than in most countries, much more significant than in the home markets of any other 'international' news agencies. The Parisian press, which in the immediate post-war period had the great bulk of French daily sales, gradually declined; the winners – as in the 1930s – were big commercial dailies in places like Toulouse, Bordeaux and some twenty other big provincial centres which steadily established impregnable regional monopolies, characterized by many local 'editions' (or pages) and border warfare of a largely ritual nature often against a rival monopoly daily 100 miles or more away. In one or two places, notably Marseilles, some vestiges of competition remained. But even in Marseilles a mildly competitive local situation included a cartel carving-up of the entire Marseilles–Lyon–Grenoble region of southeast France,[2] plus some rather Machiavellian printing arrangements – which would be known as a 'joint operating agreement' in US parlance. These French provincial monopolies are in many cases deliberately built on US models as well as made-in-USA printing plant.

The Paris-based press was, as in the inter-war period, at first sustained by the cartel distribution arrangements, but eventually strangled by them. Here is a comment from Jean Louis, one of the formidable Servan-Schreiber brothers, militant opponents of Hachette and its cartel control of kiosk sales:

In France, the distribution structure and the not very prosperous situation of the press stems for the most part from the outrageous monopoly held by the Nouvelles Messageries de la Presse Parisienne (NMPP) and the news-stand dealers. Theoretically a co-operative, the NMPP is dominated by France's biggest publishing concern, Hachette, whose newspapers traditionally have been badly managed. Those powerful lobbies (the NMPP and the vendors) have united to effectively block any innovation which might inconvenience them. In this way, three developments that could have put the French press on a really sound footing and prevented the current 'press crisis' were nipped in the bud: subscriptions for magazines, direct delivery of dailies to customers and large-scale distribution of Sunday papers.[3]

The Servan-Schreiber brothers were two among a small group of American-oriented journalists and press entrepreneurs who led the struggle against the entrenched forces of the French press. The main winners were the provincial dailies; the main combatants were three types of Parisian publication which did not depend on national daily distribution – Parisian evenings, consumer magazines and news-magazines.

Paris-Soir was reborn as *France-Soir*; it was again edited by Pierre Lazareff and for over twenty years was the French daily circulation leader. Lazareff and his wife, Hélène, had spent the Second World War in New York and Hélène, as editor of *Elle*, was to be the leading single influence on post-war consumer magazines in France:

Hélène Lazareff was a remarkable professional. And she was light-years ahead of her French contemporaries, because she had just spent five years in the United States working on the best paper in the world, the *New York Times*, and then on a woman's magazine.
On the technical plane, for instance, she mastered the use of color photos, which was completely unknown in France. . . . All the material was imported from the States. . . .[4]

This quotation is from Françoise Giroud, who subsequently played a prominent part in another import, the news magazine. In such news magazines as *L'Express*, American styles have been explicitly copied in considerable detail. The conversion of *L'Express* in 1964 to the news magazine format was the key event. Subsequently *Le Nouvel Observateur* followed this lead; in 1972 Hachette launched another news magazine, *Le Point*, which differed from the other two in being modelled not on *Time* but on its competitor *Newsweek*. Further American news magazine influences have come into French journalism by way of *Der Spiegel*. While these magazines often editorially oppose United States policies, their journalists – whose reputations stand high in France – tend to revere the more exalted elements of the American press.[5]

Such American-format magazines were successful not only in the sales but in the advertising market. During the 1950s the American invasion of Parisian advertising steadily increased. American advertising agencies have been less prominent than in Britain or West Germany, but they grew rapidly enough to be closely associated with major changes in the French media. As elsewhere, the politically

partisan daily newspapers have not been favoured with much spending via American-owned agencies. In sharp contrast to the largest
French agencies, Havas and Publicis (both of which have traditional
alliances with the French government), spending through American
advertising agencies in Paris goes first to magazines and television,
then radio, and only fourthly to newspapers.[6]

In radio, the French public had a choice. There were either the
government-controlled channels from Paris or the border stations
based in Monte Carlo, Andorra, Luxembourg and Saarland which
pumped into France the pop–news–commercials style of American
radio; in due course the French government bought financial control
in these stations, via SOFIRAD, but the alternative format largely remained, and remained popular; as elsewhere, the official government
radio also tried to beat the opposition by joining it.

Television provided the fiercest political clashes of the 1960s because
here the French public had no alternative to which they could switch.
But border overlaps were quite enough for millions of French voters
to know that British, Belgian, German, Swiss and Italian television
at times were more revealing about French politics than was the
Parisian television news. French press journalists also, like journalists
elsewhere, were quite ready to lambast French television for its sub-
servience to government control. These conflicts surfaced for even the
least observant to see, when during the 'events' of 1968, the majority
of French television news journalists went on strike against political
interference. They did not win this battle – many were fired – but
their cause at least half won the war. The news, not to mention the
advertising, on French television has grown steadily more like Anglo-
American models. There are also, not vast, but substantial imports of
programming.*

And what of the French film industry? It still exists on a substantial
scale, but like other film industries it suffers from a shortage of domestic revenue. The French film industry never had a domestic boom
around 1950 on the scale of Italy, Britain or some other European
countries – because it never had their number of cinema visits. Even
in 1948 the average French person only went to the cinema nine times
a year (against 29 in Britain).[7] The French government has continued
the inter-war policy of modest import limitation and modest support
for domestic production. The majority of films shown in France in
the early 1970s were still imports, with American imports in the lead.
What was quite different, however, from the 1930s was the difficulty
of knowing how French a 'French' feature was. In 1972 France made

* According to Tapio Varis (1973) French television in 1970–1 imported
about 500 hours of programming, the majority of which was American and
British.

Strip cartoons in translation

Blondie in Turkish

Modesty Blaise in French

Jules Feiffer in Italian

News magazines' international format

169 feature films, but only 71 of these were 'entirely French'; 98 were co-productions, in half of which French, and in half of which foreign, participation predominated.[8] Most of this foreign involvement was with Hollywood or the Italian film industry (or Hollywood in Rome).

The French film industry, in short, depended heavily on the American industry for world distribution and production finance. Moreover outside its own ex-colonies, the French industry had few distinctive export markets. In at least 16 non-colonial countries the French industry in 1972 accounted for over 10 per cent of film imports; these countries were mostly in western and eastern Europe, but also included Canada, Lebanon and Argentina.* However, in these good markets for French films, Italian films accounted for a similar proportion of imports (13 per cent) – just ahead of Britain (9 per cent) and far behind the USA (40 per cent).

FRENCH CULTURAL EMPIRE

French media influence is exceptionally powerful in the ex-French west African colonies, where, however, the media in general are exceptionally weak. Behind this paradox lies the rather narrow influence of French media in the world.

Thirteen separate nations in ex-French west and equatorial Africa had in 1975 a total population of about 40 million. These countries in general lack both large cities and affluent agriculture. In some the media consist mainly of one big radio station, much of its output in French, with very little indeed in the way of a local press. There is a tiny but highly French-educated élite; in most of these countries relatively little media (or educational) effort is made in the local African languages. If you are an educated African you can rely heavily on French media. Daily newspapers as well as many weekly magazines are flown in from France.

Senegal in media terms is one of the more developed of these countries, with a substantial ex-patriate population. Senegal had been used by the French from 1939 to provide coverage for the whole Francophone west African region. Senegal is also somewhat unusual among these countries in having long actually boasted a daily press of its own. In 1972 the main Senegalese newspaper was *Le Soleil*, selling 5,000 copies a day (in a nation of 4 million). There is almost no local-language press – and the radio also is dominated by French. Senegalese television, however, was devoted throughout its early years entirely to Unesco-assisted educational broadcasting – all of it

* The countries were Lebanon, Japan, Switzerland, Luxembourg, Canada, West Germany, Spain, UK, Czechoslovakia, Hungary, Poland, Yugoslavia, Argentina, Netherlands, Norway, Portugal. Based on Unesco (1975).

in Wolof, an unwritten local language; as with many educational TV projects, however, its goals were unclear and its achievements unimpressive.

Senegal in 1972 was importing 80 per cent of its (now no longer educational) TV programming from France, 80 per cent of the feature films shown in Senegal's 60 cinemas and much of its print media consumption (three-quarters of print sales were in Dakar, the capital). *Le Monde*, *France-Soir* and *Le Figaro* together had daily sales half as big as the local Dakar daily; magazine sales were dominated by French publications.[9] In Senegal, also, as elsewhere in Francophone Africa, AFP was the dominant news agency, Havas the main advertising agency, and an Hachette subsidiary dominated the distribution of French publications.

Typical of the more backward west African countries would be Niger; a Sahara nation to the north of Nigeria, Niger is twice the size of France. In 1972 its four million people boasted one daily paper with a sale of 2,000 copies. Radio was the only medium with a real national presence – the radio was in French and five vernacular languages. Television was confined to a small-scale educational exercise – with sets in some 20 schools near the capital; this educational experiment was entirely devoted to teaching the French language and it was heavily dependent on assistance from France.[10]

The apparently vice-like grip of French language, culture and media in Francophone west Africa stands in sharp contrast to the position of French media in the world. The most impressive French media performance of continental proportions is probably the position of Agence France-Presse throughout Latin America, where it – and not Reuters – provides the competition to UPI and AP. In a few places – notably French Canada, the Lebanon and Greece – French culture has lived on and French media have done well. But in terms of the world market, each of these is lowly populated and even in each of these places Anglo-American media and media influences are as strong as, or stronger than, the French. In Belgium also French media – including daily newspapers – do quite well, although only with the French-speaking part of the population. In Europe at large France is well behind Germany as a media exporter.

But in one other region French media are still strong – north Africa. This is no less true of the two more populated Maghreb countries, Morocco and Algeria, than of Tunisia and Libya. In these countries, however, French media exports have to contend with serious rivals – domestic French-language media, domestic Arabic-language media (which are growing increasingly strong) and imported Arabic-language media. These four countries tend to conduct love-hate relationships with each other, with France and also with

Egypt – resulting in shifting alliances in the media, as in politics generally. Egyptian radio played a major part in the struggle for independence, especially in Algeria.

The continuing strength of French culture is perhaps most remarkable in Algeria where one of the most savage of all the wars of independence was fought. Yet in the same Algiers cafés, which in the late 1950s had been a major target for bombing, in the mid-1960s one could see Algerians reading *Le Monde* and *Le Figaro*.

In Morocco French influence remains strong, but the bulk of the French-language newspaper sales are of Moroccan-produced dailies. The Arabic daily press is growing and there is also a Spanish press. Morocco has quite elaborate radio arrangements; it does transmit domestic radio in French, but also in Arabic, in several Berber dialects and in Spanish and English; Morocco at independence even had some privately owned commercial radio.[11] Morocco had the first television station in Africa, from 1954 to 1956; when television began again in 1962 it was on a much firmer footing than in west Africa – and in 1965 it was hooked into Eurovision.* This enables Morocco (like the other Maghreb countries) to receive programming from France – but also, of course, from other European countries. In the news agency field Agence France-Presse is strong but there is a domestic Moroccan agency and UPI and Reuters also have Moroccan customers.[12] The trend in Morocco (and Algeria) seems to be that French media influence will remain strong but will gradually diminish in the face of competition from Arabic and non-French western media influences.

The Algerian media in the wake of the bitter independence struggle fell behind those of Morocco, but Algeria, with its oil revenues, shows signs of taking the lead and indeed of developing television on something like the Iranian pattern. This includes the manufacture of receiving sets and elaborate plans for both micro-wave links and a satellite system. Algerian television seems to exhibit the Foreign Metropolitan v. Local Authentic dilemma in an especially acute form. The history of television in Algeria is one of original French installation and programming, leading later to Arab personnel being trained in France. By the 1970s there were also powerful strains towards Arabic programming and some senior personnel lacking French education. From where can the non-French material come? The obvious answer is from Egypt, but Algeria has been a rival of Egypt and often preferred to import materials from the Lebanon; thus Algeria preferred commercially produced non-political fare in

---

* Of ORTF's 1971 total TV exports of 9,000 hours, 65 per cent went to Africa and the Indian Ocean, and only 4 per cent to west Europe. Tapio Varis (1973), p. 40.

preference to material from a fellow socialist, but rival, neighbour.

In 1973 Algeria imported just over half its television programming, of which nearly a third was in Arabic and seven-tenths in French. This may look like the continuance of French cultural domination. But less than half of the French-language imports were French-made programming; about half of these 'French' imports were American and British programming dubbed into French, presumably Parisian French. Moreover some of the 'Arabic' programming was also Anglo-American material, dubbed into apparently Lebanese Arabic. Only 30 per cent of Algerian TV imports were truly French;[13] of the remaining 70 per cent the bulk was Anglo-American material (dubbed into French or Arabic) and some of the remainder was clearly entertainment material more or less influenced by Anglo-American models. Algeria was also quite well supplied with cinemas and had a high rate of cinema attendance. In 1971 it imported 104 feature films 'mainly from France, the USA, Italy, India, the UK, Egypt, Lebanon and USSR'; Algeria has also been making a few feature films each year – some of them co-productions with Italy or France.[14] Here again, then, the foreign influences go far beyond merely French ones.

Thus French dominance of its ex-colonial territories seems to remain strong only so long as the connection is a *cultural* one involving French language and education plus the air-freighting of French media. When these ex-French territories start to develop their own media, the ties with France are very considerably weakened. Cultural imperialism is not replaced by an equally dominant media imperialism. French materials in the future will also clearly have to compete with a wider range of domestic Algerian media as well as with a wider range of media available from other African countries (ex-British and ex-French) and from the Middle East.

Meanwhile, the more media-developed ex-French territories – notably Morocco and Algeria – show a substantial penetration of Anglo-American materials. But in Nigeria – whose population alone nearly equals that of all the ex-French African territories – the penetration of French media is negligible.

FRANCE AS MEDIA IMPERIALIST

There are several possible ways of interpreting both the strength of French media in her former colonies and the rapid decline in the more developed Maghreb countries.

An obvious cause of weakness is the continuing salience of *governmental* influence within the French media industry. After the 1944 'rebirth', the pre-war constellation of governmentally linked media organizations was also reborn and re-established in the colonies: Havas and Publicis, the governmentally linked advertising agencies; the official radio and television as well as the peripheral radio stations controlled by the government through SOFIRAD; Agence France-Presse, an international agency dependent on government finance; Hachette, the newspaper-book-magazine combine and controller of distribution. Yet other companies, such as the electronics manufacturer Thomson-CSF (active in Senegal and other ex-French colonies), give the impression of extremely close ties to the French government. All of these organizations can work powerfully together in an ex-colony which wishes to maintain close ties with French culture; when the same country decides to search for its own national culture, the whole structure is much weaker. Moreover in the rest of the world most governments and businessmen are reluctant to import media from other governments – Soviet or French, distant or neighbouring. There are exceptions – for example in the news field there may be a demand for a 'French view' distinct from competing Anglo-American views. But even this has its dangers; if that is the demand, it may disappear when French views are no longer distinctive.

There is a great ambivalence in attitudes of the French media towards the American media. Even the great government-linked commercial media interests are involved in importing American media. Hachette, for example, not only produces American-style publications but also imports American comics for French translation and sale. Even the great French film directors often acknowledge clear American influences. Clair and Renoir both worked in Hollywood; Truffaut sees in Hitchcock more to admire than do most Americans or Britons. Even Jean-Luc Godard's films are full of American influences. The same is the case with French journalists, advertising men, and market researchers. The broadcasters who went on strike in 1968 were demanding standards, and proclaiming values, which had never really existed in French broadcasting but which were known to exist in the USA, Britain and West Germany.

CHAPTER SIXTEEN

The media are American

Since no concise statement of the 'media imperialism thesis' existed, an attempt was made to provide one in Chapter Two. Further difficulties remain in assessing its validity, one of which is the weak state of the data. But even if some factual common ground is established – such as that in the tables at the end of this book – it can still be agreed, or denied, that these add up to media imperialism.

If American multi-national companies are regarded as instruments of neo-imperialism, then a company like RCA–NBC, also a defence contractor, is clearly one such instrument.* If the fact of certain people in New York and Washington planning a world-wide sales strategy – including tactics for persuading governments to change their minds – constitutes media imperialism, then this has happened repeatedly. There undoubtedly has been a military element in these overseas sales – although one which the media imperialism thesis seeks to exaggerate in the Cold War era and to underplay in earlier periods. Again the thesis ignores the enormous significance of the British Empire, among others.

There is much room for disagreement over the *motives* surrounding media exports and the subjective attitudes of exporters, intermediaries and audiences. Did the enormous scale of media exporting result from carefully laid Machiavellian plans, or was it an innocent accident which surprised importers and exporters alike? Were commercial middlemen and government officials in importing countries engaged in corrupt agreements or unseemly conspiracies? Some businessmen's most ambitious plans worked, while others did not. In some cases a nonsense, or chaos, view of history would be viable.

The response of the audience is left especially unclear in the media imperialism thesis. There is a strong case for arguing that these media have been dumped at low prices, that in some cases the only effective choice has been between cheap alternatives from the same one or two countries. Clearly recipients in many countries have been on the receiving end of a 'one-way flow'. But the media imperialism thesis does not propose a clear alternative. Should African or Asian com-

* In 1971, RCA had defence contracts worth $250 million, while AT and T had $1,199 millions worth. See *Variety*, 12th July 1972.

municators give the audience more local fare, even if this is more costly or less popular? If all media imports are not to be forbidden what is a reasonable level of imports and does it differ between media and between countries?

Both the proponents and opponents of the media imperialism thesis implicitly argue that the media constitute one more example, or one more refutation, of a wider neo-Marxist case. The central thesis of the present book, however, is that the media are not just one more example of any general thesis. The media are about politics, and commerce and ideas. This is a strange enough combination even when the media stay at home. But as an item of international trade the combination is even more unusual. When a government allows news importation it is in effect importing a piece of another country's politics – which is true of no other import. The media also set out to entertain and intrigue – to make people laugh or cry – they have an emotional appeal unlike other products. And because the media also deal in ideas, their influence can be unpredictable in form and strength.

The media become quickly encrusted with fixed traditions, which makes the original patterning especially important. This has given an enormous influence over other media systems to a country which has consistently led development of new media.

In retrospect the eagerness of so many countries to copy and adopt so many American media patterns seems to have an air both of inevitability and of accident. Time and time again particular countries have seemed likely to 'escape' American influence, not to repeat their own reflexes, and then – quite accidentally – they step once more on to the American path.

The media can be heavily skewed in particular countries in particular directions. The media are the consequence of *political* decisions – whether or not to tax, censor, control or subsidize. The media are also skewed heavily by *advertising* revenue or its absence. And a particular medium tends to skew other media because for audiences media are partly interchangeable.

THE MEDIA ARE POLITICS

The United States media emerged from, and reflect the assumptions of, American politics. The US media do not merely 'fit' neatly into the US political system, the US media are an important, indeed essential, part of that system. All other nations in the world have borrowed American press models and then subsequent media models; but this does not mean that more or less American-style media 'fit' so neatly into, or constitute such an important part of, other political systems.

Through the press, de Tocqueville said, the American parties, without actually meeting, listen and argue with one another. This is a different conception of party from the communist one, or the conception of party in that majority of the world's states which have a dominant governing party.

The enormous proliferation of media which the USA developed (and which is now found with modifications in all other industrialized nations) assumed the American type of political party – a loose coalition of local parties and factions which met together mainly for electioneering. The American media also reflect the division of powers – the American press, taken out of the hands of government, was thus taken from the executive branch and given if not to the Congress, then to the *legislators*, whose interests the press especially still tends to reflect.

The executive branch has had to seek ways of influencing a press whose natural allies are the local Senators and Congressmen. The executive branch has done this by courting the *national* media – the agencies, the networks, the magazines – and by expanding government control of information through an enormous army of public relations personnel.

The American media emphasis on personalities derives partly from the stress which American politics gave to individual, rather than party, seekers of office. The American media reflect both the constitutional provision of 'no law' on the press and also the wider common law tradition of allowing new fields to expand unfettered by special laws.

'Freedom of the press' seems a safe conservative doctrine to most Americans because it implies a mixture of news and entertainment, of politics and advertising, which has never seriously been challenged, but rather has been adapted to the later media. However, such conceptions of news and entertainment and advertising when adopted in other countries may there seem much different. For example there is a common complaint in other nations that Anglo-American news values are negative and destructive. In other countries the offerings of AP and UPI are not seen alongside the more positive stories in the local American media about the successes of the local Chamber of Commerce of the local Congressman; moreover traditional American suspicion of Washington, the executive branch and the rascality of politicians as a species – which underlies news values – may appear much less conservative and reassuring when seen applied to diplomatic or foreign news in some other country.

THE MEDIA ARE COMMERCE

Commercial assumptions, based on the US domestic market, also lie behind all American media, for they assume large proportions of advertising revenue, and a major concern with directing media content towards the preferences and buying behaviour of customers and advertisers. These media are also paced and packaged to compete for audience attention.

Entertainment products coming from the United States are even more deeply entwined with advertising and marketing than are soap or packaged food. Consumer products merely use heavy doses of advertising to achieve sales. But television series and other entertainment media products have the unique distinction of selling advertising itself.

Moreover, the dispensers abroad of American entertainment conform to classic commercial industrial patterns. A single Hollywood company typically offers entertainment in three forms – feature films, television series and records/tapes. A broadcasting organization in an importing country is offered by the salesmen of such companies material to fulfil all of its annual import requirements. Each particular company may not stock the entire entertainment range; but RCA also offers equipment, and the BBC – while not as yet offering feature films – does have television series, sound programming, records and books.

Some fifteen American and five British organizations each offering a variety of materials and services, together sell the entire media range from foreign news to hit songs, and from feature films to comic strips. Just three or four Anglo-American organizations may dominate the media imports of any particular country. Each of these three or four organizations can offer bulk discounts and free extras across a wide range of media; each organization carries a certain aura of technological and management sophistication and presents a list of its prominent customers in other countries.

These few organizations often find themselves dealing in any single country with a range of customers and government departments which are internally divided and antagonistic. Even in countries where the government dominates the media, conflicting decisions are often made by Ministers of Information, Education, Rural Development and Finance – and subsequently altered in the Presidential Palace. Often the various politicians and government officials may not be aware of commercial assumptions in the background. In some countries American-owned advertising agencies insist on placing their advertising in segments of imported programming. They may have 'rational' reasons – such as the desired international image of the product, the more affluent audiences which watch foreign programming and so on. But such policies clearly favour more importing.

These tough commercial facts only seem improper or surprising if one forgets the essentially commercial nature of American entertainment media. This, however, is often forgotten – imports are cheaper than home-made alternatives and much media policy is formed by government officials; it is typical of such rather confused official media policy-making that advertising agencies are often thought to be outside the mainstream of the media.

THE MEDIA ARE TECHNOLOGY

The media are also technology and undeniably a significant connection exists between media exporting and technology. Technical innovations were involved in the American development of the popular press in the 1830s, the emergence of AP as a domestic news agency and Reuters as an international agency, in silent and talkie films, in radio and television. Clearly also current developments in the media focus upon a new electronic revolution – computers, space satellites, cable, photo-composition in the press, and so on. The United States is once again prominent in these new forms of media hardware. But the question of whether such technologies determine particular consequences crosses many disputatious areas within social science, within Marxism, within politics and in the world at large.

One argument is that the new technology does determine the media patterns which subsequently follow in the importing nation: Once RCA has sold you the new technological pill and you've swallowed it, then the rest follows; your media system is soon permeated by the refreshing draught, or the poison. Such views, like most other sweeping statements about the media, have been propounded in both left-wing and right-wing versions. Both the left and right versions tend to imply that, Yes, the media are American – because importers have first imported American technology. Versions of this media-technological-imperatives view are held not only by writers of the left and right but by relevant government officials in Washington and Moscow and Paris and by businessmen in companies like RCA. These arguments lay behind the French sale and Soviet purchase of the SECAM colour television system.

Another version of media technological determinism, however, takes the reverse view of the significance of American media, and media technology, in the world. In this view the media follow inevitably from industrialization and the United States thus led in the media because from 1880 or so it led in industrialization; Germany or Japan

or China followed in the American media path, not because they
were importing media technology or ideas, but because they were a
little later at industrializing everything including the media. This
view is implicitly accepted by many historians of the media, for
example the press historians who typically give chronological
accounts of a single nation's press related to the same country's
political and economic history.

Another school of thought usually concludes that there is a strong
correlation between the development of different media, levels of
literacy, and general levels of economic development. The implication here is that in practice each of the media separately, and also all
of the media collectively, are related to the level of industrialization
and division of labour.

Such arguments have some broad strength and some obvious
weaknesses. Clearly there are obvious examples of countries
which swallowed the RCA technological pill with American media
consequences. But many contrary examples can also be found:
some countries have imported little American technology
and much American programming, while other countries did the
reverse.

That an American pattern of media follows more or less automati-
cally from industrialization is very broadly true. All highly industrialized countries have a highly developed press, for example. But com-
pare Britain, Germany and France in 1900 or many neighbouring
pairs of countries in Latin America, Africa or Asia today. Both the
scale of the media and their character do vary enormously between
countries of similar levels of economic development. Differences are
especially noticeable between eastern and western Europe, between
ex-French and ex-British colonies in Africa and between countries
in south-east Asia.

The correlation of indicators of media development has some very
general validity. These correlations are strongest between groups of
countries all of which for example have television services. But what
about the small countries which still do not have television, or the
larger countries which could, but do not, make feature films? These
are enormous differences in themselves, and have very big implications for media importing.

The most dramatic recent technological innovation has been the
space satellite. The technology is American (and Soviet) and is clearly
related to the military significance of space. The configuration of the
technology reflects primarily the requirements of American telephone
users and electronics companies; in its original phase the United
States did own 'more than half' of INTELSAT. On the other hand the
Soviet Union got into the satellite game at the same time, and

satellites do differ in other significant ways from any previous media innovation.

The public relations and 'image' considerations present in the satellite issue are common to new media technology, and help to explain why the acquisition of domestic space satellites in the 1970s produces strong echoes of the introduction of television into many countries in the 1950s. The notion of having their own domestic space satellite seems in the 1970s to have an irresistible appeal for nations such as India, Brazil, Iran, Indonesia, Nigeria and Algeria. A coalition of various powerful groups in each country favours the idea. 'Educational' goals and literacy campaigns are much to the fore; satellites are a way of bypassing the shortage of teachers, and achieving national identity. Politicians point to the encouraging stimulus this will give to the domestic electronics industry; the benefits which strong central communications will give to the governing party and to the chief executive presumably are recognized. Several of these countries have military regimes and the military favour satellites – necessary for efficient internal communications to threatened border areas and in line with the technically advanced image of the national armed forces. The Hughes Aircraft Company, the ITU, Unesco, NASA and the US State Department are also in favour – and on hand with easy terms for paying the admittedly high initial cost. This satellite debate does not merely have echoes of the earlier introduction of television – it is directly related to television. The argument is made that satellites are the only practical way of taking television out of the big cities and into the vast hinterland; satellites are expensive, yes, although much cheaper for a large country than endless numbers of micro-wave links bouncing TV signals from one range of hills to the next. But the temptation to accept both the satellite and the micro-wave plan is difficult to resist, even if difficult to finance.

Satellites are indeed cheaper for some purposes, although the main use has been for telephone calls rather than television. Canada has shown that a domestic satellite can tie in small remote population clusters to the main population centres – although at a rather high cost. Nevertheless the lead of the USA and USSR in this technology and its aura of prestige appear to be the key to the enthusiasm of so many countries. The strength of general enthusiasm and the uncertainty about specific goals are illustrated when the satellite's arrival is imminent. Educational experiments, military uses, social welfare demonstrations, evaluation research projects are rapidly and vociferously assembled. Opposing cases are criticized. Is the objective really to help the teachers or is it to replace teachers by some more politically reliable central source? Will satellite communication really help the military or will it be too cumbersome and vulnerable? Does central government enthusiasm reflect a willingness to develop the interior or a wish to dominate it yet further? What language will be used – that of the capital city élite or the vernacular of the region? Will space satellites strengthen national identity or merely increase dependence on foreign media? Will not satellites mainly benefit businessmen and users of telephones? Will the satellite help to develop a domestic electronics industry, or will it not lead to the importation of educational technology gadgets which will moulder at the quayside because nobody can quite remember who wanted them for what?

Such debates and struggles over satellites illustrate the strength of prestige and image, the prevalence of public relations strategies. The American companies are often concerned less with profits than in looking good domestically – good works and spreading the American way in the Third World as a means of building up their public relations image in Washington. Unesco and its inevitable experts also seem vocally enthusiastic even if privately more doubtful; the thing looks as though it's going to happen anyway – scattering research contracts, evaluation projects and international commuting tickets in its wake – so it's only realistic to step aboard. And in the recipient countries it is, as usual, difficult to distinguish between seducers and seduced. Even if the Education Ministry thinks the satellite will not provide value for money, its very probable failure may seem a useful way of highlighting the educational needs which do exist and which perhaps can, after all, only be met with conventional methods and teachers. Economic planners may admit that it might be better to spend the money on rural newspapers or radio stations, but may also point out that were the satellite cancelled the funds would not be so spent.

It remains difficult to forecast how satellites and other new technology will affect media importing in the future. This is largely because of the enormous importance of political decisions, which in turn are so often based on vague or conflicting public relations and prestige grounds. But new technology, or some sorts of it, will probably continue to have the same hypnotic attraction as in the past – partly because the political conflicts and weaknesses which lie behind the attraction are unlikely to go away. Imports of media hardware may well continue to be followed by imports of media software from the same sources – not because technology determines all but because the same prestige and public relations appeals and economic relationships lie behind the purchase of both the hardware and the software. And media imports will continue to be a source of such images of technology.

THE PERILS OF IMPERIALISM: BRITAIN

Almost everyone who argues for or against the practice of media imperialism, or the fact of media exporting, seems to assume that it must benefit the exporter. In Britain it is generally assumed that media exports are good for Britain; those who are aware of the extent of exports by the BBC, Reuters, Visnews, ITC, EMI, British book publishers and others, almost invariably see this as one of the few areas in which Britain remains a clear world leader, or as a key means by which Britain maintains her still extensive diplomatic and financial influence in the world.

National media policy-making in Britain is even less co-ordinated, or thought about at all, than in most other west European countries. There is no single ministry involved; the main Cabinet responsibility is shifted about in line with the current Prime Minister's perceptions of, and relationships with, his senior colleagues. The media are as elsewhere divided between several domestic ministries, with the foreign ministry having general responsibility for media overseas. But the British Foreign Office is in an unusual position since it has no formal control, and only some informal influence over Reuters – the main projector of the British image abroad. The Foreign Office does have some influence over the BBC, especially through its financial control of the BBC's external services. The significance of the control is always down-played and this element of the BBC is traditionally excluded from the various Committees on Broadcasting whose recommendations have largely shaped the domestic BBC. The Foreign Office has no control over, and little interest in, such media exports as pop songs, commercial television series or magazines. These latter are merely regarded as commercial export fields; titles and Queen's Awards for Industry are handed out for media exporting success on this commercial basis.

Do British media exports as such favour Britain? It seems at least possible that these exports have unfortunate consequences both at home and abroad. The 'undeserved' prominence of Britain in the world flow of news and entertainment may in the 1950s and 1960s have encouraged Britain to retain unrealistic military and diplomatic goals abroad. The continuing strength of British media in the Commonwealth might encourage importing countries' wish to show their independence in other ways – such as by buying industrial imports from Britain's competitors.

It could also be argued that the large scale of British media exports is bought at too high a price in the scale of British importing of American media which may be doing all the things that media imports are claimed to do elsewhere – undermining national identity, producing unrealistic consumer demands and so on. Nobody in Britain has collected the most elementary relevant information; clearly in terms of audience time, American imports take up much more than the supposed 14 per cent of British television – because these American imports get higher than average audiences and because some American items, such as short inserts and interviews, are not counted in the quota.

A third possibility is that some other more vital British interests suffer from the general position of Britain as the junior media partner to the United States. This may have damaged Britain by aligning her reputation in the eyes of the world too closely with that of the USA. It could lead to Britain getting exaggerated quantities of bad publicity in the US and around the world, as American correspondents based in London search for dramatic news among the often not very dramatic supply available in the domestic British media. Another possibility is that their place in the Anglo-American media encourages, in London-based media personnel, values and attitudes which in the long run damage British industry or political harmony.

As with media importing in any other country the costs and benefits are difficult to evaluate because these can only be assessed in the light of wider national goals (which would need first to be defined) and because key pieces of information, even then, would not exist.

However, mention of the possibility that Britain's gains in media exporting might be outweighed by losses raises the question of just how much American media exporting does rely upon an Anglo-American partnership. The answer may be that this reliance is heavy, especially if one considers examples of national media policies which Britain might adopt. British membership of the EEC raises the possibility – however remote – that the EEC might try to become a rival media force to the media of the United States. This might have very large repercussions especially if the EEC countries were to set out to try to induce Asian, African and – perhaps most of all – Latin American countries to substitute imports of EEC media for US media.

Such examples seem unlikely at present and may be contrary to British interests. They are suggested here merely to illustrate that Anglo-American public relations could, as is sometimes the way with PR, have misled those out of whose mouths it came.

THE PERILS OF IMPERIALISM: UNITED STATES

In the early days of Hollywood exporting there was some anxiety in Washington as to its possible unfortunate consequences for the

American reputation abroad. From time to time such anxieties have again surfaced; some surveys have shown that familiarity with Hollywood products does not necessarily induce love of the United States. Occasionally foreign regimes – including those of Hitler and Stalin – have used careful selections of especially unsavoury Hollywood films, deliberately to reflect discredit on the USA. But it is much more common to accept the opposite arguments – that American media exporting not only reflects but also strengthens United States commercial, military and diplomatic influence around the world. It is difficult to be sure because once again the relevant national goals are unclear and much relevant evidence lacking; there is now still less evidence than there used to be – the USA's practice of conducting opinion polls about the local inhabitants' views on the United States, itself became a controversial subject.

Much has been said and written about the role of the American media in the Vietnam War – especially to the effect that extensive media coverage eventually in the late 1960s sapped domestic political support. But it could also be argued that this media coverage more diffusely in the mid and late 1960s helped to lengthen and deepen American involvement. The predominant position of the United States in the world-wide flow of media may have drawn more attention to US involvement in Vietnam than it 'deserved', made Washington excessively conscious of its international image, and thus increased US official reluctance to leave as well as the international hostility which the USA attracted. Or similar points might be made about, say, multinational companies – that exaggerated criticism of them results from international concern and interest in, and antagonism towards, the multi-national US media corporations.

One other point, if point it be, may be mentioned. Can the United States continue to be an exception to the general rule that major media exporters are also major media importers? As in any other aspect of media in the future, prediction is difficult because political decisions are so important and so unpredictable. But the US market has for some time been attractive to Britain and Mexico; there are some signs also that Canada – for so long a massive importer from the USA – may do more exporting into the US domestic market. The pattern of Hollywood-financed films being made in Italy, Britain and France has switched somewhat to include Mexico, Spain and West Germany; but all of these runaway and co-production arrangements have shown that films made outside the United States can attract big audiences there – and can be shown subsequently on network television. The missing ingredient for any European invasion of the domestic US market is the absence of convincing distribution; however the pattern of made-in-Europe television series pioneered by Lew

Grade has been slowly extended to include national television organizations like the Italian RAI. The main European television networks
could pose a very serious threat to the US market, were they to combine for that purpose and for world-wide distribution; a key point
about a network like RAI in Italy is that it has a monopoly in its home
television market – potentially an impregnable base from which to
attack a domestic US market which has the unique attraction of paying high prices for series, plus a formal disapproval of monopoly.
Such a pattern of events would require some legal changes in
Europe and might induce other legal and trade union responses in
the USA.

More European involvement in the US market seems likely to occur
in at least some fields – and it could occur in some apparently im-
probable fields such as comic strips or more newspaper chains (along
the Thomson lines). Nevertheless this is not necessarily a serious
peril for the USA; such European media would have to be tailored for
US markets and could perhaps be seen more as further evidence of the
Americanization of Europe than of European dominance of America.

THE AMERICANIZATION OF THE WORLD?

At least two contrary trends can be foreseen: First, there may be an
increasing tendency for films and television and media generally
around the world to be put into primarily American packages. The
more media each country has the more each bit of the media must
compete, the more each country must either import or imitate competitive American practices. Whatever else current and future communications revolutions produce they will produce the increased
internationalization of consumption, leisure patterns, youth culture,
education, language and consciousness generally. In this view the
Americanization of everyone still has a long way to go. Such im-
probable sights as hot-dogs, American-style drum majorettes, blue
jeans and T-shirts saying 'Ohio State University' will be found not
only in small provincial French towns but around the entire world.
Even newspapers may go international; regional editions of the *Wall
Street Journal* will circle the world.*

There is, however, another argument, that the world is splitting up
into smaller units and ethnic identities. Other trends in the media –
such as cable television, cheap videotape cameras, offset printing,
small record companies, underground news agencies and newpapers,
local radio, film industries in small African countries, the nationalization of foreign media, the increasing ease of media piracy – all these

* In 1976 the *Wall Street Journal* launched an Asian edition based in Hong-
Kong, and printed also in Japan, Singapore and Malaysia.

will encourage localism, separatism, talking back to, and switching off from, authority, the centre, the national and foreign media.

Both trends seem likely to continue. The probable future is that within each country there will be broadly three media levels. At one extreme there will be 'international' media which will remain primarily Anglo-American in flavour – and will appeal especially to the urban and affluent. At the other extreme there will also be an expansion, probably a bigger expansion, of the small, the local, the ethnic and the traditional; this seems likely on all continents and in almost all countries – the United States, Britain and the USSR not excluded. But there must also be a middle level in between – which can be called 'national' (rather than international or local), and will almost certainly be hybrid.

It is these hybrid media which may have the biggest growth. They will be on the pattern of the Indian,* Hong-Kong, Egyptian or Mexican film industries (and their numerous would-be imitators) and the Zambian or Thai versions of 'country and western' or the Brazilian or Argentinian telenovela. Of these media it will become more and more difficult to deny that there is a local authentic element (since media imitations so quickly become local traditions) but it will be equally difficult to deny that these hybrid forms are linked to the international media.

All three forms already appear together in many local newspaper and radio offerings – international news and hit tunes; national talk and hybrid music; local gossip and advertising. If this occurs, the level and trend of Anglo-American influence will depend more and more upon precise definitions of what constitutes such media and such influence.

AUDIENCES AND AMBIGUITY

It is characteristic of much media content – of Anglo-American media especially – that there is a large element of ambiguity. The same is true of media audiences, although for different reasons.

Little research is conducted on what audiences think of foreign media, and even less is published. On the whole, research is only commissioned where there is some potential competitive advantage in doing so. Most organizations which import or use foreign media materials want to conceal such information. Usually other factors – such as the price, or the official government quota – are much more

---

* Although they went to many countries India's film exports in 1974 earned only $8 million (*Variety*, 14th May 1975). With the increasing numbers of national film industries which now have export ambitions, failure must be widespread.

important considerations than marginal differences in audience attraction.

Data from some countries do exist. These often show – in the case of films, records, radio and television – that the most popular materials are the leading local hybrid forms, the local imitation of *Peyton Place* perhaps. The most popular imports tend to feature strongly in the second dozen on the list. But it is difficult to say which is more popular; so much depends on pricing, distribution, time slots, the opposition on other channels and the broad strategy of schedules. Most broadcast schedulers want to demonstrate that domestic programming gets the highest figures – and, even though this might well happen anyway, it can be made certain through scheduling. Often the most popular imports are not quite so popular as the local imitations of them; but the imports may be scheduled for different purposes – to attract advertisers into particular commercial breaks, or to build up the early evening audience for the peak-time local product.

The questions which can be asked of audiences present problems too. Imports are of certain things – foreign news, foreign-language songs, feature films and series – and the home production is of other things. Like is not being compared with like.

Nevertheless it still would be possible to investigate this topic more systematically than is normally done; in the meanwhile the general lack of such investigations is itself an interesting reflection of the sensitivity of the subject as well as a cause of continuing disagreement as to the appeals of media imports.

GOVERNMENT, KNOWLEDGE AND PUBLIC RELATIONS

Three predictions can safely be made about the future of media in general and Anglo-American media exports particularly. Government involvement will increase; research will increase; and public relations will increase.

All governments are interested in the media and probable national and international developments must extend that interest. Continuing growth is especially noticeable in the electronic media which is where government involvement is greatest. Government involvement in the press will also increase partly because of the increasing trend to public subsidy, even in western Europe; the electronic revolution in the press is merging the technology of the press with telecommunications generally. Since film and television are also becoming increasingly intertwined, governments will be unable to avoid further involvement in film as well. The internationalization of the media, as well as the trend to regional groupings of governments, will also further such interest. Of all these inter-governmental groups the

European Economic Community is the one which so far has had the largest effect in furthering Anglo-American media exports, but could also in the future change their shape the most.

Research will increase partly because governments will seek more information with which to reduce the level of policy confusion and inconsistency. They will also be faced with the repercussions of media policy in wider and wider other areas of policy. For instance it seems inevitable that the presence of American-owned advertising agencies will be challenged in an increasing number of countries. The wider economic repercussions of such policies will require study.

Finally the continued expansion of public relations activity (and research) will derive partly from increased government involvement in the media – governments everywhere being great users of public relations. The increase in research will also lead to increased emphasis on the presentation of research findings to public and governments. But the more governments and researchers investigate Anglo-American media in the world, the more they may conclude that public relations is the one area in which Americans – politicians and advertising men, media tycoons and media academics – are still most clearly superior. The inevitable response will be to reply in kind.

Of the construction of media images for the media there will be no end.

Tables

TABLE 1. IMPORTED PROGRAMMING AS A PERCENTAGE OF TELEVISION TIME 197

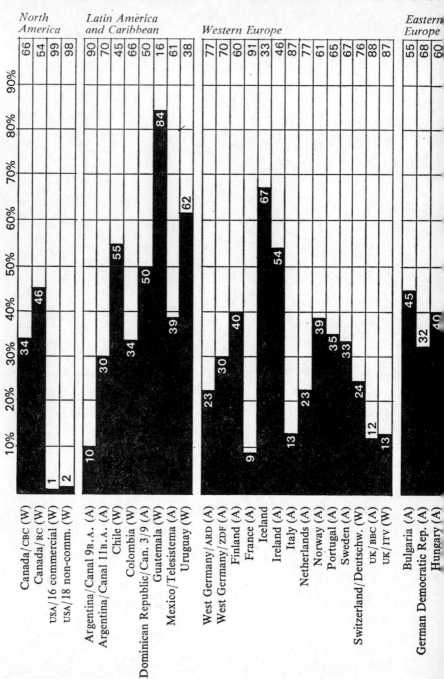

Source: Tapio Varis (1974) 'Global Traffic in Television'

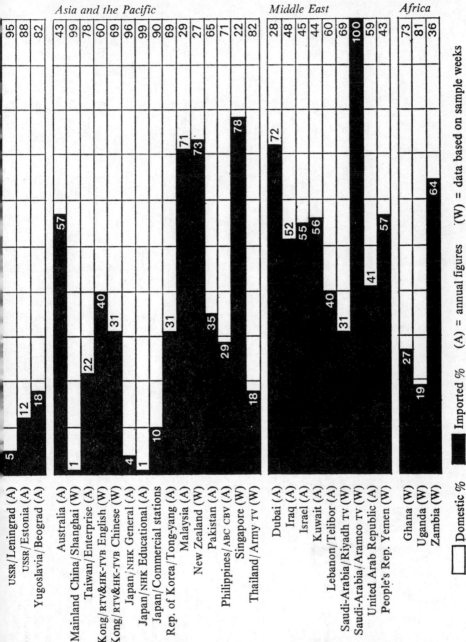

Asia and the Pacific

Station	Domestic %	Imported %
USSR/Leningrad (A)	95	5
USSR/Estonia (A)	88	12
Yugoslavia/Beograd (A)	82	18
Australia (A)	43	57
Mainland China/Shanghai (W)	99	1
Taiwan/Enterprise (A)	78	22
Hong Kong/RTV&HK-TVB English (W)	60	40
Hong Kong/RTV&HK-TVB Chinese (W)	69	31
Japan/NHK General (A)	96	4
Japan/NHK Educational (A)	99	1
Japan/Commercial stations	90	10
Rep. of Korea/Tong-yang (A)	69	31
Malaysia (A)	29	71
New Zealand (W)	27	73
Pakistan (A)	65	35
Philippines/ABC CBV (A)	71	29
Singapore (W)	22	78
Thailand/Army TV (W)	82	18

Middle East

Station	Domestic %	Imported %
Dubai (A)	28	72
Iraq (A)	48	52
Israel (A)	45	55
Kuwait (A)	44	56
Lebanon/Telibor (A)	60	40
Saudi-Arabia/Riyadh TV (W)	69	31
Saudi-Arabia/Aramco TV (W)	100	100
United Arab Republic (A)	59	41
People's Rep. Yemen (W)	43	57

Africa

Station	Domestic %	Imported %
Ghana (W)	73	27
Uganda (W)	81	19
Zambia (W)	36	64

■ Imported %   (A) = annual figures   (W) = data based on sample weeks

□ Domestic %

TABLE 2: SOURCES OF FEATURE FILM IMPORTS INTO 54 NATIONS, 1971–2

Feature film imports by these countries (in percentages)

Sources of film imports	7 EEC countries	13 Other W. Europe and developed countries	7 East European countries	3 Latin American countries	7 African countries	7 Middle-East countries	10 South Asian countries	Total of 54 countries
USA	45	39	10	61	26	38	38	34·6
Italy	13	12	8	7	28	15	10	13·2
UK	14	13	3	6	10	7	7	8·8
France	12	10	8	7	15	5	3	8·7
West Germany	6	5	1	2	2	1	2	2·8
4 EEC COUNTRIES	44	41	21	22	54	28	23	33·5
Japan	1	1	3	2	1	—	2	1·1
Spain	1	1	1	4	2	2	—	·9
Greece	—	1	—	—	—	—	—	·6
Sweden	1	1	—	—	—	—	—	·4
4 OTHER W. EUROPEAN AND DEVELOPED	3	4	4	7	3	2	2	3·0
USSR	1	2	19	2	2	1	3	3·6
Czechoslovakia	—	—	6	—	—	—	—	·8
East Germany	—	—	7	—	—	—	—	·8
Poland	—	—	6	—	—	—	—	·7
Hungary	—	—	4	—	—	—	—	·5
Romania	—	—	4	—	—	—	—	·5
Yugoslavia	—	—	3	—	—	—	—	·4

7 EAST EUROPE	7·3	3	1	2	2	49	2	1
Mexico	·5	—	—	—	2	1	1	1
Egypt	1·0	—	5	3	—	1	—	—
Turkey	·6	—	4	—	—	—	—	—
Iran	·4	2	—	—	—	—	—	—
3 MID-EAST	2·0	2	9	3	—	1	—	—
India	4·5	17	5	9	—	—	—	—
Hong-Kong	1·0	7	—	—	—	—	—	—
2 FAR EAST	5·5	24	5	9	—	—	—	—
ALL OTHERS	13·6	8	27	3	6	14	13	6

Source: Unesco (1975), *World Communications*

Note: These figures incorporate the 54 countries for which Unesco's *World Communications* details the origins of feature film imports. In many cases the total number of feature films imports is indicated, but incomplete details are provided for country of origin. This is unlikely to distort figures for the top half of the table but probably does underestimate the weight of exports from the lesser exporters in the bottom half of the table.

The least reliable figures are for imports into the three Latin American nations (Costa Rica, Mexico, Argentina), the seven African nations (Ethiopia, Madagascar, Somalia, Ghana, Ivory Coast, Sudan, Tunisia) and the six Middle-East nations (Bahrein, Cyprus, Israel, Kuwait, Egypt, Iran, Lebanon).

Mexican film exports are certainly underestimated, as are those of Egypt; this occurs mainly because sufficiently detailed data are not available from the smaller central and south American and the smaller Middle-East nations which provide Mexico's and Egypt's strongest film export markets. These discrepancies, however, merely inflate the bottom 'all others' line of the table.

For most importing nations the figures relate to 1972 or 1971, but in some cases to an earlier year – usually 1970.

TABLE 3: ORIGINS OF FEATURE FILM IMPORTS INTO SOME MAJOR FILM EXPORTING NATIONS, 1971–2

Feature film imports by these countries (in percentages)

Source of film imports	Italy	UK	West Germany	Japan	Spain	USSR	Czecho-slovakia	Mexico	Egypt	India	Hong-Kong
USA	53	52	35	49	30	—	9	49	46	69	31
Italy	*	10	22	10	22	5	7	7	20	10	14
UK	10	*	12	11	11	—	—	13	—	3	12
France[1]	9	11	11	11	12	6	10	7	8	5	5
West Germany	8	3	*	10	1	—	—	4	—	—	—
USA, Italy, UK, France, West Germany combined:	80	76	80	91	76	11	26	80	74	87	62
Japan	3	2	3	*	—	—	—	6	—	5	—
Spain	2	2	2	—	*	—	—	9	—	—	—
USSR	—	—	—	3	—	*	20	—	—	7	—
Czechoslovakia	—	—	—	—	—	9	*	—	—	—	—
Other Socialist countries	—	—	—	—	—	50	33	—	—	—	—
Mexico	2	—	—	—	6	—	—	*	—	—	—
Egypt	—	—	—	—	—	5	—	—	*	—	—
India	—	—	—	—	—	—	—	—	—	*	7
Total imports	100	100	100	100	100	100	100	100	100	100	100
Total imports number	261	297	290	283	398	92	142	327	357	125	483

Domestic production number	294	89	94	390	103	234	36	124	64	433	133
Total imports +Domestic production	555	386	384	673	501	326	178	451	421	558	616
Domestic Production as percentage of Domestic production plus imports	53	23	24	58	21	72	20	22	15	78	22

Source: Unesco (1975) *World Communications*

[1]Data on French imports are not provided in this source.

TABLE 4: THE HOLLYWOOD SHARE IN FOREIGN FILM
MARKETS, 1925, 1928, 1937

	% of all Hollywood foreign film market revenue 1925	*Hollywood feature films as % of all films shown*		
		1925	*1928*	*1937*
UK	35	95	81	65
Germany	10	60	47	18
Australia	} 8	} 95	82	75
New Zealand			90	
Scandinavia	6	85	65	
Argentina	5	90	90	70
Canada	5	95	95	75
France	3	70	63	45
Japan	3	30	22	34
Brazil	3	95	85	85
Austria	} 3	} 70	50	
Hungary			80	
Czechoslovakia			48	
Italy	2	65	70	75
Spain and Portugal	2	90	85	
Mexico	2	90	95	80
China				85
Colombia				80
Egypt				76
India				46
Total foreign revenue of all Hollywood films		$50m.	$70m.	

Sources: For 1925 and 1928, William Victor Strauss, 'Foreign Distribution of American Motion Pictures', *Harvard Business Review*, 1930; for 1937, US Department of Commerce (1937) *Review of Foreign Film Markets*.

TABLE 5: LANGUAGES SPOKEN IN WESTERN EUROPE 1969
(IN PERCENTAGES)

	West Germany	Italy	France	Netherlands	Belgium	Great Britain	Spain	Sweden	Western Europe*
Adults† who speak‡									
ENGLISH:									
Aged 25–	37	9	27	62	30	100	9	85	42
Aged 25+	19	5	9	37	11	100	5	32	28
Adults who speak									
GERMAN:									
Aged 25–	100	2	6	60	13	13	–	41	32
Aged 25+	100	3	7	44	15	6	1	21	31
Adults who speak									
FRENCH:									
Aged 25–	10	28	100	24	37	24	13	13	29
Aged 25+	10	9	100	15	45	14	11	5	27

Source: Reader's Digest (1970) *A Survey of Europe To-Day*, pp. 60–1.

* 'Western Europe' includes also Luxembourg, Portugal, Austria, Switzerland, Denmark, Norway, Finland and Ireland – 16 countries in all.
† 'Adult' was defined as 18 years and over. There were an estimated 226 million adults in the 16 countries in 1969.
‡ The survey question was: 'Which languages can you speak fairly fluently – enough to make yourself understood?' 17,681 interviews were completed in the 16 countries – between 1,000 and 1,700 in each of the countries detailed above.

TABLE 6: RADIO SETS IN LEADING RADIO COUNTRIES
IN 1930 AND 1948

	Total no. of radio sets	*No. of radio sets per thousand population*	
	1930	*1930*	*1948*
Denmark	343,000	100	285
USA	10,500,000	85	566
Sweden	450,000	74	298
UK	3,093,000	70	227
Austria	371,011	57	180
Austratia	311,322	56	237
Germany	3,066,682	49	144
Canada	423,557	43	237
Argentina	400,000	37	92
France	1,500,000	37	178
New Zealand	52,124	37	229
Hungary	240,000	29	57
Norway	75,000	28	251
Finland	90,232	25	164
Spain	500,000	23	14
Czechoslovakia	300,000	21	166
Netherlands	152,000	20	185
Switzerland	77,959	20	214
Latvia	33,000	18	—
Estonia	14,426	13	—
Peru	70,000	13	74
WORLD TOTAL 1930	24,297,561		

Source: For 1930: Lawrence D. Batson ed. (1930) *Radio Markets of the World – 1930*, US Department of Commerce, Trade Promotion series – No. 109. Washington: Government Printing Office; for 1948: Unesco (1950) *World Communications*

TABLE 7: UNITED STATES DOMINANCE IN NEWSPRINT
CONSUMPTION, FEATURE FILM PRODUCTION, AND
TELEVISION, 1948

	Newsprint con- sumption	Newsprint production	No. of feature films produced	No. of TV trans- mitters	No. of TV receivers
USA	100	100	100	100	100
UK	8	39	16	2	7
USSR	7	40	4	2	1
Canada	6	575	1	—	—
France	5	35	25	2	1
Germany (all)	3	21	14	—	—
Argentina	3	—	10	—	—
Sweden	2	38	8	—	—
Japan	2	13	28	—	—
Australia	2	—	1	—	—
Belgium	1	—	1	—	—
Netherlands	1	—	1	—	—
Switzerland	1	—	1	—	—
Czecho- slovakia	1	—	3	—	—
Denmark	1	—	3	—	—
Poland	1	—	—	—	—
Finland	1	4	3	—	—
Norway	1	2	1	—	—
India	—	—	58	—	—
Mexico	—	—	19	—	—
Italy	—	—	12	—	—
China	—	—	12	—	—
Burma	—	—	10	—	—
Philippines	—	—	10	—	—
Egypt	—	—	8	—	—
Spain	—	—	8	—	—
Austria	—	—	6	—	—

Source: Unesco (1950) *World Communications*.

Note: — indicates no information provided in source, but the quantity was probably below 1 % of the USA level.
In 1948 only four nations had television services.

TABLE 8: DAILY NEWSPAPERS IN 1948

	Copies daily per 1,000 inhabitants	Daily sales (thousands)	Average number of pages per daily	Cities with dailies	Annual newsprint consumption (thousand metric tons)
1 UK	570	28,503	4–6	66	412·5
2 Norway	472	1,500	14–16	—	23·9
3 Luxembourg	445	130	8–12	3	1·7
4 Australia	438	3,350	16	43	90·8
5 Denmark	403	1,700	12–14	25	36·6
6 Sweden	382	2,630	18–20	62	109·3
7 New Zealand	374	688	8–12	40	23·6
8 USA	357	52,285	over 24	1,400*	4,765·4
9 Switzerland	355	1,637	16	59	50·3
10 Belgium	316	2,700	10–12	13	65·7
11 Netherlands	285	2,800	6	52	57·4
12 France	284	11,790	6	70	216·0
13 Finland	275	1,088	14	22	27·4
14 Canada	261	4,519	24	—	278·0
15 Austria	259	1,800	6–8	7	23·0
16 Germany (all)	243	16,500	8	—	165·3
17 Japan	230	18,423	2	—	101·0
18 Iceland	219	30	—	2	·6
19 Argentina	212	3,460	8–10	87	128·5
20 Israel	191	136	—	2	3·0
21 Czechoslovakia	190	2,400	8	7	40·8
22 Uruguay	172	400	14–16	9	16·3
23 USSR	161	31,107†	—	—	327·9
24 Ireland	153	460	4–8	3	18·1
25 Romania	141	2,250	—	17	7·7
26 Poland	121	2,900	6–8	14	31·2
27 Bulgaria	113	800	—	6	13·6

Source: Unesco (1950) *World Communications*.

* Approximate figure based on Edwin Emery, *The Press and America* (1972), p. 621.

† 'Total for all newspapers', presumably including non-dailies.

TABLE 9: SOURCES OF FEATURE FILMS, 1948

% of all exhibited feature films originated from these countries

Films exhibited in these countries	USA	Italy	UK	France	Sweden	USSR	Mexico	Argen-tina	Egypt	India	China	Domestic
AFRICA												
Egypt	35	—	9	—	—	—	—	—	(50)	—	—	50
S. Africa	81	—	16	—	—	—	—	—	—	3	—	—
Algeria	35	—	—	45	—	—	—	—	9	—	—	—
Tunisia	60	—	—	17	—	—	—	—	13	—	—	—
NORTH AMERICA												
Canada	77	—	5	—	—	—	—	—	—	—	—	—
Costa Rica	63	—	—	—	—	—	25	12	—	—	—	—
Cuba	75	—	—	—	—	—	8	10	—	—	—	—
Dominican Republic	70	—	—	30	—	—	20	10	—	—	—	—
Haiti	70	—	—	—	—	—	10	5	—	—	—	—
Honduras	80	—	4	—	—	—	(60)	—	—	—	—	—
Mexico	35	—	—	—	—	—	—	—	—	—	—	60
USA	(95)	—	—	—	—	—	—	—	—	—	—	95
Guadeloupe	50	—	—	50	—	—	—	—	—	—	—	—
Martinique	50	—	—	50	—	—	—	—	—	—	—	—

continued ...

TABLE 9 (cont.)

% of all exhibited feature films originated from these Countries

Films Exhibited in these countries	USA	Italy	UK	France	Sweden	USSR	Mexico	Argentina	Egypt	India	China	Domestic
SOUTH AMERICA												
Argentina	50						5	(35)				35
Bolivia	65–70						15–20	10–15				10
Brazil	70	4	12									
Chile	50		10				—	6				
Colombia	50						10	10				
Ecuador	70						15	10				
Paraguay	70						5	20				
Peru	72						18	6				
Uruguay	58			9			12	11				
Venezuela	70						15	8				
ASIA												
Afghanistan	50									50		
Burma	44		16							41		9
Ceylon	50									32		
India	5		12							(90)		90
Iraq	60								15			
Israel	55		25			20						
S. Korea	95		5									
Lebanon	40		5	5					50			
Pakistan	15					10				80		
Persia	76			9								
Philippines	50		6									40
Syria	60	3	2	8					18		10	
Thailand	90										8	
Turkey	70								5			
Indonesia	65		20									10

EUROPE											
Austria	30	—	10	25	—	20	—	—	—	—	15
Belgium	80	—	4	12	—	—	—	—	—	—	3
Czechoslovakia	18	—	19	11	—	23	—	—	—	—	3
Denmark	76	—	8	7	—	9	—	—	—	—	5
Finland	57	—	10	9	7	—	—	—	—	—	24
France	40	—	—	(24)	—	—	—	—	—	—	—
Greece	70	—	13	8	—	30	—	—	—	—	—
Hungary	25	—	15	15	—	—	—	—	—	—	—
Ireland	79	—	19	—	—	—	—	—	—	—	11
Italy	64	(11)	9	7	—	—	—	—	—	—	—
Luxembourg	70	—	—	10	—	—	—	—	—	—	—
Netherlands	67	—	16	7	—	—	—	—	—	—	14
Norway	49	—	17	13	12	—	—	—	—	—	10
Spain	67	—	9	—	—	—	9	—	—	—	—
Sweden	50	—	10	10	—	—	—	—	—	—	23
Switzerland	55	6	9	19	—	—	—	—	—	—	9
United Kingdom[1]	68	1	(23)	4	—	—	—	—	—	—	—
Yugoslavia	—	—	—	—	—	65	—	—	—	—	—
OCEANIA											
New Caledonia	48	—	—	52	—	—	—	—	25	—	—
Fiji	70	—	5	—	—	—	—	—	—	—	—

[1] These UK figures are for 1949 and are taken from Thomas Guback (1969), p. 44.

% of feature films from the USA only as follows:

98% British Honduras
97% Leeward Islands
95% Netherlands West Indies, Bermuda, Leeward Islands, Puerto Rico
90% Ethiopia, Angola, Bahamas, Surinam

continued ....

TABLE 9 (cont.)

%	
85%	Australia
83%	New Zealand and Nicaragua
80%	Portugal, Barbados, British Guiana
77%	Trinidad and Tobago
75%	Panama
70%	Mozambique, Iceland
66%	Nigeria
60%	Kenya
56%	Trieste
55%	Gold Coast, Tangier
50%	US Zone of Germany, Belgian Congo, French Guiana
40%	French West Africa
35%	Malta
30%	Japan, Hong-Kong
25%	Gibraltar

Source: Unesco (1950) *World Communications*

Note: In most cases these percentages refer to number of films distributed, but in some cases to percentages of screen time, attendance or receipts.

TABLE 10: AMERICAN LEADERSHIP IN WORLD TELEVISION, 1954

	No. of TV sets per thousand population	Total No. of TV sets thousands
1 USA	199	32,500
2 UK	81	4,156
3 Canada	74	1,125
4 Cuba	22	135
5 Venezuela	6	35
6 Belgium	5	40
7 Dominican Republic	3	7
7 France	3	125
7 Mexico	3	93
10 Argentina	2	33
10 Brazil	2	125
10 West Germany	2	81
10 Italy	2	88
10 USSR	2	450
15 Netherlands	1·4	15
16 Colombia	1·0	10
16 Switzerland	1·0	4·5
18 Denmark	0·6	2·6
19 Japan	0·5	40
20 Czechoslovakia	0·3	3·8
21 Philippines	0·2	3·5
21 Sweden	0·2	1·5
23 East Germany	0·1	2·3
23 Luxembourg	0·1	·03
25 Hungary	0·02	·2
26 Austria	0·01	·1
26 Thailand	0·01	·1

Source: Unesco (1963) *Statistics on Radio and Television 1950–1960*, Paris: Unesco, pp. 77–82.

TABLE 11: ADVERTISING EXPENDITURE BY WORLD REGION
IN THE NON-COMMUNIST WORLD (81 MAJOR ADVERTISING
COUNTRIES), 1972

	Advertising expenditure			% of world region's advertising expenditure by media		
	Total advertising expenditure (millions of US dollars)	*Per capita advertising expenditure*	*% of world advertising expenditure*	*in print*	*in television*	*in radio*
USA & Canada	24,375	105·7	61	40	17	7
Europe	9,374	27·7	24	55	12	3
Asia	3,411	3·2	8	40	31	6
Latin America	1,520	5·5	4	23	24	12
Australia & New Zealand	629	39·8	2	54	24	10
Middle East & Africa	589	1·9	1	42	5	9
Total non-communist world 81 countries*	39,898	17·8	100	43	17	6

Source: Starch, INRA, Hooper (1974) *Advertising Expenditures around the World, 1972*, New York.

* The figures for expenditure by media are from 63 countries.

TABLE 12: TOTAL ADVERTISING EXPENDITURE IN
SELECTED COUNTRIES, 1972

	(*in $ US millions*)
USA	23,130·0
Japan	2,963·9
W. Germany	2,339·7
UK	1,734·6
France	1,660·0
Canada	1,245·1
Brazil	560·0
Italy	550·0
Netherlands	549·5
Australia	538·1
Spain	512·8
Switzerland	490·4
Sweden	326·3
Mexico	246·9
Venezuela	230·5
South Africa	222·2
Argentina	193·5
Turkey	147·0
India	93·6
New Zealand	91·0
Colombia	53·4
Iran	34·5
Egypt	32·8
Indonesia	30·8
Lebanon	20·1
Nigeria	19·1
Pakistan	12·1
Zambia	8·4
Kenya	8·0
Morocco	6·6
Saudi Arabia	4·9
Syria	3·0
Non-communist world total	39,898

Source: Starch, INRA, Hooper (1974) *Advertising Expenditures around the World, 1972*, New York.

TABLE 13: ADVERTISING EXPENDITURE PLACED BY FOUR
LEADING UNITED STATES ADVERTISING AGENCIES IN
SELECTED FOREIGN COUNTRIES, 1975

Country	Figures represent $ US millions of advertising placed (bracketed figure represents order of size in country)			
	McCann-Erickson	J. Walter Thompson	Young & Rubicam	Ogilvy & Mather
Argentina	1·1 (8)	2·2 (3)		
Australia	43·7 (2)	34·3 (5)	17·3 (11)	26·0 (7)
Brazil	45·5 (1)	36·3 (2)	4·0 (20)	12·6 (11)
Canada	30·0 (11)	44·5(4)	13·8 (16)	23·5 (14)
France	23·3 (12)	18·4 (18)	37·9 (4)	9·0 (27)
India	5·9 (2)			4·5 (3)
Italy	21·1 (3)	22·2 (2)	24·0 (1)	3·5 (26)
Japan	55·5 (12)	31·8 (15)	7·5 (26)	
Mexico	14·2 (3)	15·5 (2)	11·6 (4)	
South Africa	18·0 (3)	18·7 (2)		
Spain	8·9 (4)	12·4 (3)	5·4 (10)	
Sweden	8·7 (15)	4·0 (22)	17·0 (6)	
UK	72·6 (2)	112·0 (1)	52·6 (7)	61·7 (4)
W. Germany	95·2 (1)	74·5 (2)	59·2 (5)	42·5 (8)

Source: *Advertising Age*, 29th March 1976.

TABLE 14: ADVERTISING EXPENDITURE PLACED BY LEADING
UNITED STATES ADVERTISING AGENCIES OUTSIDE THE USA,
1960–5–70–5

Company	Total advertising expenditure placed outside USA (*in $ US millions*)				Total advertising expenditure placed inside USA (*in $ US millions*)
	1960 (1960 rank)	1965	1970	1975	1975 only
McCann-Erickson	102·0 (2)	161·0	300·4	544·3	230·8
J. Walter Thompson	135·0 (1)	191·0	328·0	467·3	432·8
Young & Rubicam	37·0 (3)	77·2	163·8	324·3	476·6
Ted Bates	10·9 (7)	68·3	160·2	323·7	280·2
Ogilvy & Mather	—	70·9	91·3	315·5	266·1
Leo Burnett	4·9 (10)	10·4	106·0	223·0	400·0
SSC & B	—	—	96·2	179·0	135·0
BBD & O	11·3 (6)	16·8	26·0	155·1	369·8
Norman, Craig, Kummel	2·1 (12)	34·8	86·0	140·6	79·6
Foote, Cone & Belding	20·4 (5)	52·0	61·6	121·2	275·3
Total for these 10 advertising agencies	323·6	682·4	1,419·5	2,794·0	2,946·2

Source: *Advertising Age.*

TABLE 15: PERCENTAGE OF ADVERTISING EXPENDITURE
PLACED IN PRINT, RADIO AND TELEVISION, 1972

	Total print	Only news-papers	radio	television	Advertising as % of GNP
Argentina	33·1%	22·2%	13·3%	25·2%	0·71%
Australia	51·0	39·1	10·0	26·4	1·07
Brazil	23·8	15·0	9·7	22·9	1·13
Canada	39·8	34·3	11·8	12.7	1·21
Colombia	23·8	19·9	25·7	26·8	0·68
Egypt	77·1	47·4	1·1	2·4	0·40
France	36·1	12·6	5·1	7·7	0·76
India	77·9	—	6·6	—	0·16
Indonesia	7·5	6·8	16·5	2·7	0·29
Iran	52·8	30·9	8·0	24·5	0·20
Italy	60·8	24·5	9·2	17·2	0·45
Japan	39·8	34·4	4·9	32·4	0·88
Mexico	30·6	18·0	19·1	39·2	0·61
New Zealand	74·2	51·0	13·2	12·0	0·94
Nigeria	27·6	21·0	18·8	3·3	0·22
Pakistan	43·8	36·4	9·1	20·7	0·20
South Africa	56·8	38·9	10·5	—	1·05
Sweden	64·7	38·0	—	—	0·75
Turkey	13·9	9·6	9·5	5·4	0·86
UK	70·3	47·0	0·1	24·9	1·14
USA	40·2	30·3	6·7	17·7	2·00
West Germany	65·6	33·2	3·3	10·6	0·82
Zambia	40·5	—	6·0	7·1	0·47

Source: Starch, INRA, Hooper (1974) *Advertising Expenditure around the World, 1972*, New York.

TABLE 16: HOLLYWOOD'S FOREIGN MARKETS FOR THEATRICAL
FILM SHOWINGS, 1963-74

16(a) HOLLYWOOD'S 15 LARGEST FOREIGN MARKETS
(IN RANK ORDER OF REVENUE)

Country	1963	1968	1973	1974*	1975
Canada	6	3	2	1	1
Italy	2	2	1	2	3
Australia	8	7	7	3	7
Japan	5	5	6	4	2
UK	1	1	4	5	6
W. Germany	3	6	3	6	5
France	4	4	5	7	4
Spain	7	8	10	8	8
South Africa	11	10	8	9	10
Brazil	10	9	9	10	9
Mexico	9	11	11	11	11
Sweden	15	13	12	12	12
Argentina	12	12	15	13	40
Venezuela	14	16	14	14	15
Netherlands	22	20	16	15	14

*In 1974 the first 10 countries accounted for 65% of Hollywood's film
revenue abroad, the next 5 countries for a further 9% – the first 15
countries thus making up 74%.

16(b) THE HOLLYWOOD MAJOR COMPANIES' FOREIGN
AND US EARNINGS FOR FILMS

	1963	1968	1973	1975
	$m.	$m.	$m.	$m.
Foreign	293	339	415	592
USA	239	372	390	628
Total	532	711	806	1,220
In 1963 stable dollar value	532	626	555	694

16(c) HOLLYWOOD MAJOR COMPANIES' SHARES OF
US FILMS' FOREIGN REVENUE, 1972–4

	1972		1974	
Company	*Home*	*Foreign*	*Home*	*Foreign*
Warner Bros	17·6%	13·0%	23·2%	22·5%
Universal	5·0	9·0	18·6	17·0
20th C. Fox	9·1	16·5	10·9	12·0
Paramount	21·6	14·5	10·0	10·0
United Artists	15·0	21·0	8·5	16·0
Columbia	9·1	12·0	7·0	14·0

Source: Motion Picture Export Association of América, published in *Variety*, 15th May 1974, 25th June 1975, 6th August 1975, 1st September 1976.

TABLE 17: PRICES CHARGED FOR US TELEVISION SERIES
AND FOR TELEVISION SHOWINGS OF FEATURE FILMS, 1976

Country	Price range half-hour episode	Price range feature film
CANADA	$	$
CBC	2,500–4,000	8,500–12,000
CBC (French Net)	2,000–3,500	4,500–5,500
CTV Network	1,500–2,500	10,000–40,000
LATIN AMERICA & CARIBBEAN		
Argentina	500–800	1,600–4,000
Bermuda	30–45	90–150
Brazil	2,000–3,000	5,000–10,000
Chile	65–70	350–400
Colombia	190–200	700–1,000
Costa Rica	60–70	250–500
Dominican Republic	100–150	225–300
Ecuador	55–75	200–250
El Salvador	50–55	400–450
Guatemala	70–80	250–400
Haiti	20–25	75–100
Honduras	30–35	135–150
Jamaica	60–65	200–400
Mexico	900–1,100	1,000–5,000
Netherlands Antilles	50–55	90–100
Nicaragua	40–50	200–300
Panama	60–70	350–500
Peru	120–125	750–1,100
Puerto Rico	500–600	3,000–3,750
Trinidad & Tobago	55–60	150–200
Uruguay	75–85	350–550
Venezuela	500–600	2,000–3,500
WESTERN EUROPE		
Austria	400–425	1,400–1,800
Belgium	500–650	1,200–2,000
Denmark	200–250	1,500–2,500
Finland	250–350	1,600–2,500
France	4,200–5,000	14,000–20,000
West Germany	4,900–5,300 (undubbed)	24,000–32,000 (dubbed)

continued ...

Country	Price range half-hour episode	Price range feature film
Gibraltar	26–35	75–125
Greece	200–210	200–210
Ireland	185–190	500–600
Italy	1,500–2,000	10,000–12,000
Luxembourg	500–600	800–1,000
Malta	28	no sales
Monaco	200–250	575–700
Netherlands	1,000–1,200	2,200
Norway	150–175	800–1,200
Portugal	150–200	500–600
Spain	450–550	4,500–5,000
Sweden	1,000–1,100	3,000–5,500
Switzerland	250–300	900–1,500
UK	3,500–5,000	25,000–70,000
EASTERN EUROPE	$	$
Bulgaria	65–100	300–400
Czechoslovakia	250–300	1,800–2,000
East Germany	500–1,000	2,000–5,000
Hungary	100–160	1,000–1,200
Poland	150–200	800–1,000
Rumania	150–200	400–500
USSR	120–300	6,000–8,000
Yugoslavia	175–250	800–1,000
MIDDLE EAST AND SOUTH ASIA		
Cyprus	30–35	100–150
Egypt	200–225	600–800
India	no sales	no sales
Iran	300–400	1,200–2,000
Iraq	300–500	200–250
Israel	75–200	500
Kuwait	100–135	400–500
Lebanon	85–125	300–425
Saudi-Arabia	375–500	1,500–2,000
Syria	50–70	90–120
AFRICA		
Algeria	90–100	no sales
Kenya	25–30	no sales
Nigeria	35–40	80–100
Rhodesia	no sales	no sales
Uganda	25–30	no sales
Zambia	50	100

FAR EAST		
Australia		15,000–30,000
Hong-Kong	60–85	200–400
Japan	3,000–3,500	20,000–60,000
South Korea	50–80	250–350
Singapore	50–60	175–200
Malaysia	50–60	175–200
New Zealand	300–350	1,300–1,700
Philippines	200–275	1,000–1,200
Ryukyu Islands (Okinawa)	50–60	100–125
Taiwan	60–100	250–300
Thailand	125–175	600–800

Note: 'US television exporters anticipate a total foreign gross of between $125,000,000 and $150,000,000 for 1976, reflecting a market characterized by relative stability. The total estimate includes sales of public affairs shows, cartoons, etc., as well as series and feature film product, but the major part of the total is for vidfilm product. One-hour series generally bring twice the half-hour price.'

Source: *Variety,* 21st April 1976

References

1. WORLD NEWS: MADE IN USA AND UK

1. Alexis de Tocqueville (1835), pp. 224–9.
2. Wesley E. Rich (1924), pp. 182–3.
3. Frank Luther Mott (1962), pp. 220–6.
4. Finis H. Capps (1966), p. 229.
5. Carl Wittke (1957), pp. 201–2, 75.
6. Karl Arndt and May Olson (1961), p. 10.
7. Edward C. Kemble (1962), pp. 130–1.
8. Einar Östgaard (1965), p. 42.
9. Richard A. Schwarzlose (1965), p. 396.
10. Robert A. Rutland (1973), p. 135.
11. James P. Wood (1949), pp. 157–72.
12. Paul Bairoch (1973), p. 472.
13. William Stott (1973).
14. Ibid., p. 129.
15. Raymond Fielding (1972).
16. Robert E. Park, 'News and the Human Interest Story' (1940).
17. Edward J. Epstein, *News from Nowhere* (1973), Vintage Edition (1974), p. 241.

2. MEDIA IMPERIALISM?

1. The present author first came across this phenomenon in the case of British advertising agencies. See Jeremy Tunstall (1964), pp. 33–5, 140–1, 156–7, 224–6.
2. The shortage of Marxist empirically based accounts of this topic is illustrated in *Marxism and the Mass Media: Towards a Basic Bibliography 3* (1974) which contains 453 references.
3. Alan Wells (1972), p. 121.
4. Kaarle Nordenstreng and Tapio Varis (1974), p. 14.
5. Tapio Varis (1974), p. 107.
6. E. Katz, E. G. Wedell et al. (1977).
7. Michael A. Barkočy (1963).
8. 'Profiles of the European Executive Market'. Survey conducted in 11 west European countries for Newsweek International by Conrad Jameson Associates (London, 1973).
'Foreign Circulation of Representative US Publications 1964–65' (New York: Magazine Publishers' Association).

10. This passage on foreign correspondents in the USA is based on John Hohenberg's (1967) account of how Asian foreign correspondents operate in the USA, upon the author's experience of interviewing foreign correspondents of British media in New York and Washington in 1965 and upon questionnaires completed by 37 such British correspondents in 1968 and reported in *Journalists at Work* (1971).
11. Robert Windeler (1975), pp. 119–20.
12. Isaiah Litvak and Christopher Maule (1974), pp. 19–20.
13. *Advertising Age*, 25th March 1974.
14. Leon Bramson (1961).

3. ENTERTAINMENT: OCCUPATIONAL AND INDUSTRIAL STRUCTURE

1. Isaac Goldberg (1930), p. 320.
2. W. A. Swanberg (1967), pp. 189–90.
3. Robert Park (1922), p. 8.
4. Rachel Low (1949), p. 119.
5. Terry Ramsaye (1926), p. 660.
6. Rachel Low (1948), p. 28.
7. Jay Leyda (1960), p. 172.
8. Leo Rosten (1941), p. 7.
9. Benjamin B. Hampton (1931), pp. 64–82.
10. Leo Rosten (1941), p. 177.
11. Ian Whitcomb (1973), p. 44.
12. This information is derived from Robert Thompson's standard work on the American telegraph industry, 1832–66. See especially Thompson (1972), pp. 336, 440–6.
13. 'The Newspaper Preservation Act'. The multi-volume report of the US Senate Subcommittee on Anti-Trust and Monopoly (1967–8) is called *The Failing Newspaper Act* – and constitutes a mine of information on local newspaper monopoly and competition.
14. Unesco (1953), p. 68.
15. Robert Houlton (1973).

4. IMMIGRANT DREAMS, EXPORT SALES

1. Kent Cooper (1942).
2. Norman Zierold (1969), p. 19.
3. Eugene Lyons (1966), pp. 60, 245–8, 259, 263.
4. M. De Fleur (1964).
5. M. Wolfenstein and N. Leites (1950).
6. Rudolph Arnheim (1944).
7. L. Handel (1950).
8. Leo Lowenthal (1944); Theodore P. Greene (1970).
9. C. Wright Mills (1956), p. 74.
10. Isaac Goldberg (1930), pp. 293–4.

11. Robert C. Toll (1974), pp. 270–3.
12. Erik Barnouw (1966), pp. 225–31.
13. Edward Jay Epstein (1973), pp. 222–3.

5. BRITAIN AND THE WHITE COMMONWEALTH

1. W. H. G. Armytage (1951); Donald Read (1961), pp. 69–71; William Ames (1972).
2. Patricia Hollis (1970).
3. G. D. H. Cole (1947), pp. 48–68.
4. *The History of the Times*, Volume 2, pp. 295–6.
5. R. K. Webb (1955), p. 22.
6. Ibid., pp. 50–2.
7. Allen Hutt (1973), p. 71.
8. Guinevere L. Griest (1970) passim.
9. Ibid., pp. 31–2.
10. Reginald Pound and Geoffrey Harmsworth (1959), pp. 241–2.
11. L. Elthan Ellis (1960).
12. Edwin Emery (1972), p. 343.
13. T. P. O'Connor (1889).
14. Graham Storey (1951), pp. 107–11.
15. Allen Hutt (1973), p. 71.
16. Asa Briggs (1965), pp. 169–84.
17. Asa Briggs (1970), p. 684.
18. Ibid., p. 315.
19. Ibid., pp. 564, 567, 560.
20. Ibid., pp. 567–8.
21. Ibid., pp. 403, 509, 404.
22. Elaine Potter (1974).
23. Ibid.
24. Details on ownership of radio and television companies for Canada: Report of the Special Senate Committee on Mass Media (Chairman: Keith Davey), *The Uncertain Mirror* Volume One, 1970 (Ottawa: Information Canada). For Australia: Australian Broadcasting Control Board, *Twenty-Fifth Annual Report for the year ended 30 June 1973* (Canberra: Australian Government Publishing Service).
25. Samuel E. Moffett (1907), pp. 53–67, 95–103. Moffett's study was the first major work on the Americanization of Canada.
26. Ibid., p. 96.
27. Unesco, *Television: A World Survey* (1953), pp. 74–6.
28. Ibid., p. 38.
29. Australian Broadcasting Control Board, *Twenty-Fifth Annual Report for Year Ended 30th June, 1973*, pp. 117–19. Two years later (1974–5) 74 per cent of imports were from USA and 23 per cent from Britain. See *Variety*, 5th May 1976.
30. Unesco, *Statistics on Radio and Television, 1950–60* (1963), pp. 80–2.

6. EX-BRITISH AFRICA AND INDIA

1. J. D. Chick (1967), pp. 234–7, 473–4.
2. Rosalynde Ainslie (1966), pp. 203–4.
3. Unesco (1950), p. 49. This Unesco report has a rather proconsular tone and refers to the six languages as 'native dialects'.
4. I would like to thank George Wedell and Michael Pilsworth for letting me see drafts of their reports on Tanzanian and Nigerian broadcasting.
5. Bill Harris (1963), p. 27.
6. Christine Dobbin (1972), pp. 195–202.
7. Prodipto Roy et al. in *Agricultural Innovation among Indian Farmers* (1968).
8. This and other factual statements on the Indian media are based on information kindly supplied by the media directors of two major advertising agencies in Bombay in 1972.
9. M. R. Dua (1968).
10. Christine Dobbin (1972), pp. 198–201.
11. *Report of the Indian Cinematograph Committee, 1927–28*, p. 29.
12. Ibid., p. 103.
13. *Report of the Film Enquiry Committee 1951*, pp. 123–5.
14. Lionel Fielden (1960), p. 204.
15. Interview with Mr Kailash C. Jain, chairman and managing-director, National Advertising Service (Bombay) 18th October 1972.
16. K. E. Eapen (1969), p. 192.
17. Manfred Lohman (1971), p. 95.
18. G. C. Awasthy (1965), p. 135.
19. Manfred Lohman (1971), p. 96.

7. ENGLISH LANGUAGE, BRITISH INVASION, ANGLO-AMERICAN MEDIA

1. Robert W. Desmond (1937).
2. Llewellyn White and Robert D. Leigh (1946), passim.
3. Wilfred Whiteley (1969).
4. R. R. Mehrotra (1975), p. 114.
5. Ibid., p. 122.
6. James J. Barnes (1974).
7. Ian Whitcomb (1973), pp. 170–1, 189.

8. THE HIGH TIDE OF AMERICAN MEDIA, 1943–53

1. Erik Barnouw (1966), pp. 57–61.
2. Edward Jay Epstein, 'Power is Essential . .', (London) *Sunday Times Magazine*, 14th December 1975.
3. See the approved history of *Reader's Digest* by James Playsted Wood (1958), pp. 169–72.

4. Unesco (1950), pp. 150–61.
5. Unesco (1955), pp. 20–1.

9. FORCED TO BE FREE: ITALY, GERMANY AND JAPAN

1. The information for Germany is from Peter de Mendelssohn (*Zeitungs-stadt Berlin*). According to Alberto Albertini (*Vita di Luigi Albertini*, p. 104) the circulation of the *Corriere della sera* in 1900 was only 75,000. According to John Lent ('History of the Japanese Press', p. 21) the leading circulations in Japan in 1905 were *Osaka Asahi* with 350,000 and *Osaka Mainichi* with 320,000.
2. H. Erman (1954), pp. 66–72.
3. H. Ullstein (1943), pp. 88–9.
4. Franz Ullstein stated this in an inverview in the *New York Times*, 18th September 1912, quoted by Modris Eksteins (1975), p. 21.
5. Max Ascoli (1938), p. 236.
6. Alberto Albertini (1945).
7. *Dizionario Biografico degli Italiani*.
8. William Woodruff (1975), p. 54.
9. Grace Fox (1969), pp. 455–6.
10. Kisaburō Kawabé (1921), pp. 104–13.
11. Joseph Anderson and Donald Richie (1960), pp. 40–7.
12. NHK (1967), p. 46.
13. 641,774 out of 676,171: Lawrence D. Batson (1930), pp. 12–13.
14. Céleste Herbericks (1967), pp. 357–61.
15. John P. Diggins (1972), pp. 42–57.
16. John Lent (1968), p. 27.
17. Otto Kriegk (1943), pp. 95–6.
18. Otto Kriegk, in his *Der Deutsche Film im Spiegel der Ufa* (Berlin, 1943) makes many such comments. This account of UFA is strongly anti-Semitic and anti-American.
19. Istvan Deak (1968), pp. 23, 28–9.
20. I am indebted to Frank Turfus for this particular interpretation and for wading through a large number of relevant German-language books and articles. Most of these sources are of low quality and a number are rabidly anti-Semitic. The chaotic nature of the political events, the lack of audited circulation figures, the secretive and con-spiratorial behaviour of many owning companies, and the prevalent conflict of interests (for instance within a single company dealing in news, advertising and PR) make for obvious difficulties in studying this period. I would also like to thank Hanno Hardt for his help on Germany.
21. Modris Eksteins (1975), p. 79.
22. Arbeits Gemeinschaft Deutscher Werbungsmittler (1955), p. 63.
23. Modris Eksteins (1975), pp. 80–1.
24. Ibid., pp. 112–13, 133.
25. Marcus S. Phillips (1974), pp. 41–6.

26. Unesco, *Report of the Commission on Technical Needs*, Volume 2, 1950 supplement.
27. Newspaper circulation figures for Italy are notoriously unreliable. According to one advertising agency source, Italy's third, fourth and fifth largest *daily* sales in 1973 were all sports newspapers. Benton and Bowles Associates Pubblicità Italiana, *Advertising in Italy* (1974).
28. Sergio de Claricini (1965), p. 49.
29. Henry Pilgert (1953), pp. 19–20.
30. Ernst Meier (1954), p. 228.
31. Henry Pilgert (1953), p. 47.
32. Anna J. Merritt and Richard L. Merritt, eds (1974).
33. Claus Jacobi (1953–4), p. 329. Jacobi was, at this time, co-editor of *Der Spiegel*.
34. Ronald Bunn (1968), pp. 3–11.
35. The main findings of these surveys for the years 1945–9 are summarized in Anna J. Merritt and Richard L. Merritt, eds (1970).
36. Henry Pilgert (1953), pp. 39, 59.
37. Seven of the ten largest German agencies in 1973 had American names. *Advertising Age*, 25th March 1974.
38. Lafe Allen (1947), p. 329.
39. Joseph Anderson and Donald Richie (1960), p. 175.
40. NHK (1967), pp. 207–8.
41. *Advertising Age*, 25th March 1974.
42. *Variety*, 7th January 1976, p. 42.

10. THE OTHER AMERICA

1. Evelyn P. Stevens (1974), pp. 30–6, 40.
2. Spanish-language historical material on Mexico and Argentina was collected by Robert Gibbs, although all interpretations are the author's.
3. John W. White (1942), pp. 183–8.
4. Unesco (1949) *Press, Film, Radio: Report of the Commission on Technical Needs. Volume 3.* (Unesco publication 436), pp. 62–4.
5. See Unesco, *World Communications* (1950), pp. 152–3.
6. Jacques Kayser (1953); Paul R. Hoopes (1966); James W. Markham (1961).
7. Lawrence D. Batson and E. D. Schutrumpf, eds, *Broadcast Advertising in Latin America* (1931), pp. 3–6.
8. Marvin Alisky (1954). *a*.
9. Lawrence D. Batson and E. D. Schutrumpf, eds, *Broadcast Advertising in Latin America* (1931), pp. 26–8.
10. Julian Hale (1975), p. 102.
11. Unesco (1953), p. 52.
12. Televisa's schedule for 21st–27th May 1973.
13. Inravision's programme schedule for 1973.
14. This revealing phrase is from Donald B. Easum (1951), p. 235.
15. Joe Alex Morris (1957), pp. 102–9.

16. Vernon L. Fluharty (1957), pp. 263–4.
17. This paragraph is based largely on a draft of the Elihu Katz and Dov Shinar case study report on Brazil (part of the Katz and Wedell study of the role of broadcasting in national development) which describes the situation in Brazil in late 1974.
18. Unesco (1953), pp. 52–3.

11. COMMUNIST NATIONS, DEFENSIVE POSTURE

1. This paragraph is based mainly on Unesco, *Report of the Committee on Technical Needs* (1947) and supplement.
2. This figure is derived from an anonymous British article: Scythicus (1900). St Petersburg had a prestige paper called *Novoe Vremia*, which was controlled by Aleksei Suvorin, whose other media interests included cheap books, pamphlets, calendars and dictionaries. See Robert A. Bartol (1974).
3. Paxton Hibben (1925).
4. Unesco (1963), p. 27.
5. Jaroslaw W. Piekalkiewicz (1972).
6. Antonina Kloskowska (1964).
7. Unesco (1964).
8. Tapio Varis (1973), pp. 111–12.
9. Frank H. H. King and Prescott Clarke, *A Research Guide to China Coast Newspapers, 1822–1911*, pp. 76–97. There were also 'overland' weekly editions of the dailies and at least one Shanghai newspaper published solely for mailing to the USA.
10. Robert W. Desmond (1937), p. 340.
11. Vernon Nash (1931).
12. Vernon Nash (1933), p. 317.
13. Lee-hsia Hsu Ting (1974), pp. 98–9.
14. Ibid, pp. 134–5.
15. James Markham (1967).
16. US Department of Commerce (1937), p. 56.
17. Jay Leyda (1972), pp. 22–5, 35, 61–2, 64.
18. Lawrence D. Batson and E. D. Schutrumpf, eds (1932) *Broadcast Advertising in Asia, Africa, Australia and Oceania*, pp. 4–5.
19. This was reported by Michael Bromhead, an EMI executive, who had just returned from selling some films in Peking. See *Variety*, 29th October 1975.
20. Jay Leyda (1972), p. 334.
21. Ibid., p. 247.
22. *BBC Handbook 1970*, p. 99.
23. Maury Lisann (1975), pp. 160–72.
24. Mark W. Hopkins (1970); Gayle Durham Hollander (1972); David E. Powell (1975).
25. Maury Lisann (1975), pp. 51–3.

12. MEDIA KNOWLEDGE, PROFESSIONALISM AND VALUE NEUTRALITY

1. For a world-wide study of both media research and communicator training within Universities, see May Katzen (1975).
2. Paul Lazarsfeld (1969), p. 332.
3. In 1939 the *Journal of Applied Psychology* published a special issue on radio research, including an article by Charles Osgood about brand names in advertising. Many other such articles appeared in *Public Opinion Quarterly* which had, from its outset, close ties with market research and public relations. During 1937–47 *POQ* published no less than 55 articles on public relations: See Eleanor Singer (1970), p. 424; and Paul Lazarsfield (1969), p. 330.
4. T. V. Sathyamurthy (1964), p. 165.
5. Unesco, *Developing Information Media in Africa* (1962) p. 27.
6. Robert P. Knight (1970), p. 222.
7. W. F. Coleman et al. (1968).
8. Raymond B. Nixon (1970), p. 13–19. Professor Nixon refers to the CIA as 'an agency of the United States government'.
9. Frank Barton (1969).
10. Chia-Shih Hsu, Crispin Maslog and Tong-Jae Cho (1972).
11. Kurt Lang (1974).
12. Robert O. Blanchard (1974), p. 231.
13. J. W. C. Johnstone, E. J. Slawski and W. W. Bowman (1972–3), pp. 531–2.
14. Unesco (1958), pp. 51, 139.
15. Information supplied by Peter Golding.
16. John A. Kracmar (1971), p. 12.
17. J. F. Wilkinson (1972), p. 178.
18. Anju Chaudhary (1974).
19. Gaye Tuchman (1972) and Jeremy Tunstall (1971).

13. US GOVERNMENT MEDIA AND MEDIA POLICY

1. Thomas Guback (1969), pp. 124–41.
2. Report of the Presidential Study Commission on International Radio Broadcasting (1973) p. 69 [See Bibliog.].
3. Maury Lisann (1975), p. 163.
4. S. J. Tambiah, 'Literacy in a Buddhist village in North-East Thailand', in Jack Goody, ed. (1968), p. 115.
5. Philip Agee (1975).
6. Julian Hale (1975), p. 102.

14. ARABS, MOSLEMS, MIDDLE EAST

1. Daniel Lerner (1958), pp. 237–40.
2. Unesco (1950), p. 37.

3. Ibrahim Abu-Lughod (1963).
4. E. E. Elder (1931).
5. Jacob M. Landau (1958), p. 158.
6. George Sadoul (1966), p. 72.
7. Jacob M. Landau (1958), pp. 170–2.
8. US Department of Commerce (1937), p. 104.
9. Lawrence D. Batson and E. D. Shutrumpf, eds (1930) Part 2, pp. 8–9.
10. M. Abdel-Kader Hatem (1974), p. 250.
11. Based on interviews with international news agency correspondents conducted by Oliver Boyd-Barrett in Cairo, Beirut and other eastern Mediterranean capitals in December 1971 and January 1972.
12. Tapio Varis (1973), p. 170.
13. K. E. Eapen and John Lent in John Lent, ed. (1976).
14. Abdulrahman S. Shobaili (1971), p. 128. Almost all of the material in this passage on Saudi-Arabia comes from the 300-page Ohio State University doctoral thesis of Dr Shobaili who had himself previously been a radio and television presenter in Saudi-Arabia.
15. A. S. Shobaili (1971), pp. 244–5.
16. Ibid., p. 195.
17. Majid Tehranian, in *InterMedia*, October 1975, pp. 16–17.

15. FRANCE: THE PERILS OF IMPERIALISM

1. US Department of Commerce (1937).
2. Emmanuel Derieux and Jean C. Texier (1974).
3. Jean-Louis Servan-Schreiber (1974), pp. 249–50.
4. Françoise Giroud (1974), p. 105.
5. For this last point, I am indebted to Jean C. Texier.
6. *Advertising Age*, 24th March 1974.
7. Unesco (1950).
8. Unesco (1975), p. 387.
9. Gilles Faysse (1973).
10. Unesco (1975), pp. 90–1.
11. On broadcasting in Francophone West and Equatorial Africa and in the Maghreb see the pieces by R. Arnold Gibbon and Ali Z. Elgabri in Sydney W. Head, ed. *Broadcasting in Africa* (1974).
12. William A. Hachten (1971), pp. 104–5.
13. This information for Algeria in 1973 is taken from the 'Algerian Case Study' of E. G. Wedell and M. J. Pilsworth based on their visit to Algeria in April 1974. The interpretation is of course the present author's.
14. Unesco (1975), p. 39.

Bibliography

Abu-Lughod, Ibrahim (1962) 'International News in the Arabic Press: A Comparative Content Analysis', *Public Opinion Quarterly* 26 pp. 600–12

Abu-Lughod, Ibrahim (1963) 'The Mass Media and Egyptian Village Life', *Social Forces* 42 pp. 97–104 [Reprinted (1970) in Tunstall, Jeremy, ed. *Media Sociology* pp. 322–34]

Agee, Philip (1975) *Inside the Company: CIA Diary*, Harmondsworth: Penguin

Ainslie, Rosalynde (1966) *The Press in Africa*, London: Gollancz

Albertini, Alberto (1945) *Vita di Luigi Albertini*, Rome: Mondadori

Alisky, Marvin (1954) *a*. 'Early Mexican Broadcasting', *Hispanic American Historical Review* 34 pp. 513–26

Alisky, Marvin (1954) *b*. 'Radio's Role in Mexico: A First-Hand Survey', *Journalism Quarterly* 31 pp. 66–72

Alisky, Marvin (1960) 'Growth of Newspapers in Mexico's Provinces', *Journalism Quarterly* 37 pp. 75–82.

Alisky, Marvin and Hoopes, Paul R. (1968) 'Argentina's Provincial Dailies', *Journalism Quarterly* 45 pp. 95–105

Allen, Lafe E. (1947) 'Effect of the Allied Occupation on the Press of Japan', *Journalism Quarterly* 24 pp. 323–31

Almaney, Adnan (1972) 'Government Control of the Press in the United Arab Republic, 1952–70', *Journalism Quarterly* 49 pp. 340–8

Altick, Richard D. (1963) *The English Common Reader*, University of Chicago Press, Phoenix Books

Ames, William E. (1972) *A History of the National Intelligencer*, Chapel Hill: University of North Carolina Press

Anderson, Joseph L. and Richie, Donald (1960) *The Japanese Film*, New York: Evergreen

Anonymous (1969) *Svoboda: The Press in Czechoslovakia 1968*, Zürich: International Press Institute

Arbeits Gemeinschaft Deutscher Werbungsmittler (1955) *Der Mittler in der Werbung, 1855–1955*, Frankfurt-am-Main

Armytage, W. H. G. (1951) 'The Editorial Experience of Joseph Gales', *North Carolina Historical Review* 28 pp. 332–61

Armytage, W. H. G. (1967) *The American Influence on English Education*, London: Routledge & Kegan Paul

Arndt, Karl J. R. and Olson, May E. (1961) *German-American Newspapers and Periodicals, 1732–1955*, Heidelberg: Quelle & Meyer

Arnheim, Rudolph (1944) 'The World of the Daytime Serial', in Lazarsfeld and Stanton, eds, *Radio Research 1942–43*

Ascoli, Max (1938) 'The Press and the Universities in Italy', *Annals of the American Academy of Political and Social Science* 200 pp. 235–53

Aspen Institute (1974) *Control of the Direct Broadcast Satellite: Values in Conflict*, Palo Alto: Aspen Institute for Humanistic Studies

Awasthy, G. C. (1965) *Broadcasting in India*, Bombay: Allied Publishers

Azikiwe, Nnamdi (1970) *My Odyssey: An Autobiography*, London: C. Hurst

Bagdikian, Ben H. (1974) 'Congress and the Media: Partners in Propaganda', *Columbia Journalism Review* 12 January/February, pp. 3–10

Bairoch, Paul (1973) 'Agriculture and the Industrial Revolution', in Cipolla, Carlo M., ed., *The Fontana Economic History of Europe. Vol. 3 The Industrial Revolution*, London: Fontana pp. 452–506

Baran, Paul A. and Sweezy, Paul M. (1968) *Monopoly Capital*, Harmondsworth: Penguin

Barker, Ronald and Escarpit, Robert (1973) *The Book Hunger*, Paris: Unesco and London: Harrap

Barkočy, Michael A. (1963) 'Censorship Against *Time* and *Life* International Editions', *Journalism Quarterly* 40 pp. 517–24

Barnes, James J. (1974) *Authors, Publishers and Politicians*, London: Routledge & Kegan Paul

Barnouw, Erik and Kishnaswamy, S. (1963) *Indian Film*, New York: Columbia University Press

Barnouw, Erik (1966) *A Tower in Babel*, New York: Oxford University Press

Barnouw, Erik (1968) *The Golden Web*, New York: Oxford University Press

Barnouw, Erik (1970) *The Image Empire*, New York: Oxford University Press

Bartol, Robert A. (1974) 'Aleksei Suvorin: Russia's Millionaire Publisher', *Journalism Quarterly* 51 pp. 411–17 and 462

Barton, Frank (1969) *African Assignment*, Zürich: International Press Institute

Batson, Lawrence D. and Schutrumpf, E. D., eds (1930–2) *World Broadcast Advertising: Four Reports* (us Department of Commerce) [Reprinted (1971) New York: Arno Press]

Belfagor (1952) 'La Stampa a Rotocalco', *Belfagor* 7 pp. 450–66

Bellanger, C.; Godechot, J.; Guiral, P.; and Terrou, F. (1972) *Histoire Générale de la Presse Française, Tome 3 De 1871 à 1940*, Paris: PUF

Berelson, Bernard and Slater, Patricia L. (1946) 'Majority and Minority Americans: An Analysis of Magazine Fiction', *Public Opinion Quarterly* 10 pp. 168–90

Berger, Peter and Luckmann, Thomas (1967) *The Social Construction of Reality*, London: Allen Lane, The Penguin Press

Bernays, Edward L. (1965) *Biography of an Idea: Memoirs of Public Relations Counsel, Edward L. Bernays*, New York: Simon & Schuster

Bernstein, Robert L. *et al.* (1970) *Book Publishing in the USSR*, Cambridge, Mass.: Harvard University Press

Bishop, Michael E. (1973) 'Media Use and Democratic Political Orientation in Lima, Peru', *Journalism Quarterly* 50 pp. 60–7 and 101

Black, Peter (1972) *The Mirror in the Corner*, London: Hutchinson

Blanchard, Robert O., ed. (1974) *Congress and the News Media*, New York: Hastings House

Blumenfeld, R. D. (1930) *R.D.B.'s Diary. 1887–1914*, London: Heinemann

Blumenfeld, R. D. (1933) *The Press in My Time*, London: Rich & Cowan

Boehlert, Sherwood L. (1968) 'Telling the Congressman's Story', in Hiebert and Spitzer, eds *The Voice of Government*, pp. 129–40

Bogart, Leo (1959) 'Changing Markets and Media in Latin-America', *Public Opinion Quarterly* 23 pp. 159–67

Bogart, Leo (1972) *Silent Politics: Polls and the Awareness of Public Opinion*, New York: Wiley Interscience

Bok, Edward (1921) *The Americanization of Edward Bok*, New York: Charles Scribner's

Borchardt, Kurt (1970) *Structure and Performance of the U.S. Communications Industry*, Boston: Graduate School of Business Administration, Harvard University

Boris, George (1935) 'The French Press', *Foreign Affairs* 13 pp. 319–27

Bower, Robert T. (1973) *Television and the Public*, New York: Holt, Rinehart & Winston

Boyd, Douglas A. (1970–1) 'Saudi Arabian Television', *Journal of Broadcasting* 15 pp. 73–8

Boyle, Andrew (1972) *Only the Wind will listen: Reith of the BBC*, London: Hutchinson

Braddon, Russell (1965) *Roy Thomson of Fleet Street*, London: Collins

Bramson, Leon (1961) *The Political Context of Sociology*, Princeton University Press

Briggs, Asa (1961) *The Birth of Broadcasting*, London: Oxford University Press

Briggs, Asa (1965) *The Golden Age of Wireless*, London: Oxford University Press

Briggs, Asa (1970) *The War of Words*, London: Oxford University Press

Brown, Les (1971) *Televi$ion: The Business behind the Box*, New York: Harcourt, Brace, Jovanovich

Browne, Don R. (1968) 'The American Image as Presented Abroad by U.S. Television', *Journalism Quarterly* 45 pp. 307–18

Browne, Don R. (1971) 'The BBC and the Pirates: a phase in the life of a prolonged monopoly', *Journalism Quarterly* 48 pp. 85–99

Browne, Don. R. (1973) 'Citizen Involvement in Broadcasting – some European Experiences', *Public Telecommunications Review* 1 pp. 16–28

Bryan, Carter R. (1966) 'The Press System of Jugoslavia: Communism with a difference', *Journalism Quarterly* 43 pp. 291–9

Budd, Richard W. (1964) 'US News in the Press Down Under', *Public Opinion Quarterly* 28 pp. 30–56

Bunn, Ronald (1968) *German Politics and the Spiegel Affair*, Baton Rouge: Louisiana State University Press

Burrage, Michael (1969) 'Two Approaches to the Study of Mass Media', *Archives Européennes de Sociologie* 10 pp. 238–53

Bush, Chilton R. (1966) *News Research for Better Newspapers*, New York: American Newspaper Publishers Association Foundation

Butler, David and Freeman, Jennie (1968) *British Political Facts 1900–1967*, London: Macmillan

Buzek, Antony (1964) *How the Communist Press Works*, London: Pall Mall Press

Canham, Erwin D. (1971) 'The World Flow of News', *Nieman Reports* March pp. 7–11

Cantor, Muriel (1972) *The Hollywood TV Producer: His Work and His Audience*, New York: Basic Books

Cantril, Hadley (1940) *The Invasion from Mars: A Study in the Psychology of Panic*, Princeton University Press [Reprinted (1966) in Harper Torchbooks]

Cantril, Hadley (1967) *The Human Dimension: Experiences in Policy Research*, New Brunswick: Rutgers University Press

Capps, Finis Herbert (1966) *From Isolation to Involvement: The Swedish Immigrant Press in America, 1914–1945*, Chicago: Swedish Pioneer Historical Society

Carey, Arthur C. (1974) 'Effects of the Pony Express and the Transcontinental Telegraph upon Selected California Newspapers', *Journalism Quarterly* 51 pp. 320–3

Carroll, Wallace (1948) *Persuade or Perish*, Boston: Houghton Mifflin

Carter, Felix (1968) 'The Press in Kenya', *Gazette* 14 pp. 85–8

Casanova, Pablo Gonzales (1970) *Democracy in Mexico*, London: Oxford University Press

Ceppi, Marco B. (1965) 'Press Advertising in Italy', *Gazette* 11 pp. 27–42.

Chaudhary, Anju (1974) 'Comparative News Judgement of Indian and American Journalists', *Gazette* 20 pp. 233–47.

Chayes, Abram; Fawcett, James; Ito, Masami; and Kiss, Alexandre-Charles (1973) *Satellite Broadcasting*, London: Oxford University Press for the International Broadcast Institute and the Royal Institute of International Affairs

Chick, J. D. (1967) ' "The White Press": A Study of the Role of Foreign-Owned Newspapers in Ghana, Nigeria and Sierra Leone 1946–65' (Unpublished Ph.D. thesis, Manchester University)

Chu, James C. Y. and Fang, William (1972) 'The Training of Journalists in Communist China', *Journalism Quarterly* 49 pp. 489–97

Coase, R. H. (1974) 'The Market for Goods and the Market for Ideas', *American Economic Review* 64 pp. 384–91

Coatman, John (1951) 'The BBC, Government and Politics', *Public Opinion Quarterly* 15 pp. 287–98

Cohen, Wilbur J. (1968), 'Communication in a Democratic Society', in Hiebert and Spitzer, eds, *The Voice of Government* pp. 13–23

Cole, G. D. H. (1947) *The Life of William Cobbett*, London: Home & Van Thal

Cole, Richard R. (1971) 'Top Songs in the Sixties: A Content Analysis of Popular Lyrics', *American Behavioral Scientist* 14 pp. 389–400

Cole, Richard R. (1972) 'The Mass Media of Mexico: Ownership and Control' (Unpublished Ph.D. thesis, University of Minnesota)

Coleman, W. F.; Opoku, A. A.; and Abel, Helen C. (1968) *An African Experiment in Radio Forums in Rural Development: Ghana 1964–1965*, Paris: Unesco

Conant, Michael (1960) *Antitrust in the Mo.ion Picture Industry*, Berkeley: University of California Press

Cooper, Kent (1942) *Barriers Down: The Story of the News Agency Epoch*, New York: Farrar & Rinehart

Cudlipp, Hugh (1962) *At Your Peril*, London: Weidenfeld & Nicolson

Curran, James and Tunstall, Jeremy (1973) 'Mass Media and Leisure', in Smith, Michael; Parker, Stanley; and Smith, Cyril, eds, *Leisure and Society in Britain*, London: Allen Lane pp. 199–213

Dajani, Nabil H. (1971) 'The Press in Lebanon', *Gazette* 17 pp. 152–74

Dajani, Nabil H. (1973) 'Media Exposure and Mobility in Lebanon', *Journalism Quarterly* 50 pp. 297–305

Damle, Y. B. (1956) 'Communication of Modern Ideas and Knowledge in Indian Villages', *Public Opinion Quarterly* 20 pp. 257–70

Darnton, Robert (1975) 'Writing News and Telling Stories', *Daedalus* 104 pp. 175–94

Davis, Clive (1975) *Clive: Inside the Record Business*, New York: William Morrow

Day, J. Lawrence (1966) 'How Ciespal Seeks to Improve Latin American Journalism', *Journalism Quarterly* 43 pp. 525–30

Day, J. Lawrence (1968) 'The Latin American Journalist: A Tentative Profile', *Journalism Quarterly* 45 pp. 509–15

Day, Robin (1961) *Television: A Personal Report*, London: Hutchinson

Deak, Istvan (1968) *Weimar Germany's Left-wing Intellectuals: A Political History of the Weltbühne and its Circle*, Berkeley: University of California Press

De Blowitz, Henri (1903) *My Memoirs*, London: Edward Arnold

De Claricini, Sergio (1965) *a*. 'Women's Weeklies in Italy', *Gazette* 11 pp. 43–56

De Claricini, Sergio (1965) *b*. 'I Lettori dei Quotidiani in Italia', *Rivista di Sociologia* pp. 109–21

De Fleur, Melvin L. (1964) 'Occupational Roles as Portrayed on Television', *Public Opinion Quarterly* 28 pp. 57–74

De Fleur, Melvin L. (1966) *Theories of Mass Communication*, New York: David McKay

Delahunty, P. G. (1967) 'Educational Broadcasting in Zambia', *EBU Review* March pp. 33–5

Delmer, Sefton (1962) *Black Boomerang*, London: Secker & Warburg

De Mendelssohn, Peter (1959) *Zeitungstadt Berlin*, Berlin: Ullstein

Derieux, Emmanuel and Texier, Jean C. (1974) *La Presse Quotidienne Française*, Paris: Armand Colin

Desai, Ashok V. (1971) *Economic Aspects of the Indian Press*, New Delhi: Press Institute of India

Desmond, Robert W. (1937) *The Press and World Affairs*, New York: Appleton-Century

De Tocqueville, Alexis (1835) *Democracy in America*, Translated by Lawrence, George, London: Fontana (1968) Vol. 1

Deutsch, Karl W. (1953) *Nationalism and Social Communication*, Cambridge, Mass.: MIT Press

Deutsch, Karl. W. and Edinger, Lewis J. (1959) *Germany Rejoins the Powers*, Stanford University Press

Deutschmann, Paul; Ellingsworth, J. Huber; and McNelly, John T. (1968) *Communication and Social Change in Latin America*, New York: Praeger

Dickens, Charles (1842) [Reprinted (1972) Harmondsworth: Penguin]

Diggins, John P. (1972) *Mussolini and Fascism: The View from America*, Princeton University Press

Dix, Robert J. (1967) *Colombia: The Political Dimensions of Change*, New Haven: Yale University Press

Dizard, Wilson P. (1966) *Television: A World View*, Syracuse Univ. Press

Dobbin, Christine (1972) *Urban Leadership in Western India*, Oxford: Clarendon Press

Dua, M. R. (1968) 'Rudyard Kipling as a Journalist: An Indian Evaluation', *Journalism Quarterly* 45 pp. 113–16

Duncan, Charles T. (1973) '*The International Herald Tribune*: Unique (World) Newspaper', *Journalism Quarterly* 50 pp. 348–53

Eapen, Kadamathu Eapen (1969) 'Journalism as a Profession in India: A Study of Two States and Two Cities' (Unpublished Ph.D. thesis in Journalism, University of Wisconsin)

Easum, Donald B. (1951) '*La Prensa* and Freedom of the Press in Argentina', *Journalism Quarterly* 28 pp. 229–37

Edelman, Maurice (1966) *The Mirror: A Political History*, London: Hamish Hamilton

Edelstein, Alex (1973) 'An Alternative Approach to the Study of Source Effects in Mass Communication', *Studies of Broadcasting* 9 pp. 5–29

Eksteins, Modris (1975) *The Limits of Reason: The German Democratic Press and the Collapse of Weimar Democracy*, London: O.U.P.

Elder, E. E. (1931) 'America in the Cairo Press', *Moslem World* 21 pp. 282–6

Elder, Robert E. (1968) *The Information Machine: The U.S. Information Agency and American Foreign Policy*, Syracuse University Press

Ellegard, Alvar (1957) *The Readership of the Periodical Press in Mid-Victorian Britain*, Göteborg: Pamphlet

Elliott, H. (1960) 'The Three-Way Struggle of Press, Radio and TV in Australia', *Journalism Quarterly* 37 pp. 266–74

Elliott, Philip and Golding, Peter (1974) 'Mass Communication and Social Change: The Imagery of Development and the Development of Imagery', in de Kadt, Emanuel and Williams, Gavin eds, *Sociology and Development*, London: Tavistock pp. 229–54

Ellis, L. Ethan (1960) *Newsprint: Producers, Publishers and Political Pressure*, New Brunswick: Rutgers University Press

Emery, Edwin (1972) *The Press and America*, New York: Prentice-Hall

Emery, Walter B. (1964) 'Broadcasting in Mexico', *Journal of Broadcasting* 8 pp. 257-74

Epstein, Edward J. (1974) *News From Nowhere: Television and the News*, New York: Vintage Books

Erlandson, Erling H. (1964) 'The Press in Mexico: Past, Present and Future', *Journalism Quarterly* 41 pp. 232-6

Erman, H. (1954) *August Scherl*, Berlin: Universitas Verlag

Evans, Harold, ed. (1961) *The Active Newsroom*, Zürich: International Press Institute

Evans, Luther H. (1963) 'Some Management Problems of Unesco', *International Organisation* 17 pp. 76-90

Eynon, Derry (1971) 'us-Based Business Periodicals for Overseas Readers', *Journalism Quarterly* 48 pp. 547-50

Falewicz, Jan (1964) 'Effects of Criticism in Urban Film Tests', *Polish Sociological Bulletin* 1 pp. 90-5

Faysse, Gilles (1973) 'Mass Media in Senegal', *The Democratic Journalist* pp. 7-10

Feinstein, Phylis (1971) *All About Sesame Street*, New York: Tower Publications

Feliciano, Gloria D. (1973) *An Overview of Communication Research in Asia: Status, Problems and Needs*, Honolulu: East–West Communication Institute

Fielden, Lionel (1960) *The Natural Bent*, London: André Deutsch

Fielding, Raymond (1959) 'Mirror of Discontent: The *March of Time* and its Politically Controversial Film Issues', *Western Political Quarterly* 12 pp. 145-52

Fielding, Raymond (1972) *The American Newsreel, 1911-1967*, Norman: University of Oklahoma Press

The Film Centre (1950) *The Film Industry in Six European Countries*, Paris: Unesco

Firestone, D. J. (1970) *The Public Persuader: Government Advertising*, Toronto: Methuen

Fishman, Joshua (1967) 'Bilingualism with and without Diglossia; Diglossia with and without Bilingualism', *Journal of Social Issues* 23 pp. 29-38

Fluharty, Vernon L. (1957) *Dance of the Millions: Military Rule and the Social Revolution in Colombia*, University of Pittsburgh Press

Foster, Brian (1968) *The Changing English Language*, London: Macmillan

Fox, Grace (1969) *Britain and Japan, 1858-1883*, Oxford: Clarendon Press

Frey, Frederick W. (1973) 'Communication and Development', in Pool, Schramm *et al.* eds, *Handbook of Communication* pp. 337-461

Friederichs, Hulda (1911) *The Life of Sir George Newnes*, London: Hodder & Stoughton

Friedrich, Otto (1972) *Decline and Fall*, London: Michael Joseph

Fulbright, Senator J. William (1970) *The Pentagon Propaganda Machine*, New York: Vintage Books

Fuller, Wayne E. (1972) *The American Mail: Enlarger of the Common Life*, University of Chicago Press

Galloway, Jonathan F. (1972) *The Politics and Technology of Satellite Communications*, Lexington, Mass.: D. C. Heath

Gans, Herbert J. (1962) 'Hollywood Films on British Screens: An Analysis of the Functions of American Popular Culture Abroad', *Social Problems* 9 pp. 324–8

Gardner, Leroy, W. (1961) 'A Content Analysis of Japanese and American Television', *Journal of Broadcasting* 6 pp. 45–52

Gardner, Mary A. (1960) 'The Argentine Press Since Perón', *Journalism Quarterly* 37 pp. 426–30

Gardner, Mary A. (1967) *The Inter-American Press Association*, Austin: University of Texas Press

Geertz, Clifford (1973 *The Interpretation of Cultures*, New York: Basic Books

Gerald, U. Edward (1956) *The British Press Under Government Economic Controls*, Minneapolis: University of Minnesota Press

Gerbner, George (1964) 'Ideological Perspectives and Political Tendencies in News Reporting', *Journalism Quarterly* 41 pp. 495–516

Gillett, Charlie (1971) *The Sound of the City*, London: Sphere Books

Giroud, Françoise (1974) *I Give You My Word*, London: Weidenfeld & Nicolson [First published as *Si Je Mens – Conversations avec Claude Gleyman* (1973) Paris: Editions Stock]

Gohdes, Clarence (1944) *American Literature in Nineteenth Century England*, New York: Columbia University Press

Goldberg, Isaac (1930) *Tin Pan Alley*, New York: John Day

Goldhamer, Herbert (1972) *The Foreign Powers in Latin America*, Princeton University Press

Goldsborough, James O. (1974) 'An American in Paris: The International Herald Tribune', *Columbia Journalism Review* July/August pp. 37–45

Goldsen, Rose K. (1971) 'NBC's Make-Believe Research on TV Violence', *Transaction* October pp. 28–35

Goldsen, Rose K. and Bibliowicz, Azriel (1974) 'Mindlessness in *Plaza Sesamo*' (Paper at International Broadcast Institute Conference in Mexico City)

Goody, Jack ed. (1968) *Literacy in Traditional Societies*, London: Cambridge University Press

Goulden, Joseph C. (1970) *Monopoly*, New York: Pocket Books

Gramling, Oliver (1940) *AP: The Story of the News*, New York: Farrar & Rinehart

Grant, Marcia A. M. (1975) 'The Nigerian Press and Politics since Independence' (Unpublished Ph.D. thesis, University of London)

Green, Timothy (1972) *The Universal Eye: World Television in the Seventies*, London: Bodley Head

Greene, Theodore P. (1970) *America's Heroes: the changing models of success in American magazines*, New York: Oxford University Press

Greenfield, Robert (1975) *A Journey through America with the Rolling Stones*, St. Albans: Panther

Griest, Guinevere L. (1970) *Mudie's Circulating Library and the Victorian Novel*, Newton Abbot: David & Charles

Griffith, Mrs. D. W. (1925) *When the Movies were Young*, New York: E. P. Dutton [Reprinted (1969) New York: Dover Publications]

Groombridge, Brian (1972) *Television and the People*, Harmondsworth: Penguin

Gross, John (1969) *The Rise and Fall of the Man of Letters: English Literary Life Since 1800*, London: Weidenfeld & Nicolson

Guback, Thomas H. (1967) 'American Interests in the British Film Industry', *The Quarterly Review of Economics and Business* 7

Guback, Thomas H. (1969) *The International Film Industry*, Bloomington: Indiana University Press

Guback, Thomas H. (1971) 'Film and Cultural Pluralism', *Journal of Aesthetic Education* Vol. 5 2 pp. 35–51

Guback, Thomas H. (1973) 'Film as International Business' (Unpublished paper)

Guback, Thomas H. (1974) 'Cultural Identity and Film in the European Economic Community' (Paper delivered at conference on 'Film in Europe', Polytechnic of Central London)

Gunaratne, Shelton A. (1970) 'Government-Press Conflict in Ceylon: Freedom versus Responsibility', *Journalism Quarterly* 47 pp. 530–43 and 552

Haacke, Wilmont (1938) 'The German Magazine: Its Origin and Development', *Journalism Quarterly* 45 pp. 706–12

Hachten, William (1968) 'The Training of African Journalists', *Gazette* 14 pp. 101–110

Hachten, William (1971) *a. Muffled Drums: The News Media in Africa*, Ames: Iowa State University Press

Hachten, William (1971) *b.* 'Moroccan news media reflect divisive forces while unifying', *Journalism Quarterly* 48 pp. 100–10

Hale, Julian (1975) *Radio Power: Propaganda and International Broadcasting*, London: Paul Elek

Hall, Alex (1974) *a.* 'The Kaiser, the Wilhelmine State and Lèse-Majesté', *German Life and Letters* January pp. 101–14

Hall, Alex (1974) *b.* 'By Other Means: The Legal Struggle Against the SPD in Wilhelmine Germany 1890–1900', *The Historical Journal* 17 pp. 365–86

Halloran, J. D.; Elliot, Philip; and Murdock, Graham (1970) *Communications and Demonstrations: A Case Study*, Harmondsworth: Penguin

Halloran, Richard (1967) 'Chrysanthemum Curtain', *Columbia Journalism Review* Fall pp. 39–42

Hampton, Benjamin B. (1931) *History of the American Film Industry from its Beginnings to 1931* [Reprinted (1970) New York: Dover Publications]

Handel, L. (1950) *Hollywood Looks at its Audience: A Report on Film Audience Research*, Urbana: University of Illinois Press

Hansen, Harry L. (1945) 'Hollywood and International Understanding', *Harvard Business Review* 25 pp. 28–45

Hanson, Philip (1971) *The Development of Advertising in the Soviet Union*, London: The Advertising Association

Hanson, Philip (1973) *The Development of Advertising in Eastern Europe*, London: The Advertising Association

Hardy, Alexander G. (1967) *Hitler's Weapon: the Managed Press and Propaganda Machine of Nazi Germany*, New York: Vantage Press

Harkness, Ross (1963) *J. E. Atkinson of the Star*, University of Toronto Press

Harley, J. E. (1940) *World-Wide Influence of the Cinema*, Los Angeles: University of Southern California Press

Harris, Bill (1963) 'Kenya Broadcasting Corporation', *European Broadcasting Union Review* 81B pp. 24–7

Harris, Charles R. S. (1957) *Allied Military Administration of Italy*, London: HMSO

Harris, Paul (1968) *When Pirates Rule the Waves*, London: Impulse Books

Hart, Jim A. (1963) 'The Flow of News Between the United States and Canada', *Journalism Quarterly* 40 pp. 70–4

Hartmann, Paul and Husband, Charles (1974) *Racism and the Mass Media*, London: Davis Poynter

Hatem, M. Abdel-Kader (1974) *Information and the Arab Cause*, London: Longman

Head, Sydney W. (1972) *Broadcasting in America: A Survey of Television and Radio*, Boston: Houghton Mifflin

Head, Sydney W., ed. (1974) *Broadcasting in Africa*, Philadelphia: Temple University Press

Hellmuth, William F. Jnr. (1950) 'The Motion Picture Industry' in Adams, Walter, ed., *The Structure of American Industry*, New York: Macmillan pp. 267–304

Henderson, John W. (1969) *The United States Information Agency*, New York: Praeger

Herberichs, Céleste (1967) 'The *Corriere della Sera* and Fascism: A Chapter from Italian Press History', *Gazette* 4 pp. 348–61

Herd, Harold (1952) *The March of Journalism*, London: Allen & Unwin

Hester, Albert L. (1974) 'The News from Latin America via a World News Agency', *Gazette* 20 pp. 82–98

Hibben, Paxton (1925) 'The Movies in Russia', *The Nation* 11th November pp. 539–40

Hiebert, Ray Eldon (1966) *Courtier to the Crowd: The Story of Ivy Lee and the Development of Public Relations*, Ames: Iowa State University Press

Hiebert, Ray Eldon and Spitzer, Carlton E. eds (1968) *The Voice of Government*, New York: John Wiley

Hill, Lord (1974) *Behind the Screen*, London: Sidgwick & Jackson

Hill and Knowlton International (1967) *Handbook on International Public Relations Vol. 1: Western Europe*, New York: Frederick & Praeger

Hills, Lee (1969) 'The Story of the IAPA', *Nieman Reports* 23 pp. 3–7

Hindley, Geoffrey and Diana (1972) *Advertising in Victorian England 1837–1901*, London: Wayland

Hindustan Thompson (1972) *Media in India '72*, Bombay: Hindustan Thompson Associated

Hirsch, Paul M. (1969) *The Structure of the Popular Music Industry*, Ann Arbor: Survey Research Center, University of Michigan

Hirsch, Paul M. (1971) 'Sociological Approaches to the Pop Music Phenomenon', *American Behavioral Scientist* 14 pp. 371–88

Hirsch, Paul M. (1972) 'Processing Fads and Fashions: An Organization-Set Analysis of Cultural Industry Systems', *American Journal of Sociology* 77 pp. 639–59

Hirschmann, Edwin (1966) 'The Problems of the Press in Multilingual Bombay', *Journalism Quarterly* 43 pp. 519–24 and 557

Hohenberg, John (1964) *Foreign Correspondence: The Great Reporters and Their Times*, New York: Columbia University Press

Hohenberg, John (1967) *Between Two Worlds: Policy, Press, and Public Opinion in Asian-American Relations*, New York: Praeger

Holden, W. Sprague (1961) *Australia Goes to Press*, Detroit: Wayne State University Press

Holden, W. Sprague (1968) 'Metropolitan Newspapers in Australia To-Day', *Journalism Quarterly* 45 pp. 713–23

Hollander, Gayle Durham (1972) *Soviet Political Indoctrination*, New York: Praeger

Hollis, Patricia (1970) *The Pauper Press: A Study in Working Class Radicalism of the 1830s*, London: Oxford University Press

Holt, Robert T. (1958) *Radio Free Europe*, Minneapolis: University of Minnesota Press

Hoopes, Paul R. (1966) 'Content Analysis of News in Three Argentine Dailies', *Journalism Quarterly* 43 pp. 543–7

Hopkins, Jerry (1974) *Elvis*, London: Abacus

Hopkins, Mark W. (1970) *Mass Media in the Soviet Union*, New York: Pegasus

Horton, Donald (1957) 'The Dialogue of Courtship in Popular Songs', *American Journal of Sociology* 62 pp. 569–78

Houlton, Robert (1967) 'The Process of Innovation: Magnetic Recording and the Broadcasting Industry in the USA,' *Bulletin of the Oxford University Institute of Economics and Statistics* 29 pp. 41–59

Houlton, Robert (1973) 'Innovation, Intervention and Media Analysis: An Examination of the Pattern of Change in the US Mass Entertainment Industry with Special Reference to the Post-1940 Period' (Unpublished Ph.D. thesis in Sociology, University of Leeds)

Howell, W. (1960) 'Program Production at Radio Moscow', *Journal of Broadcasting* 4 pp. 327–38

Høyer, Svennik; Hadenius, Stig; and Weibull, Lennart (1975) *The Politics and Economics of the Press: A Developmental Perspective*, Beverly Hills: Sage Publications

Hsu, Chia-shih; Maslog, Crispin; and Cho, Tong-jae (1972) 'Journalism Education in Asia: A Symposium', *Journalism Quarterly* 49 pp. 116–22 and 128

Hull, W. H. N. (1962) 'The Public Control of Broadcasting: The Canadian and Australian Experiences', *Canadian Journal of Economics and Political Science* 28 pp. 114–26

Hultén, Olof (1974) 'The Uses of Intelsat', in Wells, Alan, ed. *Mass Communications: A World View* pp. 198–206

Hutt, Allen (1973) *The Changing Newspaper: Typographic Trends in Britain and America, 1622–1972*, London: Gordon Fraser

Hyman, Sidney (1969) *The Lives of William Benton*, Chicago: University of Chicago Press

Inkeles, Alex (1971) *Social Change in Soviet Russia*, New York: Simon & Schuster-Clarion

Inkeles, Alex and Smith, David H. (1974) *Becoming Modern: Individual Change in Six Developing Countries*, London: Heinemann

Innes, Harold (1948) *The Press: A Neglected Factor in the Economic History of the Twentieth Century*, London: Athlone Press for the University of London

Innes, Harold (1950) *Empire and Communications*, London: Oxford University Press

International Press Institute (1952) *The News from Russia*, Zürich: IPI

International Press Institute (1953) *The Flow of News*, Zürich: IPI

International Press Institute (1954) *The News from the Middle East*, Zürich: IPI

International Press Institute (1956) *News in Asia*, Zürich: IPI

International Telecommunications Union (1965) *From Semaphore to Satellite*, Geneva: ITU

Jacobi, Claus (1953–54) 'The New German Press', *Foreign Affairs* 32 pp. 323–30

Jain, Rikhab Dass (1960) *The Economic Aspects of the Film Industry in India*, Delhi: Atma Ram

Johnstone, John W. C.; Slawski, Edward J.; and Bowman, W. W. (1972) 'Professional Values of American Newsmen', *Public Opinion Quarterly* 36 pp. 522–40

Kane, Joseph F. (1951) 'The Totalitarian Pattern in Perón's Press Campaign', *Journalism Quarterly* 28 pp. 237–43

Katz, Elihu and Lazarsfeld, Paul F. (1955) *Personal Influence*, Glencoe: Free Press

Katz, Elihu (1971) *a.* 'Television Comes to the Middle East', *Transaction* 8th June pp. 42–8

Katz, Elihu (1971) *b.* 'Television Comes to the People of the Book' in Horowitz, Irving Louis ed., *The Use and Abuse of Social Science*, New Brunswick: Transaction Books pp. 249–71

Katz, Elihu (1973) 'News from the Global Village', *The Listener* 18th January pp. 68–9

Katz, E.; Wedell, E. G.; Pilsworth, M. J. and Shinar, D. (1976) *Broadcasting and National Development*, Manuscript

Katzen, May (1975) *Mass Communication: Teaching and Studies at Universities, A World Wide Survey*, Paris: Unesco

Kawabé, Kisaburō (1921) *The Press and Politics in Japan*, University of Chicago Press

Kayser, Jacques (1953) *One Week's News*, Paris: Unesco

Kemble, Edward C. (1858) *A History of California Newspapers, 1846–1858* [Reprinted (1962) Los Gatos, California: Talisman Press]

Kieve, Jeffrey (1973) *The Electric Telegraph*, Newton Abbot: David & Charles

Kim, Young Hum, ed. (1968) *The Central Intelligence Agency*, Lexington, Mass.: D. C. Heath

Kimball, Penn T. (1969) 'Congressional Candidates and the Broadcast Media in the 1968 Campaign' in *The Alfred I. DuPont–Columbia University Survey of Broadcast Journalism 1968–1969*, New York: Grosset & Dunlap

King, Frank H. H. and Clarke, Prescott (1965) *A Research Guide to China-Coast Newspapers 1822–1911*, Cambridge, Mass.: East Asian Research Center, Harvard University

Klapper, Joseph T. (1960) *The Effects of Mass Communication*, New York: Free Press

Kloskowska, Antonina (1964) 'Mass Culture in Poland', *Polish Sociological Bulletin* 2 pp. 106–15

Knight, Robert P. (1970) 'Unesco's International Communication Activities' in Fischer, Heinz-Dietrich and Merrill, John C., eds, *International Communication*, New York: Hastings House

Kobler, John (1968) *Henry Luce: His Time, Life and Fortune*, London: Macdonald

Kolade, Christopher (1975) 'Nigeria's Cultural Identity', *Inter Media* August pp. 28–9

Kondo, Mitsugi (1956) 'Newspaper Competition in Japan', *Gazette* 2 pp. 97–112

Koszyk, Kurt (1970) 'The Development of the International Press Institute' in Fischer and Merrill, eds, *International Communication* pp. 227–32

Kracauer, Siegfried (1947) *From Caligari to Hitler: A Psychological History of the German Film*, Princeton University Press

Kracauer, Siegfried (1949) 'National Types as Hollywood Presents Them', *Public Opinion Quarterly* 13 pp. 53–72

Kracmar, John A. (1971) *Marketing Research in Developing Countries*, New York: Praeger

Kriegk, Otto (1943) *Der Deutsche Film im Spiegel der Ufa*, Berlin

Kruglak, Theodore E. (1962) *The Two Faces of Tass*, Minneapolis: University of Minnesota Press

Kulik, Karol (1975) *Alexander Korda: The Man Who Could Work Miracles*, London: W. H. Allen

Kuo-Sin, Chang (1968) *A Survey of the Chinese Language Daily Press*, Hong-Kong: International Press Institute, Asian Programme

Kuppuswamy, B. (1972) *Social Change in India*, Delhi: Vikas Publications

Landau, Jacob M. (1958) *Studies in the Arab Theater and Cinema*, Philadelphia: University of Pennsylvania Press

Lang, Kurt (1974) 'Images of Society: Media Research in Germany', *Public Opinion Quarterly* 38 pp. 335–51

Lasswell, Harold D. (1948) 'The Structure and Function of Communication in Society' [Reprinted (1966) in Berelson, Bernard and Janowitz, Morris eds, *Reader in Public Opinion and Communication* New York: Free Press pp. 178–90]

Lasswell, Harold D. (1927) *Propaganda Technique in World War I* [Reprinted (1971) Cambridge, Mass.: MIT Press]

Lazarsfeld, Paul F. (1941) 'Remarks on Administrative and Critical Communication Research', *Studies in Philosophy and Social Science* 9 pp. 2–16

Lazarsfeld, Paul F. (1969) 'An Episode in the History of Social Research: A Memoir' in Fleming, Donald and Bailyn, Bernard, eds, *The Intellectual Migration*, Cambridge, Mass.: Belknap Press for Harvard University Press pp. 270–337

Lazarsfeld, Paul F.; Berelson, Bernard; and Gaudet, Hazel (1948) *The People's Choice*, New York: Columbia University Press

Lazarsfeld, Paul F. and Field, Harry (1946) *The People Look at Radio*, Chapel Hill: University of North Carolina Press

Lazarsfeld, Paul F. and Kendall, Patricia L. (1948) *Radio Listening in America*, New York: Prentice Hall

Lazarsfeld, Paul F. and Stanton, Frank N. (1941) *Radio Research 1941*, New York: Duell, Sloan & Pearce

Lazarsfeld, Paul F. and Stanton, Frank N., eds (1944) *Radio Research 1942–43*, New York: Duell, Sloan & Pearce

LeDuc, Don R. (1973) *Cable Television and the FCC: A Crisis in Media Control*, Philadelphia: Temple University Press

Lee, Linda (1975) *The Life and Tragic Death of Bruce Lee*, London: W. H. Allen

Lent, John A. (1968) 'History of the Japanese Press', *Gazette* 14 pp. 7–36

Lent, John A. ed. (1971) *The Asian Newspapers' Reluctant Revolution*, Ames: Iowa State University Press

Lent, John A. ed. (1976) *Broadcasting in Asia and the Pacific*, Manuscript

Leprehon, Pierre (1972) *The Italian Cinema*, London: Secker & Warburg

Lerner, Daniel, ed. (1951) *Propaganda in War and Crisis: Materials for American Policy*, New York: George W. Stewart

Lerner, Daniel (1958) *The Passing of Traditional Society: Modernizing the Middle East*, Glencoe: Free Press

Lerner, Daniel (1949) *Sykewar*, New York: George W. Stewart [Reprinted (1971) as *Psychological Warfare against Nazi Germany*, Cambridge, Mass.: MIT Press]

Lerner, Daniel and Schramm, Wilbur, eds (1967) *Communication and Change in the Developing Countries*, Honolulu: East–West Center Press

Levin, Harvey J. (1971) *The Invisible Resource: Use and Regulation of the Radio Spectrum*, Baltimore: Johns Hopkins University Press

Lewels, Francisco J. (1974) *The Uses of the Media by the Chicano Movement*, New York: Praeger

Lewis, Boyd (1971) 'The Syndicates and How They Grew'; *Saturday Review* 11th December pp. 67–9

Leyda, Jay (1960) *Kino: A History of the Russian and Soviet Film*, London: Allen & Unwin

Leyda, Jay (1972) *Diarying: An Account of Films and Film Audiences in China*, Cambridge, Mass.: MIT Press

Leys, Colin (1975) *Underdevelopment in Kenya*, London: Heinemann Educational

Lichtheim, George (1974) *Imperialism*, Harmondsworth: Penguin

Liebich, F. K. (1969) *Removing Taxes on Knowledge*, Paris: Unesco

Lipset, Seymour M. and Bendix, Reinhard (1959) *Social Mobility in Industrial Society*, Berkeley: University of California Press

Lipski, Sam (1974) 'Distortion of US Reports', *New Journalist* (Australia) 14 pp. 8–10

Lisann, Maury (1975) *Broadcasting to the Soviet Union: International Politics and Radio*, New York: Praeger

Litvak, Isaiah and Maule, Christopher (1974) *Cultural Sovereignty: The Time and Reader's Digest Case in Canada*, New York: Praeger

Liu, Alan P. K. (1971) *Communications and National Integration in Communist China*, Berkeley: University of California Press

Lohman, Manfred (1971) 'The Role of the Journalist in the Process of Socio-Political Change in India' in Noorani, ed., *Freedom of the Press in India*

Loory, Stuart H. (1974) 'The CIA's Use of the Press–a "Mighty Wurlitzer" ', *Columbia Journalism Review* September/October pp. 9–18

Low, Rachael (1948) *The History of the British Film, 1914–1918*, London: Allen & Unwin

Low, Rachael (1949) *The History of the British Film, 1906–1914*, London: Allen & Unwin

Low, Rachael (1971) *The History of the British Film, 1918–1929*, London: Allen & Unwin

Low, Rachael and Manvell, Roger (1948) *The History of the British Film, 1896–1906*, London: Allen & Unwin

Lowenthal, Leo (1944) 'Biographies in Popular Magazines' in Lazarsfeld and Stanton, eds, *Radio Research 1942–43* pp. 507–48

Lyons, Eugene (1966) *David Sarnoff: A Biography*, New York: Harper & Row

MacCann, Richard Dyer (1973) *The People's Films: A Political History of US Government Motion Pictures*, New York: Hastings House

McCormack, Thelma H. (1959) 'Canada's Royal Commission on Broadcasting' *Public Opinion Quarterly*, 23 pp. 92–100

MacFarquhar, Roderick (1973) 'A Visit to the Chinese Press', *China Quarterly* 53 pp. 144–52

Macgowan, Kenneth (1965) *Behind the Screen: The History and Techniques of the Motion Picture*, New York: Dell Publishing

Mackay, I. K. (1957) *Broadcasting in Australia*, Melbourne University Press

McLeod, Jack and Rush, Ramona R. (1969) 'Professionalization of Latin-American and U.S. Journalists', *Journalism Quarterly* 46 pp. 583–90

*L

MacNeil, Robert (1968) *The People Machine*, London: Eyre & Spottiswoode

Machlup, Fritz (1962) *The Production and Distribution of Knowledge in the United States*, Princeton University Press

Maddison, John (1971) *Radio and Television in Literacy*, Paris: Unesco

Maddox, Brenda (1972) *Beyond Babel: New Directions in Communications*, London: André Deutsch

Malhotra, Inder (1972) 'Television in India', *Times of India* 16th October

Mannucci, Cesare (1965) 'Structure and Policy of the RAI-TV', *Gazette* 11 pp. 57–67

Manvell, Roger and Fraenkel, Heinrich (1971) *The German Cinema*, London: J. M. Dent

Marbut, Frederick W. (1951) 'The United States Senate and the Press 1838–41', *Journalism Quarterly* 28 pp. 342–50

Market Research Society (1971) *International Directory of Market Research Organizations*, London: MRS

Markham, James W. (1961) 'Foreign News in the United States and South American Press', *Public Opinion Quarterly* 25 pp. 249–62

Markham, James W. (1967) *Voices of the Red Giants: Communications in Russia and China*, Ames: Iowa State University Press

Martin, Leslie John (1949) 'Press and Radio in Palestine Under the British Mandate', *Journalism Quarterly* 26 pp. 186–93

Martin, Leslie John (1960) 'American Newsmagazines and the European Scene', *Gazette* 6 pp. 205–22

Massing, Paul W. (1953) 'Communist References to the Voice of America', *Public Opinion Quarterly* 16 pp. 618–22

Mast, Benjamin V. (1959) 'The Impact of Television on the Control of Broadcasting in Canada', *Journal of Broadcasting* 3 pp. 263–88

Mayer, Gerald M. (1947) 'American Motion Pictures in World Trade', *Annals of the American Academy of Political and Social Sciences* 254 pp. 31–6

Mayer, Henry (1964) *The Press in Australia*, London: Angus & Robertson

Mayer, Martin (1972) *About Television*, New York: Harper & Row

Mayer, Michael F. (1973) *The Film Industries*, New York: Hastings House

Mayhew, Christopher and Adams, Michael (1975) *Publish It Not . . . The Middle East Cover Up*, London: Longman

Mehrotra, R. R. (1975) 'Dimensions of a Language Policy – The Case for English' in Saberwal, ed., *Towards a Cultural Policy* pp. 112–25

Meier, Ernst (1954) 'The Licensed Press in the US Occupation Zone of Germany', *Journalism Quarterly* 31 pp. 223–31

Melody, William (1973) *Children's Television: The Economics of Exploitation*, New Haven: Yale University Press

Menanteau-Horta, Dario (1967) 'Professionalism of Journalists in Santiago de Chile', *Journalism Quarterly* 44 pp. 715–24

Merrill, John C. (1962) 'The Image of the "Yanqui" in the Mexican Press', *Gazette* 8 pp. 251–4

Merrill, John C. (1968) *The Elite Press*, New York: Pitman

Merritt, Anna J. and Richard L. (1970) *Public Opinion in Occupied*

Germany: The OMGUS Surveys, 1945–1949, Urbana: University of Illinois Press

Merritt, Richard L. (1963) 'Public Opinion in Colonial America: Content-Analysing the Colonial Press', *Public Opinion Quarterly* 27 pp. 356–71

Merritt, Richard L. ed. (1972) *Communication in International Politics*, Urbana: University of Illinois Press

Merton, Robert (1946) *Mass Persuasion: The Social Psychology of a War Bond Drive*, New York: Harper [Reprinted (1971) Westport, Conn.: Greenwood Press]

Merton, Robert (1957) *Social Theory and Social Structure*, Glencoe: Free Press

Merton, Robert; Fiske, M.; and Kendall, P. L. (1956) *The Focused Interview*, Glencoe: Free Press

Metzger, Charles R. (1947) 'Pressure Groups and the Motion Picture Industry', *Annals of the American Academy of Political and Social Science* 254 pp. 110–15

Mickelson, Sig (1972) *The Electric Mirror: Politics in an Age of Television*, New York: Dodd, Mead

Mickiewicz, Ellen (1972–3) 'Policy Applications of Public Opinion Research in the Soviet Union', *Public Opinion Quarterly* 36 pp. 556–78

Millard, William J. (1955) 'A Study in the Sociology of Communications: Determinants and Consequences of Exposure to American Motion Pictures in the Near and Middle East' (Unpublished Ph.D. thesis, Faculty of Political Science, Columbia University)

Mills, C. Wright (1956) *The Power Elite*, New York: Oxford University Press

Mintz, Morton and Cohen, Jerry S. (1972) *America Inc: Who Owns and Operates the United States*, London: Pitman Publishing

Miracle, Gordon E. (1966) *Management of International Advertising: The Role of Advertising Agencies*, Ann Arbor: University of Michigan, Graduate School of Business Administration

Mishra, Vishwa Mohan (1970) *Communication and Modernization in Urban Slums*, New York: Asia Publishing House

Mock, James R. and Larson, Cedric (1939) *Words that Won the War*, Princeton University Press

Moffett, Samuel E. (1907) *The Americanization of Canada* [Republished (1972) University of Toronto Press]

Monopolies Commission (1966) *Films: A Report on the Supply of Films for Exhibition in Cinemas*, London: HMSO (HC 206)

Monopolies Commission (1966) *Report on the Times Newspaper and the Sunday Times Newspaper*, London: HMSO (HC 273)

Morin, Edgar (1960) *The Stars: An Account of the Star System in Motion Pictures*, New York: Grove Press

Morris, Joe Alex (1957) *Deadline Every Minute: The Story of the United Press*, Garden City, N.Y.: Doubleday

Morris, Roger; Mueller, Shelley; and Jelin, William (1974) 'Through the Looking Glass in Chile: Coverage of Allende's Regime', *Columbia Journalism Review* November/December pp. 15–26

Mott, Frank Luther (1962) *American Journalism. A History 1690–1960*, New York: Macmillan

Mousseau, Jacques, ed. (1972) *Les Communications de Masse*, Paris: Centre d'Etude et de Promotion de la Lecture

Mujahid, Sharif al (1971) 'After Decline during Ayub Era, Pakistan's Press Thrives, Improves', *Journalism Quarterly* 48 pp. 526–35

Muller, Hans Dieter (1969) *Press Power: A Study of Axel Springer*, London: Macdonald

Murthy, Nadig K. (1966) *Indian Journalism*, University of Mysore

Musole, Lloyd D. ed. (1968) *Communications Satellites in Political Orbit*, San Francisco: Chandler Publishing

Myers, John (1967) *Print in a Wild Land*, Garden City, N.Y.: Doubleday

Mytton, Graham (1972) 'Report on the National Mass Media Audience Survey', Lusaka: Institute for African Studies, University of Zambia (Duplicated)

Narasimhan, V. K. (1956) 'Shaping of Editorial Policy in the Indian Press', *Journalism Quarterly* 33 pp. 208–12

Nash, Vernon (1931) 'Chinese Journalism in 1931', *Journalism Quarterly* 8 pp. 446–52

Nash, Vernon (1933) 'Journalism in China: 1933', *Journalism Quarterly* 10 pp. 316–22

Natarajan, S. (1962) *A History of the Press in India*, Bombay: Asia Publishing House

Nayer, Balder Raj (1969) *National Communication and Language Policy in India*, New York: Praeger

Neal, Wallace E. (1950) 'Italian Newspapers Restricted by Controls and Weak Economy', *Journalism Quarterly* 27 pp. 58–61

Nihon Shinbun Kyoka *The Japanese Press*, Tokyo: NSK (The Japan Newspaper Publishers' and Editors' Association) Annual

Nippon Hoso Kyokai (1967) *The History of Broadcasting in Japan*, Tokyo: History Compilation Room, Radio and TV Culture Research Institute, NHK

Nixon, Raymond B. (1970) *Education for Journalism in Latin America*, New York: Council on Higher Education in the American Republics

Noll, Roger G.; Peck, Merton J.; and McGowan, John (1973) *Economic Aspects of Television Regulation*, Washington, D.C.: The Brookings Institution

Noorani, A. G., ed. (1971) *Freedom of the Press in India*, Bombay: Nachiketa Publications

Nordenstreng, Kaarle and Varis, Tapio (1974) *Television Traffic – A One-Way Street?*, Paris: Unesco

Norman, Albert (1951) *Our German Policy: Propaganda and Culture*, New York: Vantage Press

O'Connor, T. P. (1889) 'The New Journalism', *The New Review* October pp. 423–34

Odlum, Floyd B. (1947) 'Financial Organization of the Motion Picture Industry', *Annals of the American Academy of Political and Social Sciences* 254 pp. 18–25

Olson, Kenneth E. (1966) *The History Makers: The Press of Europe from its Beginnings Through 1965*, Baton Rouge: Louisiana State University Press

Östgaard, Einar (1965) 'Factors Influencing the Flow of News', *Journal of International Peace Research* 1 pp. 39–63

Owen, Bruce M. (1973) 'Newspaper and Television Station Joint Ownership', *The Anti-Trust Bulletin* 18 pp. 787–807

Park, Robert E. (1922) *The Immigrant Press and Its Control*, New York: Harper

Park, Robert E. (1955) *Society* Vol. 3, Glencoe: Free Press

Paulu, Burton (1955) 'Audiences for Broadcasting in Britain and America', *Journalism Quarterly* 32 pp. 329–34

Paulu, Burton (1967) *Radio and Television Broadcasting on the European Continent*, Minneapolis: University of Minnesota Press

Paulu, Burton (1974) *Radio and Television Broadcasting in Eastern Europe*, Minneapolis: University of Minnesota Press

Pearl, Cyril (1958) *Wild Men of Sydney*, London: W. H. Allen

Pearson, Lester B. (1971) *The Political Implications of Satellite Communication*, London: International Broadcasting Institute

Peers, Frank W. (1969) *The Politics of Canadian Broadcasting*, University of Toronto Press

Perry, George and Aldridge, Alan (1967) *The Penguin Book of Comics*, Harmondsworth: Penguin

Phillips, Kevin P. (1975) *Mediacracy: American Parties and Politics in the Communication Age*, Garden City, N.Y.: Doubleday

Phillips, Marcus S. (1974) 'The German Film Industry and the Third Reich' (Unpublished Ph.D. thesis, University of East Anglia)

Pickerell, Albert C. (1960) 'The Press in Thailand: Conditions and Trends', *Journalism Quarterly* 37 pp. 83–96

Pickerell, Albert C. (1966) 'The English Language Press of Asia' (Unpublished report)

Pickett, Calder M. (1965) 'A Paper for the Doughboys: *Stars and Stripes* in World War I', *Journalism Quarterly* 42 pp. 60–8

Piekalkiewicz, Jaroslaw A. (1972) *Public Opinion Polling in Czechoslovakia, 1968–69*, New York: Praeger

Pierce, Robert N. (1970) 'Costa Rica's Contemporary Media Show High Popular Participation', *Journalism Quarterly* 47 pp. 544–52

Pilgert, Henry P. (1953) *Press, Radio and Film in West Germany, 1945–1953*, Office of the U.S. High Commission for Germany: Historical Division

Pleasants, Henry (1969) *Serious Music – and All That Jazz!*, London: Gollancz

Political and Economic Planning (1938) *The British Press*, London: PEP

Political and Economic Planning (1952) *The British Film Industry*, London: PEP

Pool, Ithiel de Sola (1966) 'The Necessity for Social Scientists Doing Research for Governments', *Background* 10 pp. 111–22

Pool, Ithiel de Sola; Stone, Philip; and Szalai, Alexander (1971) *Com-*

munications, Computers and Automation for Development, New York: United Nations Institute for Training and Research

Pool, Ithiel de Sola, Schramm, Wilbur, *et al.*, eds (1973) *Handbook of Communication*, Chicago: Rand McNally

Pool, Ithiel de Sola (1973) 'Communication in Totalitarian Societies', in Pool and Schramm, eds, *Handbook of Communication* pp. 462–511

Pool, Ithiel de Sola (1974) 'Direct Broadcast Satellites and the Integrity of National Cultures', in Aspen Institute, *Control of Direct Broadcast Satellites* pp. 27–56

Porter, Vincent (1974) 'TV Strategies and European Film Production', *Sight and Sound* Summer pp. 163–5 and 175

Potter, Elaine (1974) *The Press as Opposition: The Political Role of South African Newspapers*, London: Chatto & Windus

Pound, Reginald and Harmsworth, Geoffrey (1959) *Northcliffe*, London: Cassell

Powdermaker, Hortense (1951) *Hollywood, The Dream Factory*, London: Secker & Warburg

Powell, David E. (1975) 'Television in the USSR', *Public Opinion Quarterly* 39 pp. 287–300

Pratten, C. F. (1970) *The Economics of Television*, London: PEP

Presbrey, Frank (1929) *The History and Development of Advertising*, Garden City, N.Y.: Doubleday, Doran

Pye, Lucian W., ed. (1963) *Communications and Political Development*, Princeton University Press

Radio Worldwide (1966) *Ears that Hear: Some Thoughts on Missionary Radio*, London: Radio Worldwide

Rae, W. Fraser (1892) 'The Egyptian Newspaper Press', *Nineteenth Century* 32 pp. 213–23

Ramsaye, Terry (1926) *A Million and One Nights: A History of the Motion Pictures* [Reprinted (1964) London: Frank Cass]

Ransom, Harry Howe (1970) *The Intelligence Establishment*, Cambridge, Mass.: Harvard University Press

Rao, Y. V. Lakshmana (1972) *The Practice of Mass Communication: Some Lessons from Research*, Paris: Unesco

Rappaport, Joseph (1957) 'The American Yiddish Press and the European Conflict in 1914', *Jewish Social Studies* 19 pp. 113–28

Read, Donald (1961) *Press and People, 1790–1850*, London: Edward Arnold

Reader's Digest (1970) *A Survey of Europe Today*, London: Reader's Digest

Reed, O. P. E. (1966) *Training for the World's Broadcasters*, London: BBC

Registrar of Newspapers for India, *Press in India* New Delhi: Ministry of Information and Broadcasting, Annual

Reich, Donald R. (1963) 'Accident and Design: the Reshaping of German Broadcasting Under Military Government' *Journal of Broadcasting* 7 pp. 191–207

Reith, John (1924) *Broadcast Over Britain* London: Hodder & Stoughton

Report and Recommendations of the Carnegie Commission on Educational

Television (1967) *Public Television: A Program For Action*, New York: Harper & Row

Report of the Committee on Broadcasting (1973) *The Broadcasting Future of New Zealand*, Wellington: Government Printer

Report of the Film Enquiry Committee (1951) New Delhi: Government of India Press

Report of the Indian Cinematograph Committee, 1927–28 (1928) Madras: Government of India

Report of the Presidential Study Commission on International Radio Broadcasting (1973) *The Right to Know*, Washington D.C.: US Government Printing Office

Report of the Special Senate Committee on Mass Media (1970) *The Uncertain Mirror* (Vol. 1) *Words, Music and Dollars* (Vol. 2), Ottawa: Information Canada

Report to the Congress (1974) *Telling America's Story to the World – Problems and Issues: United States Information Agency*, Washington, D.C.: Comptroller General of the United States

Rice, Frank A. ed. (1962) *Study of the Role of Second Languages*, Washington, D.C.: Center for Applied Linguistics of the Modern Language Association of America

Rich, Wesley Everett (1924) *The History of the United States Post Office to the Year 1829*, Cambridge, Mass.: Harvard University Press

Richie, Donald (1971) *Japanese Cinema: Film Style and National Character*, London: Secker & Warburg

Rimberg, John D. (1959) 'The Motion Picture in the Soviet Union 1918–52: A Sociological Analysis' (Unpublished Ph.D. thesis, Faculty of Political Science, Columbia University)

Roberts, Keith (1968) 'Antitrust Problems in the Newspaper Industry', *Harvard Law Review* 82 pp. 319–66

Robinson, Gertrude J. (1969) 'Tanjug: Yugoslavia's Multi-Faceted National News Agency' (Unpublished Ph.D. thesis in Journalism, University of Illinois)

Robinson, Gertrude J. (1971) 'Foreign News is Non-Linear in Jugoslav's Tanjug Agency', *Journalism Quarterly* 48 pp. 340–51

Robinson, Gertrude J. (1974) 'Mass Media and Ethnic Strife in Multi-National Yugoslavia', *Journalism Quarterly* 51 pp. 490–7

Robinson, John P. and Converse, Philip E. (1972) 'The Impact of Television on Mass Media Usage: A Cross National Comparison' in Szalai, Alexander, ed., *The Use of Time*, The Hague: Mouton

Roetter, Charles (1974) *Psychological Warfare*, London: Batsford

Rogers, Everett M. (1969) *Modernization among Peasants: The Impact of Communication*, New York: Holt, Rinehart & Winston

Rogers, Everett M. and Shoemaker, F. Floyd (1971), *Communication of Innovations*, New York: Free Press

Rosengarten, Frank (1968) *The Italian Anti-Fascist Press 1919–1945*, Cleveland, Ohio: Case Western Reserve University Press

Rossbacher, Peter (1966) 'The Soviet Journalistic Style', *Gazette* 12 pp. 201–11

Rosten, Leo (1937) *The Washington Correspondents*, New York: Harcourt Brace

Rosten, Leo (1941) *Hollywood; The Movie Colony, The Movie Makers*, New York: Harcourt Brace

Roy, Prodipto; Fliegel, Frederick C.; Kivlin, Joseph E.; and Sen, Lalit K. (1968) *Agricultural Innovation among Indian Farmers*, Hyderabad: National Institute of Community Development

Rutland, Robert A. (1973) *The Newsmongers: Journalism in the Life of the Nation, 1690–1972*, New York: Dial Press

Saberwal, Satish, ed. (1975) *Towards a Cultural Policy*, New Delhi: Vikas Publishing

Sadoul, George (1966) *The Cinema in the Arab Countries*, Beirut: Inter Arab Centre of Cinema and Television

Sager, Peter (1966) *Moscow's Hand in India: An Analysis of Soviet Propaganda*, Berne: Swiss Eastern Institute

Sahni, J. N. (1974) *Truth About the Indian Press*, Bombay: Allied Publishers

Salmon, Edward G. (1886) 'What Girls Read', *The Nineteenth Century* 20 pp. 515–29

Sarkar, Chanchal (1969) *Challenge and Stagnation: The Indian Mass Media*, New Delhi: Vikas Publications

Sathyamurthy, T. V. (1964) *The Politics of International Co-operation*, Geneva: Librairie Droz

Schanz, J. (1932) *Die Enstehung eines Deutschen Presse-Grossverlages*, Berlin

Schicke, C. A. (1974) *Revolution in Sound: A Biography of the Recording Industry*, Boston: Little, Brown

Schickel, Richard (1968) *The Disney Version: The Life, Times, Art and Commerce of Walt Disney*, New York: Simon and Schuster

Schiller, Herbert I. (1969) *Mass Communications and American Empire*, New York: Augustus M. Kelley

Schiller, Herbert I. (1973) 'Authentic National Development versus the Free Flow of Information and the New Communications Technology' in Gerbner, George; Gross, Larry P.; and Melody, William H., eds, *Communications Technology and Social Policy*, New York: John Wiley

Schiller, Herbert and Smythe, Dallas (1972) 'Chile: An End to Cultural Colonialism', *Society* March pp. 35–40

Schramm, Wilbur, ed. (1963) *The Science of Human Communication*, New York: Basic Books

Schramm, Wilbur (1964) *Mass Media and National Development*, Stanford University Press and Paris: Unesco

Schramm, Wilbur (1968) *Communication Satellites for Education Science and Culture*, Paris: Unesco

Schwarzlose, Richard Allen (1965) 'The American Wire Service: A Study of Their Development as a Social Institution' (Unpublished Ph.D. thesis in Communications, University of Illinois)

Scott, George (1968) *Reporter Anonymous: The Story of the Press Association*, London: Hutchinson

'Scythicus' (1900) 'The Russian Press', *The National Review* (London) 35 pp. 301–18

Sears, Donald A. and Bourland, Margaret (1970) 'Journalism Makes The Style', *Journalism Quarterly* 47 pp. 504–9

Servan-Schreiber, Jean-Louis (1974) *The Power to Inform*, New York: McGraw Hill [Translation of *Le Pouvoir d'Informer* (1972) Paris: Robert Laffont]

Sharma, S. K. and Singh, Jagdish (1972) *Television in Agricultural Transformation*, New Delhi: Indian Council for Agricultural Research

Shaw, Alexander (1942) 'India and the Film', *The Asiatic Review* 38 pp. 271–9

Shaw, Donald L. (1967) 'News Bias and the Telegraph: A Study of Historical Change', *Journalism Quarterly* 44 pp. 3–12

Sherman, Charles E. and Ruby, John (1974) 'The Eurovision News Exchange', *Journalism Quarterly* 51 pp. 478–85

Shils, Edward A. and Janowitz, Morris (1966) 'Cohesion and Disintegration in the Wehrmacht' in Berelson, Bernard and Janowitz, Morris, eds, *Reader in Public Opinion and Communication*, New York: Free Press pp. 402–17

Shils, Edward A. (1972) *The Intellectuals and the Powers and Other Essays*, University of Chicago Press

Shobaili, Abdulrahman S. (1971) 'An Historical and Analytical Study of Broadcasting and the Press in Saudi Arabia' (Unpublished Ph.D. thesis, Ohio State University)

Shulman, Milton (1973) *The Ravenous Eye*, London: Collins

Silvey, Robert (1950) 'Television Viewing in Britain', *Public Opinion Quarterly* 14 pp. 148–50

Silvey, Robert (1974) *Who's Listening? The Story of BBC Audience Research*, London: Allen & Unwin

Simonis, H. (1917) *The Street of Ink*, London: Cassell

Singer, Eleanor (1970) 'Public Opinion Research – Revisited', *Public Opinion Quarterly* 34 pp. 423–5

Singletary, Michael W. (1975) 'Newspaper Use of Supplemental Services, 1960–73', *Journalism Quarterly* 42 pp. 748–51

Sington, Derrick (1961) 'Broadcasting in East Africa', *The Listener* 3rd August pp. 167–9

Skornia, Harry J. (1965) *Television and Society*, New York: McGraw-Hill

Skornia, Harry J. and Kitson, Jack William, eds (1968) *Problems and Controversies in Television and Radio*, Palo Alto: Pacific Books

Skrzpek, Stanislaw (1972) 'The Profession of Journalism in Poland: A Profile', *Journalism Quarterly* 49 pp. 123–8

Smith, Anthony (1973) *The Shadow in the Cave*, London: Allen & Unwin

Smith, Don D. (1969–70) 'America's Short Wave Audience: Twenty-Five Years Later', *Public Opinion Quarterly* 33 pp. 537–45

Smith, Roland B. (1954) 'The Genesis of the Business Press in the United States', *The Journal of Marketing* 19 pp. 146–51

Smith, R. Harris (1972) *OSS: The Secret History of America's First Central Intelligence Agency*, Berkeley: University of California Press

Soltes, Mordecai (1924) *The Yiddish Press: An Americanizing Agency,* New York: Teachers' College, Columbia University

Sorensen, Thomas C. (1968) *The Word War: The Story of American Propaganda,* New York: Harper & Row

Spell, Lota M. (1932) 'The Anglo-Saxon Press in Mexico, 1846–1848', *American Historical Review* 38 pp. 20–31

Sprager, Harva Kaaren (1952) 'Hollywood's Foreign Correspondents', *Quarterly of Film, Radio and Television* 6 pp. 274–82

Spry, Graham (1961) 'The Decline and Fall of Canadian Broadcasting' and 'The Costs of Canadian Broadcasting', *Queen's Quarterly* Summer pp. 213–25 and Winter pp. 503–13

Starch, Daniel (1923) *Principles of Advertising,* Chicago: A. W. Shaw

Steiner, Gary A. (1963) *The People Look at Television,* New York: Knopf

Stevens, Evelyn P. (1974) *Protest and Response in Mexico,* Cambridge, Mass.: MIT Press

Stockwin, Harvey (1965) 'India's Escapist Industry', *Far Eastern Economic Review* 49 pp. 433–5

Storey, Graham (1951) *Reuter's Century 1851–1951,* London: Max Parrish

Stott, William (1973) *Documentary Expression and Thirties America,* New York: Oxford University Press

Strauss, William Victor (1930) 'Foreign Distribution of American Motion Pictures', *Harvard Business Review* 8 pp. 307–15

Swanberg, W. A. (1967) *Pulitzer,* New York: Charles Scribner's

Taubert, Sigfred, ed. (1972) *The Book Trade of the World: Europe and International Section,* London: André Deutsch

Taylor, A. J. P. (1972) *Beaverbrook,* London: Hamish Hamilton

Taylor, Peggy and Redmont, Bernard (1969) 'French Television: A Changing Image', *Television Quarterly* 8 pp. 39–48

Tebbel, John (1952) *The Life and Good Times of William Randolph Hearst,* New York: E. P. Dutton

Tebbel, John (1962) 'U.S. Television Abroad: Big New Business', *Saturday Review* 14th July [Reprinted (1968) in Skornia and Kitson, eds, *Problems and Controversies in Television and Radio* pp. 435–9

Tebbel, John (1968) 'Newest Boom: Spanish Language Stations', *Saturday Review* 8th June

Tebbel, John (1974) *The Media in America,* New York: Thomas Y. Crowell

Thomas, Bob (1972) *Selznick,* New York: Pocket Books

Thompson, Robert Luther (1972) *Wiring a Continent: The History of the Telegraph Industry in the United States 1832–1866,* New York: Arno Press

Thomson, C. A. H. (1948) *Overseas Information Service of the U.S. Government,* Washington, D.C.: The Brookings Institution

Ting, Lee-hsia Hsu (1974) *Government Control of the Press in Modern China, 1900–1949,* Cambridge, Mass.: Harvard University Press

Toll, Robert C. (1974) *Blacking Up: The Minstrel Show in Nineteenth Century America,* New York: Oxford University Press

Toogood, Alex (1969–70) 'New Zealand Broadcasting: A Monopoly in Action', *Journal of Broadcasting* 14 pp. 13–24

Tsai, Michael Kuan (1970) 'Some Effects of American Television Programs on Children in Formosa', *Journal of Broadcasting* 14 pp. 229–38

Tuchman, Gaye (1972) 'Objectivity as Strategic Ritual: An Examination of Newsmen's Notions of Objectivity', *American Journal of Sociology* 77 pp. 660–79

Tunstall, Jeremy (1964) *The Advertising Man in London Advertising Agencies*, London: Chapman & Hall

Tunstall, Jeremy (1970) *The Westminster Lobby Correspondents*, London: Routledge & Kegan Paul

Tunstall, Jeremy, ed. (1970) *Media Sociology*, London: Constable, and Urbana: University of Illinois

Tunstall, Jeremy (1971) *Journalists at Work*, London: Constable, and Beverly Hills: Sage Publications

Tunstall, Jeremy, ed. (1974) *The Open University Opens*, London: Routledge & Kegan Paul, and Amherst: University of Massachusetts Press

Ullstein, Hermann (1943) *The Rise and Fall of the House of Ullstein*, London: Nicholson & Watson

Unesco (1948, 1949) *Press, Film, Radio: Report of the Commission on Technical Needs*, Vols 2 and 3 Paris: Unesco

Unesco (1950) *World Communications: Press, Radio, Film*, Paris: Unesco

Unesco (1953) *Television: A World Survey*, Paris: Unesco

Unesco (1956) *The Problems of Transmitting Press Messages*, Paris: Unesco

Unesco (1958) *The Training of Journalists: A Worldwide Survey on the Training of Personnel for the Mass Media*, Paris: Unesco

Unesco (1963) *Statistics on Radio and Television 1950–1960*, Paris: Unesco

Unesco (1964) *World Communications: Press, Radio, Television, Film*, Paris: Unesco

Unesco (1975) *World Communications: A 200-Country Survey of Press, Radio, Television and Film*, Paris: Unesco

us Department of Commerce (1937) *Review of Foreign Film Markets*

United States House of Representatives (1974) *The Board for International Broadcasting, Radio Free Europe and Radio Liberty: Hearings Before the Committee on Foreign Affairs (H.R. 14780)*, Washington, D.C.: us Government Printing Office

United States Senate (1967–8) *The Failing Newspaper Act: Hearings before the Subcommittee on Antitrust and Monopoly of the Committee on the Judiciary (S.1312)*, Washington, D.C.: us Government Printing Office 7 Vols

United States Senate (1973) *Radio Free Europe and Radio Liberty: Hearings before the Committee on Foreign Relations (S.1914)*, Washington, D.C.: us Government Printing Office

Varis, Tapio (1970) 'The Control of Information by Jamming Radio Broadcasts', *Co-operation and Conflict* 3 pp. 168–84

Varis, Tapio (1973) *International Inventory of Television Programme Structure and the Flow of TV Programmes Between Nations*, University of Tampere: Institute of Journalism and Mass Communication

Varis, Tapio (1974) 'Global Traffic in Television', *Journal of Communication* 24 pp. 102–9

Varis, Tapio (1975) 'The Impact of Transnational Corporations on Communication' Tampere Peace Research Institute (Unpublished)

Vernon, Raymond (1971) *Sovereignty at Bay: the Multinational Spread of U.S. Enterprises*, London: Longman

Vickery, Raymond E. (1967) 'The Ceylonese Press and the Fall of the Sirimavo Bandaranaike Government', *South Atlantic Quarterly* 46 pp. 424–39

Vidura (1972) 'Special Section on the Language Press in India', *Vidura* (Press Institute of India) 9 pp. 298–342

Vidura (1973) 'Press Foundation of Asia since its Evolution', *Vidura* February pp. 3–8

Viorst, Milton (1974) 'Egypt and Israel: Two Nations and Their Press', *Columbia Journalism Review* May/June pp. 32–7

Voyene, Bernard (1971) *La Presse dans la Société Contemporaine*, Paris: Armand Colin

Wadsworth, A. P. (1955) *Newspaper Circulations, 1800–1954*, Manchester: Manchester Statistical Society

Wale, Michael (1972) *Vox Pop: Profiles of the Pop Process*, London: Harrap

Wallace, Irving (1960) *The Fabulous Showman*, London: Hutchinson

Watts, Ronald A. (1968) 'African Journalism Institute', *Gazette* 14 pp. 153–64

Wayne, Ivor (1956) 'American and Soviet Themes and Values: A Content Analysis of Pictures in Popular Magazines', *Public Opinion Quarterly* 20 pp. 214–20

Weakland, John H. (1966) 'Themes in Chinese Communist Films', *American Anthropologist* 68 pp. 477–84

Webb, R. K. (1955) *The British Working Class Reader: 1790–1848*, London: Allen & Unwin

Weigall, Arthur (1921) 'The Influence of the Kinematograph upon National Life', *The Nineteenth Century* April pp. 661–72

Weinberg, Arthur and Lila, eds (1961) *The Muckrakers*, New York: Simon & Schuster

Weir, E. Austin (1965) *The Struggle for National Broadcasting in Canada*, Toronto: McClelland & Stewart

Weiss, Ignazio (1958) 'The Daily Press in Italy', *Gazette* 4 pp. 251–60

Weiss, Ignazio (1961) *Politica dell'Informazione*, Milan: Edizioni di Communità

Wells, Alan (1972) *Picture-Tube Imperialism? The Impact of U.S. Television on Latin-America*, Maryknoll, N.Y.: Orbis Books

Wells, Alan, ed. (1974) *Mass Communications: A World View*, Palo Alto: National Press Books

Wells, William D. (1969) 'The Rise and Fall of Television Program Types', *Journal of Advertising Research* 9 pp. 21–7

Western, J. S. and Hughes, Colin A. (1971) *The Mass Media in Australia, Use and Evaluation*, St. Lucia, Brisbane: University of Queensland Press

Whale, John (1969) *The Half Shut Eye: Television and Politics in Britain and America*, London: Macmillan

Whitcomb, Ian (1973) *After the Ball*, Harmondsworth: Penguin

White, Cynthia L. (1970) *Women's Magazines 1693–1968*, London: Michael Joseph

White, John W. (1942) *Argentina: The Life Story of a Nation*, New York: Viking Press

White, Llewellyn and Leigh, Robert D. (1946) *Peoples Speaking to Peoples*, University of Chicago Press

White, Z. L. (1887) 'A Decade of American Journalism', *Westminster Review* 128 pp. 850–62

Whiteley, Wilfred (1969) *Swahili: The Rise of a National Language*, London: Methuen

Whitfield, Stephen E. (1968) *The Making of Star Trek*, New York: Ballantine

Whittemore, Edward P. (1961) *The Press in Japan Today . . . A Case Study*, Columbia: University of South Carolina Press

Whitton, John Boardman, ed. (1963) *Propaganda and the Cold War*, Washington, D.C.: Public Affairs Press

Wilcox, Dennis L. (1967) *English Language Newspapers Abroad*, Detroit: Gale Research

Wilhelm, John (1963) 'The Re-appearing Foreign Correspondent: A World Survey', *Journalism Quarterly* 40 pp. 147–68

Wilkinson, J. F. (1972) 'The BBC and Africa', *African Affairs* 71 pp. 176–85

Williams, Francis (1953) *Transmitting World News*, Paris: Unesco

Williams, Francis (1959) *Dangerous Estate*, London: Arrow Books

Williams, Francis (1969) *The Right to Know*, London: Longmans

Williams, Raymond (1961) *The Long Revolution*, London: Chatto & Windus

Williams, Raymond (1962) *Britain in the Sixties: Communications*, Harmondsworth: Penguin

Wilson, H. H. (1961) *Pressure Group: The Campaign for Commercial Television*, London: Secker & Warburg

Windeler, Robert (1975) *Mary Pickford: Sweetheart of the World*, London: W. H. Allen

Wise, T. A. (1967) 'Hill and Knowlton's World of Images', *Fortune* September pp. 98–101 and 140–4

Wittke, Carl (1957) *The German Language Press in America*, Lexington: University of Kentucky Press

Wolf, Frank (1972) *Television Programming for News and Public Affairs*, New York: Praeger

Wolfe, Wayne (1964) 'Images of the United States in the Latin American Press', *Journalism Quarterly* 41 pp. 79–86

Wolfenstein, M. and Leites, N. (1950) *Movies: A Psychological Study*, Glencoe: Free Press

Wolseley, Roland E. (1964) *Journalism in Modern India*, London: Asia Publishing

Wood, Alan (1965) *The True History of Lord Beaverbrook*, London: Heinemann

Wood, James P. (1949) *Magazines in the United States*, New York: Ronald Press

Wood, James P. (1958) *Of Lasting Interest: The Story of the Reader's Digest*, Garden City, N.Y.: Doubleday

Woodruff, William (1975) *America's Impact on the World*, London: Macmillan

WPN and Advertisers' Review (1964) 'Advertising and Marketing in Nigeria', *WPN and Advertiser's Review* 27th November pp. 55–69

Yu, Frederich T. C. (1964) *Mass Persuasion in Communist China*, London: Pall Mall Press

Yu, Frederich T. C. (1970) 'Persuasive Communications During the Cultural Revolution', *Gazette* 16 pp. 73–87 and 137–48

Zeman, Z. A. B. (1973) *Nazi Propaganda*, London: Oxford University Press

Zierold, Norman (1969) *The Hollywood Tycoons*, London: Hamish Hamilton

Zubrzycki, Herzy (1958) 'The Role of the Foreign Language Press in Migration Integration', *Population Studies* 12 pp. 73–82

Index

MISSION COLLEGE
LEARNING RESOURCE SERVICES

DATE DUE

DEC 1 4 1984		
MAY 17 '89		
DEC 1 6 2005		

DEMCO 38-297